Test Item File for

Chemistry

Sixth Edition

Test Item File for

Chemistry

Sixth Edition

Steven S. Zumdahl
Susan A. Zumdahl

Steven S. Zumdahl
University of Illinois

Susan Arena Zumdahl
University of Illinois

Donald J. DeCoste
University of Illinois

Houghton Mifflin Company • Boston • New York

Editor-in-Chief: Charles Hartford
Senior Sponsoring Editor: Richard Stratton
Associate Editor: Sara Wise
Senior Project Editor: Cathy Brooks
Editorial Assistant: Rosemary Mack
Executive Marketing Manager: Katherine Greig

Printed in the U.S.A.

ISBN: 0-618-221670

1 2 3 4 5 6 7 8 9- CRS -06 05 04 03 02

CONTENTS

Preface

This *Test Item File* consists of more than 2400 problems and questions designed to measure the level of understanding of the concepts and principles covered in the sixth edition of *Chemistry* by Steven S. Zumdahl and Susan A. Zumdahl. The questions in each chapter of the test bank are keyed to the appropriate sections in the textbook. Each chapter file contains multiple-choice, free response, true/false, and fill-in-the-blank questions.

Computerized versions of the *Test Item File* are available in IBM (for both DOS and Windows) and Macintosh versions, and a call-in test service is also available.

The multiple-choice questions have only one correct response. The responses "none of these" and "all of these" have been used sparingly.

Many of the questions in this *Test Item File* assume the availability of a periodic table and some specific information for physical constants and conversion factors. These should be provided to students with the examinations or quizzes. Acid ionization constants, standard reduction potentials, enthalpies of formation, and solubility product constants are provided within individual questions and problems.

S. S. Z.
S. A. Z.
D. J. D.

CHAPTER 1   Chemical Foundations

1. It is estimated that uranium is relatively common in the earth's crust, occurring in amounts of 4 g/metric ton. A metric ton is 1000 kg. At this concentration, what mass of uranium is present in 1.0 mg of the earth's crust?

   a) 4 nanograms
   b) 4 micrograms
   c) 4 milligrams
   d) 4×10^{-5} g
   e) 4 centigrams

   ANS: a)   4 nanograms   **PAGE:** 1.3,6

2. In 1928, 1.0 g of a new element was isolated from 660 kg of the ore molybdenite. The percent by mass of this element in the ore was:

   a) 1.5%
   b) 6.6%
   c) 1.0%
   d) 1.5×10^{-4}%
   e) 3.5×10^{-3}%

   ANS: d) 1.5×10^{-4}%   **PAGE:** 1.3,6

3. Which of the following metric relationships is incorrect?

   a) 1 microliter = 10^{-6} liters
   b) 1 gram = 10^{3} kilograms
   c) 10^{3} milliliters = 1 liter
   d) 1 gram = 10^{2} centigrams
   e) 10 decimeters = 1 meter

   ANS: b)   1 gram = 10^{3} kilograms   **PAGE:** 1.3

4. Which of the following is an example of a quantitative observation?

   a) The piece of metal is longer than the piece of wood
   b) Solution 1 is much darker than solution 2.
   c) The liquid in beaker A is blue.
   d) The temperature of the liquid is 60°C.
   e) At least two of the above (a-d) are quantitative observations.

   ANS: d)   The temperature of the liquid is 60°C.   **PAGE:** 1.2

1

5. A quantitative observation
    a) contains a number and a unit.
    b) does not contain a number.
    c) always makes a comparison.
    d) must be obtained through experimentation.
    e) none of these

    ANS: a)   contains a number and a unit.   **PAGE:** 1.3

6. Generally observed behavior which can be formulated into a statement, sometimes mathematical in nature, is called a(n)
    a) observation.
    b) measurement.
    c) theory.
    d) natural law.
    e) experiment.

    ANS: d)   natural law.   **PAGE:** 1.2

7. The statement "The total mass of materials is not affected by a chemical change in those materials" is called a(n)
    a) observation.
    b) measurement.
    c) theory.
    d) natural law.
    e) experiment.

    ANS: d)   natural law.   **PAGE:** 1.2

8. What is the measure of resistance an object has to a change in its state of motion?
    a) mass
    b) weight
    c) volume
    d) length
    e) none of these

    ANS: a)   mass   **PAGE:** 1.3

9. Express 0.00560 in exponential notation.
    a) 5.60×10^3
    b) 5.6×10^{-3}
    c) 5.60×10^{-3}
    d) 5.60
    e) none of these

    ANS: c) 5.60×10^{-3} **PAGE:** 1.5

10. A titration was performed to find the concentration of hydrochloric acid with the following results:

Trial	Molarity
1	1.25 ± 0.01
2	1.24 ± 0.01
3	1.26 ± 0.01

The actual concentration of HCl was determined to be 1.000 M; the results of the titration are:

a) both accurate and precise.

b) accurate but imprecise.

c) precise but inaccurate.

d) both inaccurate and imprecise.

e) accuracy and precision are impossible to determine with the available information.

ANS: c)   precise but inaccurate   PAGE: 1.4

11. Which of the following is the least probable concerning five measurements taken in the lab?

a) The measurements are accurate and precise.

b) The measurements are accurate but not precise.

c) The measurements are precise but not accurate.

d) The measurements are neither accurate nor precise.

e) All of these are equally probable.

ANS: b)   The measurements are accurate but not precise.   PAGE: 1.4

12. We generally report a measurement by recording all of the certain digits plus ____ uncertain digit(s).

a) no

b) one

c) two

d) three

e) four

ANS: b)   one   PAGE: 1.4

13. The amount of uncertainty in a measured quantity is determined by:

a) both the skill of the observer and the limitations of the measuring instrument.

b) neither the skill of the observer nor the limitations of the measuring instrument.

c) the limitations of the measuring instrument only.

d) the skill of the observer only.

e) none of these

ANS: a)   both the skill of the observer and the limitations of the measuring instrument.   PAGE: 1.4

14. A scientist obtains the number 0.045006700 on a calculator. If this number actually has four (4) significant figures, how should it be written?

    a)   0.4567
    b)   0.4501
    c)   0.045
    d)   0.04500
    e)   0.04501

ANS: e)   0.04501   **PAGE:** 1.5

15. How many significant figures are there in the number 3.1400?

    a)   1
    b)   2
    c)   3
    d)   4
    e)   5

ANS: e)   5   **PAGE:** 1.5

16. A piece of indium with a mass of 16.6 g is submerged in 46.3 cm^3 of water in a graduated cylinder. The water level increases to 48.6 cm^3. The correct value for the density of indium from these data is:

    a)   7.217 g/cm^3
    b)   7.2 g/cm^3
    c)   0.14 g/cm^3
    d)   0.138 g/cm^3
    e)   more than 0.1 g/cm^3 away from any of these values.

ANS: b)   7.2 g/cm^3 **PAGE:** 1.5,8

17. Express 165,000 in exponential notation.

    a) 1.65000×10^5
    b) 1.65×10^5
    c) 1.6500×10^{-5}
    d) 1.65×10^{-5}
    e) 165×10^3

ANS: b) 1.65×10^5 **PAGE:** 1.5

18. A metric unit for length is

    a) gram.
    b) milliliter.
    c) yard.
    d) kilometer.
    e) pound.

    ANS: d) kilometer.   **PAGE:** 1.3

19. One kilogram contains this many grams:

    a) 100
    b) 1000
    c) 10
    d) 1/10
    e) 1/1000

    ANS: b) 1000   **PAGE:** 1.3

20. Using the rules of significant figures, calculate the following:

    $$\frac{6.167 + 83}{5.10}$$

    a) 17.5
    b) 18
    c) 17
    d) 20
    e) 17.48

    ANS: c) 17   **PAGE:** 1.5

21. Using the rules of significant figures, calculate the following: $4.0021 - 0.004$

    a) 3.998
    b) 4
    c) 3.9981
    d) 4.00
    e) 4.0

    ANS: a) 3.998   **PAGE:** 1.5

22. How many significant figures are there in the number 0.04560700?

    a) 4
    b) 5
    c) 7
    d) 8
    e) 9

ANS: c)   7   **PAGE:** 1.5

23. Convert 5687.4 g to mg.

    a) 5.6874 mg
    b) 56.784 mg
    c) 568.74 mg
    d) 5.6874×10^3 mg
    e) 5.6874×10^6 mg

ANS: e) 5.6874×10^6 mg   **PAGE:** 1.3

24. Express the volume 245 cm^3 in liters.

    a) 245 L
    b) 24.5 L
    c) 2.45 L
    d) 0.245 L
    e) 0.0245 L

ANS: d)   0.245 L   **PAGE:** 1.3

25. The mass of 24 kg equals

    a) 0.024 g
    b) 0.24 g
    c) 240 g
    d) 2400 g
    e) 2.4×10^4 g

ANS: e) 2.4×10^4 g   **PAGE:** 1.3

26. Convert 0.6571 m to mm.

    a) 657.1 mm
    b) 6.571×10^{-3} mm
    c) 6.571×10^{-4} mm
    d) 0.06571 mm
    e) none of these

ANS: a)   657.1 mm   **PAGE:** 1.3

27. One second contains this many picoseconds.

    a) 1×10^{12}

    b) 1×10^{-12}

    c) 1×10^{-9}

    d) 1×10^{9}

    e) 1×10^{15}

ANS: a) 1×10^{12} **PAGE:** 1.3

28. 100 seconds contain this many nanoseconds.

    a) 1×10^{7}

    b) 1×10^{11}

    c) 1×10^{10}

    d) 1×10^{12}

    e) 1×10^{8}

ANS: b) 1×10^{11} **PAGE:** 1.3

29. How many significant figures are there in the number 0.0006042?

    a) 7

    b) 3

    c) 8

    d) 4

    e) 0

ANS: d) 4   **PAGE:** 1.5

30. The degree of agreement among several measurements of the same quantity is called
_____. It reflects the reproducibility of a given type of measurement.

    a) accuracy

    b) error

    c) precision

    d) significance

    e) certainty

ANS: c) precision   **PAGE:** 1.4

31. The agreement of a particular value with the true value is called

    a) accuracy.

    b) error.

    c) precision.

    d) significance.

    e) certainty.

ANS: a) accuracy.   **PAGE:** 1.4

32. Convert 4301 mL to qts. (1 L = 1.06 qt)

    a) 4559 qts
    b) 4.058 qts
    c) 4058×10^{-3} qts
    d) 4058 qts
    e) 4.559 qts

    ANS: e) 4.559 qts   **PAGE:** 1.6

33. Convert 16.8 lb to g. (1 lb = 453.6 g)

    a) 762.0 g
    b) 3.70×10^4 g
    c) 76.2 g
    d) 7621 g
    e) 7620 g

    ANS: e) 7620 g   **PAGE:** 1.6

34. Convert 761 mi to km. (1 m = 1.094 yds, 1 mi = 1760 yds)

    a) 832 km
    b) 1470 km
    c) 1.22×10^9 km
    d) 696 km
    e) 1220 km

    ANS: e) 1220 km   **PAGE:** 1.6

35. Convert 0.092 ft^3 to L. (2.54 cm = 1 in., 1 L = 1 dm^3)

    a) 26 L
    b) 2.6 L
    c) 3.2×10^{-3} L
    d) 1.8 L
    e) 0.40 L

    ANS: b) 2.6 L   **PAGE:** 1.6

36. Convert 6.0 kg to lb. (1 kg = 2.205 lb)

    a) 13 lbs
    b) 1.3 lbs
    c) 2.7 lbs
    d) 10. lbs
    e) 13.23 lbs

    ANS: a) 13 lbs   **PAGE:** 1.5,1.6

8

37. 423 Kelvin equals

    a)   150. °F

    b)   273. °F

    c)   696. °F

    d)   150. °C

    e)   696. °C

ANS: d) 150. °C   **PAGE:** 1.7

38. The melting point of lead is 327°C. What is this on the Fahrenheit scale?
        $(T_F = T_C \times (9°F/5°C) + 32°F)$

    a)   620.6°F

    b)   600°F

    c)   895°F

    d)   621°F

    e)   547°F

ANS: d) 621°F   **PAGE:** 1.5,1.7

39. The state of matter for an object that has a definite volume but not a definite shape is

    a)   solid state.

    b)   liquid state.

    c)   gaseous state.

    d)   elemental state.

    e)   mixed state.

ANS: b) liquid state.   **PAGE:** 1.9

40. Manganese makes up 1.3×10^{-4} percent by mass of the elements found in a normal healthy body. How many grams of manganese would be found in the body of a person weighing 183 lb? (2.2 lb = 1.0 kg)

    a)   1100 g

    b)   0.11 g

    c)   11 g

    d)   0.24 g

    e)   none of these is correct

ANS: b) 0.11 g   **PAGE:** 1.6

41. In 1928, rhenium cost $10,000/kg. It now costs $40/troy ounce. What is the present cost of a gram of rhenium? (1 troy ounce = 31.10 g)

    a) less than $1.00
    b) between $1.00 and $10
    c) between $10 and $50
    d) between $50 and $100
    e) over $100

    ANS: b)   between $1.00 and $10   **PAGE:** 1.6

42. You measure water in two containers: a 10-mL graduated cylinder with marks at every mL, and a 1-mL pipet marked at every 0.1 mL. If you have some water in each of the containers, and add them together, to what decimal place could you measure the total?

    a) 0.01 mL
    b) 0.1 mL
    c) 1 mL
    d) 10 mL
    e) none of these

    ANS: b)   0.1 mL   **PAGE:** 1.4,5

43. What data would you need to estimate the money you would spend on gas to drive your car from Los Angeles to Chicago? Provide a sample calculation.

    ANS: average price per gallon of gasoline, average MPG of the car,
          mileage of trip   **PAGE:** 1.6

44. In a recent accident some drums of uranium hexafluoride were lost in the English Channel. The melting point of uranium hexafluoride is 64.5°C. What is the melting point of uranium hexafluoride on the Fahrenheit scale? ($T_F = T_C \times (9°F/5°C) + 32°F$)

    a) 1.35°F
    b) 82.3°F
    c) 116°F
    d) 122°F
    e) 148°F

    ANS: e)   148°F   **PAGE:** 1.7

45. In a recent accident, some drums of uranium hexafluoride were lost in the English Channel, which is known for its cold water (about 17°C). The melting point of uranium hexafluoride is 148°F. In what physical state is the uranium hexafluoride in these drums? ($T_F = T_C \times (9°F/5°C) + 32°F$)

    a) solid
    b) liquid
    c) gas
    d) a mixture of solid and liquid
    e) not enough information

    ANS: a) solid   **PAGE:** 1.7,9

46. The melting point of indium is 156.2°C. At 323°F, what is the physical state of indium? ($T_F = T_C \times (9°F/5°C) + 32°F$)

    a) solid
    b) liquid
    c) gas
    d) not enough information
    e) At 323°F, the indium is partially solid and partially liquid; there is an equilibrium between the two states.

    ANS: d) not enough information   **PAGE:** 1.7,9

47. Convert: -40.0 °C = _____ °F. ($T_F = T_C \times (9°F/5°C) + 32°F$)

    ANS: -40.0 °F   **PAGE:** 1.7

48. The calibration points for the linear Reaumur scale are the usual melting point of ice and boiling point of water, which are assigned the values 0°R and 80°R, respectively. The normal body temperature of humans is 98.6°F. What is this temperature in °R?

    a) 37.0
    b) 28.0
    c) 29.0
    d) 29.6
    e) none of these

    ANS: d) 29.6   **PAGE:** 1.7

49. A monolayer containing 3.20×10^{-6} g of oleic acid has an area of 20.0 cm². The density of oleic acid is 0.895 g/mL. What is the thickness of the monolayer (the length of an oleic acid molecule)?

    a) 2.86×10^{-6} cm
    b) 3.58×10^{-6} cm
    c) 5.59×10^{-6} cm
    d) 1.79×10^{-7} cm
    e) 1.43×10^{-7} cm

ANS: d) 1.79×10^{-7} cm   **PAGE:** 1.8

50. The density of gasoline is 0.7025 g/mL at 20°C. When gasoline is added to water:

    a)   it will float on top.
    b)   it will sink to the bottom.
    c)   it will mix so you can't see it.
    d)   the mixture will improve the running of the motor.
    e)   none of these things will happen.

ANS: a)   it will float on top.   **PAGE:** 1.8

51. The density of a liquid is determined by successively weighing 25, 50, 75, 100, and 125 mL of the liquid in a 250-mL beaker. If volume of liquid is plotted along the horizontal axis, and total mass of beaker plus liquid is plotted on the vertical axis:

    a)   the x, or horizontal, intercept is the negative value of the weight of the beaker.
    b)   the y, or vertical, intercept is the weight of the empty beaker.
    c)   the slope of the line is 1.0.
    d)   the line will pass through the origin.
    e)   the slope of the line is independent of the identity of the liquid.

ANS: b)   the y, or vertical, intercept is the weight of the empty
              beaker.   **PAGE:** 1.8

52. Consider the plot in Question 51. Which of the following is true?

    a)   The plot should be rather linear because the slope measures the density of a liquid.
    b)   The plot should be curved upward because the slope measures the density of a liquid.
    c)   The plot should be curved upward because the mass of the liquid is higher in successive trials.
    d)   The plot should be linear because the mass of the beaker stays constant.
    e)   none of the above

ANS: a)   The plot should be rather linear because the slope
              measures the density of a liquid.   **PAGE:** 1.8

53. All physical changes are accompanied by chemical changes.

    ANS: False   **PAGE:** 1.9

54. The boiling of water is a
    a) physical change because the water merely disappears.
    b) physical change because the gaseous water is chemically the same as the liquid.
    c) chemical change because heat is needed for the process to occur.
    d) chemical change because a gas (steam) is given off.
    e) chemical and physical damage.

    ANS: b)   physical change because the gaseous water is chemically
    the same as the liquid.   **PAGE:** 1.9

55. A freighter carrying a cargo of uranium hexafluoride sank in the English Channel in late August 1984. The cargo of uranium hexafluoride weighed 2.25×10^8 kg and was contained in 30 drums, each having a volume of 1.62×10^6 L. What is the density (g/mL) of uranium hexafluoride?
    a)   1.39 g/mL
    b)   4.63 g/mL
    c)   1.39 g/mL
    d)   46.3 g/mL
    e)   41.7 g/mL

    ANS: b)   4.63 g/mL   **PAGE:** 1.8

56. The state of matter for an object that has both definite volume and definite shape is
    a)   solid state.
    b)   liquid state.
    c)   gaseous state.
    d)   elemental state.
    e)   mixed state.

    ANS: a)   solid state.   **PAGE:** 1.9

57. _____ are substances with constant composition that can be broken down into elements by chemical processes.
    a)   Solutions
    b)   Mixtures
    c)   Compounds
    d)   Quarks
    e)   Heterogeneous mixtures

    ANS: c)   Compounds   **PAGE:** 1.9

58. A method of separation that employs a system with two phases of matter, a mobile phase and a stationary phase, is called

    a) filtration.
    b) chromatography.
    c) distillation.
    d) vaporization.
    e) homogenization.

    ANS: b) chromatography.   **PAGE:** 1.9

59. A solution is also called a

    a) homogeneous mixture.
    b) heterogeneous mixture.
    c) pure mixture.
    d) compound.
    e) distilled mixture.

    ANS: a) homogeneous mixture.   **PAGE:** 1.9

60. An example of a pure substance is

    a) elements.
    b) compounds.
    c) pure water.
    d) carbon dioxide.
    e) all of these

    ANS: e) all of these   **PAGE:** 1.9

61. Which of the following is *not* a unit in the SI system?

    a) ampere
    b) candela
    c) Kelvin
    d) meter
    e) calorie

    ANS: e) calorie   **PAGE:** 1.3

62. What are the components of the scientific method?

    ANS: See Sec. 1.2 of Zumdahl, *Chemistry*.   **PAGE:** 1.2

63. Garfield (weighing 24 lbs) took a flight to the moon on the space shuttle. As usual he stuffed himself with lasagna during the entire flight and napped when he wasn't eating. Much to his delight when he got to the moon he found he weighed only 6 lbs. He immediately proclaimed a quick weight loss diet. Explain the fallacy in his reasoning. Assume gravity on the moon to be about 1/6 that of Earth.

   ANS: See Sec. 1.2 of Zumdahl, *Chemistry*.   **PAGE:** 1.2

64. Contrast the terms precision and accuracy.

   ANS: See Sec. 1.4 of Zumdahl, *Chemistry*.   **PAGE:** 1.4

65. A 20.0-mL sample of glycerol has a mass of 25.2 grams. What is the mass of a 53-mL sample of glycerol?

   ANS: (25.2 g/20.0 mL) (53 mL) = 66.8 g = 67 g to 2 sig. figs.   **PAGE:** 1.6

66. A 20.0-mL sample of glycerol has a mass of 25.2 grams. What is the density of glycerol in ounces/quart? (1.00 ounce = 28.4 grams, and 1.00 liter = 1.06 quarts)

   ANS: (25.2 g/20.0 mL) (10^3 mL/1 L) (1 L/1.06 qt) (1 oz/28.4 g) =
   41.9 oz/qt   **PAGE:** 1.6,8

67. Suppose that you purchased a water bed that has dimensions 2.55 m × 2.53 dm × 230 cm. What mass of water does this bed contain?

   ANS: 1.48×10^6 g   **PAGE:** 1.8

68. On a new temperature scale (°Z), water boils at 120.0 °Z and freezes at 40.0 °Z. Calculate the normal human body temperature using this temperature scale. On the Celsius scale, normal human body temperature is 37 °C, and water boils at 100.0 °C and freezes at 0.00 °C.

   ANS: 69.6 °Z   **PAGE:** 1.7

69. On a new temperature scale (°Y), water boils at 155.0 °Y and freezes at 0.00 °Y. Calculate the normal human body temperature using this temperature scale. On the Fahrenheit scale, normal human body temperature is 98.6 °F, and water boils at 212.0 °F and freezes at 32.0 °F.

   ANS: 57.3 °Y   **PAGE:** 1.7

15

70. As warm water sits in a cool room, you measure the temperature change. Which of the following is true?

    a)   The temperature change is bigger if you are measuring in °F.
    b)   The temperature change is bigger if you are measuring in °C.
    c)   The temperature change will be the same regardless of the scale you use.
    d)   Answer a or b is correct, depending on the difference in temperature between the water and the room.
    e)   none of the above

    ANS: a)   The temperature change is bigger if you are measuring in °F.   **PAGE:** 1.7

71. Explain the main differences between a compound and a mixture.

    ANS: See Sec. 1.9 of Zumdahl, *Chemistry*.   **PAGE:** 1.9

72. Color changes always indicate a chemical change.

    ANS: False   **PAGE:** 1.9

73. Explain how Archimedes might have used the concept of density to determine whether the king's crown was pure gold. (density of gold = 19.32 g/cm^3)

    ANS: See Sec. 1.8 of Zumdahl, *Chemistry*.   **PAGE:** 1.8

74. Give three physical methods used by chemists to separate mixtures and identify the type of mixture best suited for each process.

    ANS: See Sec. 1.9 of Zumdahl, *Chemistry*.   **PAGE:** 1.9

75. Name three methods for the separation of mixtures.

    ANS: See Sec. 1.9 of Zumdahl, *Chemistry*.   **PAGE:** 1.9

76. A chemical theory that has been known for a long time becomes a law.

    ANS: False   **PAGE:** 1.2

1. According to the law of multiple proportions:

    a) if the same two elements form two different compounds, they do so in the same ratio.
    b) it is not possible for the same two elements to form more than one compound.
    c) the ratio of the masses of the elements in a compound is always the same.
    d) the total mass after a chemical change is the same as before the change.
    e) none of these

    ANS: e)   none of these   **PAGE:** 2.2

2. Which of the following pairs of compounds can be used to illustrate the law of multiple proportions?

    a) NH_4 and NH_4Cl
    b) ZnO_2 and $ZnCl_2$
    c) H_2O and HCl
    d) NO and NO_2
    e) CH_4 and CO_2

    ANS: d) NO and NO_2 **PAGE:** 2.2

3. Many classic experiments have given us indirect evidence of the nature of the atom. Which of the experiments listed below did not give the results described?

    a) The Rutherford experiment proved the Thomson "plum-pudding" model of the atom to be essentially correct.
    b) The Rutherford experiment was useful in determining the nuclear charge on the atom.
    c) Millikan's oil-drop experiment showed that the charge on any particle was a simple multiple of the charge on the electron.
    d) The electric discharge tube proved that electrons have a negative charge.

    ANS: a)   The Rutherford experiment proved the Thomson "plum-pudding" model of the atom to be essentially correct.   **PAGE:** 2.4

4. Which of the following statements from Dalton's atomic theory is no longer true, according to modern atomic theory?

    a) Elements are made up of tiny particles called atoms.
    b) Atoms are not created or destroyed in chemical reactions.
    c) All atoms of a given element are identical.
    d) Atoms are indivisible in chemical reactions.
    e) All of these statements are true according to modern atomic theory.

    ANS: c)   All atoms of a given element are identical.   **PAGE:** 2.3

5. The first people to attempt to explain why chemical changes occur were

    a) alchemists.

    b) metallurgists.

    c) physicians.

    d) physicists.

    e) the Greeks.

    ANS: e) the Greeks.   **PAGE:** 2.1

6. The Greeks proposed that matter consisted of four fundamental substances:

    a) fire, earth, water, air

    b) fire, metal, water, air

    c) earth, metal, water, air

    d) atoms, fire, water, air

    e) atoms, metal, fire, air

    ANS: a) fire, earth, water, air   **PAGE:** 2.1

7. The first chemist to perform truly quantitative experiments was

    a) Paracelsus.

    b) Boyle.

    c) Priestly.

    d) Bauer.

    e) Lavoisier.

    ANS: b) Boyle.   **PAGE:** 2.1

8. The scientist who discovered the law of conservation of mass and is also called the father of modern chemistry is

    a) Proust.

    b) Boyle.

    c) Priestly.

    d) Bauer.

    e) Lavoisier.

    ANS: e) Lavoisier.   **PAGE:** 2.2

9. Which of the following pairs can be used to illustrate the law of multiple proportions?

    a) SO and SO_2

    b) CO and $CaCo_3$

    c) H_2O and $C_{12}H_{22}O_{11}$

    d) H_2SO_4 and H_2S

    e) KCl and $KClO_2$

    ANS: a) SO and SO_2 **PAGE:** 2.2

10. The chemist credited for inventing a set of symbols for writing elements and a system for writing the formulas of compounds (and for discovering selenium, silicon, and thorium) is

   a) Boyle.
   b) Lavoisier.
   c) Priestly.
   d) Berzelius.
   e) Dalton.

   ANS: d) Berzelius.   **PAGE:** 2.3

11. What element (in trace amounts) has been shown to help in protecting against heart disease and cancer?

   a) silicon
   b) oxygen
   c) selenium
   d) copper
   e) potassium

   ANS: c) selenium   **PAGE:** 2.3

12. The first scientist to show that atoms emit any negative particles was

   a) J. J. Thomson.
   b) Lord Kelvin.
   c) Ernest Rutherford.
   d) William Thomson.
   e) John Dalton.

   ANS: a) J. J. Thomson.   **PAGE:** 2.4

13. The scientist whose alpha-particle scattering experiment led him to conclude that the nucleus of an atom contains a dense center of positive charge is

   a) J. J. Thomson.
   b) Lord Kelvin.
   c) Ernest Rutherford.
   d) William Thomson.
   e) John Dalton.

   ANS: c) Ernest Rutherford.   **PAGE:** 2.4

14. Which one of the following statements about atomic structure is false?

    a) The electrons occupy a very large volume compared to the nucleus.
    b) Almost all of the mass of the atom is concentrated in the nucleus.
    c) The protons and neutrons in the nucleus are very tightly packed.
    d) The number of protons and neutrons is always the same in the neutral atom.
    e) All of the above statements (a-d) are true.

    ANS: d)   The number of protons and neutrons is always the same in
    the neutral atom.   **PAGE:** 2.4,5

15. If the Thomson model of the atom had been correct, Rutherford would have observed

    a) alpha particles going through the foil with little or no deflection.
    b) alpha particles greatly deflected by the metal foil.
    c) alpha particles bouncing off the foil.
    d) positive particles formed in the foil.
    e) None of the above observations is consistent with the Thomson model of the
       atom.

    ANS: a)   alpha particles going through the foil with little or no
    deflection.   **PAGE:** 2.4

16. Rutherford's experiment was important because it showed that:

    a) radioactive elements give off alpha particles.
    b) gold foil can be made to be only a few atoms thick.
    c) a zinc sulfide screen scintillates when struck by a charged particle.
    d) the mass of the atom is uniformly distributed throughout the atom.
    e) an atom is mostly empty space.

    ANS: e)   an atom is mostly empty space.   **PAGE:** 2.4

17. Which of the following name(s) is(are) correct?

       1. sulfide S^{2-}
       2. ammonium chloride NH_4Cl
       3. acetic acid $HC_2H_3O_2$
       4. barium oxide BaO
    a) all
    b) none
    c) 1, 2
    d) 3, 4
    e) 1, 3, 4

    ANS: a)   all   **PAGE:** 2.8

18. Which of the following atomic symbols is incorrect?

   a) $^{14}_{6}C$

   b) $^{37}_{17}Cl$

   c) $^{32}_{15}P$

   d) $^{39}_{19}K$

   e) $^{14}_{8}N$

   ANS: e) $^{14}_{8}N$ **PAGE:** 2.5

19. The element rhenium (Re) exists as two stable isotopes and 18 unstable isotopes. Rhenium-185 has in its nucleus

   a)   75 protons, 75 neutrons.
   b)   75 protons, 130 neutrons.
   c)   130 protons, 75 neutrons.
   d)   75 protons, 110 neutrons.
   e)   not enough information is given.

   ANS: d)   75 protons, 110 neutrons.   **PAGE:** 2.5

20. Which statement is *not* correct?

   a)   The mass of an alpha particle is 7300 times that of the electron.
   b)   An alpha particle has a 2+ charge.
   c)   Three types of radioactive emission are gamma rays, beta rays, and alpha particles.
   d)   A gamma ray is high-energy ñlight.î
   e)   There are only three types of radioactivity known to scientists today.

   ANS: e)   There are only three types of radioactivity known to
                  scientists today.   **PAGE:** 2.4

21. $^{40}_{20}Ca^{2+}$ has

   a)   20 protons, 20 neutrons, and 18 electrons.
   b)   22 protons, 20 neutrons, and 20 electrons.
   c)   20 protons, 22 neutrons, and 18 electrons.
   d)   22 protons, 18 neutrons, and 18 electrons.
   e)   20 protons, 20 neutrons, and 22 electrons.

   ANS: a)   20 protons, 20 neutrons, and 18 electrons.   **PAGE:** 2.5

22. Which of the following has 61 neutrons, 47 protons, and 46 electrons?

    a) $^{80}_{61}Pm$

    b) $^{108}_{47}Ag^+$

    c) $^{108}_{46}Pd^-$

    d) $^{108}_{47}Cd^+$

    e) $^{108}_{47}Ag$

    ANS: b) $^{108}_{47}Ag^+$ **PAGE:** 2.5

23. The numbers of protons, neutrons, and electrons in $^{39}_{19}K^+$ are:

    a) 20 p, 19 n, 19 e
    b) 20 p, 19 n, 20 e
    c) 19 p, 20 n, 20 e
    d) 19 p, 20 n, 19 e
    e) 19 p, 20 n, 18 e

    ANS: e)   19 p, 20 n, 18 e   **PAGE:** 2.5

24. All of the following are true *except*:

    a) Ions are formed by adding electrons to a neutral atom.
    b) Ions are formed by changing the number of protons in an atom's nucleus.
    c) Ions are formed by removing electrons from a neutral atom.
    d) An ion has a positive or negative charge.
    e) Metals tend to form positive ions.

    ANS: b)   Ions are formed by changing the number of protons in an
    atom's nucleus.   **PAGE:** 2.6, 2.7

25. Which of the following statements is (are) true?

    a) $^{18}_{8}O$ and $^{19}_{9}F$ have the same number of neutrons.

    b) $^{14}_{6}C$ and $^{14}_{7}N$ are isotopes of each other because their mass numbers are the same.

    c) $^{18}_{8}O^{2-}$ has the same number of electrons as $^{20}_{10}Ne$.

    d) a and b

    e) a and c

    ANS: e)   a and c   **PAGE:** 2.5

26. Which among the following represent a set of isotopes? Atomic nuclei containing:

    I.   20 protons and 20 neutrons.
    II. 21 protons and 19 neutrons.
    III. 22 neutrons and 18 protons.
    IV. 20 protons and 22 neutrons.
    V.   21 protons and 20 neutrons.
    a)   I, II, III
    b)   III, IV
    c)   I, V
    d)   I, IV and II, V
    e)   No isotopes are indicated.

    ANS: d)   I, IV and II, V   **PAGE:** 2.5

27. By knowing the number of protons a neutral atom has, you should be able to determine

    a)   the number of neutrons in the neutral atom.
    b)   the number of electrons in the neutral atom.
    c)   the name of the atom.
    d)   two of the above.
    e)   none of the above

    ANS: d)   two of the above.   **PAGE:** 2.5

28. The number of neutrons in an atom is the same for all neutral atoms of that element.

    ANS: False   **PAGE:** 2.5

29. The average mass of a carbon atom is 12.011. Assuming you were able to pick up only one carbon unit, the chances that you would randomly get one with a mass of 12.011 is

    a)   0%.
    b)   0.011%.
    c)   about 12%.
    d)   12.011%.
    e)   greater than 50%.

    ANS: a)   0%.   **PAGE:** 2.5

30. The number of electrons in an atom is the same for all neutral atoms of that element.

    ANS: True   **PAGE:** 2.5,2.6

31. An ion is formed
    a) by either adding or subtracting protons from the atom.
    b) by either adding or subtracting electrons from the atom.
    c) by either adding or subtracting neutrons from the atom.
    d) All of the above are true.
    e) Two of the above are true.

    ANS: b)   by either adding or subtracting electrons from the atom.   **PAGE:** 2.6

32. Which of the following statements are *true* of uranium-238?
    I. Its chemical properties will be exactly like those of uranium-235.
    II. Its mass will be slightly different from that of an atom of uranium-235.
    III. It will contain a different number of protons that an atom of uranium-235.
    IV. It is more plentiful in nature than uranium-235.
    a) III, IV
    b) I, II, III
    c) I, II, IV
    d) II, III, IV
    e) all of these

    ANS: c) I, II, IV   **PAGE:** 2.5

33. An isotope, *X*, of a particular element has an atomic number of 7 and a mass number of 15. Therefore,
    a) *X* is an isotope of nitrogen.
    b) *X* has 8 neutrons per atom.
    c) *X* has an atomic mass of 14.0067.
    d) a and b
    e) a, b, and c

    ANS: d)   a and b   **PAGE:** 2.5

34. Write the symbol for each of the following elements.
    a) silver   _____
    b) calcium   _____
    c) iodine   _____
    d) copper   _____
    e) phosphorus   _____

    ANS: a) Ag   b) Ca   c) I   d) Cu   e) P   **PAGE:** 2.7,8

35. How many oxygen atoms are there in one formula unit of $Ca_3(PO_4)_2$?

    a) 2
    b) 4
    c) 6
    d) 8
    e) none of these

    ANS: d) 8   **PAGE:** 2.8

36. The formula of water, H_2O, suggests

    a) there is twice as much mass of hydrogen as oxygen in each molecule.
    b) there are two hydrogen atoms and one oxygen atom per water molecule.
    c) there is twice as much mass of oxygen as hydrogen in each molecule.
    d) there are two oxygen atoms and one hydrogen atom per water molecule.
    e) none of these

    ANS: b)   there are two hydrogen atoms and one oxygen atom per
                  water molecule.   **PAGE:** 2.8

37. Which of the following are incorrectly paired?

    a) K, alkali metal
    b) Ba, alkaline earth metal
    c) O, halogen
    d) Ne, noble gas
    e) Ni, transition metal

    ANS: c)   O, halogen   **PAGE:** 2.7

38. Which of the following are incorrectly paired?

    a) Phosphorus, Pr
    b) Palladium, Pd
    c) Platinum, Pt
    d) Lead, Pb
    e) Potassium, K

    ANS: a)   Phosphorus, Pr   **PAGE:** 2.7

39. Which of the following are incorrectly paired?

    a) Copper, Cu
    b) Carbon, C
    c) Cobalt, Co
    d) Calcium, Ca
    e) Cesium, Ce

    ANS: e)   Cesium, Ce   **PAGE:** 2.7

40.   All of the following are characteristics of metals *except*:

    a)   good conductors of heat
    b)   malleable
    c)   ductile
    d)   often lustrous
    e)   tend to gain electrons in chemical reactions

ANS: e)   tend to gain electrons in chemical reactions   **PAGE:** 2.7

41.   All of the following are characteristics of nonmetals *except*:

    a)   poor conductors of electricity
    b)   often bond to each other by forming covalent bonds
    c)   tend to form negative ions in chemical reactions with metals
    d)   appear in the upper left-hand corner of the periodic table
    e)   do not have a shiny (lustrous) appearance

ANS: d)   appear in the upper left-hand corner of the periodic table   **PAGE:** 2.7

42.   What are the forms of elemental carbon?

    a)   graphite and diamond
    b)   graphite, diamond, and buckminsterfullerene
    c)   graphite and buckminsterfullerene
    d)   diamond and buckminsterfullerene
    e)   diamond, graphite, and carbonite

ANS: b)   graphite, diamond, and buckminsterfullerene   **PAGE:** 2.8

43.   Which metals form cations with varying positive charges?

    a)   transition metals
    b)   Group 1 metals
    c)   Group 2 metals
    d)   Group 3 metals
    e)   metalloids

ANS: a)   transition metals   **PAGE:** 2.7,2.8

44.   A species with 12 protons and 10 electrons is

    a) Ne^{2+}
    b) Ti^{2+}
    c) Mg^{2+}
    d) Mg
    e) Ne^{2-}

ANS: c) Mg^{2+} **PAGE:** 2.5

45. The correct name for LiCl is

   a) lithium monochloride
   b) lithium (I) chloride
   c) monolithium chloride
   d) lithium chloride
   e) monolithium monochloride

   ANS: d)   lithium chloride   **PAGE:** 2.8

46. The correct name for FeO is

   a) iron oxide
   b) iron (II) oxide
   c) iron (III) oxide
   d) iron monoxide
   e) iron (I) oxide

   ANS: b)   iron (II) oxide   **PAGE:** 2.8

47. The correct name for Ca^{2+} is

   a) calcium
   b) calcium (II) ion
   c) calcium ion
   d) calcium (I) ion
   e) monocalcium ion

   ANS: c)   calcium ion   **PAGE:** 2.8

48. The formula for calcium bisulfate is

   a) $Ca(SO_4)_2$
   b) CaS_2
   c) $Ca(HSO_4)_2$
   d) Ca_2HSO_4
   e) Ca_2S

   ANS: c) $Ca(HSO_4)_2$ **PAGE:** 2.8

49. Which of the following is incorrectly named?

   a) $Pb(NO_3)_2$, lead(II) nitrate
   b) NH_4ClO_4, ammonium perchlorate
   c) PO_4^{3-}, phosphate ion
   d) $Mg(OH)_2$, magnesium hydroxide
   e) NO^{3-}, nitrite ion

   ANS: e) NO^{3-}, nitrite ion   **PAGE:** 2.8

27

50. All of the following are in aqueous solution. Which is incorrectly named?

   a) H_2SO_4, sulfuric acid
   b) H_2CO_3, carbonic acid
   c) H_3PO_4, phosphoric acid
   d) HCN, cyanic acid
   e) HCl, hydrochloric acid

   ANS: d)   HCN, cyanic acid   **PAGE:** 2.8

51. All of the following are in aqueous solution. Which is incorrectly named?

   a) $HC_2H_3O_2$, acetic acid
   b) HBr, bromic acid
   c) H_2SO_3, sulfurous acid
   d) HNO_2, nitrous acid
   e) $HClO_3$, chloric acid

   ANS: b)   HBr, bromic acid   **PAGE:** 2.8

52. Which of the following pairs is incorrect?

   a) NH_4Br, ammonium bromide
   b) K_2CO_3, potassium carbonate
   c) $BaPO_4$, barium phosphate
   d) CuCl, copper(I) chloride
   e) MnO_2, manganese (IV) oxide

   ANS: c) $BaPO_4$, barium phosphate   **PAGE:** 2.8

53. Write the names of the following compounds:

   a) $FeSO_4$ _____
   b) $NaC_2H_3O_2$ _____
   c) KNO_2 _____
   d) $Ca(OH)_2$ _____
   e) $NiCO_3$ _____

   ANS: a)   iron(II) sulfate
         b)   sodium acetate
         c)   potassium nitrite
         d)   calcium hydroxide
         e)   nickel(II) carbonate   **PAGE:** 2.8

54. Write the chemical formulas for the following compounds or ions.

   a) nitrate ion _____
   b) aluminum oxide _____
   c) ammonium ion _____
   d) perchloric acid _____
   e) copper(II) bromide _____

   ANS: a) NO_3^- b) Al_2O_3 c) NH_4^+ d) $HClO_4$ e) $CuBr_2$ **PAGE:** 2..8

55. How many atoms (total) are there in one formula unit of $Ca_3(PO_4)_2$?

   ANS: 13   **PAGE:** 2.8

56. Three samples of a solid substance composed of elements A and Z were prepared. The first contained 4.31 g A and 7.69 g Z. The second sample was 35.9% A and 64.1% Z. It was observed that 0.718 g A reacted with Z to form 2.00 g of the third sample. Show that these data illustrate the law of definite composition.

   ANS: See Sec. 2.2 of Zumdahl, *Chemistry*.   **PAGE:** 2.2

57. Explain how Dalton's atomic theory accounts for:

   a) the law of conservation of mass.
   b) the law of definite composition.
   c) the law of multiple proportion.

   ANS: See Sec. 2.3 of Zumdahl, *Chemistry*.   **PAGE:** 2.3

58. Complete the following table.

Symbol	# protons	# neutrons	# electrons	Net Charge
$^{206}_{82}Pb$				
	31	38		3$^+$
	52	75	54	
Mn		29		2$^+$

ANS:

Symbol	# protons	# neutrons	# electrons	Net Charge
$^{206}_{82}Pb$	82	124	82	0
Ga	31	38	28	3$^+$
Te	52	75	54	2$^-$
Mn	25	29	23	2$^+$

PAGE: 2.5

59. Complete the following table.

Symbol	$^{69}Ga^{+3}$	
Number of protons		34
Number of neutrons		46
Number of electrons		
Atomic number		
Mass number		
Net charge		0

ANS:

Symbol	$^{69}Ga^{+3}$	^{80}Se
Number of protons	31	34
Number of neutrons	38	46
Number of electrons	28	34
Atomic number	31	34
Mass number	69	80
Net charge	+3	0

PAGE: 2.5

60. Arsenopyrite is a mineral containing As, Fe, and S. Classify each element as metal, nonmetal, or metalloid.

   ANS: As = metalloid, Fe = metal, S = nonmetal   **PAGE:** 2.7

61–70. Name the following compounds:

61. $Al_2(SO_4)_3$

   ANS: aluminum sulfate   **PAGE:** 2.8

62. NH_4NO_3

   ANS: ammonium nitrate   **PAGE:** 2.8

63. NaH

   ANS: sodium hydride   **PAGE:** 2.8

64. $K_2Cr_2O_7$

   ANS: potassium dichromate   **PAGE:** 2.8

65. CCl_4

   ANS: carbon tetrachloride   **PAGE:** 2.8

66. AgCl

   ANS: silver chloride   **PAGE:** 2.8

67. $CaSO_4$

   ANS: calcium sulfate   **PAGE:** 2.8

68. HNO_3

   ANS: nitric acid   **PAGE:** 2.8

69. N_2O_3

   ANS: dinitrogen trioxide   **PAGE:** 2.8

70. SnI_2

   ANS: tin(II) iodide   **PAGE:** 2.8

71-80. Write the formula for:

71. sodium dichromate

   ANS: $Na_2Cr_2O_7$ **PAGE:** 2.8

72. iron (III) oxide

   ANS: Fe_2O_3 **PAGE:** 2.8

73. dinitrogen trioxide

   ANS: N_2O_3 **PAGE:** 2.8

74. cobalt (II) chloride

   ANS: $CoCl_2$ **PAGE:** 2.8

75. aluminum hydroxide

   ANS: $Al(OH)_3$ **PAGE:** 2.8

76. hydrosulfuric acid

   ANS: H_2S **PAGE:** 2.8

77. sulfurous acid

   ANS: H_2SO_3 **PAGE:** 2.8

78. nitric acid

   ANS: HNO_3 **PAGE:** 2.8

79. phosphoric acid

   ANS: H_3PO_4 **PAGE:** 2.8

80. acetic acid

   ANS: CH_3COOH **PAGE:** 2.8

31

CHAPTER 3   Stoichiometry

1. Bromine exists naturally as a mixture of bromine-79 and bromine-81 isotopes. An atom of bromine-79 contains

    a)   35 protons, 44 neutrons, 35 electrons.
    b)   34 protons and 35 electrons, only.
    c)   44 protons, 44 electrons, and 35 neutrons.
    d)   35 protons, 79 neutrons, and 35 electrons.
    e)   79 protons, 79 electrons, and 35 neutrons.

    ANS: a)   35 protons, 44 neutrons, 35 electrons.   **PAGE:** 3.1

2. The atomic mass of rhenium is 186.2. Given that 37.1% of natural rhenium is rhenium-185, what is the other stable isotope?

    a) $^{183}_{75} \text{Re}$

    b) $^{187}_{75} \text{Re}$

    c) $^{189}_{75} \text{Re}$

    d) $^{181}_{75} \text{Re}$

    e) $^{190}_{75} \text{Re}$

    ANS: b) $^{187}_{75} \text{Re}$ **PAGE:** 3.1

3. Consider the element indium, atomic number 49, atomic mass 114.8 g. The nucleus of an atom of indium-112 contains

    a)   49 protons, 63 neutrons, 49 electrons.
    b)   49 protons, 49 neutrons.
    c)   49 protons, 49 alpha particles.
    d)   49 protons, 63 neutrons.
    e)   49 protons, 112 neutrons.

    ANS: d)   49 protons, 63 neutrons.   **PAGE:** 3.1

4. Gallium consists of two isotopes of masses 68.95 amu and 70.95 amu with abundances of 60.16% and 39.84%, respectively. What is the average atomic mass of gallium?

    a)   69.95
    b)   70.15
    c)   71.95
    d)   69.75
    e)   69.55

    ANS: d)   69.75   **PAGE:** 3.1

5. Naturally occurring iron contains 5.82% $^{54}_{26}$Fe, 91.66% $^{56}_{26}$Fe, 2.19% $^{57}_{26}$Fe, and 0.33% $^{58}_{26}$Fe. The respective atomic masses are 53.940 amu, 55.935 amu, 56.935 amu, and 57.933 amu. Calculate the average atomic mass of iron.

ANS: 55.85 amu   **PAGE:** 3.1

6. What is the mass of one atom of copper in grams?
    a) 63.5 g
    b) 52.0 g
    c) 58.9 g
    d) 65. 4 g
    e) 1.06 x 10^{-22} g

    ANS: e)   1.06 x 10^{-22} g   **PAGE:** 3.2

7. Iron is biologically important in the transport of oxygen by red blood cells from the lungs to the various organs of the body. In the blood of an adult human, there are approximately 2.60×10^{13} red blood cells with a total of 2.90 g of iron. On the average, how many iron atoms are present in each blood cell? (molar mass (Fe) = 55.85 g)
    a) 8.33×10^{-10}
    b) 1.20×10^9
    c) 3.12×10^{22}
    d) 2.60×10^{13}
    e) 5.19×10^{-2}

    ANS: b) 1.20×10^9 **PAGE:** 3.2

8. Naturally occurring copper exists in two isotopic forms: ^{63}Cu and ^{65}Cu. The atomic mass of copper is 63.55 amu. What is the approximate natural abundance of ^{63}Cu?
    a) 63%
    b) 90%
    c) 70%
    d) 50%
    e) 30%

    ANS: c)   70%   **PAGE:** 3.1

9. Naturally occurring element X exists in three isotopic forms: X-28 (27.977 amu, 92.21% abundance), X-29 (28.976 amu, 4.70% abundance), and X-30 (29.974 amu, 3.09% abundance). Calculate the atomic weight of X.
    a) 28.1 amu
    b) 54.0 amu
    c) 29 amu
    d) 72.7 amu
    e) 36.2 amu

    ANS: a)   28.1 amu   **PAGE:** 3.1

10. A sample of ammonia has a mass of 56.6 g. How many molecules are in this sample?

    a) 3.32 molecules
    b) 17.03×10^{24} molecules
    c) 6.78×10^{23} molecules
    d) 2.00×10^{24} molecules
    e) 1.78×10^{24} molecules

    ANS: d) 2.00×10^{24} molecules   **PAGE:** 3.3

11. How many moles of hydrogen sulfide are contained in a 35.0-g sample of this gas?

    a) 2.16 mol
    b) 1.03 mol
    c) 7.43 mol
    d) 10.4 mol
    e) 6.97 mol

    ANS: b) 1.03 mol   **PAGE:** 3.3

12. What is the molar mass of ethanol (C_2H_5OH)?

    a) 45.07
    b) 38.90
    c) 46.07
    d) 34.17
    e) 62.07

    ANS: c) 46.07   **PAGE:** 3.3

13. For which compound does 0.256 mole weigh 12.8 g?

    a) C_2H_4O
    b) CO_2
    c) CH_3Cl
    d) C_2H_6
    e) none of these

    ANS: c) CH_3Cl **PAGE:** 3.3

14. Roundup, an herbicide manufactured by Monsanto, has the formula $C_3H_8NO_5P$. How many moles of molecules are there in a 500.-g sample of Roundup?

    a) 0.338
    b) 1.75
    c) 2.96
    d) 84.5
    e) none of these

    ANS: c) 2.96   **PAGE:** 3.3

15. Phosphorus has the molecular formula P_4 and sulfur has the molecular formula S_8. How many grams of phosphorus contain the same number of molecules as 6.41 g of sulfur?

    a) 3.10 g
    b) 3.21 g
    c) 6.19 g
    d) 6.41 g
    e) none of these

    ANS: a) 3.10 g   **PAGE:** 3.3

16. A given sample of xenon fluoride contains molecules of a single type XeF_n, where n is some whole number. Given that 9.03×10^{20} molecules of XeF_n weigh 0.311 g, calculate n.

    a) 1
    b) 2
    c) 4
    d) none of these

    ANS: c) 4   **PAGE:** 3.3

17–19. Phosphoric acid can be prepared by reaction of sulfuric acid with "phosphate rock" according to the equation:

$$Ca_3(PO_4)_2 + 3H_2SO_4 \rightarrow 3CaSO_4 + 2H_3PO_4$$

17. What is the molar mass of $Ca_3(PO_4)_2$?

    a) 310.18 g/mol
    b) 87.05 g/mol
    c) 135.05 g/mol
    d) 118.02 g/mol
    e) 166.02 g/mol

    ANS: a) 310.18 g/mol   **PAGE:** 3.3

35

18. How many oxygen atoms are there in 1.55 ng of $Ca_3(PO_4)_2$?

    a) 3.01×10^{12}
    b) 1.20×10^{13}
    c) 3.01×10^{18}
    d) 1.21×10^{16}
    e) 2.41×10^{13}

    ANS: e) 2.41×10^{13} **PAGE:** 3.3

19. Suppose the reaction is carried out starting with 103 g of $Ca_3(PO_4)_2$ and 75.0 g of H_2SO_4. Which substance is the limiting reactant?

    a) $Ca_3(PO_4)_2$
    b) H_2SO_4
    c) $CaSO_4$
    d) H_3PO_4
    e) none of these

    ANS: b) H_2SO_4 **PAGE:** 3.9

20. How many grams are in a 6.94-mol sample of sodium hydroxide?

    a) 40.0 g
    b) 278 g
    c) 169 g
    d) 131 g
    e) 34.2 g

    ANS: b)   278 g   **PAGE:** 3.3

21. How many atoms of hydrogen are present in 6.0 g of water?

    a) 2.0×10^{23}
    b) 7.2×10^{24}
    c) 1.1×10^{24}
    d) 4.0×10^{23}
    e) 0.66

    ANS: d) 4.0×10^{23} **PAGE:** 3.3

22. What is the molar mass of cryolite (Na_3AlF_6)?

    a) 209.9
    b) 185.3
    c) 210.0
    d) 104.2
    e) 68.97

    ANS: c)   210.0   **PAGE:** 3.3

23. The molar mass of calcium phosphate is

    a) 325.0 g/mol
    b) 310.2 g/mol
    c) 175.1 g/mol
    d) 135.1 g/mol
    e) none of these

    ANS: b) 310.2 g/mol   **PAGE:** 3.3

24. Which compound contains the highest percent by mass of hydrogen?

    a) HCl
    b) H_2O
    c) H_2SO_4
    d) H_2S
    e) HF

    ANS: b) H_2O **PAGE:** 3.4

25. A substance contains 35.0 g nitrogen, 5.05 g hydrogen, and 60.0 g of oxygen. How many grams of hydrogen are there in a 185-g sample of the substance?

    a) 9.34 g
    b) 18.7 g
    c) 10.6 g
    d) 5.05 g
    e) 36.6 g

    ANS: a) 9.34 g   **PAGE:** 3.4

26. How many grams of potassium are in 12.5 g of K_2CrO_7?

    a) 2.02 g
    b) 8.80 g
    c) 4.04 g
    d) 78.2 g
    e) 25.0 g

    ANS: c) 4.04 g   **PAGE:** 3.4

27. Nitric acid contains what percent hydrogen by mass?

    a) 20.0%
    b) 10.0%
    c) 4.50%
    d) 1.60%
    e) 3.45%

    ANS: d) 1.60%   **PAGE:** 3.4

28. In balancing an equation, we change the _____ to make the number of atoms on each side of the equation balance.

    a)   formulas of compounds in the reactants
    b)   coefficients of compounds
    c)   formulas of compounds in the products
    d)   subscripts of compounds
    e)   none of these

    ANS: b)   coefficients of compounds   **PAGE:** 3.6

29. What is the coefficient for water when the following equation is balanced?

$$As(OH)_3(s) + H_2SO_4(aq) \rightarrow As_2(SO_4)_3(aq) + H_2O(l)$$

    a)   1
    b)   2
    c)   4
    d)   6
    e)   12

    ANS: d)   6   **PAGE:** 3.7

30. One molecule of a compound weighs 2.03×10^{-22} g. Its molar mass is:

    a)   48.0 g/mol
    b)   92.1 g/mol
    c)   114 g/mol
    d)   122 g/mol
    e)   none of these

    ANS: d)   122 g/mol   **PAGE:** 3.3

31. A compound is composed of element X and hydrogen. Analysis shows the compound to be 80% X by mass, with three times as many hydrogen atoms as X atoms per molecule. Which element is element X?

    a)   He
    b)   C
    c)   F
    d)   S
    e)   none of these

    ANS: b)   C   **PAGE:** 3.4

32. You take an aspirin tablet (a compound consisting solely of carbon, hydrogen, and oxygen) with a mass of 1.00 g, burn it in air, and collect 2.20 g of carbon dioxide and 0.400 g water. The molar mass of aspirin is between 170 and 190 g/mol. The molecular form of aspirin is

   a) $C_6H_8O_5$
   b) $C_9H_8O_4$
   c) $C_8H_{10}O_5$
   d) $C_{10}H_6O_4$
   e) none of these

   ANS: b) $C_9H_8O_4$ **PAGE:** 3.5

33. Oxides of copper include CuO and Cu_2O. You heat 1.51 g of one of these copper oxides in the absence of air and obtain 1.21 g of Cu. True or false: You must have had CuO.

   ANS: True   **PAGE:** 3.4

34. You heat 3.970 g of a mixture of Fe_3O_4 and FeO to form 4.195 g Fe_2O_3. The mass percent of FeO originally in the mixture was:

   a) 12.1%
   b) 28.7%
   c) 71.3%
   d) 87.9%
   e) none of these

   ANS: b) 28.7%   **PAGE:** 3.4

35. You heat 3.970 g of a mixture of Fe_3O_4 and FeO to form 4.195 g Fe_2O_3. The mass of oxygen reacted is

   a) 0.225 g.
   b) 0.475 g.
   c) 1.00 g.
   d) cannot be determined
   e) none of these

   ANS: a) 0.225 g.   **PAGE:** 3.8

36. A mixture of KCl and KNO_3 is 44.20% potassium by mass. The percent of KCl in the mixture is closest to

   a) 40%
   b) 50%
   c) 60%
   d) 70%
   e) 80%

   ANS: a) 40%   **PAGE:** 3.4

39

37. The limiting reactant in a reaction

    a) has the lowest coefficient in a balanced equation.
    b) is the reactant for which you have the fewest number of moles.
    c) has the lowest ratio of moles available/coefficient in the balanced equation.
    d) has the lowest ratio of coefficient in the balanced equation/moles available.
    e) none of these

    ANS: c)   has the lowest ratio of moles available/coefficient in the
    balanced equation.   **PAGE:** 3.9

38. Given the equation $3A + B \rightarrow C + D$, you react 1 mole of A with 3 moles of B. True or false: A is the limiting reactant because you have fewer moles of A than B.

    ANS: False   **PAGE:** 3.9

39. Suppose the reaction $Ca_3(PO_4)_2 + 3H_2SO_4 \rightarrow 3CaSO_4 + 2H_3PO_4$ is carried out starting with 103 g of $Ca_3(PO_4)_2$ and 75.0 g of H_2SO_4. How much phosphoric acid will be produced?

    a) 74.9 g
    b) 50.0 g
    c) 112 g
    d) 32.5 g
    e) 97.6 g

    ANS: b)   50.0 g   **PAGE:** 3.9

40. A substance, A_2B, has the composition by mass of 60% A and 40% B. What is the composition of AB_2 by mass?

    a) 40% A, 60% B
    b) 50% A, 50% B
    c) 27% A, 73% B
    d) 33% A, 67% B
    e)   none of these

    ANS: c)   27% A, 73% B   **PAGE:** 3.3,4

41. Cortisone consists of molecules, each of which contains 21 atoms of carbon (plus other atoms). The mass percentage of carbon in cortisone is 69.98%. What is the molar mass of cortisone?

    a) 176.5 g/mol
    b) 252.2 g/mol
    c) 287.6 g/mol
    d) 312.8 g/mol
    e) 360.4 g/mol

    ANS: e)   360.4 g/mol   **PAGE:** 3.3,5

42. A substance contains 23.0 g sodium, 27.0 g aluminum, and 114 g fluorine. How many grams of sodium are there in a 120.-g sample of the substance?

    a) 14.0 g
    b) 23.0 g
    c) 16.8 g
    d) 27.6 g
    e) none of these

ANS: c)   16.8 g   PAGE: 3.4

43. $NaHCO_3$ is the active ingredient in baking soda. How many grams of oxygen are in 0.35 g of $NaHCO_3$?

    a) 0.012 g
    b) 0.022 g
    c) 0.067 g
    d) 0.15 g
    e) 0.20 g

ANS: e)   0.20 g   PAGE: 3.3

44. An oxide of iron has the formula Fe_3O_4. What mass percent of iron does it contain?

    a) 0.72%
    b) 28%
    c) 30.%
    d) 70.%
    e) 72%

ANS: e)   72%   PAGE: 3.4

45. Which of the following compounds has the same percent composition by mass as styrene, C_8H_8?

    a) acetylene, C_2H_2
    b) benzene, C_6H_6
    c) cyclobutadiene, C_4H_4
    d) α-ethyl naphthalene, $C_{12}H_{12}$
    e) all of these

ANS: e)   all of these   PAGE: 3.4

46. The molar mass of an insecticide, dibromoethane, is 187.9. Its molecular formula is $C_2H_4Br_2$. What percent by mass of bromine does dibromoethane contain?

    a)   37.8%
    b)   42.5%
    c)   50.0%
    d)   85.0%
    e)   89.3%

    ANS: d)   85.0%   **PAGE:** 3.4

47. Ammonium carbonate contains what percent nitrogen by mass?

    a)   14.6%
    b)   17.9%
    c)   29.2%
    d)   34.8%
    e)   none of these

    ANS: c)   29.2%   **PAGE:** 3.4

48. A chloride of rhenium contains 63.6% rhenium. What is the formula of this compound?

    a)   ReCl
    b) $ReCl_3$
    c) $ReCl_5$
    d) $ReCl_7$
    e) Re_2Cl_3

    ANS: b) $ReCl_3$ **PAGE:** 3.5

49. A 2.00-g sample of an oxide of bromine is converted to 2.936 g of AgBr. Calculate the empirical formula of the oxide. (molar mass for AgBr = 187.78)

    a) BrO_3
    b) BrO_2
    c)   BrO
    d) Br_2O
    e)   none of these

    ANS: a) BrO_3 **PAGE:** 3.5

50. A hydrocarbon (a compound consisting solely of carbon and hydrogen) is found to be 85.6% carbon by mass. What is the empirical formula for this compound?

    a) CH
    b) CH_2
    c) C_3H
    d) C_6H
    e) CH_6

    ANS: b) CH_2 **PAGE:** 3.5

51. The empirical formula of a group of compounds is CHCl. Lindane, a powerful insecticide, is a member of this group. The molar mass of lindane is 290.8. How many atoms of carbon does a molecule of lindane contain?

    a) 2
    b) 3
    c) 4
    d) 6
    e) 8

    ANS: d) 6   **PAGE:** 3.5

52. The empirical formula of styrene is CH; its molar mass is 104.1. What is the molecular formula of styrene?

    a) C_2H_4
    b) C_8H_8
    c) $C_{10}H_{12}$
    d) C_6H_6
    e) none of these

    ANS: b) C_8H_8 **PAGE:** 3.5

53. Adipic acid contains 49.32% C, 43.84% O, and 6.85% H by mass. What is the empirical formula?

    a) $C_3H_5O_2$
    b) $C_3H_3O_4$
    c) C_2HO_3
    d) $C_2H_5O_4$
    e) C_3HO_3

    ANS: a) $C_3H_5O_2$ **PAGE:** 3.5

54. Vitamin C contains the elements C, H, and O. It is known to contain 40.9% C and 4.58% H by mass. The molar mass of vitamin C has been found to be about 180. The molecular formula for vitamin C is:

    a) $C_2H_3O_2$
    b) $C_3H_4O_3$
    c) $C_4H_6O_4$
    d) $C_6H_8O_6$

    ANS: d) $C_6H_8O_6$ **PAGE:** 3.5

55. A 0.4647-g sample of a compound known to contain only carbon, hydrogen, and oxygen was burned in oxygen to yield 0.8635 g of CO_2 and 0.1767 g of H_2O. What is the empirical formula of the compound?

    a) CHO
    b) C_2H_2O
    c) $C_3H_3O_2$
    d) $C_6H_3O_2$
    e) $C_3H_6O_2$

    ANS: c) $C_3H_3O_2$ **PAGE:** 3.5

56. The hormone epinephrine is released in the human body during stress and increases the body's metabolic rate. Epinephrine, like many biochemical compounds, is composed of carbon, hydrogen, oxygen, and nitrogen. The percentage composition of the hormone is 56.8% C, 6.56% H, 28.4% O, and 8.28% N. Determine the empirical formula.

    ANS: $C_8H_{11}O_3N$ **PAGE:** 3.5

57. The characteristic odor of pineapple is due to ethyl butyrate, a compound containing carbon, hydrogen, and oxygen. Combustion of 2.78 g of ethyl butyrate leads to formation of 6.32 g of CO_2 and 2.58 g of H_2O. The properties of the compound suggest that the molar mass should be between 100 and 150. What is the molecular formula?

    ANS: $C_6H_{12}O_2$ **PAGE:** 3.5

58. Balanced chemical equations imply which of the following?

    a) Numbers of molecules are conserved in chemical change.
    b) Numbers of atoms are conserved in chemical change.
    c) Volume is conserved in chemical change.
    d) a and b
    e) b and c

    ANS: b)   Numbers of atoms are conserved in chemical change.   **PAGE:** 3.6

44

59. What is the coefficient for oxygen when the following equation is balanced?

$$NH_3(g) + O_2(g) \rightarrow NO_2(g) + H_2O(g)$$

   a) 3
   b) 6
   c) 7
   d) 12
   e) 14

   ANS: c) 7   **PAGE:** 3.7

60. When 125.0 g of ethylene (C_2H_4) burns in oxygen to give carbon dioxide and water, how many grams of CO_2 are formed?

   a) 392.2 g
   b) 250.0 g
   c) 57.50 g
   d) 425.6 g
   e) 327.0 g

   ANS: a) 392. g   **PAGE:** 3.8

61. How many of the following statements are true concerning chemical equations?

   I. Coefficients can be fractions.
   II. Subscripts can be fractions.
   III. Coefficients represent the relative masses of the reactants and/or products.
   IV. Changing the subscripts to balance an equation can only be done once.
   V. Atoms are conserved when balancing chemical equations.
   a) 1
   b) 2
   c) 3
   d) 4
   e) 5

   ANS: b) 2   **PAGE:** 3.7

62. Determine the coefficient for O_2 when the following equation is balanced in standard form (smallest whole number integers)

$$C_4H_{10}(g) + O_2(g) \rightarrow CO_2(g) + H_2O(g)$$

   a) 4
   b) 8
   c) 10
   d) 13
   e) 20

   ANS: d) 13   **PAGE:** 3.7

45

63. What is the sum of the coefficients of the following equation when it is balanced using smallest whole number integers?

$$NaNH_2 + NaNO_3 \rightarrow NaN_3 + NaOH + NH_3$$

a) 5
b) 6
c) 7
d) 8
e) 9

ANS: e) 9

PAGE: 3.7

64. Hydrocortisone valerate is an ingredient in hydrocortisone cream, prescribed for skin problems. Its empirical formula is $C_{26}H_{38}O_6$. What is the percent by mass of carbon in hydrocortisone valerate?

a) 69.9%
b) 43.6%
c) 54.2%
d) 76.9%
e) 60.1%

ANS: a) 69.9%

PAGE: 3.4

65. $$wPCl_5 + xH_2O \rightarrow yPOCl_3 + zHCl$$

The above equation is properly balanced when

a) $w = 1, x = 2, y = 2, z = 4$
b) $w = 2, x = 2, y = 2, z = 2$
c) $w = 2, x = 2, y = 2, z = 1$
d) $w = 1, x = 1, y = 1, z = 2$
e) none of these

ANS: d) $w = 1, x = 1, y = 1, z = 2$

PAGE: 3.7

66. Potassium forms an oxide containing 1 oxygen atom for every 2 atoms of potassium. What is the coefficient of oxygen in the balanced equation for the reaction of potassium with oxygen to form this oxide?

a) 0
b) 1
c) 2
d) 3
e) 4

ANS: b) 1

PAGE: 3.7

67. What is the subscript of aluminum in the formula of aluminum phosphate?

    a) 1
    b) 2
    c) 3
    d) 4
    e) 0

    ANS: a)   1   **PAGE:** 3.7

68. Indium reacts with chlorine to form $InCl_3$. In the balanced equation for this reaction, the coefficient of the indium trichloride is

    a) 1
    b) 2
    c) 3
    d) 4
    e) 6

    ANS: b)   2   **PAGE:** 3.7

69. Give (in order) the correct coefficients to balance the following reaction:

    $$H_2SnCl_6 + H_2S \rightarrow SnS_2 + HCl$$

    a) 1, 2, 1, 6
    b) 1, 2, 2, 2
    c) 1, 1, 1, 6
    d) 6, 2, 1, 1
    e) 2, 4, 2, 6

    ANS: a)   1, 2, 1, 6   **PAGE:** 3.7

70. What would be the g Al/mole S ratio for the product of a reaction between aluminum and sulfur?

    a) 26.98 g Al/mol S
    b) 53.98 g Al/mol S
    c) 80.94 g Al/mol S
    d) 17.99 g Al/mol S
    e) 40.47 g Al/mol S

    ANS: d)   17.99 g Al/mol S   **PAGE:** 3.7,8

71. In the balanced equation for the reaction

    $[A]P_4O_6 (s) + [B]H_2O(1) \rightarrow [C]H_3PO_3 (aq)$

    if [A] equals 2, the coefficient [C] equals

    a) 2
    b) 4
    c) 6
    d) 10
    e) none of these

    ANS: e)   none of these   **PAGE:** 3.7

72. When the equation $C_4H_{10} + O_2 \rightarrow CO_2 + H_2O$ is balanced with the smallest set of integers, the sum of the coefficients is

    a) 4
    b) 28
    c) 33
    d) 15
    e) 30

    ANS: c)   33   **PAGE:** 3.7

73. Which of the following equations correctly describes the combustion of CH_4 and O_2 to produce water (H_2O) and carbon dioxide (CO_2)?

    a) $CH_4 + (1/2)O_2 \rightarrow CO_2 + H_2O$
    b) $CH_4 + O_2 \rightarrow CO_2 + 2H_2O$
    c) $CH_4 + 2O_2 \rightarrow CO_2 + 2H_2O$
    d) $CH_4 + 3O_2 \rightarrow 2CO_2 + H_2O$

    ANS: c) $CH_4 + 2O_2 \rightarrow CO_2 + 2H_2O$ **PAGE:** 3.7

74. A reaction occurs between sodium carbonate and hydrochloric acid producing sodium chloride, carbon dioxide, and water. The correct set of coefficients, respectively, for the balanced reaction is:

    a) 3 6 6 3 4
    b) 8 6 5 10 5
    c) 5 10 10 5 5
    d) 1 2 2 1 1
    e) none of these

    ANS: d)   1 2 2 1 1   **PAGE:** 3.7

75. Which of the following equations is not balanced?

    a) $4Al + 3O_2 \rightarrow 2Al_2O_3$

    b) $C_2H_6 + \dfrac{7}{2} O_2 \rightarrow 2CO_2 + 3H_2O$

    c) $2KClO_3 \rightarrow 2KCl + \dfrac{3}{2} O_2$

    d) $4P_4 + 5S_8 \rightarrow 4P_4S_{10}$

    e) $P_4 + 5O_2 \rightarrow P_4O_{10}$

ANS: c) $2KClO_3 \rightarrow 2KCl + \dfrac{3}{2} O_2$ **PAGE:** 3.6

76. When the following equation is balanced, what is the sum of the coefficients?

    $$Al_2(SO_4)_3 + Ca(OH)_2 \rightarrow Al(OH)_3 + CaSO_4$$

    a) 4
    b) 9
    c) 8
    d) 3
    e) 10

ANS: b)   9   **PAGE:** 3.7

77. The Claus reactions, shown below, are used to generate elemental sulfur from hydrogen sulfide.

    $$2H_2S + 3O_2 \rightarrow 2SO_2 + 2H_2O$$

    $$SO_2 + 2H_2S \xrightarrow{Fe_2O_3} 3S + 2H_2O$$

    How much sulfur (in grams) is produced from 48.0 grams of O_2?

    a) 16.0 g
    b) 32.1 g
    c) 48.1 g
    d) 96.2 g
    e) none of these

ANS: d)   96.2 g   **PAGE:** 3.8

78. A 6.32-g sample of potassium chlorate was decomposed according to the following equation: $2KClO_3 \rightarrow 2KCl + 3O_2$

How many moles of oxygen are formed?

   a) 1.65 g
   b) 0.051 moles
   c) 0.0344 moles
   d) 0.0774 moles
   e) none of these

ANS: d)   0.0774 moles   **PAGE:** 3.8

79. How many grams of $Ca(NO_3)_2$ can be produced by reacting excess HNO_3 with 7.40 g of $Ca(OH)_2$?

   a) 10.2 g
   b) 16.4 g
   c) 32.8 g
   d) 8.22 g
   e) 7.40 g

ANS: b)   16.4 g   **PAGE:** 3.8

80. How many grams of H_2O will be formed when 32.0 g H_2 is mixed with 32.0 g O_2 and allowed to react to form water?

   a) 36.0 g
   b) 288 g
   c) 18.0 g
   d) 64.0 g
   e) 144 g

ANS: a)   36.0 g   **PAGE:** 3.8,9

81. Sulfuric acid may be produced by the following process:

$$4FeS_2 + 11O_2 \rightarrow 2Fe_2O_3 + 8SO_2$$

$$2SO_2 + O_2 \rightarrow 2SO_3$$

$$SO_3 + H_2O \rightarrow H_2SO_4$$

How many moles of H_2SO_4 will be produced form 5.00 moles of FeS_2?

   a) 6.11
   b) 5.00
   c) 10.00
   d) 12.22
   e) 20.00

ANS: c)   10.00   **PAGE:** 3.8

82.   Reaction of methane with oxygen really proceeds in two steps:

$$CH_4 + \left(\frac{3}{2}\right) O_2 \rightarrow CO + 2H_2O$$

$$CO + \left(\frac{1}{2}\right) O_2 \rightarrow CO_2$$

A sample of CH_4 is burned in an excess of O_2 to give 2.2 moles of H_2O. How many moles of CH_4 were in the original sample?

   a)   1.1
   b)   1.8
   c)   2.2
   d)   0.60
   e)   none of these (a-d)

ANS: a)   1.1   **PAGE:** 3.8,9

83.   Iron is produced from its ore by the reactions:

$$2C(s) + O_2(g) \rightarrow 2CO(g)$$

$$Fe_2O_3(s) + 3CO(g) \rightarrow 2Fe(s) + 3CO_2(g)$$

How many moles of $O_2(g)$ are needed to produce 1 mole of $Fe(s)$?

   a)   0.5 mole O_2
   b)   0.75 mole O_2
   c)   1 mole O_2
   d)   1.5 mole O_2
   e)   none of these

ANS: b)   0.75 mole O_2 **PAGE:** 3.8

84.   The refining of aluminum from bauxite ore (which contains 50.% Al_2O_3 by mass) proceeds by the overall reaction $2Al_2O_3 + 3C \rightarrow 4Al + 3CO_2$. How much bauxite ore is required to give the 5.0×10^{13} g of aluminum produced each year in the United States? (Assume 100% conversion.)

   a) 1.3×10^{13} g
   b) 5.3×10^{13} g
   c) 1.9×10^{14} g
   d) 7.6×10^{14} g
   e)   none of these

ANS: c) 1.9×10^{14} g   **PAGE:** 3.8

51

85. Consider the following reaction:

$$CH_4(g) + 4Cl_2(g) \rightarrow CCl_4(g) + 4HCl(g)$$

What mass of CCl_4 is formed by the reaction of 8.00 g of methane with an excess of chlorine?

   a)   1.42 g
   b)   7.10 g
   c)   14.2 g
   d)   76.7 g
   e)   none of these

ANS: d)   76.7 g   **PAGE:** 3.8

86. One commercial system removes SO_2 emissions from smoke at 95.0°C by the following set of balanced reactions:

$$SO_2(g) + Cl_2 \rightarrow SO_2Cl_2(g)$$

$$SO_2Cl_2 + 2H_2O \rightarrow H_2SO_4 + 2HCl$$

$$H_2SO_4 + Ca(OH)_2 \rightarrow CaSO_4(s) + 2H_2O$$

Assuming the process is 95.0% efficient, how many grams of $CaSO_4$ may be produced from 1.00×10^2 grams of SO_2 (molar masses: SO_2, 64.1 g/mol; $CaSO_4$, 136 g/mol)?

   a)   44.8 g
   b)   47.1 g
   c)   87.2 g
   d)   202 g
   e)   212 g

ANS: d)   202 g   **PAGE:** 3.8

87. When rubidium metal is exposed to air, one atom of rubidium, Rb, combines with two atoms of oxygen. If 1.75 grams of rubidium is exposed to air, what will be the mass of the product in grams?

   a)   0.328 g
   b)   0.655 g
   c)   1.37 g
   d)   2.08 g
   e)   2.41 g

ANS: e)   2.41 g   **PAGE:** 3.8

88. The following two reactions are important in the blast furnace production of iron metal from iron ore (Fe_2O_3):

$$2C(s) + O_2(g) \rightarrow 2CO(g)$$

$$Fe_2O_3 + 3CO(g) \rightarrow 2Fe + 3CO_2(g)$$

Using these balanced reactions, how many moles of O_2 are required for the production of 5.00 kg of Fe?

   a) 67.1 moles
   b) 29.8 moles
   c) 7.46 moles
   d) 89.5 moles
   e) 16.8 moles

ANS: a)   67.1 moles   **PAGE:** 3.8

89. SO_2 reacts with H_2S as follows:

$$2H_2S + SO_2 \rightarrow 3S + 2H_2O$$

When 7.50 g of H_2S reacts with 12.75 g of SO_2, which statement applies?

   a) 6.38 g of sulfur are formed.
   b) 10.6 g of sulfur are formed.
   c) 0.0216 moles of H_2S remain.
   d) 1.13 g of H_2S remain.
   e) SO_2 is the limiting reagent.

ANS: b)   10.6 g of sulfur are formed.   **PAGE:** 3.9

90. A 15-g sample of lithium is reacted with 15 g of fluorine to form lithium fluoride: $2Li + F_2 \rightarrow 2LiF$. After the reaction is complete, what will be present?

   a) 2.16 moles lithium fluoride only
   b) 0.789 moles lithium fluoride only
   c) 2.16 moles lithium fluoride and 0.395 moles fluorine
   d) 0.789 moles lithium fluoride and 1.37 moles lithium
   e) none of these

ANS: d)   0.789 moles lithium fluoride and 1.37 moles lithium   **PAGE:** 3.9

91. Consider the fermentation reaction of glucose:

$$C_6H_{12}O_6 \rightarrow 2C_2H_5OH + 2CO_2$$

A 1.00-mole sample of $C_6H_{12}O_6$ was placed in a vat with 100 g of yeast. If 46 grams of C_2H_5OH was obtained, what was the percent yield of C_2H_5OH?

a) 50.%
b) 56%
c) 100%
d) 42%
e) none of these

ANS: a)   50.%   **PAGE:** 3.9

92. A 5.95-g sample of $AgNO_3$ is reacted with $BaCl_2$ according to the equation

$$2AgNO_3(aq) + BaCl_2(aq) \rightarrow 2AgCl(s) + Ba(NO_3)_2(aq)$$

to give 4.00 g of AgCl. What is the percent yield of AgCl?

a) 21.4%
b) 39.8%
c) 67.2%
d) 79.7%
e) 93.5%

ANS: d)   79.7%   **PAGE:** 3.9

93. The reaction of 11.9 g of $CHCl_3$ with excess chlorine produced 12.6 g of CCl_4, carbon tetrachloride: $2CHCl_3 + 2Cl_2 \rightarrow 2CCl_4 + 2HCl$. What is the percent yield?

a) 100%
b) 27.4%
c) 82.2%
d) 113%
e) 46.2%

ANS: c)   82.2%   **PAGE:** 3.9

94. When 20.0 g C_2H_6 and 60.0 g O_2 react to form CO_2 and H_2O, how many grams of water are formed?

a) 14.5 g
b) 18.0 g
c) 58.0 g
d) 20.0 g
e) none of these

ANS: e)   none of these   **PAGE:** 3.9

54

95. Given the equation $3A + B \rightarrow C + D$, you react 2 moles of A with 1 mole of B. Which of the following is true?

    a) A is the limiting reactant because of its higher molar mass.
    b) A is the limiting reactant because you need 3 moles of A and have 2.
    c) B is the limiting reactant because you have fewer moles of B than A.
    d) B is the limiting reactant because 3 A molecules react with 1 B molecule.
    e) Neither reactant is limiting.

    ANS: b) A is the limiting reactant because you need 3 moles of A and have 2.   **PAGE:** 3.9

96. Consider the following reaction:

    $$CH_4(g) + 4Cl_2(g) \rightarrow CCl_4(g) + 4HCl(g)$$

    What mass of CCl_4 will be formed if 1.20 moles of methane react with 1.60 moles of chlorine?

    a) 229 g
    b) 171 g
    c) 114 g
    d) 61.5 g
    e) 17.1 g

    ANS: d)   61.5 g   **PAGE:** 3.9

97. The limiting reactant in a reaction

    a) is the reactant for which there is the least amount in grams.
    b) is the reactant which has the lowest coefficient in a balanced equation.
    c) is the reactant for which there is the most amount in grams.
    d) is the reactant for which there is the fewest number of moles.
    e) none of the above

    ANS: e)   none of the above   **PAGE:** 3.9

98. The limiting reactant is the reactant

    a) for which you have the lowest mass in grams.
    b) which has the lowest coefficient in the balanced equation.
    c) which has the lowest molar mass.
    d) which is left over after the reaction has gone to completion.
    e) none of the above

    ANS: e)   none of the above   **PAGE:** 3.9

99. Consider the following reaction:

$$2A + B \rightarrow 3C + D$$

3.0 mol A and 2.0 mol B react to form 4.0 mol C. What is the percent yield of this reaction?

   a)   50%
   b)   67%
   c)   75%
   d)   89%
   e)   100%

ANS: d)   89%   **PAGE:** 3.9

100. One of the major commercial uses of sulfuric acid is in the production of phosphoric acid and calcium sulfate. The phosphoric acid is used for fertilizer. The reaction is $Ca_3(PO_4)_2 + 3H_2SO_4 \rightarrow 3CaSO_4 + 2H_3PO_4$. What mass of concentrated H_2SO_4 (98% by mass) must be used to react completely with 100.00 g of calcium phosphate?

ANS: 96.770 g H_2SO_4 **PAGE:** 3.8

101. In a metallurgical process the mineral pyrite, FeS_2, is roasted in air:

$$FeS_2 + O_2 \rightarrow Fe_2O_3 + SO_2$$

The SO_2 is then converted into H_2SO_4 in the following reactions:

$$2SO_2 + O_2 \rightarrow 2SO_3$$
$$SO_3 + H_2SO_4 \rightarrow H_2S_2O_7$$
$$H_2S_2O_7 + H_2O \rightarrow 2H_2SO_4$$

Assuming the mineral is 24.0% FeS_2 and the remainder is inert, what mass of H_2SO_4 is produced if 155 g of the mineral is used?

ANS: 60.8 g H_2SO_4 **PAGE:** 3.8

102. Vitamin B_{12}, cyanocobalamin, is essential for human nutrition. It's concentrated in animal tissue but not in higher plants. People who abstain completely from animal products may develop anemia so cyanocobalamin is used in vitamin supplements. It contains 4.38% cobalt by mass. Calculate the molar mass of cyanocobalamin assuming there is one cobalt per molecule.

ANS: 1345 g/mol   **PAGE:** 3.4

103. The molecular formula always represents the total number of atoms of each element present in a compound.

ANS: True   **PAGE:** 3.5

104. When balancing a chemical equation, it is generally best to start with the least complicated molecules.

    ANS: False   **PAGE:** 3.6

105. To balance a chemical equation, the coefficients must not be changed.

    ANS: False   **PAGE:** 3.6

106. The reactant with the highest molar mass is always the limiting reactant.

    ANS: False   **PAGE:** 3.9

107. The reactant which, when used up completely, can produce the least amount of product, is the limiting reactant.

    ANS: False   **PAGE:** 3.9

108. In order to determine the molecular formula from the empirical formula, we must know the _____.

    ANS: molar mass   **PAGE:** 3.5

109. In a chemical equation, the _____ are written on the left side of the arrow, and the _____ are written on the right side of the arrow.

    ANS: reactants, products   **PAGE:** 3.6

110. The _____ in a chemical equation represent the number of atoms in a particular molecule or formula unit.

    ANS: subscripts   **PAGE:** 3.6

111. The _____ in a balanced equation represent numbers of molecules.

    ANS: coefficients   **PAGE:** 3.7

112. The percent yield is a ratio of the _____ yield to the _____ yield, multiplied by 100%.

    ANS: actual, theoretical   **PAGE:** 3.9

1. An unknown substance dissolves readily in water but not in benzene (a nonpolar solvent). Molecules of what type are present in the substance?

    a) neither polar nor nonpolar
    b) polar
    c) either polar or nonpolar
    d) nonpolar
    e) none of these

   ANS: b) polar   **PAGE:** 4.1

2. A 20.0-g sample of HF is dissolved in water to give 2.0×10^2 mL of solution. The concentration of the solution is:

    a) 1.0 M
    b) 3.0 M
    c) 0.10 M
    d) 5.0 M
    e) 10.0 M

   ANS: d) 5.0 M   **PAGE:** 4.3

3. 1.00 mL of a 3.50×10^{-4} M solution of oleic acid is diluted with 9.00 mL of petroleum ether, forming solution A. 2.00 mL of solution A is diluted with 8.00 mL of petroleum ether, forming solution B. How many grams of oleic acid are 5.00 mL of solution B? (molar mass for oleic acid = 282 g/mol)

    a) 4.94×10^{-4} g
    b) 7.00×10^{-6} g
    c) 4.94×10^{-5} g
    d) 1.97×10^{-6} g
    e) 9.87×10^{-6} g

   ANS: e) 9.87×10^{-6} g   **PAGE:** 4.3

4. How many grams of NaCl are contained in 350. mL of a 0.250 M solution of sodium chloride?

    a) 41.7 g
    b) 5.11 g
    c) 14.6 g
    d) 87.5 g
    e) none of these

   ANS: b) 5.11 g   **PAGE:** 4.3

5. Which of the following aqueous solutions contains the greatest number of ions?

   a) 400.0 mL of 0.10 M NaCl
   b) 300.0 mL of 0.10 M $CaCl_2$
   c) 200.0 mL of 0.10 M $FeCl_3$
   d) 200.0 mL of 0.10 M KBr
   e) 800.0 mL of 0.10 M sucrose

   ANS: b)   300.0 mL of 0.10 M $CaCl_2$ **PAGE:** 4.3

6. What mass of calcium chloride, $CaCl_2$, is needed to prepare 2.850 L of a 1.56 M solution?

   a) 25.9 g
   b) 60.8 g
   c) 111 g
   d) 203 g
   e) 493 g

   ANS: e)   493 g   **PAGE:** 4.3

7. A 54.8 g sample of $SrCl_2$ is dissolved in 112.5 mL of solution. Calculate the molarity of this solution.

   a) 0.346 M
   b) 3.07 M
   c) 3.96 M
   d) 8.89 M
   e) none of these

   ANS: b)   3.07 M   **PAGE:** 4.3

8. What mass of solute is contained in 256 mL of a 0.895 M ammonium chloride solution?

   a) 12.3 g
   b) 13.7 g
   c) 47.9 g
   d) 53.5 g
   e) none of these

   ANS: a)   12.3 g   **PAGE:** 4.3

9. A 51.24-g sample of $Ba(OH)_2$ is dissolved in enough water to make 1.20 liters of solution. How many mL of this solution must be diluted with water in order to make 1.00 liter of 0.100 molar $Ba(OH)_2$?

    a) 400. mL
    b) 333 mL
    c) 278 mL
    d) 1.20×10^3 mL
    e) none of these

    ANS: a)   400. mL   **PAGE:** 4.3

10. What volume of 18.0 M sulfuric acid must be used to prepare 15.5 L of 0.195 M H_2SO_4?

    a) 168 mL
    b) 0.336 L
    c) 92.3 mL
    d) 226 mL
    e) none of these

    ANS: a)   168 mL   **PAGE:** 4.3

11. How many grams of NaOH are contained in 5.0×10^2 mL of a 0.80 M sodium hydroxide solution?

    a) 16 g
    b) 80. g
    c) 20. g
    d) 64 g
    e) none of these

    ANS: a)   16 g   **PAGE:** 4.3

12. A 230.-mL sample of a 0.275 M solution is left on a hot plate overnight; the following morning the solution is 1.10 M. What volume of solvent has evaporated from the 0.275 M solution?

    a) 58.0 mL
    b) 63.3 mL
    c) 172 mL
    d) 230. mL
    e) 288 mL

    ANS: c)   172 mL   **PAGE:** 4.3

13. The net ionic equation for the reaction of aluminum sulfate and sodium hydroxide contains which of the following species?

   a) $3Al^{3+}(aq)$

   b) $OH^-(aq)$

   c) $3OH^-(aq)$

   d) $2Al^{3+}(aq)$

   e) $2Al(OH)_3(s)$

   ANS: c) $3OH^-(aq)$ **PAGE:** 4.6,8

14. The net ionic equation for the reaction of calcium bromide and sodium phosphate contains which of the following species?

   a) $Ca^{2+}(aq)$

   b) $PO_4^{3-}(aq)$

   c) $2Ca_3(PO_4)2(s)$

   d) $6NaBr(aq)$

   e) $3Ca^{2+}(aq)$

   ANS: e) $3Ca^{2+}(aq)$ **PAGE:** 4.6,8

15. Which of the following is a strong acid?

   a) HF
   b) KOH
   c) $HClO_4$
   d) HClO
   e) HBrO

   ANS: c) $HClO_4$ **PAGE:** 4.2

16. All of the following are weak acids *except*

   a) HCNO
   b) HBr
   c) HF
   d) HNO_2
   e) HCN

   ANS: b) HBr   **PAGE:** 4.2

61

17. Which of the following is *not* a strong base?

   a) $Ca(OH)_2$
   b) KOH
   c) NH_3
   d) LiOH
   e) $Sr(OH)_2$

   ANS: c) NH_3 **PAGE:** 4.2

18. Which of the following is paired incorrectly?

   a) HI – strong acid
   b) HNO_3 – weak acid
   c) $Ba(OH)_2$ – strong base
   d) HBr – strong acid
   e) NH_3 – weak acid

   ANS: b) HNO_3 – weak acid   **PAGE:** 4.2

19. The interaction between solute particles and water molecules, which tends to cause a salt to fall apart in water, is called

   a) hydration.
   b) polarization.
   c) dispersion.
   d) coagulation.
   e) conductivity.

   ANS: a) hydration   **PAGE:** 4.1

20. Consider two organic molecules, ethanol and benzene. One dissolves in water and the other does not. Why?

   a) They have different molar masses.
   b) One is ionic, the other is not.
   c) One is an electrolyte, the other is not.
   d) Ethanol contains a polar $O-H$ bond, and benzene does not.
   e) Two of these.

   ANS: d) Ethanol contains a polar $O-H$ bond, and benzene does
           not.   **PAGE:** 4.1,2

21. When sodium chloride and lead(II) nitrate react in an aqueous solution, which of the following terms will be present in the balanced molecular equation?

    a) $PbCl(s)$
    b) $Pb_2Cl(s)$
    c) $NaNO_3(aq)$
    d) $2NaNO_3(aq)$
    e) $2PbCl_2(s)$

    ANS: d) $2NaNO_3(aq)$ **PAGE:** 4.5,6

22. When solutions of phosphoric acid and iron(III) nitrate react, which of the following terms will be present in the balanced molecular equation?

    a) $HNO_3(aq)$
    b) $3HNO_3(aq)$
    c) $2FePO_4(s)$
    d) $3FePO_4(s)$
    e) $2HNO_3(aq)$

    ANS: b) $3HNO_3(aq)$ **PAGE:** 4.5,6

23. When solutions of cobalt(II) chloride and carbonic acid react, which of the following terms will be present in the net ionic equation?

    a) $CoCO_3(s)$
    b) $H^+(aq)$
    c) $2CoCO_3(s)$
    d) $2Cl^-(aq)$
    e)   two of these

    ANS: a) $CoCO_3(s)$ **PAGE:** 4.5,6

24. You have exposed electrodes of a light bulb in a solution of H_2SO_4 such that the light bulb is on. You add a dilute solution and the bulb grows dim. Which of the following could be in the solution?

    a) $Ba(OH)_2$
    b) $NaNO_3$
    c) K_2SO_4
    d) $Ca(NO_3)_2$
    e)   none of these

    ANS: a) $Ba(OH)_2$ **PAGE:** 4.2,5,8

25. You mix 260. mL of 1.20 M lead(II) nitrate with 300. mL of 1.90 M potassium iodide. The lead(II) iodide is insoluble. Which of the following is false?

   a)   The final concentration of Pb^{2+} ions is 0.0482 M.
   b)   You form 131 g of lead(II) iodide.
   c)   The final concentration of K^+ is 1.02 M.
   d)   The final concentration of NO_3^- is 1.02 M.
   e)   All are true.

   ANS: d)   The final concentration of NO_3^- is 1.02 M.   **PAGE:** 4.5-7

26. The concentration of a salt water solution which sits in an open beaker decreases over time.

   ANS: False   **PAGE:** 4.3

27. You have 2 solutions of chemical *A*. To determine which has the highest concentration of *A* in molarity, what is the minimum number of the following you must know?

   I.   the mass in grams of *A* in each solution
   II. the molar mass of *A*
   III. the volume of water added to each solution
   IV. the total volume of the solution
   a)   0
   b)   1
   c)   2
   d)   3
   e)   You must know all of them.

   ANS: c)   2   **PAGE:** 4.3

28. The following reactions:

   $$Pb^{2+} + 2I^- \rightarrow PbI_2$$

   $$2Ce^{4+} + 2I^- \rightarrow I_2 + 2Ce^{3+}$$

   $$HOAc + NH_3 \rightarrow NH_4^+ + OAc^-$$

   are examples of

   a)   acid-base reactions.
   b)   unbalanced reactions.
   c)   precipitation, acid-base, and redox reactions, respectively.
   d)   redox, acid-base, and precipitation reactions, respectively.
   e)   precipitation, redox, and acid-base reactions, respectively.

   ANS: e)   precipitation, redox, and acid-base reactions, respectively.   **PAGE:** 4.4-9

29. In writing the total ionic equation for the reaction (if any) that occurs when aqueous solutions of KOH and $Mg(NO_3)_2$ are mixed, which of the following would *not* be written as ionic species?

   a) KOH
   b) $Mg(NO_3)_2$
   c) $Mg(OH)_2$
   d) KNO_3
   e) All of the above would be written as ionic species.

   ANS: c) $Mg(OH)_2$ **PAGE:** 4.4,6

30–32. Aqueous solutions of barium chloride and silver nitrate are mixed to form solid silver chloride and aqueous barium nitrate.

30. The balanced molecular equation contains which one of the following terms?

   a) $AgCl(s)$
   b) $2AgCl(s)$
   c) $2Ba(NO_3)_2$
   d) $BaNO_3$
   e) $3AgCl(s)$

   ANS: b) $2AgCl(s)$ **PAGE:** 4.5,6

31. The balanced complete ionic equation contains which of the following terms?

   a) $2Ba^{2+}(aq)$
   b) $Cl^-(aq)$
   c) $2Ag^+(aq)$
   d) $NO_3^-(aq)$
   e) $3NO_3^-(aq)$

   ANS: c) $2Ag^+(aq)$ **PAGE:** 4.5,6

32. The net ionic equation contains which of the following terms?

   a) $Ag^+(aq)$
   b) $Ba^{2+}(aq)$
   c) $NO_3^-(aq)$
   d) $2NO_3^-(aq)$
   e) none of these

   ANS: a) $Ag^+(aq)$ **PAGE:** 4.5,6

33. The man who discovered the essential nature of acids through solution conductivity studies is

    a) Priestly.
    b) Boyle.
    c) Einstein.
    d) Mendeleev.
    e) Arrhenius.

    ANS: e)   Arrhenius.   **PAGE:** 4.2

34. The following reactions

    $$2K(s) + Br_2(l) \rightarrow 2KBr(s)$$

    $$AgNO_3(aq) + NaCl(aq) \rightarrow AgCl(s) + NaNO_3(aq)$$

    $$HCl(aq) + KOH(aq) \rightarrow H_2O(l) + KCl(aq)$$

    are examples of

    a) precipitation reactions.
    b) redox, precipitation, and acid-base, respectively.
    c) precipitation (two) and acid-base reactions, respectively.
    d) redox reactions.
    e) none of these

    ANS: b)   redox, precipitation, and acid-base, respectively.   **PAGE:** 4.4–9

35. Aqueous solutions of sodium sulfide and copper(II) chloride are mixed together. Which statement is correct?

    a) Both NaCl and CuS precipitate from solution.
    b) No precipitate forms.
    c) CuS will precipitate from solution.
    d) NaCl will precipitate from solution.
    e) No reaction will occur.

    ANS: c)   CuS will precipitate from solution.   **PAGE:** 4.5

36. Which of the following salts is insoluble in water?

    a) Na_2S
    b) K_3PO_4
    c) $Pb(NO_3)_2$
    d) $CaCl_2$
    e) All of these are soluble in water.

    ANS: e)   All of these are soluble in water.   **PAGE:** 4.5

37. How many of the following salts are expected to be insoluble in water?

sodium sulfide   barium nitrate
ammonium sulfate   potassium phosphate

   a) none
   b) 1
   c) 2
   d) 3
   e) 4

ANS: a)   none   PAGE: 4.5

38. When NH_3(aq) is added to Cu^{2+}(aq), a precipitate initially forms. Its formula is:

   a) $Cu(NH_3)_4^{2+}$

   b) $Cu(NO_3)_2$

   c) $Cu(OH)_2$

   d) $Cu(NH_3)_2^{2+}$

   e) CuO

ANS: c) $Cu(OH)_2$ PAGE: 4.5

39. Which of the following ions is most likely to form an insoluble sulfate?

   a) K^+
   b) Li^+
   c) Ca^{2+}
   d) S^{2-}
   e) Cl^-

ANS: c) Ca^{2+} PAGE: 4.5

40. Which of the following compounds is soluble in water?

   a) $Ni(OH)_2$
   b) K_3PO_4
   c) $BaSO_4$
   d) $CoCO_3$
   e) $PbCl_2$

ANS: b) K_3PO_4 PAGE: 4.5

41. A solution contains the ions Ag^+, Pb^{2+}, and Ni^{2+}. Dilute solutions of NaCl, Na_2SO_4, and Na_2S are available to separate the positive ions from each other. In order to effect separation, the solutions should be added in which order?

    a) Na_2SO_4, NaCl, Na_2S

    b) Na_2SO_4, Na_2S, NaCl

    c) Na_2S, NaCl, Na_2SO_4

    d) NaCl, Na_2S, Na_2SO_4

    e) NaCl, Na_2SO_4, Na_2S

ANS: a) Na_2SO_4, NaCl, Na_2S **PAGE:** 4.5

42. Which pair of ions would *not* be expected to form a precipitate when dilute solutions of each are mixed?

    a) Al^{3+}, S^{2-}

    b) Pb^{2+}, Cl^-

    c) Ba^{2+}, PO_4^{3-}

    d) Pb^{2+}, OH^-

    e) Mg^{2+}, SO_4^{2-}

ANS: e) Mg^{2+}, SO_4^{2-} **PAGE:** 4.5

43. In the balanced molecular equation for the neutralization of sodium hydroxide with sulfuric acid, the products are:

    a) $NaSO_4 + H_2O$

    b) $NaSO_3 + 2H_2O$

    c) $2NaSO_4 + H_2O$

    d) $Na_2S + 2H_2O$

    e) $Na_2SO_4 + 2H_2O$

ANS: e) $Na_2SO_4 + 2H_2O$ **PAGE:** 4.6,8

44. If all of the chloride in a 5.000-g sample of an unknown metal chloride is precipitated as AgCl with 70.90 mL of 0.2010 M $AgNO_3$, what is the percentage of chloride in the sample?

    a) 50.55%

    b) 10.10%

    c) 1.425%

    d) 20.22%

    e) none of the above

ANS: b) 10.10%   **PAGE:** 4.7

45. Which of the following do you need to know to be able to calculate the molarity of a salt solution?

     I.   the mass of salt added
    II.   the molar mass of the salt
   III.   the volume of water added
   IV.   the total volume of the solution

    a)   I, III
    b)   I, II, III
    c)   II, III
    d)   I, II, IV
    e)   You need all of the information.

ANS: d)   I, II, IV   **PAGE:** 4.3

46. You mix 60.0 mL of 1.0 M silver nitrate with 25.0 mL of 0.80 M sodium chloride. What mass of silver chloride should you form?

    a)   2.9 g
    b)   5.8 g
    c)   8.7 g
    d)   9.6 g
    e)   none of these

ANS: a)   2.9 g   **PAGE:** 4.7

47. You have separate solutions of HCl and H_2SO_4 with the same concentrations in terms of molarity. You wish to neutralize a solution of NaOH. Which acid solution would require more volume (in mL) to neutralize the base?

    a)   the HCl solution
    b)   the H_2SO_4 solution
    c)   You need to know the acid concentrations to answer this question.
    d)   You need to know the volume and concentration of the NaOH solution answer this question.
    e)   c and d

ANS: a)   the HCl solution   **PAGE:** 4.8

48. What mass of NaOH is required to react exactly with 25.0 mL of 1.2 M H_2SO_4?

    a)   1.2 g
    b)   1.8 g
    c)   2.4 g
    d)   3.5 g
    e)   none of these

ANS: c)   2.4 g   **PAGE:** 4.8

49. A 3.00-g sample of an alloy (containing only Pb and Sn) was dissolved in nitric acid (HNO_3). Sulfuric acid was added to this solution, which precipitated 2.93 g of $PbSO_4$. Assuming that all of the lead was precipitated, what is the percentage of Sn in the sample? (molar mass of $PbSO_4$ = 303.3 g/mol)

   a)   33.3% Sn
   b)   17.7% Sn
   c)   50.0% Sn
   d)   66.7% Sn
   e)   2.00% Sn

   ANS: a)   33.3% Sn   **PAGE:** 4.7

50. A mixture contained no fluorine compound except methyl fluoroacetate, FCH_2COOCH_3 (molar mass = 92.1 g/mol. When chemically treated, all the fluorine was converted to CaF_2 (molar mass = 78.1 g/mol). The mass of CaF_2 obtained was 12.1 g. Find the mass of methyl fluoroacetate in the original mixture.

   a)   92.0 g
   b)   28.5 g
   c)   24.2 g
   d)   14.3 g
   e)   12.1 g

   ANS: b)   28.5 g   **PAGE:** 4.7

51. A 1.000-g sample of a metal chloride, MCl_2, is dissolved in water and treated with excess aqueous silver nitrate. The silver chloride that formed weighed 1.286 g. Calculate the atomic mass of M.

   a)   222.8 g
   b)   76.00 g
   c)   152.0 g
   d)   304.0 g
   e)   none of these

   ANS: c)   152.0 g   **PAGE:** 4.7

52-55. You have 75.0 mL of a 2.50 M solution of Na_2CrO_4(aq). You also have 125 mL of a 2.50 M solution of $AgNO_3$(aq). Calculate the concentrations of the following ions when the two solutions are added together.

52. Na^+

   a)   0 M
   b)   0.938 M
   c)   1.88 M
   d)   2.50 M
   e)   5.00 M

   ANS: c)   1.88 M   **PAGE:** 4.7

53. CrO_4^{2-}

    a) 0 M
    b) 0.156 M
    c) 0.188 M
    d) 0.938 M
    e) 2.50 M

    ANS: b) 0.156 M   **PAGE:** 4.7

54. Ag^+

    a) 0 M
    b) 0.800 M
    c) 1.00 M
    d) 1.50 M
    e) 1.80 M

    ANS: a) 0 M   **PAGE:** 4.7

55. NO_3^-

    a) 0 M
    b) 0.313 M
    c) 1.56 M
    d) 3.13 M
    e) 2.50 M

    ANS: c) 1.56 M   **PAGE:** 4.7

56. A 0.307-g sample of an unknown triprotic acid is titrated to the third equivalence point using 35.2 mL of 0.106 M NaOH. Calculate the molar mass of the acid.

    a) 247 g/mol
    b) 171 g/mol
    c) 165 g/mol
    d) 151 g/mol
    e) 82.7 g/mol

    ANS: a) 247 g/mol   **PAGE:** 4.8

71

57. Sulfamic acid, HSO_3NH_2 (molar mass = 97.1 g/mol), is a strong monoprotic acid that can be used to standardize a strong base:

$$HSO_3NH_2(aq) + KOH(aq) \rightarrow KSO_2NH_2(aq) + H_2O(l)$$

A 0.179-g sample of HSO_3NH_2 required 19.4 mL of an aqueous solution of KOH for complete reaction. What is the molarity of the KOH solution?

   a) 9.25 M

   b) 9.50×10^{-5} M

   c) 0.0950 M

   d) 0.194 M

   e) none of these

ANS: c) 0.0950 M   **PAGE:** 4.8

58. A student weighs out 0.568 g of KHP (molar mass = 204 g/mol) and titrates to the equivalence point with 36.78 mL of a stock NaOH solution. What is the concentration of the stock NaOH solution? KHP is an acid with one acidic proton.

   a) 0.100 M

   b) 3.15 M

   c) 0.943 M

   d) 0.0757 M

   e) none of these

ANS: d) 0.0757 M   **PAGE:** 4.8

59. In which of the following does nitrogen have an oxidation state of +4?

   a) HNO_3

   b) NO_2

   c) N_2O

   d) NH_4Cl

   e) $NaNO_2$

ANS: d) NO_2 **PAGE:** 4.9

60. Which of the following statements is *not* true?

   a) When a metal reacts with a nonmetal, an ionic compound is formed.

   b) A metal-nonmetal reaction can always be assumed to be an oxidation-reduction reaction.

   c) Two nonmetals can undergo an oxidation-reduction reaction.

   d) When two nonmetals react, the compound formed is ionic.

   e) A meal-nonmetal reaction involves electron transfer.

ANS: d) When two nonmetals react, the compound formed is ionic.   **PAGE:** 4.9

61. The following reactions

$$ZnBr_2(aq) + 2AgNO_3(aq) \rightarrow Zn(NO_3)_2(aq) + 2AgBr(s)$$

$$KBr(aq) + AgNO_3(aq) \rightarrow AgBr(s) + KNO_3(aq)$$

are examples of

   a)   oxidation-reduction reactions.
   b)   acid-base reactions.
   c)   precipitation reactions.
   d)   a and c
   e)   none of these

   ANS: c)   precipitation reactions.   **PAGE:** 4.4-9

62. All of the following reactions

$$2Al(s) + 3Br_2(l) \rightarrow 2AlBr_3(s)$$

$$2Ag_2O(s) \rightarrow 4Ag(s) + O_2(g)$$

$$CH_4(l) + 2O_2(g) \rightarrow CO_2(g) + 2H_2O(g)$$

can be classified as

   a)   oxidation-reduction reactions.
   b)   combustion reactions.
   c)   precipitation reactions.
   d)   a and b
   e)   a and c

   ANS: a)   oxidation-reduction reactions.   **PAGE:** 4.4-9

63. In the reaction $2Ca(s) + O_2(g) \rightarrow 2CaO(s)$, which species is oxidized?

   a) O_2
   b) O^{2-}
   c)   Ca
   d) Ca^{2+}
   e)   none of these

   ANS: c)   Ca   **PAGE:** 4.9

64. In the reaction $2Cs(s) + Cl_2(g) \rightarrow 2CsCl(s)$, Cl_2 is

   a)   the reducing agent.
   b)   the oxidizing agent.
   c)   oxidized.
   d)   the electron donor.
   e)   two of these

   ANS: b)   the oxidizing agent.   **PAGE:** 4.9

65. In the reaction $N_2(g) + 3H_2(g) \rightarrow 2NH_3(g)$, N_2 is

    a) oxidized.
    b) reduced.
    c) the electron donor.
    d) the reducing agent.
    e) two of these

    ANS: b)   reduced.   **PAGE:** 4.9

66. In the reaction $P_4(s) + 10Cl_2(g) \rightarrow 4PCl_5(s)$, the reducing agent is

    a) chlorine.
    b) PCl_5.
    c) phosphorus.
    d) Cl^-.
    e) none of these

    ANS: c)   phosphorus.   **PAGE:** 4.9

67. In the reaction $C(s) + O_2(g) \rightarrow CO_2(g)$ carbon is _____.

    a) the reducing agent
    b) the electron acceptor
    c) reduced
    d) the oxidizing agent
    e) more than one of these

    ANS: a)   the reducing agent   **PAGE:** 4.9

68. Diabetics often need injections of insulin to help maintain the proper blood glucose levels in their bodies. How many moles of insulin are needed to make up 45 mL of 0.0052 M insulin solution?

    a) 4.6×10^{-4} mol
    b) 5.0×10^{-3} mol
    c) 1.7×10^{-4} mol
    d) 6.0×10^2 mol
    e) 2.3×10^{-4} mol

    ANS: e) 2.3×10^{-4} mol   **PAGE:** 4.3

69. For the reaction of sodium bromide with chlorine gas to form sodium chloride and bromine, the appropriate half-reactions are (ox = oxidation and re = reduction):

     a)   ox: $Cl_2 + 2e^- \rightarrow 2Cl^-$;   re: $2Br^- \rightarrow Br_2 + 2e^-$
     b)   ox: $2Br^- \rightarrow Br_2 + 2e^-$;   re: $Cl_2 + 2e^- \rightarrow 2Cl^-$
     c)   ox: $Cl + e^- \rightarrow Cl^-$;   re: $Br \rightarrow Br^- + e^-$
     d)   ox: $Br + 2e^- \rightarrow Br^{2-}$;   re: $2Cl^- \rightarrow Cl_2 + 2e^-$
     e)   ox: $2Na^+ + 2e^- \rightarrow 2Na$;   re: $2Cl^- \rightarrow Cl_2 + 2e^-$

ANS: b)   ox: $2Br^- \rightarrow Br_2 + 2e^-$;   re: $Cl_2 + 2e^- \rightarrow 2Cl^-$ **PAGE:** 4.10

70. Which of the following reactions does *not* involve oxidation-reduction?

     a) $CH_4 + 3O_2 \rightarrow 2H_2O + CO_2$
     b) $Zn + 2HCl \rightarrow ZnCl_2 + H_2$
     c) $2Na + 2H_2O \rightarrow 2NaOH + H_2$
     d) $MnO_2 + 4HCl \rightarrow Cl_2 + 2H_2O + MnCl_2$
     e)   All are oxidation-reduction reactions.

ANS: e)   All are oxidation-reduction reactions.   **PAGE:** 4.9

71. Which of the following are oxidation-reduction reactions?

     I. $PCl_3 + Cl_2 \rightarrow PCl_5$
     II. $Cu + 2AgNO_3 \rightarrow Cu(NO_3)_2 + 2Ag$
     III. $CO_2 + 2LiOH \rightarrow Li_2CO_3 + H_2O$
     IV. $FeCl_2 + 2NaOH \rightarrow Fe(OH)_2 + 2NaCl$
     a)   III
     b)   IV
     c)   I and II
     d)   I, II, and III
     e)   I, II, III, and IV

ANS: c)   I and II   **PAGE:** 4.9

72. Which of the following statements is(are) *true*? Oxidation and reduction

     a)   cannot occur independently of each other.
     b)   accompany all chemical changes.
     c)   describe the loss and gain of electron(s), respectively.
     d)   result in a change in the oxidation states of the species involved.
     e)   a, c, and d are true

ANS: e)   a, c, and d are true   **PAGE:** 4.9

73. In the reaction $Zn + H_2SO_4 \rightarrow ZnSO_4 + H_2$, which, if any, element is oxidized?

   a) zinc
   b) hydrogen
   c) sulfur
   d) oxygen
   e) none of these

   ANS: a) zinc   **PAGE:** 4.9

74. In the following reaction, which species is oxidized?

   $$8NaI + 5H_2SO_4 \rightarrow 4I_2 + H_2S + 4Na_2SO_4 + 4H_2O$$

   a) sodium
   b) iodine
   c) sulfur
   d) hydrogen
   e) oxygen

   ANS: b) iodine   **PAGE:** 4.9

75. How many of the following are oxidation-reduction reactions?

   $$NaOH + HCl \rightarrow NaCl + H_2O$$

   $$Cu + 2AgNO_3 \rightarrow 2Ag + Cu(NO_3)_2$$

   $$Mg(OH)_2 \rightarrow MgO + H_2O$$

   $$N_2 + 3H_2 \rightarrow 2NH_3$$

   a) 0
   b) 1
   c) 2
   d) 3
   e) 4

   ANS: c) 2   **PAGE:** 4.9

76. In the reaction shown below, what species is oxidized?

   $$2NaI + Br_2 \rightarrow 2NaBr + I_2$$

   a) Na^+
   b) I^-
   c) Br_2
   d) Br^-
   e) I_2

   ANS: b) I^- **PAGE:** 4.9

77. Given the following reaction in acidic media:

$$Fe^{2+} + Cr_2O_7^{2-} \rightarrow Fe^{3+} + Cr^{3+}$$

answer the following question: The coefficient for water in the balanced reaction is

a)   1.
b)   3.
c)   5.
d)   7.
e)   none of these

ANS: d)   7   **PAGE:** 4.10

78. Balance the following oxidation-reduction reaction using the half-reaction method:

$$Fe^{3+} + I^- \rightarrow Fe^{2+} + I_2$$

In the balanced equation, the coefficient of Fe^{2+} is

a)   1.
b)   2.
c)   3.
d)   4.
e)   none of these

ANS: b)   2   **PAGE:** 4.10

79. The following unbalanced equation represents a reaction that occurs in basic solution:

$$MnO_4^{2-} + C_2O_4^{2-} \rightarrow MnO_2 + CO_3^{2-}$$

How many moles of MnO_4^{2-} are required to produce 1 mole of CO_3^{2-}?

a)   4
b)   3
c)   2
d)   1
e)   none of these

ANS: e)   none of these   **PAGE:** 4.10

77

80–82. The following reaction occurs in aqueous acid solution:

$$NO_3^- + I^- \rightarrow IO_3^- + NO_2$$

80. The oxidation state of iodine in IO_3^- is:

   a)   0
   b)   +3
   c)   −3
   d)   +5
   e)   −5

   ANS: d)   +5   **PAGE:** 4.9

81. In the balanced equation the coefficient of NO_3^- is:

   a)   2
   b)   3
   c)   4
   d)   5
   e)   6

   ANS: e)   6   **PAGE:** 4.10

82. In the balanced equation the coefficient of water is:

   a)   1
   b)   2
   c)   3
   d)   4
   e)   5

   ANS: c)   3   **PAGE:** 4.10

83. When the equation $Cl_2 \rightarrow Cl^- + ClO_3^-$ (basic solution) is balanced using the smallest whole-number coefficients, the coefficient of OH^- is:

   a)   1
   b)   2
   c)   3
   d)   4
   e)   6

   ANS: e)   6   **PAGE:** 4.10

84. When the following reaction is balanced in acidic solution, what is the coefficient of I_2?

$$IO_3^- + I^- \rightarrow I_2$$

   a) 1
   b) 2
   c) 3
   d) 4
   e) none of these

   ANS: c) 3   **PAGE:** 4.10

85. The MnO_4^- is often used to analyze for the Fe^{2+} content of an aqueous solution via the reaction $MnO_4^- + Fe^{2+} \rightarrow Fe^{3+} + Mn^{2+}$ in acidic solution. What is the ratio of MnO_4^- : Fe^{2+} in the balanced equation?

   a) 1 : 1
   b) 2 : 1
   c) 3 : 1
   d) 4 : 1
   e) 5 : 1

   ANS: e) 5 : 1   **PAGE:** 4.10

86. Balance the following oxidation–reduction reaction using the half-reaction method.

$$Cr_2O_7^{2-} + I_2 \rightarrow Cr^{3+} + IO_3^-$$

   In the balanced equation, the coefficient of water is:

   a) 4
   b) 17
   c) 11
   d) 7
   e) 6

   ANS: b) 17   **PAGE:** 4.10

87. With what volume of 5.0 M HF will 7.4 g of calcium hydroxide react completely, according to the reaction $2HF + Ca(OH)_2 \rightarrow CaF_2 + 2H_2O$?

   a) 20. mL
   b) 50. mL
   c) 30. mL
   d) 40. mL
   e) 1.0×10^2 mL

   ANS: d) 40. mL   **PAGE:** 4.8

79

88. For the redox reaction $2Fe^{2+} + Cl_2 \rightarrow 2Fe^{3+} + 6Cl^-$ which of the following are the correct half-reactions?

   I. $Cl_2 + 2e^- \rightarrow 2Cl^-$

   II. $Cl \rightarrow Cl^- + e^-$

   III. $Cl_2 \rightarrow 2Cl^- + 2e^-$

   IV. $Fe^{2+} \rightarrow Fe^{3+} + e^-$

   V. $Fe^{2+} + e^- \rightarrow Fe^{3+}$

   a) I and IV

   b) I and V

   c) II and IV

   d) II and V

   e) III and IV

ANS: a) I and IV   **PAGE:** 4.10

89. The following equation describes the oxidation of ethanol to acetic acid by potassium permanganate:

$$3C_2H_5OH + 4KMnO_4 \rightarrow 3HC_2H_3O_2 + 4MnO_2 + 4KOH + H_2O$$

5.0 g of ethanol and an excess of aqueous $KMnO_4$ are reacted, and 5.9 g $HC_2H_3O_2$ result. What is the percent yield?

   a) 100%

   b) 91%

   c) 67%

   d) 30.%

   e) 5.9 g $HC_2H_3O_2$ is impossible since it represents more than a 100% yield.

ANS: b) 91%   **PAGE:** 3.9, 4.10

90. Given the reaction

$$2MnO_4^- + 5H_2O_2 + 6H^+ \rightarrow 2Mn^{2+} + 8H_2O + 5O_2$$

determine the number of electrons involved in this reaction.

   a) 10

   b) 8

   c) 6

   d) 4

   e) 2

ANS: a) 10   **PAGE:** 4.10

80

Selecting from the following reagents, indicate which reagents would be mixed to give the compounds in Questions 91 and 92.

$CuSO_4(aq)$	$Fe_2(CO_3)_3(s)$	$NH_3(aq)$
$CuCO_3(s)$	$FeCl_3(aq)$	$Na_2SO_4(aq)$
$Cr(OH)_3(s)$	$H_2SO_4(aq)$	

91. $Cu(OH)_2$

　　 ANS: $CuSO_4(aq)$ and $NH_3(aq)$　　　　　　　　　　　**PAGE:** 4.5,6

92. $FeCl_3(aq) + Na_2SO_4(aq)$

　　 ANS: $FeCl_3(aq) + Na_2SO_4(aq)$　　　　　　　　　　　**PAGE:** 4.5,6

Write balanced equations for each of the processes in Questions 93 through 97, choosing from the following substances as reactants:

$BaCl_2$	O_2	H_2SO_4	HNO_3
C_2H_5OH	H_2O	$Ca(OH)_2$	K
Na_2CrO_4	KOH	$Pb(NO_3)_2$	

93. Precipitation of $BaSO_4$ from solution

　　 ANS: $H_2SO_4 + BaCl_2 \rightarrow BaSO_4 + 2HCl$　　　　　　　**PAGE:** 4.5,9

94. Formation of hydrogen gas

　　 ANS: $2K + H_2O \rightarrow 2KOH + H_2$　　　　　　　　　　**PAGE:** 4.5,9

95. Neutralization of sulfuric acid

　　 ANS: $H_2SO_4 + 2KOH \rightarrow K_2SO_4 + 2H_2O$　　　　　　　**PAGE:** 4.5,9

96. Combustion reaction

　　 ANS: $C_2H_5OH + 3O_2 \rightarrow 2CO_2 + 3H_2O$　　　　　　　**PAGE:** 4.5,9

97. Dissolution of calcium hydroxide with another reagent

　　 ANS: $Ca(OH)_2 + 2HCl \rightarrow CaCl_2 + 2H_2O$　　　　　　　**PAGE:** 4.5,9

98–103. Balance each of the following equations.

98. $C_3H_5(NO_3)_3 \rightarrow N_2 + CO_2 + H_2O + O_2$

　　 ANS: $4C_3H_5(NO_3)_3 \rightarrow 6N_2 + 12CO_2 + 10H_2O + O_2$　　**PAGE:** 4.10

99. $KI + HNO_3 \rightarrow KNO_3 + NO + I_2 + H_2O$

　　 ANS: $6KI + 8HNO_3 \rightarrow 6KNO_3 + 2NO + 3I_2 + 4H_2O$　　**PAGE:** 4.10

100. $Cr_2O_7^{2-} + I^- \rightarrow Cr^{3+} + IO_3^-$ (acid)

　　 ANS: $8H^+ + Cr_2O_7^{2-} + I^- \rightarrow 2Cr^{3+} + IO_3^- + 4H_2O$　　**PAGE:** 4.10

　　　　81

101. $Zn + As_2O_3 \rightarrow AsH_3 + Zn^{2+}$ (acid)

   ANS: $12H^+ + 6Zn + As_2O_3 \rightarrow 2AsH_3 + 6Zn^{2+} + 3H_2O$ **PAGE:** 4.10

102. $MnO_4^- + Br^- \rightarrow MnO_2 + BrO_3^-$ (base)

   ANS: $H_2O + 2MnO_4^- + Br^- \rightarrow 2MnO_2 + BrO_3^- + 2OH^-$ **PAGE:** 4.10

103. $Bi(OH)_3 + SnO_2^{2-} \rightarrow Bi + SnO_3^{2-}$ (base)

   ANS: $2Bi(OH)_3 + 3SnO_2^{2-} \rightarrow 2Bi + 3SnO_3^{2-} + 3H_2O$ **PAGE:** 4.10

104.   Polar molecules have an unequal distribution of charge within the molecule.

   ANS: True   **PAGE:** 4.1

105.   An acid is a substance that produces OH^- ions in water.

   ANS: False   **PAGE:** 4.2

106.   The filtrate is the solid formed when two solutions are mixed.

   ANS: False   **PAGE:** 4.5

107.   A chemical that changes color at the endpoint of a reaction is called a colorimeter.

   ANS: False   **PAGE:** 4.8

108.   Oxidation is the gain of electrons.

   ANS: False   **PAGE:** 4.9

109.   A reducing agent is an electron donor.

   ANS: True   **PAGE:** 4.9

110.   A molecule with an unequal charge distribution is said to be a _____ molecule.

   ANS: polar   **PAGE:** 4.1

111.   Soluble ionic compounds containing the hydroxide ion are called strong _____.

   ANS: bases   **PAGE:** 4.1

112.   A _____ is a substance dissolved in a liquid to make a solution.

   ANS: solute   **PAGE:** 4.2

113.   A _____ electrolyte dissociates to a great extent in an aqueous solution.

   ANS: strong   **PAGE:** 4.2

114.   Molarity is defined as _____ of solute per volume of solution in _____.

   ANS: moles, liters   **PAGE:** 4.6

1. A glass column is filled with mercury and inverted in a pool of mercury. The mercury column stabilizes at a height of 735 mm above the pool of mercury. What is the pressure of the atmosphere?

   a) 0.697 atm
   b) 0.735 atm
   c) 0.967 atm
   d) 1.03 atm
   e) 194 atm

   ANS: c)   0.967 atm   **PAGE:** 5.1

2–4. Consider three 1-L flasks at STP. Flask A contains NH_3 gas, flask B contains NO_2 gas, and flask C contains N_2 gas.

2. Which contains the largest number of molecules?

   a) flask A
   b) flask B
   c) flask C
   d) all are the same
   e) none

   ANS: d)   all are the same   **PAGE:** 5.2

3. In which flask are the molecules least polar and therefore most ideal in behavior?

   a) flask A
   b) flask B
   c) flask C
   d) all are the same
   e) none

   ANS: c)   flask C   **PAGE:** 5.8

4. In which flask do the molecules have the highest average velocity?

   a) flask A
   b) flask B
   c) flask C
   d) all are the same
   e) none

   ANS: a)   flask A   **PAGE:** 5.6

83

5. You and a friend have gas samples in open manometers as shown:

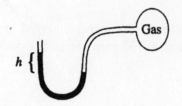

You have Hg(l) in your manometer and your friend has water. The height h is the same in both manometers. Which of the following statements is true?

a) Your sample of gas has the higher pressure.
b) Your friend's sample of gas has the higher pressure.
c) Both samples of gas have the same pressure.
d) There is not enough information to answer the question.
e) None of these is correct.

ANS: a) Your sample of gas has the higher pressure.   **PAGE:** 5.1

6–7. You have two samples of the same gas in the same size container, with the same pressure. The gas in the first container has a kelvin temperature four times that of the gas in the other container.

6. The ratio of the number of moles of gas in the first container compared to that in the second is

a) 1 : 1
b) 4 : 1
c) 1 : 4
d) 2 : 1
e) 1 : 2

ANS: c) 1 : 4   **PAGE:** 5.3

7. The ratio of number of collisions with the wall in the first container compared to that in the second is

a) 1 : 1
b) 4 : 1
c) 1 : 4
d) 2 : 1
e) 1 : 2

ANS: e) 1 : 2   **PAGE:** 5.6

8. The air pressure in the inner tube of a tire on a typical racing bike is held at a pressure of 115 psi. Convert this pressure to atm.

    a)   0.151 atm
    b)   7.83 atm
    c)   1690 atm
    d)   32.6 atm
    e)   115 atm

    ANS: b)   7.83 atm   **PAGE:** 5.1

9. A gas sample is held at constant pressure. The gas occupies 3.62 L of volume when the temperature is 21.6°C. Determine the temperature at which the volume of the gas is 3.45 L.

    a)   309 K
    b)   281 K
    c)   20.6 K
    d)   294 K
    e)   326 K

    ANS: b)   281 K   **PAGE:** 5.2

10. Gaseous chlorine is held in two separate containers at identical temperature and pressure. The volume of container 1 is 1.30 L and it contains 6.70 mol of the gas. The volume of container 2 is 2.20 L. How many moles of the gas are in container 2.

    a)   11.3 mol
    b)   19.2 mol
    c)   0.427 mol
    d)   3.96 mol
    e)   none of these

    ANS: a)   11.3 mol   **PAGE:** 5.2

11. A balloon has a volume of 1.20 liters at 24.0°C. The balloon is heated to 48.0°C. Calculate the new volume of the balloon.

    a)   1.20 L
    b)   1.30 L
    c)   1.70 L
    d)   2.10 L
    e)   2.40 L

    ANS: b)   1.30 L   **PAGE:** 5.2

85

12–13. Three 1.00-L flasks at 25°C and 725 torr contain the gases CH_4 (flask A), CO_2 (flask B), and C_2H_6 (flask C).

12. In which flask is there 0.039 mol of gas?

    a) flask A
    b) flask B
    c) flask C
    d) all
    e) none

ANS: d) all   **PAGE:** 5.3

13. In which single flask do the molecules have the greatest mass, the greatest average velocity, *and* the highest kinetic energy?

    a) flask A
    b) flask B
    c) flask C
    d) all
    e) none

ANS: e) none   **PAGE:** 5.6

14. A gas sample is heated from –20.0°C to 57.0°C and the volume is increased from 2.00 L to 4.50 L. If the initial pressure is 0.125 atm, what is the final pressure?

    a) 0.189 atm
    b) 0.555 atm
    c) 0.0605 atm
    d) 0.247 atm
    e) none of these

ANS: e) none of these   **PAGE:** 5.3

15. A sample of oxygen gas has a volume of 4.50 L at 27°C and 800.0 torr. How many oxygen molecules does it contain?

    a) 1.16×10^{23}
    b) 5.8×10^{22}
    c) 2.32×10^{24}
    d) 1.16×10^{22}
    e) none of these

ANS: a) 1.16×10^{23} **PAGE:** 5.3

16. The valve between a 5-L tank containing a gas at 9 atm and a 10-L tank containing a gas at 6 atm is opened. Calculate the final pressure in the tanks.

    a) 3 atm
    b) 4 atm
    c) 7 atm
    d) 15 atm
    e) none of these

    ANS: c) 7 atm   **PAGE:** 5.3,5

17. You fill a balloon with 2.50 moles of gas at 28°C at a pressure of 1.20 atm. What is the volume of the balloon?

    a) 4.79 L
    b) 22.4 L
    c) 51.5 L
    d) 56.0 L
    e) 61.8 L

    ANS: c) 51.5 L   **PAGE:** 5.3

18. A sample of helium gas occupies 12.4 L at 23°C and 0.956 atm. What volume will it occupy at 40°C and 1.20 atm?

    a) 0.488 L
    b) 6.28 L
    c) 12.4 L
    d) 10.4 L
    e) 17.2 L

    ANS: d) 10.4 L   **PAGE:** 5.3

19. A 6.35-L sample of carbon monoxide is collected at 55°C and 0.892 atm. What volume will the gas occupy at 1.05 atm and 20°C?

    a) 1.96 L
    b) 5.46 L
    c) 4.82 L
    d) 6.10 L
    e) none of these

    ANS: c) 4.82 L   **PAGE:** 5.3

20. Body temperature is about 308 K. On a cold day, what volume of air at 273 K must a person with a lung capacity of 2.00 L breathe in to fill the lungs?

   a)   2.26 L
   b)   1.77 L
   c)   1.13 L
   d)   3.54 L
   e)   none of these

   ANS: b)   1.77 L

PAGE: 5.3

21. Mercury vapor contains Hg atoms. What is the volume of 200. g of mercury vapor at 822 K and 0.500 atm?

   a)   135 L
   b)   82.2 L
   c)   329 L
   d)   67.2 L
   e)   none of these

   ANS: a)   135 L

PAGE: 5.3

22. What volume is occupied by 19.6 g of methane (CH_4) at 27°C and 1.59 atm?

   a)   1.71 L
   b)   18.9 L
   c)   27.7 L
   d)   302 L
   e)   not enough data to calculate

   ANS: b)   18.9 L

PAGE: 5.3

23. An automobile tire is filled with air at a pressure of 30 lb/in² at 25°C. A cold front moves through and the temperature drops to 5°C. Assuming no change in volume, what is the new tire pressure?

   a)   6.0 lb/in²
   b)   28 lb/in²
   c)   32 lb/in²
   d)   20. lb/in²
   e)   4.0 lb/in²

   ANS: b)   28 lb/in.²

PAGE: 5.3

24. You are holding two balloons, an orange balloon and a blue balloon. The orange balloon is filled with neon (Ne) gas and the blue balloon is filled with argon (Ar) gas. The orange balloon has twice the volume of the blue balloon. Which of the following best represents the mass ratio of Ne:Ar in the balloons?

   a) 1:1
   b) 1:2
   c) 2:1
   d) 1:3
   e) 3:1

   ANS: a)   1:1   **PAGE: 5.3**

25. Given reaction $2NH_3(g) + 3Cl_2(g) \rightarrow N_2(g) + 6HCl(g)$, you react 5.0 L of NH_3 with 5.0 L of Cl_2 measured at the same conditions in a closed container. Calculate the ratio of pressures in the container ($P_{final}/P_{initial}$).

   a) 0.75
   b) 1.00
   c) 1.33
   d) 1.50
   e) none of these

   ANS: c)   1.33   **PAGE: 5.4**

26. Given reaction $N_2 + 3H_2 \rightarrow 2NH_3$, you mix 1 mol each of nitrogen and hydrogen gases under the same conditions in a container fixed with a piston. Calculate the ratio of volumes of the container ($V_{final}/V_{initial}$).

   a) 0.67
   b) 1.00
   c) 1.33
   d) 1.50
   e) none of these

   ANS: a)   0.67   **PAGE: 5.4**

27. You have 26.4 g of O_2 gas in a container with twice the volume as one with CO_2 gas. The pressure and temperature of both containers are the same. Calculate the mass of carbon dioxide gas you have in the container.

   a) 36.3 g
   b) 26.4 g
   c) 18.2 g
   d) 13.2 g
   e) none of these

   ANS: c)   18.2 g   **PAGE: 5.4**

28–29. You have a 400-mL container containing 55.0% He and 45.0% Ar by mass at 25°C and 1.5 atm total pressure. You heat the container to 100°C.

28. Calculate the total pressure.

   a)   1.20 atm
   b)   1.50 atm
   c)   1.88 atm
   d)   2.01 atm
   e)   none of these

   ANS: c)   1.88 atm   **PAGE:** 5.2-4

29. Calculate the ratio of $P_{He} : P_{Ar}$.

   a)   1/1.22
   b)   1.22/1
   c)   1/12.2
   d)   12.2/1
   e)   none of these

   ANS: d)   12.2/1   **PAGE:** 5.2-4

30. Hydrogen and chlorine gases react to form HCl. You and a friend are on opposite sides of a long hallway, you with H_2 and your friend with Cl_2. You both want to form HCl in the middle of the room. Which of the following is true?

   a)   You should release the H_2 first.
   b)   Your friend should release the Cl_2 first.
   c)   You both should release the gases at the same time.
   d)   You need to know the length of the room to answer this question.
   e)   You need to know the temperature to answer this question.

   ANS: b)   Your friend should release the Cl_2 first.   **PAGE:** 5.7

31. Which of the following is the best qualitative graph of P versus molar mass of a 1-g sample of different gases at constant volume and temperature?

a)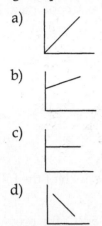

b)

c)

d)

e)   None of these

ANS: e)   none of these

32. Which conditions of P, T, and n, respectively, are most ideal?

a)   high P, high T, high n
b)   low P, low T, low n
c)   high P, low T, high n
d)   low P, high T, high n
e)   low P, high T, low n

ANS: e)   low P, high T, low n **PAGE:** 5.4

33. A 4.40-g piece of solid CO_2 (dry ice) is allowed to sublime in a balloon. The final volume of the balloon is 1.00 L at 300 K. What is the pressure of the gas?

a)   2.46 atm
b)   246 atm
c)   0.122 atm
d)   122 atm
e)   none of these

ANS: a)   2.46 atm   **PAGE:** 5.3

34. A sample of gas is in a 50.0-mL container at a pressure of 645 torr and a temperature of 25ÁC. The entire sample is heated to a temperature of 35°C and transferred to a new container whose volume is 65.0 mL. The pressure of the gas in the second container is:

   a)   867 torr
   b)   694 torr
   c)   480. torr
   d)   760. torr
   e)   none of these

   ANS: e)   none of these   **PAGE:** 5.3

35. Given a cylinder of fixed volume filled with 1 mol of argon gas, which of the following is correct? (Assume all gases obey the ideal gas law.)

   a)   If the temperature of the cylinder is changed from 25°C to 50°C, the pressure inside the cylinder will double.
   b)   If a second mole of argon is added to the cylinder, the ratio T/P would remain constant.
   c)   A cylinder of identical volume filled with the same *pressure* of helium must contain more atoms of gas because He has a smaller atomic radius than argon.
   d)   Two of the above.
   e)   None of the above.

   ANS: e)   None of the above.   **PAGE:** 5.3

36–41. Four identical 1.0-L flasks contain the gases He, Cl_2, CH_4, and NH_3, each at 0°C and 1 atm pressure.

36. Which gas has the highest density?

   a)   He
   b) Cl_2
   c) CH_4
   d) NH_3
   e)   all gases the same

   ANS: b) Cl_2 **PAGE:** 5.4

37. For which gas do the molecules have the highest average velocity?

   a)   He
   b) Cl_2
   c) CH_4
   d) NH_3
   e)   all gases the same

   ANS: a)   He   **PAGE:** 5.6

38. Which gas sample has the greatest number of molecules?

    a) He
    b) Cl_2
    c) CH_4
    d) NH_3
    e) all gases the same

    ANS: e)   all gases the same   **PAGE:** 5.4

39. For which gas are the molecules diatomic?

    a) He
    b) Cl_2
    c) CH_4
    d) NH_3
    e) all gases the same

    ANS: b) Cl_2 **PAGE:** 2.7,5.6

40. For which gas are the collisions elastic?

    a) He
    b) Cl_2
    c) CH_4
    d) NH_3
    e) all gases the same

    ANS: e)   all gases the same   **PAGE:** 5.6

41. For which gas do the molecules have the smallest average kinetic energy?

    a) He
    b) Cl_2
    c) CH_4
    d) NH_3
    e) all gases the same

    ANS: e)   all gases the same   **PAGE:** 5.6

42-44. A plastic bag is weighed and then filled successively with two gases, X and Y. The following data are gathered:

> Temperature: 0.0°C (273 K)
> Pressure: 1.00 atmosphere
> Mass of empty bag: 20.77 g
> Mass of bag filled with gas X: 24.97 g
> Mass of 1.12 liters of air at conditions given: 1.30 g
> Volume of bag: 1.12 liter
> Molar volume at STP: 22.4 liters

93

42. The mass of 1.12 liters of gas Y is found to be 6.23 g. The density of gas Y is

a) 10.6 g/L
b) 5.56 g/L
c) 15.6 g/L
d) 0.200 g/L
e) 0.180 g/L

ANS: b)   5.56 g/L   **PAGE:** 5.4

43. The molar mass of gas Y is

a) 56.0 g/mol
b) 89.0 g/mol
c) 125 g/mol
d) 140. g/mol
e) 157 g/mol

ANS: c)   125 g/mol   **PAGE:** 5.4

44. The bag is emptied and refilled, successively, with gases X and Y, this time at 1 atm pressure and a temperature 30°C *higher*. Assume that the volume of the bag is the same as before. Which one of the following statements is *wrong*?

a) The full bag contains fewer molecules of each gas than it did at 0.0°C.
b) The *ratio* of the density of gas Y to the density of gas X is the same as at 0.0°C.
c) The molar masses of the two gases are the same as they were at 0.0°C.
d) The mass of each gas filling the bag is now 303/273 times the mass held at 0.0°C.
e) The average velocity of the molecules of gas X at 30°C is higher than it was at 0.0°C.

ANS: d)   The mass of each gas filling the bag is now 303/273 times
                 the mass held at 0.0°C.   **PAGE:** 5.4,6

45. Argon has a density of 1.78 g/L at STP. How many of the following gases have a density at STP *greater* than that of argon?

Cl_2 He NH_3 NO_2

a) 0
b) 1
c) 2
d) 3
e) 4

ANS: c)   2   **PAGE:** 5.4

94

46. It is found that 250. mL of gas at STP has a mass of 1.00 g. What is the molar mass?

     a)   89.6 g/mol
     b)   28.0 g/mol
     c)   14.0 g/mol
     d)   22.4 g/mol
     e)   none of these

ANS: a)   89.6 g/mol   **PAGE:** 5.4

47. When 0.72 g of a liquid is vaporized at 110°C and 0.967 atm, the gas occupies a volume of 0.559 L. The empirical formula of the gas is CH_2. What is the molecular formula of the gas?

     a) CH_2
     b) C_2H_4
     c) C_3H_6
     d) C_4H_8
     e)   none of these

ANS: c) C_3H_6 **PAGE:** 5.4

48. Gaseous C_2H_4 reacts with O_2 according to the following equation:

$$C_2H_4(g) + 3O_2(g) \rightarrow 2CO_2(g) + 2H_2O(g)$$

What volume of oxygen at STP is needed to react with 1.50 mol of C_2H_4?

     a)   4.50 L
     b)   33.6 L
     c)   101 L
     d)   67.2 L
     e)   Not enough information is given to solve the problem.

ANS: c)   101 L   **PAGE:** 5.4

49. A 4.37 gram sample of a certain diatomic gas occupies a volume of 3.00-L at 1.00 atm and a temperature of 45°C. Identify this gas.

     a) F_2
     b) N_2
     c) H_2
     d) O_2
     e) Cl_2

ANS: a) F_2 **PAGE:** 5.4

50. Air has an average molar mass of 29.0 g/mol. The density of air at 1.00 atm and 30°C is
    a) 29.0 g/L
    b) 40.0 g/mL
    c) 1.17 g/L
    d) 1.29 g/L
    e) 12 g/L

    ANS: c) 1.17 g/L   **PAGE:** 5.4

51. Calculate the density of nitrogen at STP.
    a) 0.312 g/L
    b) 0.625 g/L
    c) 0.800 g/L
    d) 1.25 g/L
    e) 1.60 g/L

    ANS: d) 1.25 g/L   **PAGE:** 5.4

52. If a 2.15-g sample of a gas occupies 750. mL at STP, what is the molar mass of the gas at 125°C?
    a) 3.07×10^{-2}
    b) 64.2
    c) 70.1
    d) 75.0
    e) Not enough information is given.

    ANS: b) 64.2   **PAGE:** 5.4

53. A 3.31-g sample of lead nitrate, $Pb(NO_3)_2$, molar mass = 331 g/mol, is heated in an evacuated cylinder with a volume of 1.62 L. The salt decomposes when heated, according to the equation

    $$2Pb(NO_3)_2(s) \rightarrow 2PbO(s) + 4NO_2(g) + O2(g)$$

    Assuming complete decomposition, what is the pressure in the cylinder after decomposition and cooling to a temperature of 300 K? Assume the PbO(s) takes up negligible volume.
    a) 0.380 atm
    b) 0.228 atm
    c) 0.0342 atm
    d) 1.38 atm
    e) none of these

    ANS: a) 0.380 atm   **PAGE:** 5.4

54. The density of nitrogen at STP is

   a) 1.60 g/cm^3
   b) 0.800 g/L
   c) 1.25 g/L
   d) 0.625 g/L
   e) Not enough information is given.

   ANS: c) 1.25 g/L **PAGE:** 5.4

55. The purity of a sample containing zinc and weighing 0.198 g is determined by measuring the amount of hydrogen formed when the sample reacts with an excess of hydrochloric acid. The determination shows the sample to be 84.0% zinc. What amount of hydrogen (measured at STP) was obtained?

   a) 0.152 L
   b) 0.0330 g
   c) $3.42 \times 10^{-3} \text{ mole}$
   d) $1.53 \times 10^{21} \text{ molecules}$
   e) $1.53 \times 10^{21} \text{ atoms}$

   ANS: d) 1.53×10^{21} molecules   **PAGE:** 5.4

56. What volume of carbon dioxide measured at STP will be formed by the reaction of 1.30 mol of oxygen with 9.00×10^{-1} mol of ethyl alcohol CH_3CH_2OH?

   a) 8.70 L
   b) 19.4 L
   c) 28.0 L
   d) 40.3 L
   e) 91.9 L

   ANS: b) 19.4 L **PAGE:** 5.4

57. What volume of $H_2O(g)$ measured at STP is produced by the combustion of 4.00 g of natural gas (CH_4) according to the following equation?

   $$CH_4(g) + 2O_2(g) \rightarrow CO_2(g) + 2H_2O(g)$$

   a) 5.60 L
   b) 11.2 L
   c) 22.4 L
   d) 33.6 L
   e) 44.8 L

   ANS: b) 11.2 L **PAGE:** 5.4

58. At 1000°C and 10. torr, the density of a certain element in the gaseous state is 2.9×10^{-3} g/L. The element is:

   a) Ne
   b) He
   c) Na
   d) Ar
   e) Hg

ANS: c)   Na   **PAGE:** 5.4

59. Into a 3.00-liter container at 25°C are placed 1.23 moles of O_2 gas and 3.20 moles of solid C (graphite). If the carbon and oxygen react completely to form CO(g), what will be the final pressure in the container at 25°C?

   a)   20.1 atm
   b)   26.1 atm
   c)   10.2 atm
   d)   1.68 atm
   e)   none of these

ANS: a)   20.1 atm   **PAGE:** 5.4

60. Calcium hydride combines with water according to the equation

$$CaH_2(s) + 2H_2O(l) \rightarrow 2H_2(g) + Ca(OH)_2(s)$$

Beginning with 84.0 g of CaH_2 and 36.0 g of H_2O, what volume of H_2 will be produced at 273 K and a pressure of 1520 torr?

   a)   22.4 L
   b)   44.8 L
   c)   89.6 L
   d)   179 L
   e)   none of these

ANS: a)   22.4 L   **PAGE:** 5.4

61. A mixture is prepared from 15.0 L of ammonia and 15.0 L chlorine measured at the same conditions, these compounds react according to the following equation:

$$2NH_3(g) + 3\,Cl_2(g) \rightarrow N_2(g) + 6HCl(g)$$

When the reaction is completed, what is the volume of each gas (NH_3, Cl_2, N_2, and HCl, respectively)? Assume the final volumes are measured under identical conditions.

   a)   0.00 L, 5.00 L, 7.50 L, 45.0 L
   b)   5.00 L, 0.00 L, 5.00 L, 30.0 L
   c)   0.00 L, 0.00 L, 7.50 L, 45.0 L
   d)   0.00 L, 0.00 L, 5.00 L, 30.0 L
   e)   0.00 L, 10.0 L, 15.0 L, 90.0 L

ANS: b)   5.00 L, 0.00 L, 5.00 L, 30.0 L   **PAGE:** 5.4

62. An excess of sodium hydroxide is treated with 1.1 L of dry hydrogen chloride gas measured at STP. What is the mass of sodium chloride formed?

    a) 0.50 g
    b) 1.8 g
    c) 2.0 g
    d) 2.9 g
    e) 22 g

    ANS: d)   2.9 g   **PAGE:** 5.4

63. A 1.00-g sample of a gaseous compound of boron and hydrogen occupies 0.820 L at 1.00 atm and 3ÁC. What is the molecular formula for the compound?

    a) BH_3
    b) B_2H_6
    c) B_4H_{10}
    d) B_3H_{12}
    e) B_5H_{14}

    ANS: b) B_2H_6 **PAGE:** 5.4

64. A mixture of KCl and $KClO_3$ weighing 1.80 grams was heated; the dry O_2 generated occupied 1.40×10^2 mL at STP. What percent of the original mixture was $KClO_3$, which decomposes as follows:

    $$2KClO_3(s) \rightarrow 2KCl(s) + 3O_2(g)$$

    a) 28.4%
    b) 37.2%
    c) 42.6%
    d) 63.8%
    e) 72.6%

    ANS: a)   28.4%   **PAGE:** 5.4

65. Given the equation

    $$2KClO_3(s) \rightarrow 2KCl(s) + 3O_2(g)$$

    A 3.00 g sample of $KClO_3$ is decomposed and the oxygen at 24.0°C and 0.982 atm is collected. What volume of oxygen gas will be collected assuming 100% yield?

    a) 304 mL
    b) 608 mL
    c) 911 mL
    d) 1820 mL
    e) none of these

    ANS: c)   911 mL   **PAGE:** 5.3,4

66. A sample of 35.1 g of methane gas has a volume of 5.20 L at a pressure of 2.70 atm. Calculate the temperature.

   a) 4.87 K
   b) 78.1 K
   c) 46.3 K
   d) 275 K
   e) 129 K

   ANS: b) 78.1 K   **PAGE:** 5.3

67–69. Zinc metal is added to hydrochloric acid to generate hydrogen gas and is collected over a liquid whose vapor pressure is the same as pure water at 20.0°C (18 torr). The volume of the mixture is 1.7 L and its total pressure is 0.810 atm.

67. Determine the partial pressure of the hydrogen gas in this mixture.

   a) 562 torr
   b) 580 torr
   c) 598 torr
   d) 616 torr
   e) 634 torr

   ANS: c) 598 torr   **PAGE:** 5.5

68. Determine the number of moles of hydrogen gas present in the sample.

   a) 42 mol
   b) 0.82 mol
   c) 1.3 mol
   d) 0.056 mol
   e) 22 mol

   ANS: d) 0.056 mol   **PAGE:** 5.3,5

69. What would happen to the average kinetic energy of the molecules of a gas sample if the temperature of the sample increased from 20°C to 40°C?

   a) It would double.
   b) It would increase.
   c) It would decrease.
   d) It would become half its value.
   e) Two of these.

   ANS: b) It would increase.   **PAGE:** 5.6

70. A 130.-mL sample of gas is collected over water at 22°C and 753 torr. What is the volume of the dry gas at STP? (The vapor pressure of water at 22°C = 20. torr.)

    a) 135 mL

    b) 119 mL

    c) 130. mL

    d) 111 mL

    e) none of these

ANS: e) none of these   **PAGE:** 5.5

71. What volume does 28.0 g of N_2 occupy at STP?

    a) 5.60 L

    b) 11.2 L

    c) 22.4 L

    d) 44.8 L

    e) none of these

ANS: c) 22.4 L   **PAGE:** 5.4

72. A vessel with a volume of 10.0 L contains 2.80 g of nitrogen gas, 0.403 g of hydrogen gas, and 79.9 g of argon gas. At 25°C, what is the pressure in the vessel?

    a) 0.471 atm

    b) 6.43 atm

    c) 3.20 atm

    d) 5.62 atm

    e) 2.38 atm

ANS: d) 5.62 atm   **PAGE:** 5.5

73. Oxygen gas, generated by the reaction $2KClO_3(s) \rightarrow 2KCl(s) + 3O_2(g)$, is collected over water at 27°C in a 2.00-L vessel at a total pressure of 760. torr. (The vapor pressure of H_2O at 27°C is 26.0 torr.) How many moles of $KClO_3$ were consumed in the reaction?

    a) 0.0790 moles

    b) 0.119 moles

    c) 0.0527 moles

    d) 0.0813 moles

    e) none of these

ANS: c) 0.0527 moles   **PAGE:** 5.5

74. A balloon contains an anesthetic mixture of cyclopropane (cp) and oxygen (O_2) at 170 torr and 570 torr, respectively. What is the ratio of the number of moles of cyclopropane to moles of oxygen?

$n_{cp}/n_{O_2} = ?$

a) 0.19
b) 0.23
c) 0.30
d) 0.39
e) 0.46

ANS: c)   0.30   **PAGE:** 5.5

75. A gaseous mixture containing 1.5 mol Ar and 3.5 mol CO_2 has a total pressure of 7.0 atm. What is the partial pressure of CO_2?

a) 1.8 atm
b) 2.1 atm
c) 3.5 atm
d) 4.9 atm
e) 2.4 atm

ANS: d)   4.9 atm   **PAGE:** 5.5

76. Which of the following is *not* a postulate of the kinetic molecular theory?

a) Gas particles have most of their mass concentrated in the nucleus of the atom.
b) The moving particles undergo perfectly elastic collisions with the walls of the container.
c) The forces of attraction and repulsion between the particles are insignificant.
d) The average kinetic energy of the particles is directly proportional to the absolute temperature.
e) All of the above are postulates of the kinetic molecular theory.

ANS: a)   Gas particles have most of their mass concentrated in the
nucleus of the atom.   **PAGE:** 5.6

77. Consider the following gas samples:

Sample A	Sample B
$S_2(g)$	$O_2(g)$
$n = 1$ mol	$n = 2$ mol
$T = 800$ K	$T = 400$ K
$P = 0.20$ atm	$P = 0.40$ atm

Which one of the following statements is *false*?

a) The volume of sample A is twice the volume of sample B.

b) The average kinetic energy of the molecules in sample A is twice the average kinetic energy of the molecules in sample B.

c) The fraction of molecules in sample A having a kinetic energy greater than some high fixed value is larger than the fraction of molecules in sample B having kinetic energies greater than that same high fixed value.

d) The mean square velocity of molecules in sample A is twice as large as the mean square velocity of molecules in sample B.

e) Assuming identical intermolecular forces in the two samples, sample A should be more nearly ideal than sample B.

ANS: d)   The mean square velocity of molecules in sample A is twice as large as the mean square velocity of molecules in sample B.   PAGE: 5.6,8

78. At 200 K, the molecules or atoms of an unknown gas, X, have an average velocity equal to that of Ar atoms at 400 K. What is X? (Assume ideal behavior.)

a) He

b) CO

c) HF

d) HBr

e) F_2

ANS: c)   HF   PAGE: 5.6

79. Which of the following is *not* an assumption of the kinetic molecular theory for a gas?

a) Gases are made up of tiny particles in constant chaotic motion.

b) Gas particles are very small compared to the average distance between the particles.

c) Gas particles collide with the walls of their container in elastic collisions.

d) The average velocity of the gas particles is directly proportional to the absolute temperature.

e) All of the above are correct.

ANS: d)   The average velocity of the gas particles is directly proportional to the absolute temperature.   PAGE: 5.6

80. A sample of N_2 gas is contaminated with a gas (A) of unknown molar mass. The partial pressure of each gas is known to be 200. torr at 25°C. The gases are allowed to effuse through a pinhole, and it is found that gas A escapes at three times the rate of N_2. The molar mass of gas A is:

    a) 3.11
    b) 252
    c) 84.0
    d) 9.33
    e) none of these

    ANS: a)   3.11   **PAGE:** 5.7

81. Use the kinetic molecular theory of gases to predict what would happen to a closed sample of a gas whose temperature increased while its volume decreased.

    a) Its pressure would decrease.
    b) Its pressure would increase.
    c) Its pressure would hold constant.
    d) The number of moles of the gas would decrease.
    e) The average kinetic energy of the molecules of the gas would decrease.

    ANS: b)   Its pressure would increase.   **PAGE:** 5.6

82. Calculate the root mean square velocity for the O_2 molecules in a sample of O_2 gas at 25.0°C. ($R = 8.3145\ J/K \cdot mol$)

    a) $2.32 \times 10^5\ m/s$
    b) $658 \times 10^2\ m/s$
    c) 482 m/s
    d) 853 m/s
    e) 97.5 m/s

    ANS: c)   482 m/s   **PAGE:** 5.6

83. Which of the following would have a higher rate of effusion than C_2H_2?

    a) N_2
    b) O_2
    c) Cl_2
    d) CH_4
    e) CO_2

    ANS: d) CH_4 **PAGE:** 5.7

84. Calculate the ratio of the effusion rates of N_2 and N_2O.

    a) 0.637
    b) 1.57
    c) 1.25
    d) 0.798
    e) 1.61

ANS: c) 1.25   **PAGE:** 5.7

85. Which of the following is true about the kinetic molecular theory?

    a) The volume of a gas particle is considered to be small – about 0.10 mL.
    b) Pressure is due to the collisions of the gas particles with the walls of the container.
    c) Gas particles repel each other, but do not attract one another.
    d) Adding an ideal gas to a closed container will cause an increase in temperature.
    e) At least two of the above statements are correct.

ANS: b) Pressure is due to the collisions of the gas particles with
             the walls of the container   **PAGE:** 5.6

86. Which of the following statements is true concerning ideal gases?

    a) The temperature of the gas sample is directly related to the average velocity of the gas particles.
    b) At STP, 1.0 L of Ar(g) contains about twice the number of atoms as 1.0 L of Ne(g) since the molar mass of Ar is about twice that of Ne.
    c) A gas exerts pressure as a result of the collisions of the gas molecules with the walls of the container.
    d) The gas particles in a sample exert attraction for one another.
    e) All of the above are false.

ANS: c) A gas exerts pressure as a result of the collisions of the gas
             molecules with the walls of the container.   **PAGE:** 5.6

87. The van der Waals equation, $nRT = [P + (n^2a/V^2)](V - nb)$, incorporates corrections to the ideal gas law in order to account for the properties of real gases. One of the corrections accounts for

    a) the possibility of chemical reaction between molecules.
    b) the finite volume of molecules.
    c) the quantum behavior of molecules.
    d) the fact that average kinetic energy is inversely proportional to temperature.
    e) the possibility of phase changes when the temperature is decreased or the pressure is increased.

ANS: b) the finite volume of molecules.   **PAGE:** 5.8

88. Which of the following properties of a real gas is related to the *b* coefficient in the van der Waals equation?

    a) Real gases consist of molecules or atoms that have volume.
    b) The average speed of the molecules o: a real gas increases with temperature.
    c) There are attractive forces between atoms or molecules of a real gas.
    d) The rate of effusion of a gas is inversely proportional to the square root of the molecular weight of the gas.

    ANS: a) Real gases consist of molecules or atoms that have volume.   **PAGE:** 5.8

89. Which of the following effects will make PV/nRT less than 1 for a real gas?

    a) The gas molecules are large enough to occupy a substantial amount of space.
    b) A large number of molecules have speeds greater than the average speed.
    c) The gas molecules have a very low molar mass.
    d) The gas molecules attract one another.
    e) none of these

    ANS: d) The gas molecules attract one another.   **PAGE:** 5.8

90. Order the following in increasing rate of effusion:

    F_2, Cl_2, NO, NO_2, CH_4

    a) $Cl_2 < NO_2 < F_2 < NO < CH_4$
    b) $Cl_2 < F_2 < NO_2 < CH_4 < NO$
    c) $CH_4 < NO_2 < NO < F_2 < Cl_2$
    d) $CH_4 < NO < F_2 < NO_2 < Cl_2$
    e) $F_2 < NO < Cl_2 < NO_2 < CH_4$

    ANS: a) $Cl_2 < NO_2 < F_2 < NO < CH_4$ **PAGE:** 5.7

91. A room is 16 ft x 12 ft x 12 ft. Would air enter or leave the room if the temperature changed from 27°C to –3°C while the pressure remained constant? Determine the volume of the air that moved in or out of the room.

    ANS: Air enters the room. 230 ft^3 of air moves.   **PAGE:** 5.2

92. Toy balloons are filled with hydrogen gas, at standard temperature, from a 10.0-liter cylinder. The initial pressure of the gas in the cylinder is exactly 100 atm. Assuming each balloon is filled to a volume of 1.0 liter at standard pressure, how many balloons could be filled?

    ANS: 999   **PAGE:** 5.2

93. A 25-g sample of Ne gas exerts a certain pressure in a container of fixed volume. What mass of Ar gas is required to exert half the pressure at the same conditions of volume and temperature?

    ANS: 25 g Ar   **PAGE:** 5.3

94. Calculate the density of F_2 gas at 26°C and 755 torr.

    ANS: 1.54 g/L   **PAGE:** 5.4

95. If equal masses of hydrogen gas and helium gas are placed in the same container, determine the ratio of partial pressure of hydrogen: partial pressure of helium.

    ANS: 2   **PAGE:** 5.5

96. In the kinetic molecular theory we assume an ideal gas has no mass.

    ANS: False   **PAGE:** 5.2

97. At the same temperature lighter molecules have a higher average kinetic energy than heavier molecules.

    ANS: False   **PAGE:** 5.6

98. The diffusion of a gas is faster than the effusion of a gas.

    ANS: False   **PAGE:** 5.7

99. Gases behave most ideally at STP.

    ANS: False   **PAGE:** 5.8

100. The pressure a gas would exert under ideal conditions is greater than the observed pressure of a real gas.

    ANS: True   **PAGE:** 5.8

1. A gas absorbs 0.0 J of heat and then performs 15.2 J of work. The change in internal energy of the gas is

   a) −24.8 J
   b) 14.8 J
   c) 55.2 J
   d) −15.2 J
   e) none of these

   ANS: d) −15.2 J   **PAGE:** 6.1

2. Calculate the work for the expansion of CO_2 from 1.0 to 2.5 liters against a pressure of 1.0 atm at constant temperature.

   a) 1.5 liter · atm
   b) 2.5 liter · atm
   c) 0
   d) −1.5 liter · atm
   e) −2.5 liter · atm

   ANS: d) −1.5 liter · atm   **PAGE:** 6.1

3. Of energy, work, enthalpy, and heat, how many are state functions?

   a) 0
   b) 1
   c) 2
   d) 3
   e) 4

   ANS: c) 2   **PAGE:** 6.1, 6.2

4. Which of the following statements correctly describes the signs of q and w for the following exothermic process at $P = 1$ atm and $T = 370$ K?

   $$H_2O(g) \rightarrow H_2O(l)$$

   a) q and w are negative.
   b) q is positive, w is negative.
   c) q is negative, w is positive.
   d) q and w are both positive.
   e) q and w are both zero.

   ANS: c) q is negative, w is positive.   **PAGE:** 6.1

5. One mole of an ideal gas is expanded from a volume of 1.00 liter to a volume of 10.00 liters against a constant external pressure of 1.00 atm. How much work (in joules) is performed on the surroundings? ($T = 300$ K; 1 L atm = 101.3 J)

   a)   456 J
   b)   912 J
   c)   2740 J
   d)   2870 J
   e)   none of these

   ANS: b)   912 J   **PAGE:** 6.1

6. For a particular process $q = 20$ kJ and $w = 15$ kJ. Which of the following statements is true?

   a)   Heat flows from the system to the surroundings.
   b)   The system does work on the surroundings.
   c) $\Delta E = 35$ kJ.
   d)   All of the above are true.
   e)   None of the above are true.

   ANS: c) $\Delta E = 35$ kJ.   **PAGE:** 6.1

7. Which statement is *true* of a process in which one mole of a gas is expanded from state A to state B?

   a)   When the gas expands from state A to state B, the surroundings are doing work on the system.
   b)   The amount of work done in the process must be the same, regardless of the path.
   c)   It is not possible to have more than one path for a change of state.
   d)   The final volume of the gas will depend on the path taken.
   e)   The amount of heat released in the process will depend on the path taken.

   ANS: e)   The amount of heat released in the process will depend on
   the path taken.   **PAGE:** 6.1

8. Which of the following statements is correct?

   a)   The internal energy of a system increases when more work is done by the system than heat was flowing into the system.
   b)   The internal energy of a system decreases when work is done on the system and heat is flowing into the system.
   c)   The system does work on the surroundings when an ideal gas expands against a constant external pressure.
   d)   All statements are true.
   e)   All statements are false.

   ANS: c)   The system does work on the surroundings when an ideal
   gas expands against a constant external pressure.   **PAGE:** 6.1

9. Which one of the following statements is *false*?

   a) The change in internal energy, ΔE, for a process is equal to the amount of heat absorbed at constant volume, q_v.

   b) The change in enthalpy, ΔH, for a process is equal to the amount of heat absorbed at constant pressure, q_p.

   c) A bomb calorimeter measures ΔH directly.

   d) If q_p for a process is negative, the process is exothermic.

   e) The freezing of water is an example of an exothermic reaction.

   ANS: c)   A bomb calorimeter measures ΔH directly.   **PAGE:** 6.1,2

10-13. Consider a gas in a 1.0 L bulb at STP that is connected via a valve to another bulb that is initially evacuated. Answer the following concerning what occurs when the valve between the two bulbs is opened.

10. What is true about the value of q?

    a) It is greater than zero.

    b) It is equal to zero.

    c) It is less than zero.

    d) More information is needed.

    e) none of these

    ANS: b)   It is equal to zero.   **PAGE:** 6.1

11. What is true about the value of ΔH?

    a) It is greater than zero.

    b) It is equal to zero.

    c) It is less than zero.

    d) More information is needed.

    e) none of these

    ANS: b)   It is equal to zero.   **PAGE:** 6.2

12. What is true about the value of w?

    a) It is greater than zero.

    b) It is equal to zero.

    c) It is less than zero.

    d) More information is needed.

    e) none of these

    ANS: b)   It is equal to zero.   **PAGE:** 6.1

13. What is true about the value of ΔE?

    a) It is greater than zero.

    b) It is equal to zero.

    c) It is less than zero.

    d) More information is needed.

    e) none of these

    ANS: b)   It is equal to zero.   **PAGE:** 6.1

14. Two metals of equal mass with different heat capacities are subjected to the same amount of heat. Which undergoes the smallest change in temperature?

    a) The metal with the higher heat capacity.
    b) The metal with the lower heat capacity.
    c) Both undergo the same change in temperature.
    d) You need to know the initial temperatures of the metals.
    e) You need to know which metals you have.

    ANS: a)   The metal with the higher heat capacity.   **PAGE:** 6.2

15. A 25.0 g piece of aluminum (which has a molar heat capacity of 24.03J/°Cmol) is heated to 82.4°C and dropped into a calorimeter containing water (specific heat capacity of water is 4.18J/g°C) initially at 22.3°C. The final temperature of the water is 24.9°C. Calculate the mass of water in the calorimeter.

    a) 118 g
    b) 6.57 g
    c) 3180 g
    d) 2120 g
    e) none of these

    ANS: a)   118 g   **PAGE:** 6.2

16. A 40.2 g sample of a metal is heated to 99.3°C and then placed in a calorimeter containing 120.0 g of water (c=4.18J/g°C) at 21.8°C. The final temperature of the water is 24.5°C. Which metal was used?

    a) Aluminum (c=0.89J/g°C)
    b) Iron (c=0.45J/g°C)
    c) Copper (c = 0.20J/g°C)
    d) Lead (c=0.14J/g°C)
    e) none of these

    ANS: b)   Iron   **PAGE:** 6.2

17. You take 200. g of a solid at 30.0°C and let it melt in 400. g of water. The water temperature decreases from 85.1°C to 30.0°C. Calculate the heat of fusion of this solid.

    a) 125 J/g
    b) 285 J/g
    c) 461 J/g
    d) 518 J/g
    e) cannot without the heat capacity of the solid

    ANS: c)   461 J/g   **PAGE:** 6.2

18. Consider a rigid insulated box containing 20.0 g of He(g) at 25.0ÁC and 1.00 atm in one compartment and 20.0 g of N_2(g) at 115.0 ÁC and 2.00 atm in the other compartment. These compartments are connected by a partition which transmits heat. What will be the final temperature in the box at thermal equilibrium? (C_v(He)= 12.5 J/K mol, C_v(N_2)= 20.7 J/K mol)

    a)   42.2°C
    b)   58.9°C
    c)   70.0°C
    d)   81.0°C
    e)   none of these

    ANS: a)   42.2°C   **PAGE:** 6.2

19. Which of the following properties is (are) intensive properties?

    I.   mass
    II. temperature
    III. volume
    IV. concentration
    V.   energy
    a)   I, III, and V
    b)   II only
    c)   II and IV
    d)   III and IV
    e)   I and V

    ANS: c)   II and IV   **PAGE:** 6.1,2

20. The enthalpy of fusion of ice is 6.020 kJ/mol. The heat capacity of liquid water is 75.4 J/mol°C. What is the smallest number of ice cubes at 0°C, each containing one mole of water, necessary to cool 500. g of liquid water initially at 20°C to 0°C?

    a)   1
    b)   7
    c)   14
    d)   15
    e)   126

    ANS: b)   7   **PAGE:** 6.2

21. 30.0 mL of pure water at 280. K is mixed with 50.0 mL of pure water at 330. K. What is the final temperature of the mixture?

   a)   290. K
   b)   311 K
   c)   320. K
   d)   326 K
   e)   405 K

   ANS: b)   311 K   **PAGE:** 6.2

22. For a particular process $q = -17$ kJ and $w = 21$ kJ. Which of the following statements is *false*?

   a)   Heat flows from the system to the surroundings.
   b)   The system does work on the surroundings.
   c) $E = +4$ kJ
   d)   The process is exothermic.
   e)   None of the above is false.

   ANS: c) $E = +4$ kJ   **PAGE:** 6.1

23. Calculate the work associated with the expansion of a gas from 152 L to 189 L at a constant pressure of 14 atm.

   a)   520 L · atm
   b)   –520 L · atm
   c)   –260 L · atm
   d)   175 L · atm
   e)   260 L · atm

   ANS: b)   –520 L · atm   **PAGE:** 6.1

24. Calculate the work associated with the compression of a gas from 121 L to 80. L at a constant pressure of 11 atm.

   a)   –450 L · atm
   b)   450 L · atm
   c)   3.7 L · atm
   d)   –3.7 L · atm
   e)   120 L · atm

   ANS: b)   450 L · atm   **PAGE:** 6.1

25. Consider the reaction

$$H_2(g) + (1/2)O_2(g) \rightarrow H_2O(l) \quad \Delta H\acute{A} = -286 \text{ kJ}$$

Which of the following is true?

    a) The reaction is exothermic.
    b) The reaction is endothermic.
    c) The enthalpy of the products is less than that of the reactants.
    d) Heat is absorbed by the system.
    e) Both a and c are true.

ANS: e)   Both a and c are true.   **PAGE:** 6.2

26. In the lab, you mix two solutions (each originally at the same temperature) and the temperature of the resulting solution decreases. Which of the following is true?

    a) The chemical reaction is releasing energy.
    b) The energy released is equal to $s \times m \times T$.
    c) The chemical reaction is absorbing energy.
    d) The chemical reaction is exothermic.
    e) More than one of these.

ANS: c)   The chemical reaction is absorbing energy.   **PAGE:** 6.2

27. What is the heat capacity of mercury if it requires 167 J to change the temperature of 15.0 g mercury from 25.0°C to 33.0°C?

    a) 6.92×10^{-3} J/g°C
    b) 1.12×10^{-2} J/g°C
    c) 0.445 J/g°C
    d) 1.39 J/g°C
    e) 313 J/g°C

ANS: d)   1.39 J/g°C   **PAGE:** 6.2

28. A 140.0-g sample of water at 25.0°C is mixed with 100.0 g of a certain metal at 100.0°C. After thermal equilibrium is established, the (final) temperature of the mixture is 29.6°C. What is the heat capacity of the metal, assuming it is constant over the temperature range concerned?

    a) 0.38 J/g°C
    b) 0.76 J/g°C
    c) 0.96 J/g°C
    d) 0.031 J/g°C
    e) none of these

ANS: a)   0.38 J/g°C   **PAGE:** 6.2

29. For the reaction $H_2O(l) \rightarrow H_2O(g)$ at 298 K, 1.0 atm, ΔH is more positive than ΔE by 2.5 kJ/mol. This quantity of energy can be considered to be

   a) the heat flow required to maintain a constant temperature.
   b) the work done in pushing back the atmosphere.
   c) the difference in the H—O bond energy in $H_2O(l)$ compared to $H_2O(g)$.
   d) the value of ΔH itself.
   e) none of these

   ANS: b)   the work done in pushing back the atmosphere.   **PAGE:** 6.2

30. Consider the reaction

   $$C_2H_5OH(l) + 3O_2(g) \rightarrow 2CO_2(g) + 3H_2O(l), \Delta H = -1.37 \times 10^3 \text{ kJ}$$

   When a 15.1-g sample of ethyl alcohol (molar mass = 46.1 g/mol) is burned, how much energy is released as heat?

   a) 0.449 kJ
   b) 2.25×10^3 kJ
   c) 4.49×10^2 kJ
   d) 1.02×10^3 kJ
   e) 196 kJ

   ANS: c) 4.49×10^2 kJ   **PAGE:** 6.2

31. $C_2H_5OH(l) + 3O_2(g) \rightarrow 2CO_2(g) + 3H_2O(l), \Delta H = -1.37 \times 10^3$ kJ

   For the combustion of ethyl alcohol as described in the above equation, which of the following is true?

   I. The reaction is exothermic.
   II. The enthalpy change would be different if gaseous water were produced.
   III. The reaction is not an oxidation–reduction one.
   IV. The products of the reaction occupy a larger volume than the reactants.

   a) I, II
   b) I, II, III
   c) I, III, IV
   d) III, IV
   e) Only I

   ANS: a)   I, II   **PAGE:** 6.2,4

32. The ΔH value for the reaction $(1/2)O_2(g) + Hg(l) \rightarrow HgO(s)$ is -90.8 kJ. How much heat is released when 32.5 g Hg is reacted with oxygen?

    a) 9.32 kJ
    b) 90.8 kJ
    c) 14.7 kJ
    d) 40.0 kJ
    e) none of these

    ANS: c)   14.7 kJ   **PAGE:** 6.2

33. If 5.0 kJ of energy is added to a 15.5-g sample of water at 10.°C, the water is

    a) boiling.
    b) completely vaporized.
    c) frozen solid.
    d) decomposed.
    e) still a liquid.

    ANS: e)   still a liquid.   **PAGE:** 6.2

34. Exactly 313.5 J will raise the temperature of 10.0 g of a metal from 25.0°C to 60.0°C. What is the specific heat capacity of the metal?

    a) 3.74 J/g°C
    b) 0.896 J/g°C
    c) 9.70 J/g°C
    d) 1.73 J/g°C
    e) none of these

    ANS: b)   0.896 J/g°C   **PAGE:** 6.2

35. The total volume of hydrogen gas needed to fill the Hindenburg was 2.00×10^8 L at 1.00 atm and 25.0°C. How much energy was evolved when it burned?

    $$H_2(g) + (1/2)O_2(g) \rightarrow H_2O(l), \Delta H = -286 \text{ kJ}$$

    a) 3.5×10^{11} kJ
    b) 8.18×10^6 kJ
    c) 2.86×10^4 kJ
    d) 2.34×10^9 kJ
    e) 5.72×10^{10} kJ

    ANS: d) 2.34×10^9 kJ   **PAGE:** 6.2

36. $CH_4 + 4Cl_2(g) \rightarrow CCl_4(g) + 4HCl(g)$, $\Delta H = -434$ kJ

Based on the above reaction, what energy change occurs when 1.2 moles of methane reacts?

a) 5.2×10^5 J are released.
b) 5.2×10^5 J are absorbed.
c) 3.6×10^5 J are released.
d) 3.6×10^5 J are absorbed.
e) 4.4×10^5 J are released.

ANS: a) 5.2×10^5 J are released.   PAGE: 6.2

37. Given the equation $S(s) + O_2(g) \rightarrow SO_2(g)$, $\Delta H = -296$ kJ, which of the following statement(s) is (are) true?

I. The reaction is exothermic.
II. When 0.500 mole sulfur is reacted, 148 kJ of energy is released.
III. When 32.0 g of sulfur are burned, 2.96×10^5 J of energy is released.

a) All are true.
b) None is true.
c) I and II are true.
d) I and III are true.
e) Only II is true.

ANS: a)   All are true.   PAGE: 6.2

38. Consider the reaction:

$$C_2H_5OH(l) + 3O_2(g) \rightarrow 2CO_2(g) + 3H_2O(l); \Delta H = -1.37 \times 10^3 \text{ kJ}$$

Consider the following propositions:

I. The reaction is endothermic
II. The reaction is exothermic.
III. The enthalpy term would be different if the water formed was gaseous.

Which of these propositions is (are) true?

a) I
b) II
c) III
d) I, II
e) II, III

ANS: e)   II, III   PAGE: 6.2,4

117

39. What is the specific heat capacity of gold if it requires 48.8 J to raise the temperature of 15 grams of gold 25°C?

   a)   29 J/g°C
   b)   0.13 J/g°C
   c)   79 J/g°C
   d)   0.011 J/g°C
   e)   none of these

   ANS: b)   0.13 J/g°C   **PAGE:** 6.2

40. The heat of formation of $Fe_2O_3(s)$ is –826 kJ/mol. Calculate the heat of the reaction $4Fe(s) + 3O_2(g) \rightarrow 2Fe_2O_3(s)$ when a 55.8-g sample of iron is reacted.

   a)   –206 kJ
   b)   –413 kJ
   c)   –826 kJ
   d)   –1650 kJ
   e) -3.30×10^3 kJ

   ANS: b)   –413 kJ   **PAGE:** 6.2,4

41. When 0.157 mol NH_3 is reacted with excess HCl, 6.91 kJ of energy is released as heat. What is ΔH for this reaction per mole of NH_3 consumed?

   a)   –22.7 J
   b)   –1.08 kJ
   c)   –44.0 kJ
   d)   +22.7 J
   e)   +44.0 kJ

   ANS: c)   –44.0 kJ   **PAGE:** 6.2

42. A 4.0-g sample of Colorado oil shale is burned in a bomb calorimeter, which causes the temperature of the calorimeter to increase by 5.0°C. The calorimeter contains 1.00 kg of water (CH_2O = 4.184 J/g°C) and the heat capacity of the empty calorimeter is 0.10 kJ/°C. How much heat is released per gram of oil shale when it is burned?

   a)   21 kJ/g
   b)   42 kJ/g
   c)   0 kJ/g
   d)   5.4 kJ/g
   e)   5.2 kJ/g

   ANS: d)   5.4 kJ/g   **PAGE:** 6.2

43. If a student performs an endothermic reaction in a calorimeter, how does the calculated value of ΔH differ from the actual value if the heat exchanged with the calorimeter is not taken into account?

   a) ΔH_{calc} would be more negative because the calorimeter always absorbs heat from the reaction.

   b) ΔH_{calc} would be less negative because the calorimeter would absorb heat from the reaction.

   c) ΔH_{calc} would be more positive because the reaction absorbs heat from the calorimeter.

   d) ΔH_{calc} would be less positive because the reaction absorbs heat from the calorimeter.

   e) ΔH_{calc} would equal the actual value because the calorimeter does not absorb heat.

   ANS: d) ΔH_{calc} would be less positive because the reaction absorbs
             heat from the calorimeter.   **PAGE:** 6.2

44. A bomb calorimeter has a heat capacity of 2.47 kJ/K. When a 0.105-g sample of ethylene (C_2H_4) was burned in this calorimeter, the temperature increased by 2.14 K. Calculate the energy of combustion for one mole of ethylene.

   a) –5.29 kJ
   b) –50.3 kJ
   c) –572 kJ
   d) –661 kJ
   e) -1.41×10^3 kJ

   ANS: e) -1.41×10^3 kJ   **PAGE:** 6.2

45. How much heat is required to raise the temperature of a 6.21-g sample of iron (specific heat = 0.450 J/(g°C) from 25.0°C to 79.8°C?

   a) 70.0 J
   b) 101 J
   c) 386 J
   d) 756 J
   e) 153 J

   ANS: e)   153 J   **PAGE:** 6.2

46. Consider the following processes:

$$2A \rightarrow 1/2B + C \qquad \Delta H_1 = 5 \text{ kJ/mol}$$

$$(3/2)B + 4C \rightarrow 2A + C + 3D \qquad \Delta H_2 = -15 \text{ kJ/mol}$$

$$E + 4A \rightarrow C \qquad \Delta H_3 = 10 \text{ kJ/mol}$$

Calculate ΔH for: $C \rightarrow E + 3D$

a) 0 kJ/mol
b) 10 kJ/mol
c) -10 kJ/mol
d) -20 kJ/mol
e) 20 kJ/mol

ANS: c)   -10 kJ/mol   **PAGE:** 6.3

47. Consider the following processes:

	ΔH (kJ/mol)
$(1/2)A \rightarrow B$	150.
$3B \rightarrow 2C + D$	-125
$E + A \rightarrow D$	350.

Calculate ΔH for: $B + D \rightarrow E + 2C$

a) 325 kJ/mol
b) 525 kJ/mol
c) -175 kJ/mol
d) -325 kJ/mol
e) none of these

ANS: c)   -175 kJ/mol   **PAGE:** 6.3

48. Which of the following does *not* have a standard enthalpy of formation equal to zero at 25°C and 1.0 atm?

a) $F_2(g)$
b) $Al(s)$
c) $H_2O(l)$
d) $H_2(g)$
e) They all have a standard enthalpy equal to zero.

ANS: c) $H_2O_{(1)}$ **PAGE:** 6.4

49. Consider the following numbered processes:

   I. $A \rightarrow 2B$

   II. $B \rightarrow C + D$

   III. $E \rightarrow 2D$

ΔH for the process $A \rightarrow 2C + E$ is

   a) $\Delta H_1 + \Delta H_2 + \Delta H_3$
   b) $\Delta H_1 + \Delta H_2$
   c) $\Delta H_1 + \Delta H_2 - \Delta H_3$
   d) $\Delta H_1 + 2\Delta H_2 - \Delta H_3$
   e) $\Delta H_1 + 2\Delta H_2 + \Delta H_3$

ANS: d) $\Delta H_1 + 2\Delta H_2 - \Delta H_3$ **PAGE:** 6.3

50. At 25°C, the following heats of reaction are known:

	ΔH (kJ/mol)
$2ClF + O_2 \rightarrow Cl_2O + F_2O$	167.4
$2ClF_3 + 2O_2 \rightarrow Cl_2O + 3F_2O$	341.4
$2F_2 + O_2 \rightarrow 2F_2O$	-43.4

At the same temperature, calculate ΔH for the reaction:

   $ClF + F_2 \rightarrow ClF_3$

   a) -217.5 kJ/mol
   b) -130.2 kJ/mol
   c) +217.5 kJ/mol
   d) -108.7 kJ/mol
   e) none of these

ANS: d)   -108.7 kJ/mol   **PAGE:** 6.3

51. Calculate $\Delta H°$ for the reaction $C_4H_4(g) + 2H_2(g) \rightarrow C_4H_8(g)$, using the following data:

   $\Delta H°_{combustion}$ for $C_4H_4(g) = -2341$ kJ/mol

   $\Delta H°_{combustion}$ for $H_2(g) = -286$ kJ/mol

   $\Delta H°_{combustion}$ for $C_4H_8(g) = -2755$ kJ/mol

   a) -128 kJ
   b) -158 kJ
   c) 128 kJ
   d) 158 kJ
   e) none of these

ANS: b)   -158 kJ   **PAGE:** 6.3

52. Given the following two reactions at 298 K and 1 atm, which of the statements is true?

$$1. \quad N_2(g) + O_2(g) \rightarrow 2NO(g) \qquad \Delta H_1$$

$$2. \quad NO(g) + (1/2)O_2(g) \rightarrow NO_2(g) \quad \Delta H_2$$

a) ΔH_f° for $NO_2(g) = \Delta H_2$
b) ΔH_f° for $NO(g) = \Delta H_1$
c) $\Delta H_f^\circ = \Delta H_2$
d) ΔH_f° for $NO_2(g) = \Delta H_2 + (1/2)\Delta H_1$
e) none of these

ANS: d) ΔH_f° for $NO_2(g) = \Delta H_2 + (1/2)\Delta H_1$ 　　　　　　　　 **PAGE:** 6.3,4

53. Given the heats of the following reactions:

		ΔH° (kJ)
I.	$P_4(s) + 6Cl_2(g) \rightarrow 4PCl_3(g)$	–1225.6
II.	$P_4(s) + 5O_2(g) \rightarrow P_4O_{10}(s)$	–2967.3
III.	$PCl_3(g) + Cl_2(g) \rightarrow PCl_5(g)$	–84.2
IV.	$PCl_3(g) + (1/2)O_2(g) \rightarrow Cl_3PO(g)$	–285.7

Calculate the value of ΔH° for the reaction below:

$$P_4O_{10}(s) + 6PCl_5(g) \rightarrow 10Cl_3PO(g)$$

a) –110.5 kJ
b) –610.1 kJ
c) –2682.2 kJ
d) –7555.0 kJ
e) None of these is within 5% of the correct answer.

ANS: b)   –610.1 kJ 　　　　　　　　　　　　　　　　 **PAGE:** 6.3

54. Given: $Cu_2O(s) + (1/2)O_2(g) \rightarrow 2CuO(s) \quad \Delta H^\circ = -144$ kJ

$$Cu_2O(s) \rightarrow Cu(s) + CuO(s) \qquad \Delta H^\circ = +11 \text{ kJ}$$

Calculate the standard enthalpy of formation of CuO(s).

a) –166 kJ
b) –299 kJ
c) +299 kJ
d) +155 kJ
e) –155 kJ

ANS: e)   –155 kJ/mol 　　　　　　　　　　　　　　　 **PAGE:** 6.3,4

55. The heat combustion of acetylene, $C_2H_2(g)$, at 25°C, is –1299 kJ/mol. At this temperature, ΔH_f° values for $CO_2(g)$ and $H_2O(l)$ are –393 and –286 kJ/mol, respectively. Calculate ΔH_f° for acetylene.

    a)   2376 kJ/mol
    b)   625 kJ/mol
    c)   227 kJ/mol
    d)   –625 kJ/mol
    e)   none of these

    ANS: c)   227 kJ/mol   **PAGE:** 6.4

56. Choose the correct equation for the standard enthalpy of formation of $CO(g)$, where ΔH_f° for CO = –110.5 kJ/mol (gr indicates graphite).

    a) $2C(gr) + O_2(g) \rightarrow 2CO(g)$, $\Delta H^\circ = -110.5$ kJ
    b) $C(gr) + O(g) \rightarrow CO(g)$, $\Delta H^\circ = -110.5$ kJ
    c) $C(gr) + (1/2)O2(g) \rightarrow CO(g)$, $\Delta H^\circ = -110.5$ kJ
    d) $C(gr) + CO_2(g) \rightarrow 2CO(g)$, $\Delta H^\circ = -110.5$ kJ
    e) $CO(g) \rightarrow C(gr) + O(g)$, $\Delta H^\circ = -110.5$ kJ

    ANS: c) $C(gr) + (1/2)O_2(g) \rightarrow CO(g)$, $\Delta H^\circ = -110.5$ kJ   **PAGE:** 6.4

57. For the reaction

    $$AgI(s) + (1/2)Br_2(g) \rightarrow AgBr(s) + (1/2)I_2(s), \quad \Delta H_{298}^\circ = -54.0 \text{ kJ}$$

    ΔH_f° for AgBr(s) = –100.4 kJ/mol

    ΔH_f° for $Br_2(g)$ = +30.9 kJ/mol

    The value of ΔH_f° (298) for AgI(s) is:

    a)   –123.5 kJ/mol
    b)   +77.3 kJ/mol
    c)   +61.8 kJ/mol
    d)   –77.3 kJ/mol
    e)   –61.8 kJ/mol

    ANS: e)   –61.8 kJ/mol   **PAGE:** 6.4

58. Using the following data, calculate the standard heat of formation of the compound ICl in kJ/mol:

		$\Delta H°$ (kJ/mol)
$Cl_2(g) \rightarrow 2Cl(g)$		242.3
$I_2(g) \rightarrow 2I(g)$		151.0
$ICl(g) \rightarrow I(g) + Cl(g)$		211.3
$I_2(s) \rightarrow I_2(g)$		62.8

a) –211 kJ/mol
b) –14.6 kJ/mol
c) 16.8 kJ/mol
d) 245 kJ/mol
e) 439 kJ/mol

ANS: c)   16.8 kJ/mol   **PAGE:** 6.3,4

59. Using the information below, calculate ΔH_f° for PbO(s)

$PbO(s) + CO(g) \rightarrow Pb(s) + CO_2(g)$ $\Delta H\text{Á} = -131.4$ kJ

ΔH_f° for $CO_2(g) = -393.5$ kJ/mol

ΔH_f° for $CO(g) = -110.5$ kJ/mol

a) –151.6 kJ/mol
b) –283.0 kJ/mol
c) +283.0 kJ/mol
d) –372.6 kJ/mol
e) +252.1 kJ/mol

ANS: a)   –151.6 kJ/mol   **PAGE:** 6.4

60. For which of the following reaction(s) is the enthalpy change for the reaction *not* equal to ΔH_f° of the product?

I. $2H(g) \rightarrow H_2(g)$
II. $H_2(g) + O_2(g) \rightarrow H_2O_2(l)$
III. $H_2O(l) + O(g) \rightarrow H_2O_2(l)$

a) I
b) II
c) III
d) I and III
e) II and III

ANS: d)   I and III   **PAGE:** 6.4

124

61. Consider the following reaction:

$$2Al(s) + 3Cl_2(g) \rightarrow 2AlCl_3(s); \quad \Delta H = -1390.81 \text{ kJ}$$

   a) Is the reaction exothermic or endothermic?
   b) Calculate the heat produced when 10.0 g $AlCl_3$ forms.
   c) How many grams of Al are required to produce 1.00 kJ of energy?

   ANS: a)   exothermic;   b)   52.2 kJ;   c)   0.0388 g Al   **PAGE:** 6.2

62, 63.   To carry out the reaction $N_2 + 2O_2 \rightarrow 2NO_2$ requires 67.7 kJ.

   To carry out the reaction $N_2 + 2O_2 \rightarrow N_2O_4$ requires 9.7 kJ.
   Consider the reaction $2NO_2 \rightarrow N_2O_4$.

62. How much energy (absolute value) is involved in the reaction $2NO_2 \rightarrow N_2O_4$?

   ANS: 58.0 kJ   **PAGE:** 6.3

63. Is the reaction endothermic or exothermic?

   ANS: exothermic   **PAGE:** 6.3

64. Consider the following data:

	ΔH (kJ)
$Ca(s) + 2C(graphite) \rightarrow CaC_2(s)$	–62.8
$Ca(s) + 1/2O_2(g) \rightarrow CaO(s)$	–635.5
$CaO(s) + H_2O(l) \rightarrow Ca(OH)_2(aq)$	–653.1
$C_2H_2(g) + (5/2)O_2(g) \rightarrow 2CO_2 + H_2O(l)$	–1300
$C(graphite) + O_2(g) \rightarrow CO_2(g)$	–393.51

Use Hess's law to find the change in enthalpy at 25°C for the following equation:

$$CaC_2(s) + 2H_2O(l) \rightarrow Ca(OH)_2(aq) + C_2H_2(g)$$

   ANS: –713 kJ   **PAGE:** 6.3

65. Consider the following standard heats of formation:

   $P_4O_{10}(s) = -3110 \text{ kJ/mol}$

   $H_2O(l) = -286 \text{ kJ/mol}$

   $H_3PO_4(s) = -1279 \text{ kJ/mol}$

Calculate the change in enthalpy for the following process:

$$P_4O_{10}(s) + 6H_2O(l) \rightarrow 4H_3PO_4(s)$$

   ANS: –290 kJ   **PAGE:** 6.4

66. The following statements concerning petroleum are all true *except*:

   a) It is a thick, dark liquid composed mostly of hydrocarbons.
   b) It must be separated into fractions (by boiling) in order to be used efficiently.
   c) Some of the commercial uses of petroleum fractions include gasoline and kerosene.
   d) It was probably formed from the remains of ancient marine organisms.
   e) All of its hydrocarbon chains contain the same number of carbon atoms.

   ANS: e) All of its hydrocarbon chains contain the same number of carbon atoms.   **PAGE:** 6.5

67. This fossil fuel was formed from the remains of plants that were buried and exposed to high pressure and heat over time. It is

   a) coal.
   b) natural gas.
   c) diesel fuel.
   d) propane.
   e) gasoline.

   ANS: a) coal.   **PAGE:** 6.5

68. The coal with the highest energy available per unit burned is

   a) lignite.
   b) subbituminous.
   c) bituminous.
   d) anthracite.
   e) They are equal in energy value.

   ANS: d) anthracite.   **PAGE:** 6.5

69. All of the following statements about the greenhouse effect are true *except*:

   a) It occurs only on earth.
   b) The molecules H_2O and CO_2 play an important role in retaining the atmosphere's heat.
   c) Low humidity allows efficient radiation of heat back into space.
   d) The carbon dioxide content of the atmosphere is quite stable.
   e) a and d

   ANS: e) a and d   **PAGE:** 6.5

70. One of the main advantages of hydrogen as a fuel is that

    a) the only product of hydrogen combustion is water.
    b) it exists as a free gas.
    c) it can be economically supplied by the world's oceans.
    d) plants can economically produce the hydrogen needed.
    e) it contains a large amount of energy per unit volume of hydrogen gas.

    ANS: a)   the only product of hydrogen combustion is water.   PAGE: 6.6

71. Which of the following is *not* being considered as an energy source for the future?

    a) ethanol
    b) methanol
    c) seed oil
    d) shale oil
    e) carbon dioxide

    ANS: e)   carbon dioxide   PAGE: 6.6

72. Acetylene (C_2H_2) and butane (C_4H_{10}) are gaseous fuels. Determine the ratio of energy available from the combustion of a given volume of acetylene to butane at the same temperature and pressure using the following data:

    The change in enthalpy of combustion for

    $C_2H_2(g) = -49.9$ kJ/g.

    The change in enthalpy of combustion for

    $C_4H_{10} = -49.5$ kJ/g.

    ANS: About 2.21 times the volume of acetylene is needed to furnish the same energy as a given volume of butane.   PAGE: 6.6

73. A property that is independent of the pathway is called an intensive property.

    ANS: False   PAGE: 6.1

74. In exothermic reaction, potential energy stored in chemical bonds is being converted to thermal energy via heat.

    ANS: True   PAGE: 6.1

75. A state function does not depend on the system's past or future.

    ANS: True   PAGE: 6.1

76. When a system performs work on the surroundings, the work is reported with a negative sign.

    ANS: True   PAGE: 6.1

77.   The change in enthalpy can always be thought of as equal to energy flow as heat.

ANS: False   PAGE: 6.2

78.   The specific heat capacities of metals are relatively low.

ANS: True   PAGE: 6.2

79.   The _____ of a system is the sum of the kinetic and potential energies of all the particles in the system.

ANS: internal energy   PAGE: 6.1

80.   _____ involves the transfer of energy between two objects due to a temperature difference.

ANS: Heat   PAGE: 6.1

CHAPTER 7   Atomic Structure and Periodicity

1. When ignited, a uranium compound burns with a green flame. The wavelength of the light given off by this flame is greater than that of

    a) red light.
    b) infrared light.
    c) radio waves.
    d) ultraviolet light.
    e) none of these

    ANS: d)   ultraviolet light.   **PAGE:** 7.1

2. Which one of the following types of radiation has the shortest wavelength, the greatest energy, and the highest frequency?

    a) ultraviolet radiation
    b) infrared radiation
    c) visible red light
    d) visible blue light
    e) none because short wavelength is associated with low energy and low frequency, not high energy and high frequency

    ANS: a)   ultraviolet radiation   **PAGE:** 7.1,2

3. Which form of electromagnetic radiation has the longest wavelengths?

    a) gamma rays
    b) microwaves
    c) radio waves
    d) infrared radiation
    e) x-rays

    ANS: c)   radio waves   **PAGE:** 7.1

4. Which of the following frequencies corresponds to light with the longest wavelength?

    a) 3.00×10^{13} s^{-1}
    b) 4.12×10^{5} s^{-1}
    c) 8.50×10^{20} s^{-1}
    d) 9.12×10^{12} s^{-1}
    e) 3.20×10^{9} s^{-1}

    ANS: b) 4.12×10^{5} s^{-1} **PAGE:** 7.1

5. Which of the following statements is (are) true?

   I.   An excited atom can return to its ground state by absorbing electromagnetic radiation.
   II. The energy of an atom is increased when electromagnetic radiation is emitted from it.
   III. The energy of electromagnetic radiation increases as its frequency increases.
   IV. An electron in the $n = 4$ state in the hydrogen atom can go to the $n = 2$ state by emitting electromagnetic radiation at the appropriate frequency.
   V.   The frequency and wavelength of electromagnetic radiation are inversely proportional to each other.

   a) II, III, IV
   b) III, V
   c) I, II, III
   d) III, IV, V
   e) I, II, IV

   ANS: d)   III, IV, V   **PAGE:** 7.1,4

6-11. From the following list of observations, choose the one that most clearly supports the following conclusion:

   a) emission spectrum of hydrogen
   b) the photoelectric effect
   c) scattering of alpha particles by metal foil
   d) diffraction
   e) cathode "rays"

6. Electrons have wave properties.

   ANS: d)   diffraction   **PAGE:** 7.2

7. Electromagnetic radiation has wave characteristics.

   ANS: d)   diffraction   **PAGE:** 7.2

8. The mass of the atom is located mainly in the nucleus.

   ANS: c)   scattering of alpha particles by metal foil   **PAGE:** 2.4,7.2

9. Atoms contain electrons.

   ANS: e)   cathode "rays"   **PAGE:** 2.4,7.2

10. Electrons in atoms have quantized energies.

   ANS: a)   emission spectrum of hydrogen   **PAGE:** 7.2,3

11. de Broglie wavelengths.

   ANS: d)   diffraction   **PAGE:** 7.2

12. Alpha particles $^{4}_{2}He^{2+}$ beamed at thin metal foil may

    a)   pass directly through without changing direction.

    b)   be slightly diverted by attraction to electrons.

    c)   be reflected by direct contact with nuclei.

    d)   a and c

    e)   a, b, and c

ANS: e)   a, b, and c   **PAGE: 2.4,7.2**

13. Green light has a wavelength of 5.50×10^2 nm. The energy of a photon of green light is

    a) 3.64×10^{-38} J

    b) 2.17×10^{5} J

    c) 3.61×10^{-19} J

    d) 1.09×10^{-27} J

    e) 5.45×10^{12} J

ANS: c) 3.61×10^{-19} J   **PAGE: 7.2**

14. In an investigation of the electronic absorption spectrum of a particular element, it is found that a photon having $\lambda = 500$ nm provides just enough energy to promote an electron from the second quantum level to the third. From this information, we can deduce

    a)   the energy of the $n = 2$ level.

    b)   the energy of the $n = 3$ level.

    c)   the sum of the energies of $n = 2$ and $n = 3$.

    d)   the difference in energies between $n = 2$ and $n = 3$.

    e)   all of these

ANS: d)   the difference in energies between $n = 2$ and $n = 3$.   **PAGE: 7.3,4**

15. What is the wavelength of light that is emitted when an excited electron in the hydrogen atom falls from n=5 to n=2?

    a) 5.12×10^{-7} m

    b) 4.34×10^{-7} m

    c) 6.50×10^{-7} m

    d) 5.82×10^{-7} m

    e)   none of these

ANS: b) 4.34×10^{-7} m   **PAGE: 7.4**

16. Which of the following is incorrectly paired?

    a) wavelength – λ
    b) frequency – ν
    c) speed of light – c
    d) hertz – s^{-1}
    e) x-rays – shortest wavelength

    ANS: e) x-rays – shortest wavelength   **PAGE:** 7.1

17. When a strontium salt is ignited, it burns with a red flame. The frequency of the light given off by this flame is greater than

    a) yellow light
    b) infrared light
    c) ultraviolet light
    d) radio waves
    e) x-rays

    ANS: b) infrared light   **PAGE:** 7.1

18. What is the wavelength of a photon of red light (in nm) whose frequency is 4.60×10^{14} Hz?

    a) 652 nm
    b) 153×10^6 nm
    c) 153 nm
    d) 460. nm
    e) none of these

    ANS: a) 652 nm   **PAGE:** 7.2

19. What is the energy of a photon of blue light that has a wavelength of 450 nm?

    a) 6.7×10^{14} J
    b) 4.4×10^{-19} J
    c) 1.5×10^5 J
    d) 1.01×10^{48} J
    e) 5.8×10^{-19} J

    ANS: b) 4.4×10^{-19} J   **PAGE:** 7.2

20. Which of the following is *incorrect*?

    a) The importance of the equation $E = mc^2$ is that energy has mass.
    b) Electromagnetic radiation can be thought of as a stream of particles called photons.
    c) All of these are correct.
    d) The energy of matter is not continuous and is actually quantized.
    e) Energy can only occur in discrete units called quanta.

    ANS: c) All of these are correct.   **PAGE:** 7.2

21–23. Consider the following portion of the energy-level diagram for hydrogen:

$n = 4$ -0.1361×10^{-18} J

$n = 3$ -0.2420×10^{-18} J

$n = 2$ -0.5445×10^{-18} J

$n = 1$ -2.178×10^{-18} J

21. For which of the following transitions does the light emitted have the longest wavelength?

   a) $n = 4$ to $n = 3$
   b) $n = 4$ to $n = 2$
   c) $n = 4$ to $n = 1$
   d) $n = 3$ to $n = 2$
   e) $n = 2$ to $n = 1$

ANS: a) $n = 4$ to $n = 3$ **PAGE: 7.4**

22. In the hydrogen spectrum, what is the wavelength of light associated with the $n = 2$ to $n = 1$ electron transition?

   a)   1.097 nm
   b)   364.9 nm
   c) 0.1097×10^{-8} cm
   d) 9.122×10^{-8} m
   e) 1.216×10^{-7} m

ANS: e) 1.216×10^{-7} m   **PAGE: 7.4**

23. The wavelength of light associated with the $n = 2$ to $n = 1$ electron transition in the hydrogen spectrum is 1.216×10^{-7} m. By what coefficient should this wavelength be multiplied to obtain the wavelength associated with the same electron transition in the Li^{2+} ion?

   a)   1/9
   b)   1/7
   c)   1/4
   d)   1/3
   e)   1

ANS: a)   1/9   **PAGE: 7.4**

24. When a hydrogen electron makes a transition from $n = 3$ to $n = 1$, which of the following statements is *true*?

    I. Energy is emitted.
    II. Energy is absorbed.
    III. The electron loses energy.
    IV. The electron gains energy.
    V. The electron cannot make this transition.

    a) I, IV
    b) I, III
    c) II, III
    d) II, IV
    e) V

ANS: b) I, III   **PAGE:** 7.4

25. Which of the following is a reasonable criticism of the Bohr model of the atom?

    a) It makes no attempt to explain why the negative electron does not eventually fall into the positive nucleus.
    b) It does not adequately predict the line spectrum of hydrogen.
    c) It does not adequately predict the ionization energy of the valence electron(s) for elements other than hydrogen.
    d) It does not adequately predict the ionization energy of the 1st energy level electrons for one-electron species for elements other than hydrogen.
    e) It shows the electrons to exist outside of the nucleus.

ANS: c) It does not adequately predict the ionization energy of the valence electron(s) for elements other than hydrogen.   **PAGE:** 7.4

26. When an electron in a 2p orbital of a lithium atom makes a transition to the 2s orbital, a photon of wavelength 670.8 nm is emitted. The energy difference between these 2p and 2s orbitals is

    a) 2.96×10^{-10} J
    b) 2.96×10^{-19} J
    c) 3.38×10^{18} J
    d) 2.96×10^{-17} J
    e) none of these

ANS: b) 2.96×10^{-19} J   **PAGE:** 7.4

27. The energy of the light emitted when a hydrogen electron goes from $n = 2$ to $n = 1$ is what fraction of its ground-state ionization energy?

    a) 3/4
    b) 1/2
    c) 1/4
    d) 1/8
    e) 1/9

ANS: a) 3/4   **PAGE:** 7.4

28. In Bohr's atomic theory, when an electron moves from one energy level to another energy level more distant from the nucleus

    a) energy is emitted.
    b) energy is absorbed.
    c) no change in energy occurs.
    d) light is emitted.
    e) none of these

ANS: b) energy is absorbed.   **PAGE:** 7.4

29. Which of the following is *not* determined by the principal quantum number, n, of the electron in a hydrogen atom?

    a) the energy of the electron
    b) the minimum wavelength of the light needed to remove the electron from the atom.
    c) the size of the corresponding atomic orbital(s)
    d) the shape of the corresponding atomic orbital(s)
    e) All of the above are determined by n.

ANS: d) the shape of the corresponding atomic orbital(s)   **PAGE:** 7.4,6

30. Which of the following statements about quantum theory is *incorrect*?

    a) The energy and position of an electron cannot be determined simultaneously.
    b) Lower energy orbitals are filled with electrons before higher energy orbitals.
    c) When filling orbitals of equal energy, two electrons will occupy the same orbital before filling a new orbital.
    d) No two electrons can have the same four quantum numbers.
    e) All of these are correct.

ANS: c) When filling orbitals of equal energy, two electrons will occupy the same orbital before filling a new orbital.   **PAGE:** 7.5–11

31. Which of the following statements is *true*?

    a)   The exact location of an electron can be determined if we know its energy.
    b)   An electron in a 2s orbital can have the same n, l, and m_l quantum numbers as an electron in a 3s orbital.
    c)   Ni has 2 unpaired electrons in its 3d orbitals.
    d)   In the buildup of atoms, electrons occupy the 4f orbitals before the 6s orbitals.
    e)   Only three quantum numbers are needed to uniquely describe an electron.

    ANS: c)   Ni has 2 unpaired electrons in its 3d orbitals.   **PAGE:** 7.5–11

32. Which of the following statements is *false*?

    a)   An orbital can accommodate at most two electrons.
    b)   The electron density at a point is proportional to psi^2 at that point.
    c)   The spin quantum number of an electron must be either +1/2 or –1/2.
    d)   A 2p orbital is more penetrating than a 2s; i.e., it has a higher electron density near the nucleus and inside the charge cloud of a 1s orbital.
    e)   In the usual order of filling, the 6s orbital is filled before the 4f orbital.

    ANS: d)   A 2 p orbital is more penetrating than a 2s; i.e., it has a higher electron density near the nucleus and inside the charge cloud of a 1s orbital.   **PAGE:** 7.5–11

33. How many f orbitals have the value $n = 3$?

    a)   0
    b)   3
    c)   5
    d)   7
    e)   1

    ANS: a)   0   **PAGE:** 7.6

34. How many electrons in an atom can have the quantum numbers $n = 3$, $l = 2$?

    a)   2
    b)   5
    c)   10
    d)   18
    e)   6

    ANS: c)   10   **PAGE:** 7.6,11

35. How many electrons can be described by the quantum numbers $n = 3, l = 3, m_l = 1$?

   a) 0
   b) 2
   c) 6
   d) 10
   e) 14

   ANS: a)   0   **PAGE: 7.6,11**

36. Which of the following is *incorrect*?

   a) The continuous spectrum of hydrogen contains only four discrete colors.
   b) Diffraction produces both constructive and destructive interference.
   c) All matter displays both particle and wavelike characteristics.
   d) Niels Bohr developed a quantum model for the hydrogen atom.
   e) The lowest possible energy state of a molecule or atom is called its ground state.

   **ANS: a)   The continuous spectrum of hydrogen contains only four
           discrete colors.**   **PAGE: 7.2,3,4**

37. How many d orbitals have $n = 3$?

   a) 2
   b) 5
   c) 10
   d) 7
   e) 18

   ANS: b)   5   **PAGE: 7.6**

38. How many electrons in an atom can have the quantum numbers $n = 4, l = 2$?

   a) 14
   b) 12
   c) 5
   d) 10
   e) 6

   ANS: d)   10   **PAGE: 7.6,11**

39. If $n = 2$, how many orbitals are possible?

   a) 3
   b) 4
   c) 2
   d) 8
   e) 6

   ANS: b)   4   **PAGE: 7.6**

40. A given set of p orbitals consists of _____ orbitals.

    a) 1
    b) 2
    c) 3
    d) 4
    e) 5

    ANS: c) 3   **PAGE:** 7.6

41. Which of the following is an incorrect designation for an atomic orbital?

    a) 1s
    b) 3d
    c) 1p
    d) 4f
    e) 6s

    ANS: c) 1p   **PAGE:** 7.6

42. The number of orbitals having a given value of l is equal to

    a) $2l + 1$
    b) $2n + 2$
    c) $3l$
    d) $l + m_l$
    e) the number of lobes in each orbital

    ANS: a) $2l + 1$ **PAGE:** 7.6

43. Which of the following combinations of quantum numbers do *not* represent permissible solutions of the Schrodinger equation for the electron in the hydrogen atom (i.e., which combination of quantum numbers is *not* allowed)?

	n	l	m	s (or m_s)
a)	9	8	–4	1/2
b)	8	2	2	1/2
c)	6	–5	–1	1/2
d)	6	5	–5	1/2
e)	All are allowed.

    ANS: c) 6   –5   –1   1/2   **PAGE:** 7.6,8

44. Which of the following atoms or ions has 3 unpaired electrons?

    a) N
    b) O
    c) Al
    d) S^{2-}
    e) Zn^{2+}

    ANS: a) N   **PAGE:** 7.11

45. The electron configuration for the barium atom is:

    a) $1s^2 2s^2 2p^6 3s^2 3p^6 3d^{10} 4s^2$
    b) $[Xe]\ 6s^2$
    c) $1s^2 2s^2 2p^6 3s^2 3p^6 4s^1$
    d) $1s^2 2s^2 2p^6 3s^2 3p^6 4s^2$
    e) none of these

    ANS: b) $[Xe]\ 6s^2$ **PAGE: 7.11**

46. The electron configuration for the carbon atom is:

    a) $1s^2 2s^2 2p^2$
    b) $[He]\ 2s^4$
    c) $[Ne]\ 2s^2 2p^2$
    d) $1s^2 2p^4$
    e) none of these

    ANS: a) $1s^2 2s^2 2p^2$ **PAGE: 7.11**

47. The electron configuration of indium is

    a) $1s^2 2s^2 2p^6 3s^2 3p^6 3d^{10} 4s^2 4p^6 4d^{10} 5s^2 5p^1 5d^{10}$
    b) $1s^2 2s^2 2p^6 3s^2 3p^6 3d^{10} 4s^2 4d^{10} 4p^1$
    c) $1s^2 3s^2 2p^6 3s^2 3p^6 4s^2 4p^6 4d^{10} 5s^2 5d^{10} 5p^1$
    d) $1s^2 2s^2 2p^6 3s^2 3p^6 3d^{10} 4s^2 4p^6 4d^{10} 5s^2 5p^1$
    e) none of these

    ANS: d) $1s^2 2s^2 2p^6 3s^2 3p^6 3d^{10} 4s^2 4p^6 4d^{10} 5s^2 5p^1$ **PAGE: 7.11**

48. If $l = 3$, how many electrons can be contained in all the possible orbitals?

    a) 7
    b) 6
    c) 14
    d) 10
    e) 5

    ANS: c)   14   **PAGE: 7.6,11**

49. Which of the following combinations of quantum numbers is not allowed?

	n	l	$m_{(l)}$	$m_{(s)}$
a)	1	1	0	1/2
b)	3	0	0	-1/2
c)	2	1	-1	1/2
d)	4	3	-2	-1/2
e)	4	2	0	1/2

    ANS: a)   1   1   0   1/2   **PAGE: 7.6,8**

50. Who was the first chemist to recognize patterns in chemical properties of the elements?

    a) Medeleev
    b) Newlands
    c) Meyer
    d) Dobereiner
    e) Bohr

ANS: d)   Dobereiner   **PAGE:** 7.10

51. The statement that "the lowest energy configuration for an atom is the one having the maximum number of unpaired electrons allowed by the Pauli principle in a particular set of degenerate orbitals" is known as

    a) the aufbau principle.
    b) Hund's rule.
    c) Heisenberg uncertainty principle.
    d) the Pauli exclusion principle.
    e) the quantum model.

ANS: b)   Hund's rule.   **PAGE:** 7.11

52. Which of the following atoms would have the largest second ionization energy?

    a) Mg
    b) Cl
    c) S
    d) Ca
    e) Na

ANS: e)   Na   **PAGE:** 7.12

53. The electron configuration of Cr^{3+} is

    a) $[Ar]4s^23d^1$
    b) $[Ar]4s^13d^2$
    c) $[Ar]3d^3$
    d) $[Ar]4s^23d^4$
    e) none of these

ANS: c) $[Ar]3d^3$ **PAGE:** 7.11

54. An element has the electron configuration $[Kr]4d^{10}5s^25p^2$. The element is a(n)

    a) nonmetal.
    b) transition element.
    c) metal.
    d) lanthanide.
    e) actinide.

ANS: c)   metal.   **PAGE:** 7.11,13

55. An element E has the electron configuration $[Kr]4d^{10}5s^25p^2$. The formula for the fluoride of E is most likely

   a) EF_{14}
   b) EF_4
   c) EF
   d) EF_6
   e) EF_8

   ANS: b) EF_4 **PAGE:** 7.11,13

56. An element with the electron configuration $[Xe]4f^{14}5d^76s^2$ would belong to which class on the periodic table?

   a) transition elements
   b) alkaline earth elements
   c) halogens
   d) rare earth elements
   e) none of the above

   ANS: a) transition elements   **PAGE:** 7.11,13

57. The electron configuration for Cr^{2+} is

   a) $[Ar]4s^23d^4$
   b) $[Ar]4s^13d^5$
   c) $[Ar]3d^4$
   d) $[Ar]4s^23d^2$
   e) none of these

   ANS: c) $[Ar]3d^4$ **PAGE:** 7.11

58. All halogens have the following number of valence electrons:

   a) 2
   b) 3
   c) 5
   d) 7
   e) none of these

   ANS: d) 7   **PAGE:** 7.11

59. Ti has _____ in its d orbitals.

   a) 1 electron
   b) 2 electrons
   c) 3 electrons
   d) 4 electrons
   e) none of these

   ANS: b) 2 electrons   **PAGE:** 7.11

60. Germanium has _____ in its 4p orbitals.

    a) 1 electron
    b) 2 electrons
    c) 3 electrons
    d) 4 electrons
    e) none of these

    ANS: b) 2 electrons   **PAGE:** 7.11

61. Fe has _____ that is (are) unpaired in its d orbitals.

    a) 1 electron
    b) 2 electrons
    c) 3 electrons
    d) 4 electrons
    e) none of these

    ANS: d) 4 electrons   **PAGE:** 7.11

62–63. Nitrogen has 5 valence electrons. Consider the following electron arrangements.

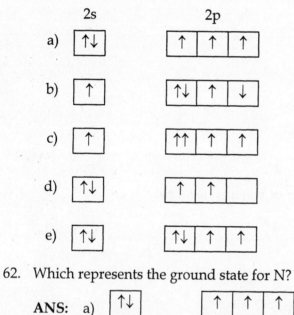

62. Which represents the ground state for N?

    ANS: a)   **PAGE:** 7.11

63. Which represents the ground state for the N⁻ ion?

    ANS: e)   **PAGE:** 7.11

64. In which groups do all the elements have the same number of valence electrons?

    a) P, S, Cl
    b) Ag, Cd, Ar
    c) Na, Ca, Ba
    d) P, As, Se
    e) none

    ANS: e)   none   **PAGE:** 7.11

65. An atom of fluorine contains 9 electrons. How many of these electrons are in s orbitals?

    a) 2
    b) 4
    c) 6
    d) 8
    e) none

    ANS: b)   4   **PAGE:** 7.11

66. How many unpaired electrons are there in an atom of sulfur in its ground state?

    a) 0
    b) 1
    c) 2
    d) 3
    e) 4

    ANS: c)   2   **PAGE:** 7.11

67. How many electrons can be contained in all of the orbitals with $n = 4$?

    a) 2
    b) 8
    c) 10
    d) 18
    e) 32

    ANS: e)   32   **PAGE:** 7.11

68. Of the following elements, which has occupied d orbitals in its ground-state neutral atoms?

    a) Ba
    b) Ca
    c) Si
    d) P
    e) Cl

    ANS: a)   Ba   **PAGE:** 7.11

69. Of the following elements, which needs three electrons to complete its valence shell?

    a) Ba
    b) Ca
    c) Si
    d) P
    e) Cl

    ANS: d) P   PAGE: 7.11

70. Which of the following electron configurations is correct?

    a) Ga: $[Kr]3d^{10}4s^24p^1$
    b) Mo: $[Kr]5s^24d^5$
    c) Ca: $[Ar]4s^13d^{10}$
    d) Br: $[Kr]3d^{10}4s^24p^7$
    e) Bi: $[Xe]6s^24f^{14}5d^{10}6p^3$

    ANS: e) Bi: $[Xe]6s^24f^{14}5d^{10}6p^3$ PAGE: 7.11

71. The electron configuration of Ti^{2+} is

    a) $[Ar]4s^2$
    b) $[Ar]4s^13d^1$
    c) $[Ar]3d^2$
    d) $[Ar]4s^23d^2$
    e) none of these

    ANS: c) $[Ar]3d^2$ PAGE: 7.11

72. $1s^22s^22p^63s^23p^64s^23d^2$ is the correct electron configuration for which of the following atoms?

    a) Ca
    b) Ti
    c) Ge
    d) Zr
    e) none of these

    ANS: b) Ti   PAGE: 7.11

73. Which of the following atoms has three electrons in p orbitals in its valence shell?

    a) Ba
    b) Ga
    c) V
    d) Bi
    e) none of these

    ANS: d) Bi   PAGE: 7.11

74. How many of the following electron configurations for the species in their ground state are correct?

    I.   Ca: $1s^22s^22p^63s^23p^64s^2$

    II. Mg: $1s^22s^22p^63s^1$

    III. V: $[Ar]\,3s^23d^3$

    IV. As: $[Ar]\,4s^23d^{10}4p^3$

    V. P: $1s^22s^22p^63p^5$

    a) 1

    b) 2

    c) 3

    d) 4

    e) 5

ANS: b)   2   **PAGE:** 7.11

75. The number of unpaired electrons in the outer subshell of a Cl atom is

    a) 0.

    b) 1.

    c) 2.

    d) 3.

    e) none of these

ANS: d)   1.   **PAGE:** 7.11

76. For which of the following elements does the electron configuration for the lowest energy state show a partially filled d orbital?

    a) Ti

    b) Rb

    c) Cu

    d) Ga

    e) Kr

ANS: a)   Ti   **PAGE:** 7.11

77. A strong line in the spectrum of atomic mercury has a wavelength of 254 nm. When mercury emits a photon of light at this wavelength, the frequency of this light is

    a) $8.46 \times 10^{-16}\ s^{-1}$

    b) $7.61 \times 10^{5}\ s^{-1}$

    c) $1.18 \times 10^{15}\ s^{-1}$

    d) $1.31 \times 10^{-6}\ s^{-1}$

    e) none of these

ANS: c) $1.18 \times 10^{15}\ s^{-1}$ **PAGE:** 7.1,2

78. Which statements about hydrogen are true?

   I.   H has a lower ionization energy than He.
   II. H⁻ is smaller than H.
   III. H bonds with the halogens to form polar covalent compounds.
   IV. H is always a metal.
   V.   H does not have a second ionization energy.
   a)   I, V
   b)   II, IV
   c)   I, III, V
   d)   II, IV, V
   e)   I, III, IV, V

   ANS: c)   I, III, V   **PAGE:** 7.12,13

79. Which of the following electron configurations are different from those expected?

   a)   Ca
   b)   Sc
   c)   Ti
   d)   V
   e)   Cr

   ANS: e)   Cr   **PAGE:** 7.11

80. When electron configurations differ from expected, it is because orbitals want to be half-filled.

   ANS: False   **PAGE:** 7.11

81. Which of the following have 10 electrons in the d orbitals?

   a)   Mn
   b)   Fe
   c)   Cu
   d)   Zn
   e)   two of the above

   ANS: e)   two of the above   **PAGE:** 7.11

82. Order the elements S, Cl, and F in terms of increasing ionization energy.

   a)   S, Cl, F
   b)   Cl, F, S
   c)   F, S, Cl
   d)   F, Cl, S
   e)   S, F, Cl

   ANS: a)   S, Cl, F   **PAGE:** 7.12

83. Order the elements S, Cl, and F in terms of increasing atomic radii.

    a) S, Cl, F
    b) Cl, F, S
    c) F, S, Cl
    d) F, Cl, S
    e) S, F, Cl

    ANS: d)   F, Cl, S   **PAGE:** 7.12

84. A gamma ray of wavelength 1.00×10^{-8} cm has enough energy to remove an electron from a hydrogen atom.

    ANS: False   **PAGE:** 7.1,4

85. Consider an atom traveling at 1% of the speed of light. The deBroglie wavelength is found to be 3.31×10^{-3} pm. Which element is this?

    a) He
    b) Ca
    c) F
    d) Be
    e) P

    ANS: b)   Ca   **PAGE:** 7.2

86. The first ionization energy of Mg is 735 kJ/mol. The second ionization energy is

    a) 735 kJ/mol
    b) less than 735 kJ/mol
    c) greater than 735 kJ/mol
    d) More information is needed to answer this question.
    e) none of these

    ANS: c)   greater than 735 kJ/mol   **PAGE:** 7.12

87. Which of the following exhibits the correct orders for both atomic radius and ionization energy, respectively?

    a) S, O, F, and F, O, S
    b) F, S, O, and O, S, F
    c) S, F, O, and S, F, O
    d) F, O, S, and S, O, F
    e) none of these

    ANS: d)   F, O, S, and S, O, F   **PAGE:** 7.12

88.   Choose the element with the highest IE.

   a)   Na
   b)   Mg
   c)   Al
   d)   P
   e)   S

ANS: d)   P   **PAGE:** 7.12

89.   On a planet where the temperature is so high, the ground state of an electron in the hydrogen atom is $n = 4$. What is the ratio of IE on this planet compared to earth?

   a) $1 : 4$
   b) $4 : 1$
   c) $1 : 16$
   d) $16 : 1$
   e) $1 : 1$

ANS: c) $1 : 16$ **PAGE:** 7.4

90.   Which of the following is the highest energy orbital for a silicon atom?

   a)   1s
   b)   2s
   c)   3s
   d)   3p
   e)   3d

ANS: e)   3d   **PAGE:** 7.11

91.   Copper exhibits the expected electron configuration.

ANS: False   **PAGE:** 7.11

92.   Which of the following concerning second IE's is true?

   a)   That of Al is higher than that of Mg because Mg wants to lose the second electron, so it is easier to take the second electron away.
   b)   That of Al is higher than that of Mg because the electrons are taken from the same energy level, but the Al atom has one more proton.
   c)   That of Al is lower than that of Mg because Mg wants to lose the second electron, thus the energy change is greater.
   d)   That of Al is lower than that of Mg because the second electron taken from Al is in a p orbital, thus it is easier to take.
   e)   The second ionization energies are equal for Al and Mg.

ANS: b)   That of Al is higher than that of Mg because the electrons are taken from the same energy level, but the Al atom has one more proton.   **PAGE:** 7.12

93. Consider the following orderings.

    I. $Al < Si < P < Cl$
    II. $Be < Mg < Ca < Sr$
    III. $I < Br < Cl < F$
    IV. $Na^+ < Mg^{2+} < Al^{3+} < Si^{4+}$

    Which of these give(s) a correct trend in ionization energy?

    a) III
    b) I, II
    c) I, IV
    d) I, III, IV
    e) none of them

    ANS: d)   I, III, IV   **PAGE: 7.12**

94. List the following atoms in order of increasing ionization energy: Li, Na, C, O, F.

    a) $Li < Na < C < O < F$
    b) $Na < Li < C < O < F$
    c) $F < O < C < Li < Na$
    d) $Na < Li < F < O < C$
    e) $Na < Li < C < F < O$

    ANS: b) $Na < Li < C < O < F$ **PAGE: 7.12**

95. Consider the ionization energy (IE) of the magnesium atom. Which of the following is *not* true?

    a) The IE of Mg is lower than that of sodium.
    b) The IE of Mg is lower than that of neon.
    c) The IE of Mg is lower than that of beryllium.
    d) The IE of Mg is higher than that of calcium.
    e) The IE of Mg is lower than that of Mg^+.

    ANS: a)   The IE of Mg is lower than that of sodium.   **PAGE: 7.12**

96. Of the following elements, which has the lowest first ionization energy?

    a) Ba
    b) Ca
    c) Si
    d) P
    e) Cl

    ANS: a)   Ba   **PAGE: 7.12**

97. Of the following elements, which is most likely to form a negative ion with charge 1-?

    a) Ba
    b) Ca
    c) Si
    d) P
    e) Cl

    ANS: e) Cl   **PAGE:** 7.12

98. Which of the following atoms has the largest ionization energy?

    a) O
    b) Li
    c) N
    d) Be
    e) K

    ANS: c) N   **PAGE:** 7.12

99. Which of the following statements is true?

    a) The first ionization potential of H is greater than that of He.
    b) The ionic radius of Fe^+ is larger than that of Fe^{3+}.
    c) The ionization energy of S^{2-} is greater than that of Cl^-.
    d) The atomic radius of Li is larger than that of Cs.
    e) All are false.

    ANS: b)   The ionic radius of Fe^+ is larger than that of Fe^{3+}.   **PAGE:** 7.12

100. Which of the following statements is false?

    a) A sodium atom has a smaller radius than a potassium atom.
    b) A neon atom has a smaller radius than an oxygen atom.
    c) A fluorine atom has a smaller first ionization energy than an oxygen atom.
    d) A cesium atom has a smaller first ionization energy than a lithium atom.
    e) All are true.

    ANS: c)   A fluorine atom has a smaller first ionization energy than
    an oxygen atom.   **PAGE:** 7.12

101. The statement that the 1st ionization energy for an oxygen atom is lower than the 1st ionization energy for a nitrogen atom is

    a) consistent with the general trend relating changes in ionization energy across a period from left to right because it is easier to take an electron from an oxygen atom than from a nitrogen atom.

    b) consistent with the general trend relating changes in ionization energy across a period from left to right because it is harder to take an electron from an oxygen atom than from a nitrogen atom.

    c) inconsistent with the general trend relating changes in ionization energy across a period from left to right and due the fact that the oxygen atom has two doubly occupied 2p orbitals and nitrogen has only one.

    d) inconsistent with the general trend relating changes in ionization energy across a period from left to right and due to the fact that oxygen has one doubly occupied 2p orbital and nitrogen does not.

    e) incorrect.

    ANS: d) inconsistent with the general trend relating changes in ionization energy across a period from left to right and due to the fact that oxygen has one doubly occupied 2p orbital and nitrogen does not. **PAGE:** 7.12

102. Sodium losing an electron is an _____ process and fluorine losing an electron is an _____ process.

    a) endothermic, exothermic
    b) exothermic, endothermic
    c) endothermic, endothermic
    d) exothermic, exothermic
    e) more information needed

    ANS: c) endothermic, endothermic **PAGE:** 7.12

103. Which of the following statements is true about the ionization energy of Mg^+?

    a) It will be equal to the ionization energy of Li.
    b) It will be equal to and opposite in sign to the electron affinity of Mg.
    c) It will be equal to and opposite in sign to the electron affinity of Mg^+.
    d) It will be equal to and opposite in sign to the electron affinity of Mg^{2+}.
    e) none of the above

    ANS: d) It will be equal to and opposite in sign to the electron affinity of Mg^{2+}. **PAGE:** 7.12

104. Photogray lenses incorporate small amounts of silver chloride in the glass of the lens. The following reaction occurs in the light, causing the lenses to darken:

$$AgCl(s) \rightarrow Ag(s) + Cl$$

The enthalpy change for this reaction is 3.10×10^2 kJ/mol. Assuming all this energy is supplied by light, what is the maximum wavelength of light that can cause this reaction?

ANS: 3.86×10^{-7} m

PAGE: 7.1

105. How does the Bohr theory explain the emission and absorption spectra of hydrogen?

ANS: See Sec. 7.4 of Zumdahl, *Chemistry*.

PAGE: 7.4

106. Give the quantum numbers for the last electron in:

a) gold
b) magnesium
c) iodine
d) cadmium

ANS: a) gold–5, 2, 2, 1/2
b) magnesium–3, 0, 0, 1/2
c) iodine–5, 1, 1, 1/2
d) cadmium–4, 2, 2, 1/2

PAGE: 7.6,8

107. How many electrons in an atom can have the following quantum numbers:

a) $n = 3$
b) $n = 2, l = 0$
c) $n = 2, l = 2, m_e = 0$
d) $n = 2, l = 0, m_e = 0, m_s = 1/2$

ANS: a) 18; b) 2; c) 0; d) 1

PAGE: 7.6,8

108. Consider the following sets of quantum numbers. Which set(s) represent(s) impossible combinations?

	n	l	m_l	m_s
Set a	1	0	1	+1/2
Set b	3	3	0	+1/2
Set c	2	1	1	−1/2
Set d	3	2	−2	−1/2
Set e	3	1	−2	−1/2
Set f	2	0	0	−1/2

ANS: Sets a and b represent impossible combinations.

PAGE: 7.6,8

109. A hydrogen 3s wave function has _____ (how many?) nodal planes and _____ (how many?) radial nodes (not counting $r = 0$)?

   ANS: 0 nodal planes and 2 radial nodes   **PAGE:** 7.7

110. The ionization energies in kcal for Mg and Ca are

	Mg	Ca
1st	176	141
2nd	346	247
3rd	1847	

   a) Indicate the reasons for the relatively high 3rd ionization energy for magnesium.
   b) Indicate the reasons for the differences in 1st ionization energies for Mg and Ca.
   c) Predict the 3rd ionization energy for calcium.

   ANS: c)   1173   **PAGE:** 7.12

111–115. Given the following electronic configuration of neutral atoms, identify the element and state the number of unpaired electrons in its ground state:

111. $[Ar]4s^23d^4$

   ANS: The element is Cr with four unpaired electrons in its ground
   state.   **PAGE:** 7.11

112. $[Ne]3s^23p^5$

   ANS: The element is Cl with one unpaired electron in its ground
   state.   **PAGE:** 7.11

113. $[Kr]5s^24d^{10}5p^4$

   ANS: The element is Te with two unpaired electrons in its ground
   state.   **PAGE:** 7.11

114. $[Ar]4s^13d^{10}$

   ANS: The element is Cu with one unpaired electron in its ground
   state.   **PAGE:** 7.11

115. $[He]2s^22p^3$

   ANS: The element is N with three unpaired electrons in its ground
   state.   **PAGE:** 7.11

116–121. Write the electron configuration for the following:

116. P

   ANS: $1s^22s^22p^63s^23p^3$ or $[Ne]3s^23p^3$ **PAGE:** 7.11

117. Ag

   ANS: $1s^22s^22p^63s^23p^64s^23d^{10}4p^65s^24d^9$ or $[Kr]5s^14d^{10}$ or $[Kr]5s^24d^9$ **PAGE:** 7.11

118. S^{2-}

   ANS: $1s^22s^22p^63s^23p^6$ or $[Ne]3s^23p^6$ **PAGE:** 7.11

119. I

   ANS: $1s^22s^22p^63s^23p^64s^23d^{10}4p^65s^24d^{10}5p^5$ or $[Kr]5s^25p^5$ **PAGE:** 7.11

120. Fe^{3+}

   ANS: $1s^22s^22p^63s^23p^64s^23d^3$ or $[Ar]4s^23d^3$ **PAGE:** 7.11

121. K^+

   ANS: $1s^22s^22p^63s^23p^6$ or $[Ar]$ **PAGE:** 7.11

122. In general the ionization energy and electron affinity increase from _____ (left to right or right to left) in a period of the periodic table. Why?

   ANS: The increase is from left to right because of the increase in nuclear charge.   **PAGE:** 7.12

123. In general, the ionization energy and electron affinity increase from _____ (top to bottom or bottom to top) in a family of the periodic table. Why?

   ANS: The increase is from bottom to top because the electrons being removed are closer to the nucleus.   **PAGE:** 7.12

124. For the set of elements Be, B, C, and N, which element has the smallest ionization energy? Explain any deviation from the expected pattern.

   ANS: B has the smallest ionization energy. The electron is in a higher p sublevel.   **PAGE:** 7.12

125. For the set of elements Li, O, Ne, and Na, which element has the largest atomic radius? Explain any deviation from the expected pattern.

   ANS: Na has the largest atomic radius. There is no deviation from the expected pattern.   **PAGE:** 7.12

126–135. Choose the correct answer for the atom using the periodic chart.

126. Larger first ionization energy, Li Be

   ANS: Be   **PAGE:** 7.12

127. Larger first ionization energy, Na Rb

   ANS: Na   **PAGE:** 7.12

154

128. Larger first ionization energy, Be B

    ANS: B   **PAGE:** 7.12

129. Larger first ionization energy, C N

    ANS: N   **PAGE:** 7.12

130. Larger second ionization energy, Na Mg

    ANS: Na   **PAGE:** 7.12

131. Larger atomic radius, P Sb

    ANS: Sb   **PAGE:** 7.12

132. Larger atomic radius, N O

    ANS: N   **PAGE:** 7.12

133. Larger atomic or ionic radius, F F⁻

    ANS: F^- **PAGE:** 7.12

134. Larger atomic or ionic radius, Mg Mg^{2+}

    ANS: Mg   **PAGE:** 7.12

135. Larger atomic radius, Fe^{2+} Fe^{3+}

    ANS: Fe^{2+} **PAGE:** 7.12

136. The calcium atom is much larger than the calcium ion, while the fluorine atom is much smaller than the fluorine ion. Explain this natural occurrence.

    ANS: See Sec. 7.13 of Zumdahl, *Chemistry*.   **PAGE:** 7.12

137. The Si unit for frequency is cycles per second.

    ANS: False   **PAGE:** 7.1

138. Diffraction results when light is scattered from a regular array of points or lines.

    ANS: True   **PAGE:** 7.2

139. All matter exhibits either particulate or wave properties exclusively.

    ANS: False   **PAGE:** 7.2

140. Bohr's model correctly describes the hydrogen atom, but no other atoms.

    ANS: False   **PAGE:** 7.4

155

141. The magnetic quantum number is related to the orientation of the orbital in space relative to the other orbitals in the atom.

      ANS: True   **PAGE:** 7.6

142. The size of an orbital is arbitrarily defined.

      ANS: True   **PAGE:** 7.7

143. The second ionization energy for calcium is smaller than the first ionization energy.

      ANS: False   **PAGE:** 7.12

144. Ionization energy increases with an increasing number of electrons.

      ANS: False   **PAGE:** 7.12

145. Electromagnetic radiation can be viewed as a stream of "particles" called _____.

      ANS: photons   **PAGE:** 7.1

146. _____ results when light is scattered from a regular array of points or lines.

      ANS: Diffraction   **PAGE:** 7.2

147. A specific wave function is called a(n) _____.

      ANS: orbital   **PAGE:** 7.5

148. The _____ quantum number is related to the size and energy of the orbital.

      ANS: principal   **PAGE:** 7.6

149. Areas of zero probability of finding an electron are called _____.

      ANS: nodes (or nodal surfaces)   **PAGE:** 7.7

150. The _____ states that in a given atom no two electrons can have the same set of four quantum numbers.

      ANS: Pauli exclusion principle   **PAGE:** 7.8

151. The _____ electrons are in the outermost principal quantum level of an atom.

      ANS: valence   **PAGE:** 7.11

CHAPTER 8   Bonding: General Concepts

1. Which of the following statements is incorrect?

    a) Ionic bonding results from the transfer of electrons from one atom to another.
    b) Dipole moments result from the unequal distribution of electrons in a molecule.
    c) The electrons in a polar bond are found nearer to the more electronegative element.
    d) A molecule with very polar bonds can be nonpolar.
    e) Linear molecules cannot have a net dipole moment.

    ANS: e)   Linear molecules cannot have a net dipole moment.   **PAGE:** 8.1,3

2. Atoms having greatly differing electronegativities are expected to form:

    a) no bonds
    b) polar covalent bonds
    c) nonpolar covalent bonds
    d) ionic bonds
    e) covalent bonds

    ANS: d)   ionic bonds   **PAGE:** 8:1,2

3. Choose the compound with the most ionic bond.

    a) LiCl
    b) KF
    c) NaCl
    d) LiF
    e) KCl

    ANS: b)   KF   **PAGE:** 8.2

4. Atoms with very similar electronegativity values are expected to form

    a) no bonds.
    b) covalent bonds.
    c) triple bonds.
    d) ionic bonds.
    e) none of these

    ANS: b)   covalent bonds   **PAGE:** 8.1,2

5. Which of the following bonds is least polar?

    a) C—O
    b) H—C
    c) S—Cl
    d) Br—Br
    e) They are all nonpolar.

    ANS: d) Br—Br   **PAGE:** 8.2

6. For the elements Rb, F, and O, the order of increasing electronegativity is:

    a) Rb < F < O
    b) Rb < O < F
    c) O < F < Rb
    d) F < Rb < O
    e) None of these

    ANS: b) Rb < O < F   **PAGE:** 8.2

7. For the elements Cs, F, and Cl, the order of increasing electronegativity is:

    a) F < Cl < Cs
    b) Cs < Cl < F
    c) Cl < Cs < F
    d) F < Cs < Cl
    e) None of these

    ANS: b) Cs < Cl < F   **PAGE:** 8.2

8. In the gaseous phase, which of the following diatomic molecules would be the most polar?

    a) CsF
    b) CsCl
    c) NaCl
    d) NaF
    e) LiF

    ANS: a) CsF   **PAGE:** 8.2

9. Based on electronegativities, which of the following would you expect to be most ionic?

    a) N_2
    b) CaF_2
    c) CO_2
    d) CH_4
    e) CF_4

    ANS: b) CaF_2 **PAGE:** 8.2

10. In which case is the bond polarity incorrect?

    a) $^{\delta+}H-F^{\delta-}$
    b) $^{\delta+}K-O^{\delta-}$
    c) $^{\delta+}Mg-H^{\delta-}$
    d) $^{\delta+}Cl-I^{\delta-}$
    e) $^{\delta+}Si-S^{\delta-}$

    ANS: d) $^{\delta+}Cl-I^{\delta-}$ **PAGE:** 8.2

11. Which of the following groups contains no ionic compounds?

    a) HCN, NO_2, $Ca(NO_3)_2$
    b) PCl_5, $LiBr$, $Zn(OH)_2$
    c) KOH, CCl_4, SF_4
    d) NaH, CaF_2, $NaNH_2$
    e) CH_2O, H_2S, NH_3

    ANS: e) CH_2O, H_2S, NH_3 **PAGE:** 8.2

12. In which pair do both compounds exhibit predominantly ionic bonding?

    a) PCl_5 and HF
    b) Na_2SO_3 and BH_3
    c) KI and O_3
    d) NaF and H_2O
    e) $RbCl$ and CaO

    ANS: e) $RbCl$ and CaO **PAGE:** 8.2

13. Metals typically have _____ electronegativity values.

    a) high
    b) low
    c) negative
    d) no
    e) two of these

    ANS: b) low   **PAGE:** 8.2

14. The electron pair in a C-F bond could be considered

    a) closer to C because carbon has a larger radius and thus exerts greater control over the shared electron pair.
    b) closer to F because fluorine has a higher electronegativity than carbon.
    c) closer to C because carbon has a lower electronegativity than fluorine.
    d) an inadequate model since the bond is ionic.
    e) centrally located directly between the C and F.

    ANS: b) closer to F because fluorine has a higher electronegativity
    than carbon.   **PAGE:** 8.2

15. Based on electronegativity differences, which of the following is most likely to be ionic?

    a) BaF_2
    b) Cl_2
    c) NH_3
    d) NO_3
    e) CH_4

    ANS: a) BaF_2 **PAGE:** 8.2

16. What is the correct order of the following bonds in terms of decreasing polarity?

    a) N-Cl, P-Cl, As-Cl
    b) P-Cl, N-Cl, As-Cl
    c) As-Cl, N-Cl, P-Cl
    d) P-Cl, As-Cl, N-Cl
    e) As-Cl, P-Cl, N-Cl

    ANS: e)   As-Cl, P-Cl, N-Cl   **PAGE:** 8.2

17. Which of the following bonds would be the most polar without being considered ionic?

    a) Mg-O
    b) C-O
    c) O-O
    d) Si-O
    e) N-O

    ANS: d)   Si-O   **PAGE:** 8.2

18. Which of the following bonds would be the least polar yet still be considered polar covalent?

    a) Mg-O
    b) C-O
    c) O-O
    d) Si-O
    e) N-O

    ANS: e)   N-O   **PAGE:** 8.2

19. How many of the following molecules possess dipole moments?

    BH_3, CH_4, PCl_5, H_2O, HF, H_2

    a) 1
    b) 2
    c) 3
    d) 4
    e) 5

    ANS: b)   2   **PAGE:** 8.3,13

20. Which of the following molecules has a dipole moment?

    a) CH_4
    b) CCl_4
    c) CO_2
    d) SO_3
    e) none of these

    ANS: d) SO_3 **PAGE:** 8.3,13

21. Select the molecule among the following that has a dipole moment.

    a) CO_2
    b) SeO_3
    c) XeF_4
    d) SF_4
    e) $BeCl_2$

    ANS: d) SF_4 **PAGE:** 8.3,13

22. Which of the following molecules (or ions) has a dipole moment?

    a) CO_2
    b) CO_3^{2-}
    c) NH_4^+
    d) PF_3
    e) two of them do

    ANS: d) PF_3 **PAGE:** 8.3, 13

23. Which of the following molecules has a dipole moment?
    a) BCl_3
    b) $SiCl_4$
    c) PCl_3
    d) Cl_2
    e) none of these

    ANS: c) PCl_3 **PAGE:** 8.3,13

24. Which of the following molecules has no dipole moment?

    a) CO_2
    b) NH_3
    c) H_2O
    d) all
    e) none

    ANS: a) CO_2 **PAGE:** 8.3,13

25. Choose the statement that best describes the $PbCl_4$ molecule in the gas phase.

    a) The bond angles are all about 109°.
    b) The molecule is polar.
    c) The molecule has a dipole moment.
    d) The bonds are nonpolar.
    e) a, b, and c

    ANS: a) The bond angles are all about 109°. PAGE: 8.3,13

26. Which of the following has a zero dipole moment?
    a) NH_3
    b) NO_2
    c) PF_5
    d) SO_2
    e) HCN

    ANS: c) PF_5 PAGE: 8.3,13

27. Which of the following has the smallest radius?

    a) Br^-
    b) S^{2-}
    c) Xe
    d) Ca^{2+}
    e) Kr

    ANS: d) Ca^{2+} PAGE: 8.4

28. Which of these is an isoelectronic series?

    a) Na^+, K^+, Rb^+, Cs^+
    b) K^+, Ca^{2+}, Ar, S^{2-}
    c) $Na^+, Mg^{2+}, S^{2-}, Cl^-$
    d) Li, Be, B, C
    e) none of these (a-d)

    ANS: b) K^+, Ca^{2+}, Ar, S^{2-} PAGE: 8.4

29. Which of the following has the smallest radius?

    a) K^+
    b) Cl^-
    c) Rb^+
    d) S^{2-}
    e) Ar

    ANS: a) K^+ **PAGE:** 8.4

30. Which of the following ionic compounds has the smallest lattice energy, i.e., the lattice energy least favorable to a stable lattice?

    a) LiF
    b) CsI
    c) NaCl
    d) BaO
    e) MgO

    ANS: b) CsI   **PAGE:** 8.5

31. Calculate the lattice energy for LiF(s) given the following:

sublimation energy for Li(s)	+166 kJ/mol
ΔH_f for F(g)	+77 kJ/mol
first ionization energy of Li(g)	+520. kJ/mol
electron affinity of F(g)	–328 kJ/mol
enthalpy of formation of LiF(s)	–617 kJ/mol

    a) 285 kJ/mol
    b) –650. kJ/mol
    c) 800. kJ/mol
    d) –1047 kJ/mol
    e) None of these

    ANS: d) –1047 kJ/mol   **PAGE:** 8.5

32. When electrons in a molecule are not found between a pair of atoms but move throughout the molecule, this is called

    a) ionic bonding.
    b) covalent bonding.
    c) polar covalent bonding.
    d) delocalization of the electrons.
    e) a dipole moment.

    ANS: d) delocalization of the electrons.   **PAGE:** 8.1,7

33. Which of the following statements concerning lattice energy is *false*?

    a) It is often defined as the energy released when an ionic solid forms from its ions.
    b) MgO has a larger lattice energy than NaF.
    c) The lattice energy for a solid with 2+ and 2– ions should be two times that for a solid with 1+ and 1– ions.
    d) MgO has a larger lattice energy than LiF.
    e) All of these are true.

    ANS: c) The lattice energy for a solid with 2+ and 2– ions should be two times that for a solid with 1+ and 1– ions.   **PAGE:** 8.5

34. Which of the following pairs is isoelectronic?

    a) Li^+ and K^+
    b) Na^+ and Ne
    c) I^- and Cl^-
    d) S^{2-} and Ne
    e) Al^{3+} and B^{3+}

    ANS: b) Na^+ and Ne   **PAGE:** 8.4

35. Which of the following arrangements is in order of increasing size?

    a) $Ga^{3+} > Ca^{2+} > K^+ > Cl^- > S^{2-}$
    b) $S^{2-} > Cl^- > K^+ > Ca^{2+} > Ga^{3+}$
    c) $Ga^{3+} > S^{2-} > Ca^{2+} > Cl^- > K^+$
    d) $Ga^{3+} > Ca^{2+} > S^{2-} > Cl^- > K^+$
    e) $Ga^{3+} > Ca^{2+} > S^{2-} > K^+ > Cl^-$

    ANS: a) $Ga^{3+} > Ca^{2+} > K^+ > Cl^- > S^{2-}$ **PAGE:** 8.4

36. Which of the following types of molecules has a dipole moment (when polar bonds are present)?

    a) linear molecules with two identical bonds
    b) tetrahedral molecules (four identical bonds equally spaced)
    c) trigonal pyramid molecules (three identical bonds)
    d) trigonal planar molecules (three identical bonds equally spaced)
    e) None has a dipole moment.

    ANS: c) trigonal pyramid molecules (three identical bonds)   **PAGE:** 8.3

37. Given the following information:

$$Li(s) \rightarrow Li(g)$$ heat of sublimation of $Li(s)$ = 166 kJ/mol

$$HCl(g) \rightarrow H(g) + Cl(g)$$ bond energy of HCl = 427 kJ/mol

$$Li(g) \rightarrow Li^+(g) + e^-$$ ionization energy of $Li(g)$ = 520. kJ/mol

$$Cl(g) + e^- \rightarrow Cl^-(g)$$ electron affinity of $Cl(g)$ = –349 kJ/mol

$$Li^+(g) + Cl^-(g) \rightarrow LiCl(s)$$ lattice energy of LiCl(s) = –829 kJ/mol

$$H_2(g) \rightarrow 2H(g)$$ bond energy of H_2 = 432 kJ/mol

calculate the net change in energy for the reaction $2Li(s) + 2HCl(g) \rightarrow 2LiCl(s) + H_2(g)$

a) 363 kJ
b) –562 kJ
c) –179 kJ
d) –73 kJ
e) None of these

ANS: b)   –562 kJ   **PAGE**: 8.5

38. The first electron affinity value for oxygen is _____ and the second electron affinity value is _____.

a) unfavorable (endothermic), favorable (exothermic)
b) unfavorable (endothermic), unfavorable (endothermic)
c) favorable (exothermic), favorable (exothermic)
d) favorable (exothermic), unfavorable (endothermic)
e) More information is needed.

ANS: d)   favorable (exothermic), unfavorable (endothermic)   **PAGE**: 8.5

39. Choose the molecule with the strongest bond.

a) F_2
b) Cl_2
c) Br_2
d) I_2
e) All are equal.

ANS: b) Cl_2 **PAGE**: 8.8

40. Choose the molecule with the strongest bond.

a) HF
b) HCl
c) HBr
d) HI
e) All are equal.

ANS: a)   HF   **PAGE**: 8.8

41. Choose the molecule with the strongest bond.

    a) CH_4
    b) H_2O
    c) NH_3
    d) HF
    e) All are equal

ANS: d) HF   **PAGE:** 8.8

42. Which of the following molecules exhibits the greatest bond energy?

    a) F_2
    b) Cl_2
    c) Br_2
    d) I_2
    e) all the same

ANS: b) Cl_2 **PAGE:** 8.8

43. As the number of bonds between two carbon atoms increases, which one of the following decreases?

    a) number of electrons between the carbon atoms
    b) bond energy
    c) bond length
    d) all of these
    e) none of these

ANS: c) bond length   **PAGE:** 8.8

44. Using the following bond energies

Bond	Bond Energy (kJ/mol)
C≡C	839
C–H	413
O=O	495
C=O	799
O–H	467

    estimate the heat of combustion for one mole of acetylene:
    $C_2H_2(g) + (5/2)O_2(g) \rightarrow 2CO_2(g) + H_2O(g)$

    a) 1228 kJ
    b) –1228 kJ
    c) –447 kJ
    d) +447 kJ
    e) +365 kJ

ANS: b) –1228 kJ   **PAGE:** 8.8

45. Which of the following species would be expected to have the lowest ionization energy?

    a) F^-
    b) Ne
    c) O^{2-}
    d) Mg^{2+}
    e) Na^+

    ANS: c) O^{2-} **PAGE:** 8.4

46. Which of the following has the smallest radius?

    a) F^-
    b) Ne
    c) O^{2-}
    d) Mg^{2+}
    e) Na^+

    ANS: d) Mg^{2+} **PAGE:** 8.4

47. Which of the following ionic compounds has the largest lattice energy (the lattice energy most favorable to a stable lattice)?

    a) BaO
    b) BeO
    c) CsI
    d) NaBr
    e) BaS

    ANS: b) BeO   **PAGE:** 8.5

48. In which of the following compounds does the bond between the central atom and bromine have the greatest ionic character?

    a) LiBr
    b) KBr
    c) $SeBr_2$
    d) $AsBr_2$
    e) $CaBr_2$

    ANS: b) KBr   **PAGE:** 8.2

49. Which of the following species is best described by drawing resonance structures?

    a) PH_3
    b) NH_4^+
    c) O_3
    d) SO_3^-
    e) HCN

    ANS: c) O_3 **PAGE:** 8.12

50. Using the following data reactions

$$\Delta H° \text{ (kJ)}$$

$$H_2(g) + Cl_2(g) \rightarrow 2HCl(g) \qquad -184$$

$$H_2(g) \rightarrow 2H(g) \qquad 432$$

$$Cl_2(g) \rightarrow 2Cl(g) \qquad 239$$

calculate the energy of an H–Cl bond.

a) 770 kJ
b) 856 kJ
c) 518 kJ
d) 326 kJ
e) 428 kJ

ANS: e) 428 kJ   **PAGE:** 6.3,8.8

51. Given the following bond energies

C–C   347 kJ/mol

C=C   614 kJ/mol

C–O   358 kJ/mol

C=O   799 kJ/mol

C–H   413 kJ/mol

O–H   463 kJ/mol

O–O   146 kJ/mol

estimate ΔH for the reaction $H_2O_2 + CH_3OH \rightarrow H_2CO + 2H_2O$.

a) –345 kJ
b) –199 kJ
c) –105 kJ
d) +199 kJ
e) +345 kJ

ANS: a) –345 kJ   **PAGE:** 8.8

168

52. Given the following information

N_2 bond energy = 941 kJ/mol

F_2 bond energy = 154 kJ/mol

$$\frac{1}{2} N_2(g) + \frac{3}{2} F_2(g) \rightarrow NF_3(g) \qquad \Delta H^\circ = -103 \text{ kJ/mol}$$

calculate the N–F bond energy.

a)   113 kJ/mol
b)   268 kJ/mol
c)   317 kJ/mol
d)   66 kJ/mol
e)   none of these

ANS: b)   268 kJ/mol   **PAGE:** 8.8

53–55. Using the following electronegativity values

C	2.5	Cl	3.2
H	2.2	N	3.0
		O	3.4

select from the following group the molecule that fits the given statement:

a) CH_3CHO
b) CO_2
c) CH_3Cl
d) C_2H_6
e)   none

53. This molecule contains a carbon atom with trigonal planar geometry.

ANS: a) CH_3CHO **PAGE:** 8.13

54. This molecule is the most polar.

ANS: a) CH_3CHO **PAGE:** 8.3,13

55. This molecule shows the smallest number of lone pairs in its Lewis structure.

ANS: d) C_2H_6 **PAGE:** 8.10

56. As indicated by Lewis structures, which of the following would probably not exist as a stable molecule?

a) CH_3OH
b) CH_2O
c) CH_3O
d) C_2H_2
e) C_3H_4

ANS: c) CH_3O **PAGE:** 8.10,11

57. Which of the following molecules is non-polar overall?

 a) SF_4
 b) SF_2
 c) CCl_4
 d) H_2S
 e) OCl_2

 ANS: c) CCl_4 **PAGE:** 8.3,13

58. Select the best Lewis structure for acetone, CH_3COCH_3.

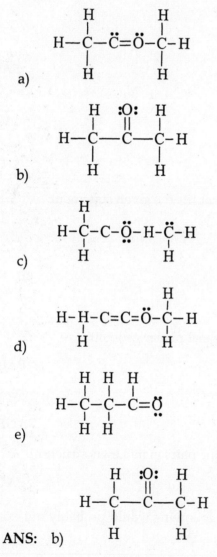

 a)

 b)

 c)

 d)

 e)

 ANS: b)   **PAGE:** 8.10,12

59. Which of the following is the correct order for molecules from most to least polar?

    a) $CH_4 > CF_2Cl_2 > CF_2H_2 > CCl_4 > CCl_2H_2$
    b) $CH_4 > CF_2H_2 > CF_2Cl_2 > CCl_4 > CCl_2H_2$
    c) $CF_2Cl_2 > CF_2H_2 > CCl_2H_2 > CH_4 = CCl_4$
    d) $CF_2H_2 > CCl_2H_2 > CF_2Cl_2 > CH_4 = CCl_4$
    e) $CF_2Cl_2 > CF_2H_2 > CCl_4 > CCl_2H_2 > CH_4$

ANS: d) $CF_2H_2 > CCl_2H_2 > CF_2Cl_2 > CH_4 = CCl_4$ **PAGES:** 8.1–3,13

60. Of the following, which molecule has the largest bond angle?

    a) O_3
    b) OF_2
    c)   HCN
    d) H_2O
    e)   More than one of the above have equally large bond angles.

ANS: c)   HCN   **PAGE:** 8.13

61. According to the VSEPR model, the arrangement of electron pairs around NH_3 and CH_4 are

    a)   different because in each case there are a different number of atoms around the central atom.
    b)   different because in each case there are a different number of electron pairs around the central atom.
    c)   the same because both nitrogen and carbon are both in the second period.
    d)   the same because in each case there are the same number of electron pairs around the central atom.
    e)   different or the same, depending on the conditions leading to maximum repulsion.

ANS: d)   the same because in each case there are the same number of electron pairs around the central atom.   **PAGE:** 8.13

62. The Cl–Kr–Cl bond angle in $KrCl_4$ is closest to

    a)   90°
    b)   109°
    c)   120°
    d)   150°
    e)   360°

ANS: a)   90°   **PAGE:** 8.13

63. Which of the following atoms cannot exceed the octet rule in a molecule?

    a) N
    b) S
    c) P
    d) I
    e) All of the atoms (a-d) can exceed the octet rule.

    ANS: a) N   **PAGE:** 8.11

64. In the cyanide ion (CN^-), the nitrogen has a formal charge of

    a) -2
    b) -1
    c) 0
    d) 2
    e) 2

    ANS: c) 0   **PAGE:** 8.10-12

65. Which has the larger N–O bond length, NO_2^- or NO_3^-?

    a) NO_2^-
    b) NO_3^-
    c) The bond lengths are the same.
    d) More information is needed.
    e) None of these (a-d)

    ANS: b) NO_3^-   **PAGE:** 8.8,10–12

66. How many of the following molecules — SF_2, SF_4, SF_6, SiO_2 — are polar?

    a) 0
    b) 1
    c) 2
    d) 3
    e) 4

    ANS: c) 2   **PAGE:** 8.1–3,13

67. Which of the following exhibits resonance?

    a) CH_4
    b) PCl_5
    c) H_2O
    d) NO_2
    e) At least two of the molecules (a-d) exhibit resonance.

    ANS: d) NO_2   **PAGE:** 8.12

68. How many resonance structures can be drawn for the molecule O_3?

    a) 1
    b) 2
    c) 3
    d) 4
    e) 5

    ANS: b)   2   **PAGES:** 8.10, 12

69. As indicated by Lewis structures, which of the following species could probably not exist as a stable molecule?

    a) NH_3
    b) N_2H_2
    c) N_2H_4
    d) N_2H_6
    e) N_2O_4

    ANS: d) N_2H_6 **PAGE:** 8.10,11

70. Choose the electron dot formula that most accurately describes the bonding in CS_2. (Hint: Consider formal charges.)

    a) $:\ddot{S}=C=\ddot{S}:$

    b) $:\ddot{C}=S=\ddot{S}:$

    c) $:\ddot{\underset{..}{S}}-C-\ddot{\underset{..}{S}}:$

    d) $:\ddot{\underset{..}{S}}-\ddot{C}=\ddot{\underset{..}{S}}:$

    e) $:\ddot{\underset{..}{S}}-C\equiv S:$

    ANS: a) $:\ddot{S}=C=\ddot{S}:$ **PAGE:** 8.10, 12

71. Which of the following has a Lewis structure most like that of CO_3^{2-}?

    a) CO_2
    b) SO_3^{2-}
    c) NO_3^-
    d) O_3
    e) NO_2

    ANS: c) NO_3^- **PAGE:** 8.10

72. Which of the following is not a valid resonance structure for N_3^-?

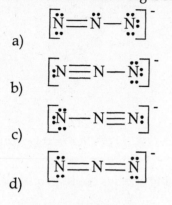

a)

b)

c)

d)

e)   all are correct

ANS: a) $\left[\ddot{N}=\ddot{N}-\ddot{N}:\right]^-$

PAGE: 8.10, 12

73. In the Lewis structure for elemental nitrogen there is (are)

a)   a single bond between the nitrogens.
b)   a double bond between the nitrogens.
c)   a triple bond between the nitrogens.
d)   three unpaired electrons.
e)   none of the above.

ANS: c)   a triple bond between the nitrogens.

PAGE: 8.10

74. Complete the Lewis structure for the molecule:

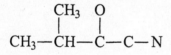

This molecule has _____ single bonds and _____ multiple bonds.

a)   4, 2
b)   6, 3
c)   11, 5
d)   11, 2
e)   13, 0

ANS: d)   11, 2

PAGE: 8.10

75–77. Draw the Lewis structures of the molecules below and use them to answer the following questions:

    I. BH_3

    II. NO_2

    III. SF_6

    IV. O_3

    V. PCl_5

75. Which of the molecules obeys the octet rule?

    a) I

    b) II

    c) III

    d) IV

    e) V

    ANS: d) IV   **PAGE:** 8.10,11

76. How many of the molecules have no dipole moment?

    a) 1

    b) 2

    c) 3

    d) 4

    e) they are all polar

    ANS: c) 3   **PAGE:** 8.3,13

77. Which of these molecules show resonance?

    a) I, II

    b) II, IV

    c) II, V

    d) III, IV

    e) III, V

    ANS: b) II, IV   **PAGE:** 8.12

78. The force between two bodies having identical electric charges

    a) is a force of repulsion.

    b) is a force of repulsion if the charges are negative, and one of attraction if they are positive.

    c) increases as the bodies are moved farther apart.

    d) is independent of the distance between them.

    e) is directly proportional to the distance between them.

    ANS: a) is a force of repulsion.   **PAGE:** 8.1

79-81. Consider the compound crotonaldehyde, whose skeleton is

$$
\begin{array}{cccc}
H & H & H & H \\
| & | & | & | \\
H-C_1-C_2-C_3-C_4-O \\
|
\end{array}
$$

H

79. How many electrons must be shown in the Lewis structure of this molecule?

    a) 12
    b) 18
    c) 24
    d) 28
    e) 32

    ANS: d)   28   **PAGE:** 8.10

80. How many nonbonding electrons appear in the Lewis structure of this molecule?

    a) 2
    b) 4
    c) 6
    d) 8
    e) 10

    ANS: b)   4   **PAGE:** 8.10

81. Which carbon in this molecule has tetrahedral bonding?

    a) 1
    b) 2
    c) 3
    d) 4
    e) all

    ANS: a)   1   **PAGE:** 8.13

82. Which of the following molecules contains a double bond?

    a) CO_2
    b) NH_3
    c) H_2O
    d) all
    e) none

    ANS: a) CO_2 **PAGE:** 8.10

83. When molten sulfur reacts with chlorine gas, a vile smelling orange liquid forms that is found to have the empirical formula SCl. Which of the following could be the correct Lewis structure for this compound?

a) $:\ddot{\text{S}}-\ddot{\text{C}}\text{l}:$

b) $:\ddot{\text{S}}=\ddot{\text{C}}\text{l}$

c) $:\ddot{\text{S}}=\ddot{\text{C}}\text{l}-\ddot{\text{C}}\text{l}=\ddot{\text{S}}:$

d) $:\ddot{\text{C}}\text{l}-\ddot{\text{S}}=\ddot{\text{S}}-\ddot{\text{C}}\text{l}$

e) $:\ddot{\text{C}}\text{l}-\ddot{\text{S}}-\ddot{\text{S}}-\ddot{\text{C}}\text{l}$

ANS: e) $:\ddot{\text{C}}\text{l}-\ddot{\text{S}}-\ddot{\text{S}}-\ddot{\text{C}}\text{l}$ **PAGE:** 8.10

84-85. Given the following Lewis structure:

$$\begin{array}{ccccc} & \text{H} & \text{H} & \text{H} & \\ & | & | & | & \\ \text{H}_2\text{C}=\text{C}-\text{C}=\text{C}-\text{CH}_3 \\ 1 & 2 & 3 & 4 & 5 \end{array}$$

84. How many unshared pairs of electrons are present in this molecule?

   a) 0
   b) 1
   c) 2
   d) 3
   e) 4

   ANS: a) 0   **PAGE:** 8.10

85. How many electrons are shared between carbons 1 and 2?

   a) 0
   b) 2
   c) 4
   d) 6
   e) 8

   ANS: c) 4   **PAGE:** 8.10

86. Which of the following compounds contains only one unshared pair of valence electrons?

   a) NH_3
   b) H_2O
   c) CH_4
   d) NaCl
   e) BeF_3

ANS: a) NH_3 **PAGE:** 8.10,11

87. In the reaction between magnesium and sulfur, the magnesium atoms

   a) become anions.
   b) become cations.
   c) become part of polyatomic ions.
   d) share electrons with sulfur.

ANS: b) become cations.   **PAGE:** 8.5

88. The Lewis structure for H_3BO_3 is

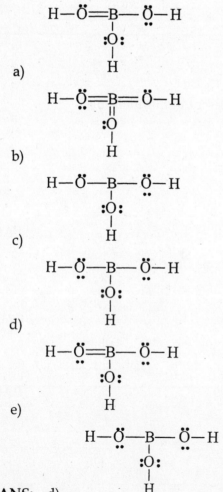

ANS: d)   **PAGE:** 8.11

89. In the Lewis structure for ICl_2^-, how many lone pairs of electrons are around the central iodine atom?

    a) 0
    b) 1
    c) 2
    d) 3
    e) 4

    ANS: d)   3   **PAGE:** 8.11

90. In the Lewis structure for SF_6, the central sulfur atom shares _____ electrons.

    a) 4
    b) 8
    c) 10
    d) 12
    e) none of the above, because SF_6 is an ionic compound

    ANS: d)   12   **PAGE:** 8.11

91–92. Consider the following molecules.

    I. BF_3
    II. $CHBr_3$ (C is the central atom)
    III. Br_2
    IV. $XeCl_2$
    V. CO
    VI. SF_4

    Select the molecule(s) that fit the given statement.

91. These molecules violate the octet rule.

    a) I, II, IV
    b) I, III, IV, VI
    c) III, V, VI
    d) I, IV, VI
    e) I, II, IV, VI

    ANS: d)   I, IV, VI   **PAGE:** 8.11

92. These molecules have a zero net dipole moment.

    a) III, V
    b) I, III, IV
    c) III, IV, V
    d) I, III, IV, VI
    e) none of them

    ANS: b)   I, III, IV   **PAGE:** 8.3,13

179

93.   Which of the following Lewis structures best describes BF_3?

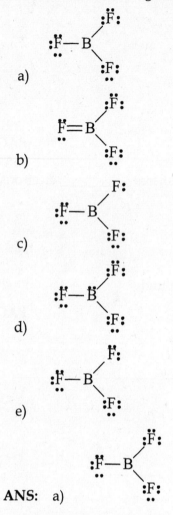

a)

b)

c)

d)

e)

ANS: a)

PAGE: 8.11

94.   Which of the following molecules has a nonlinear structure?

    a) XeF_2
    b) $BeCl_2$
    c) O_3
    d) CO_2
    e) N_2O (central atom is N)

ANS: c) O_3

PAGE: 8.13

95–100. Select the correct molecular structure for the given species from the choices below:

a) pyramidal
b) none of these
c) octahedral
d) trigonal planar
e) bent

95. $SOCl_2$

ANS: a) pyramidal   **PAGE:** 8.13

96. OF_2

ANS: e) bent   **PAGE:** 8.13

97. NCl_3

ANS: a) pyramidal   **PAGE:** 8.13

98. XeF_5^+

ANS: a) pyramidal   **PAGE:** 8.13

99. BrF_6^+

ANS: c) octahedral   **PAGE:** 8.13

100. BeF_3^-

ANS: d) trigonal planar   **PAGE:** 8.13

101. The geometry of $AsCl_5$ is

a) trigonal bipyramidal.
b) square pyramidal.
c) distorted tetrahedral.
d) octahedral.
e) none of these

ANS: a) trigonal pyramidal.   **PAGE:** 8.13

102. How many of the following molecules or ions are linear?

NH_3 NH_4^+ HCN CO_2 NO_2

a) 0
b) 1
c) 2
d) 3
e) 4

ANS: c) 2   **PAGE:** 8.13

103. The bond angles about the carbon atom in the formaldehyde molecule, $H_2C=O$, are about:

    a) 120°
    b) 60°
    c) 109°
    d) 180°
    c) 90°

    ANS: a)   120°   **PAGE:** 8.13

104. Which of the following molecules are nonlinear?

    NO_2^-, C_2H_2, N_3^-,   HCN, CO_2, H_2O_2

    a) C_2H_2, HCN
    b) CO_2, N_3^-
    c) NO_2^-, H_2O_2
    d) N_3^-, N_2^-
    e) all are linear

    ANS: c) NO_2^-, H_2O_2 **PAGE:** 8.13

105. What type of structure does the $XeOF_2$ molecule have?

    a) pyramidal
    b) tetrahedral
    c) T-shaped
    d) trigonal planar
    e) octahedral

    ANS: c)   T-shaped   **PAGE:** 8.13

106. Which of the following species has a trigonal bipyramid structure?

    a) NH_3
    b) IF_5
    c) I_3^-
    d) PCl_5
    e) none of these

    ANS: d) PCl_5 **PAGE:** 8.13

107. The bond angle in H_2Se is about:

   a)   120°
   b)   60°
   c)   180°
   d)   109°
   e)   90°

   ANS: d)   109°   **PAGE:** 8.13

108. Which ion is planar?

   a) NH_4^+
   b) CO_3^{2-}
   c) SO_3^{2-}
   d) ClO_3^-
   e)   all are planar

   ANS: b) CO_3^{2-} **PAGE:** 8.13

109–116. Select the correct molecular structure for the given species from the choices below:

   a)   pyramidal
   b)   tetrahedral
   c)   square planar
   d)   octahedral
   e)   none of these

109. PF_6^-

   ANS: d)   octahedral   **PAGE:** 8.13

110. PCl_4^+

   ANS: b)   tetrahedral   **PAGE:** 8.13

111. XeF_6

   ANS: e)   none of these   **PAGE:** 8.13

112. NI_3

   ANS: a)   pyramidal   **PAGE:** 8.13

113. SiH_4

   ANS: b)   tetrahedral   **PAGE:** 8.13

114. ClO_2

   ANS: e)   none of these   **PAGE:** 8.13

115. IF_4^-

ANS: c) square planar   **PAGE:** 8.13

116. SO_3^{2-}

ANS: a) pyramidal   **PAGE:** 8.13

117. Which of the following has an incomplete octet in its Lewis structure?

 a) SO_2
 b) ICl
 c) CO_2
 d) F_2
 e) NO

ANS: e) NO   **PAGE:** 8.11

118–125. Select the correct molecular structure for the given species from the choices below:

 a) linear
 b) trigonal planar
 c) tetrahedral
 d) bent
 e) none of these

118. H_2O

ANS: d) bent   **PAGE:** 8.13

119. CO_2

ANS: a) linear   **PAGE:** 8.13

120. $BeCl_2$

ANS: a) linear   **PAGE:** 8.13

121. SF_4

ANS: e) none of these   **PAGE:** 8.13

122. NO_3^-

ANS: b) trigonal planar   **PAGE:** 8.13

123. I_3^-

ANS: a) linear   **PAGE:** 8.13

124. PF_5

ANS: e) none of these   **PAGE:** 8.13

125. ClF_2^+

    ANS: d)   bent   **PAGE:** 8.13

126. In the molecule XeF_2, how many pairs of electrons surround Xe and what is the molecular geometry?

    a)   4, bent
    b)   4, pyramidal
    c)   5, linear
    d)   5, bent
    e)   6, linear

    ANS: c)   5, linear   **PAGE:** 8.13

127. According to VSEPR theory, which of the following species has a square planar molecular structure?

    a) $TeBr_4$
    b) BrF_3
    c) IF_5
    d) XeF_4
    e) SCl_2

    ANS: d) XeF_4 **PAGE:** 8.13

128. How many of the following molecules have all of their atoms in the same plane?

    $H_2C=CH_2$ F_2O H_2CO NH_3 CO_2 $BeCl_2$ H_2O_2

    a)   3
    b)   4
    c)   5
    d)   6
    e)   7

    ANS: c)   5   **PAGE:** 8.13

129. Which of the following sets has elements with the most nearly identical atomic radii?

    a)   Cr, Mn, Fe, Co
    b)   Mg, Ca, Sr, Ba
    c)   Ne, Ar, Kr, Xe
    d)   Be, B, C, N
    e)   C, P, Se, I

    ANS: a)   Cr, Mn, Fe, Co   **PAGE:** 8.7

130. When nonmetals chemically combine, they tend to form what type of bond?

    ANS: covalent   **PAGE:** 8.1,2

185

131. In spite of larger electronegativity differences between bonded atoms, $BeCl_2$ has no dipole while SCl_2 does. Explain fully.

   ANS: See Sec. 8.3 of Zumdahl, *Chemistry*.   **PAGE:** 8.3

132–135. For each of the following compounds:

   a) draw the Lewis structure
   b) give the shape of the molecule
   c) indicate the polarity of the molecule

132. AlF_3

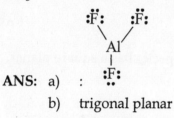

   ANS: a)
   b) trigonal planar
   c) nonpolar   **PAGE:** 8.3,10,13

133. NH_3

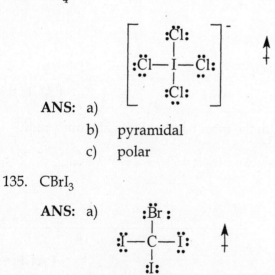

   ANS: a)
   b) pyramidal
   c) polar   **PAGE:** 8.3,10,13

134. ICl_4^-

   ANS: a)
   b) pyramidal
   c) polar   **PAGE:** 8.3,10,13

135. $CBrI_3$

   ANS: a)
   b) tetrahedral
   c) polar   **PAGE:** 8.3,10,13

136. When a metal reacts with a nonmetal a covalent bond is formed.

   ANS: False   **PAGE:** 8.1

137. A nonpolar covalent bond results from the unequal sharing of a pair of electrons between atoms in a molecule.

   ANS: False   **PAGE:** 8.1

138. The size in a series of isoelectronic ions increases as the nuclear charge increases.

   ANS: False   **PAGE:** 8.4

139. A double bond occurs when two atoms share two pairs of electrons.

   ANS: True   **PAGE:** 8.8

140. The shape of an ammonia molecule is tetrahedral.

   ANS: False   **PAGE:** 8.13

141. The shape of a carbon dioxide molecule is linear.

   ANS: True   **PAGE:** 8.13

142. The Lewis structure for $CHCl_3$ has 9 lone electron pairs.

   ANS: True   **PAGE:** 8.10

143. The ability of an atom in a molecule to attract shared electrons to itself is called _____.

   ANS: electronegativity   **PAGE:** 8.2

144. A molecule that has a center of positive charge and a center of negative charge is said to be _____.

   ANS: dipolar   **PAGE:** 8.3

145. The _____ is the change in energy that takes place when separated gaseous ions are packed together to form an ionic solid.

   ANS: lattice energy   **PAGE:** 8.5

146. The _____ of a molecule shows how the valence electrons are arranged among the atoms in the molecule.

   ANS: Lewis structure   **PAGE:** 8.10

147. Stable molecules usually contain atoms that have filled _____ orbitals.

ANS: valence   **PAGE:** 8.7

148. When several nonequivalent Lewis structures can be drawn for a molecule, _____ is used to determine the most appropriate structure(s).

ANS: formal charge   **PAGE:** 8.12

1. The hybridization of the phosphorus atom in the cation PH_2^+ is:

    a) sp^2
    b) sp^3
    c) dsp
    d) sp
    e) none of these

    ANS: a) sp^2 **PAGE:** 9.1

2. In the molecule C_2H_4 the valence orbitals of the carbon atoms are assumed to be

    a) not hybridized.
    b) sp hybridized.
    c) sp^2 hybridized.
    d) sp^3 hybridized.
    e) dsp hybridized.

    ANS: c) sp^2 hybridized.   **PAGE:** 9.1

3. Which of the following statements is (are) incorrect?

    I.   The hybridization of boron in BF_3 is sp^2.
    II. The molecule XeF_4 is nonpolar.
    III. The bond order of N_2 is three.
    IV. The molecule HCN has two pi bonds and two sigma bonds.
    a) All four statements are correct.
    b) II is incorrect.
    c) I and IV are incorrect.
    d) II and III are incorrect.
    e) II, III, and IV are incorrect.

    ANS: a)   All four statements are correct.   **PAGE:** 9.1

4. Atoms which are sp^2 hybridized form ____ pi bond(s).

    a) 0
    b) 1
    c) 2
    d) 3
    e) 4

    ANS: b)   1   **PAGE:** 9.1

5. The hybridization of the central atom in XeF_5^+ is:

   a) sp
   b) sp^2
   c) sp^3
   d) dsp^3
   e) d^2sp^3

   ANS: e) d^2sp^3 **PAGE:** 9.1

6. The hybridization of the central atom in ClF_2^+ is:

   a) sp
   b) sp^2
   c) sp^3
   d) dsp^3
   e) d^2sp^3

   ANS: c) sp^3 **PAGE:** 9.1

7. The hybridization of the central atom in I_3^- is:

   a) sp
   b) sp^2
   c) sp^3
   d) dsp^3
   e) d^2sp^3

   ANS: d) dsp^3 **PAGE:** 9.1

8. The hybridization of the central atom in O_3 is:

   a) sp
   b) sp^2
   c) sp^3
   d) dsp^3
   e) d^2sp^3

   ANS: e) sp^2 **PAGE:** 9.1

9. Which of these statements about benzene is true?

   a) All carbon atoms in benzene are sp^3 hybridized.
   b) Benzene contains only π bonds between C atoms.
   c) The bond order of each $C-C$ bond in benzene is 1.5.
   d) Benzene is an example of a molecule that displays ionic bonding.
   e) All of these statements are false.

   ANS: c) The bond order of each $C-C$ bond in benzene is 1.5.   **PAGE:** 9.1,5

10.   Which of the following molecules contains a central atom with sp^2 hybridization?

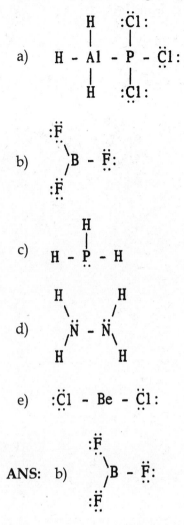

a)

$$\begin{array}{cccc} H & & :\overset{\cdot\cdot}{C}l: & \\ | & & | & \\ H - Al & - & P - \overset{\cdot\cdot}{C}l: \\ | & & | & \\ H & & :\overset{\cdot\cdot}{C}l: & \end{array}$$

b)

c)

$$\begin{array}{c} H \\ | \\ H - \overset{\cdot\cdot}{P} - H \end{array}$$

d)

e) $:\overset{\cdot\cdot}{C}l - Be - \overset{\cdot\cdot}{C}l:$

ANS: b)   PAGE: 9.1

11.   What hybridization is predicted for the nitrogen atom in the NO_3^- ion?

   a) sp^2
   b) sp^3
   c) sp^3d
   d) sp^3d^2
   e)   none of these

ANS: b) sp^2 PAGE: 9.1

191

12. Which of the following does not contain at least one pi bond?

    a) H_2CO

    b) CO_2

    c) C_2H_4

    d) C_3H_8

    e) All of the above (a-d) contain at least one pi bond.

    ANS: d) C_3H_8 **PAGE:** 9.1

13. Consider the following Lewis structure

    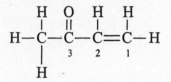

    Which statement about the molecule is false?

    a) There are 10 sigma and 2 pi bonds.

    b) C–2 is sp^2 hybridized with bond angles of 120°.

    c) Oxygen is sp^3 hybridized.

    d) This molecule contains 28 valence electrons.

    e) There are some H–C–H bond angles of about 109° in the molecule.

    ANS: c)   Oxygen is sp^3 hybridized.   **PAGE:** 9.1

14. Which statement about N_2 is false?

    a) It is a gas at room temperature.

    b) The oxidation state is +3 on one N and –3 on the other.

    c) It has one sigma and two pi bonds between the two atoms.

    d) It can combine with H_2 to form NH_3.

    e) It has two pairs of nonbonding electrons.

    ANS: b)   The oxidation state is +3 on one N and –3 on the other.   **PAGE:** 9.1

15. Consider the following Lewis structure:

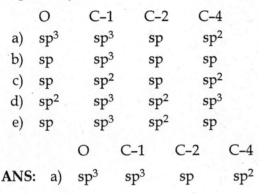

What is the hybridization of the oxygen atom and carbon atoms 1, 2, and 4, respectively?

	O	C-1	C-2	C-4
a)	sp^3	sp^3	sp	sp^2
b)	sp	sp^3	sp	sp
c)	sp	sp^2	sp	sp^2
d)	sp^2	sp^3	sp^2	sp^3
e)	sp	sp^3	sp^2	sp

	O	C-1	C-2	C-4
ANS: a)	sp^3	sp^3	sp	sp^2

PAGE: 9.1

16–19. Consider the molecule

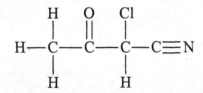

and the following hybridization choices:

a) sp
b) sp^2
c) sp^3
d) dsp^3
e) d^2sp^3

16. What is the hybridization of the carbon atom that is double bonded to oxygen?

ANS: b) sp^2 **PAGE:** 9.1

17. What is the hybridization of the carbon atom that is bonded to chlorine?

ANS: c) sp^3 **PAGE:** 9.1

18. What is the hybridization of the nitrogen atom?

ANS: a) sp **PAGE:** 9.1

19. What is the hybridization of the oxygen atom?

ANS: b) sp^2 **PAGE:** 9.1

20. The hybridization of I in IF_4^- is

   a) sp
   b) sp^2
   c) dsp^3
   d) dsp^3
   e) d^2sp^3

ANS: e) d^2sp^3 **PAGE:** 9.1

21. The hybridization of Cl in ClF_2^+ is

   a) sp
   b) sp^2
   c) sp^3
   d) $dsp3$
   e) d^2sp^3

ANS: c) sp^3 **PAGE:** 9.1

22. Consider the molecule

$$\overset{\displaystyle \overset{O}{\|}}{H_2C = CH - C - CH_2 - C \equiv N}$$

   $1 \quad 2 \quad 3 \quad 4 \quad 5$

Specify the hybridization of each carbon atom.

	C-1	C-2	C-3	C-4	C-5
a)	sp^2	sp^2	sp^2	sp^3	sp
b)	sp^2	sp^2	sp^2	sp^3	sp^3
c)	sp^2	sp^2	sp^3	sp^3	sp
d)	sp^2	sp^2	sp^3	sp^3	sp^3
e)	sp	sp	sp	sp^2	sp

	C-1	C-2	C-3	C-4	C-5
ANS: a)	sp^2	sp^2	sp^2	sp^3	sp

PAGE: 9.1

23. The hybridization of the central atom, Al, in AlBr$_3$ is

    a) sp
    b) sp^2
    c) sp^3
    d) dsp^3
    e) d^{2}sp^3

    ANS: b) sp^2 **PAGE:** 9.1

24. The hybridization of Se in SeF$_6$ is

    a) sp
    b) sp^2
    c) sp^3
    d) dsp^3
    e) d^{2}sp^3

    ANS: e) d^{2}sp^3 **PAGE:** 9.1

25. The hybridization of Br in BrF$_3$ is

    a) sp
    b) sp^2
    c) sp^3
    d) dsp^3
    e) d^{2}sp^3

    ANS: d) dsp^3 **PAGE:** 9.1

26. What is the bond order of Ne$_2$?

    a) 0
    b) 1/2
    c) 1
    d) 1 1/2
    e) 2

    ANS: a) 0   **PAGE:** 9.3

27. What is the bond order of C$_2{}^+$?

    a) 0
    b) 1/2
    c) 1
    d) 1 1/2
    e) 2

    ANS: d) 1 1/2   **PAGE:** 9.3

28. Which of the following has the greatest bond strength?

   a) B_2

   b) O_2^-

   c) CN^-

   d) O_2^+

   e) NO^-

   ANS: c) CN^- **PAGE:** 9.3

29. The hybridization of the lead atom in $PbCl_4$ is

   a) dsp^2

   b) sp^2

   c) d^2sp^3

   d) sp^2d

   e) none of these

   ANS: e) none of these **PAGE:** 9.1

30. The hybridization of the central atom in NO_3^- is

   a) p^3

   b) sp^2

   c) sp

   d) sp^2d

   e) sp

   ANS: b) sp^2 **PAGE:** 9.1

31. Which of the following statements is false?

   a) C_2 is paramagnetic.

   b) C_2 is diamagnetic.

   c) The carbon-carbon bond in C_2^{2-} is stronger than the one in CH_3CH_3.

   d) The carbon-carbon bond in C_2^{2-} is shorter than the one in CH_3CH_3.

   e) Two of the above.

   ANS: a) C_2 is paramagnetic. **PAGE:** 9.1,3

32. How many electrons are involved in pi bonding in benzene, C_6H_6?

   a) 12

   b) 30

   c) 3

   d) 6

   e) 18

   ANS: d) 6 **PAGE:** 9.1,5

33–35. Tetracyanoethylene has the skeleton shown below:

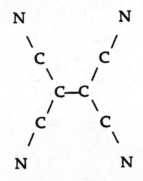

From its Lewis structure determine the following:

33. How many sigma and pi bonds are in the molecule?

   a) 5 sigma and 9 pi
   b) 6 sigma and 8 pi
   c) 9 sigma and 7 pi
   d) 9 sigma and 9 pi
   e) 5 sigma and 8 pi

   ANS: d)   9 sigma and 9 pi   **PAGE:** 9.1

34. How many of the atoms are sp² hybridized?

   a) 2
   b) 4
   c) 6
   d) 8
   e) 10

   ANS: a)   2   **PAGE:** 9.1

35. How many of the atoms are sp hybridized?

   a) 2
   b) 4
   c) 6
   d) 8
   e) 10

   ANS: d)   8   **PAGE:** 9.1

36. In which of the compounds below is there more than one kind of hybridization (sp, sp², sp³) for carbon?

    I. $CH_3CH_2CH_2CH_3$

    II. $CH_3CH = CHCH_3$

    III. $CH_2 = CH - CH = CH_2$

    IV. $H - C \equiv C - H$

    a) II and III

    b) II only

    c) III and IV

    d) I and IV

    e) III

ANS: b) II only   **PAGE:** 9.1

37. Complete the Lewis structure for the following molecule:

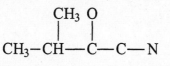

This molecule has _____ sigma and _____ pi bonds.

    a) 4, 5

    b) 6, 3

    c) 11, 5

    d) 13, 2

    e) 13, 3

ANS: e) 13, 3   **PAGE:** 9.1

38. Which of the following substances contains two pi bonds?

    a) C_2H_4

    b) C_3H_8

    c) C_2H_2

    d) C_2H_6

    e) CH_4

ANS: c) C_2H_2 **PAGE:** 9.1

39. Which of the following molecules has a bond order of 1.5?

    a) O_2^+

    b) N_2

    c) O_2^-

    d) C_2

    e) none of these

    ANS: c) O_2^- **PAGE:** 9.3

40. Consider the molecule C_2H_4. The hybridization of each C atom is

    a) sp

    b) sp^2

    c) sp^3

    d) dsp^3

    e) d^2sp^3

    ANS: b) sp^2 **PAGE:** 9.1

41–42. Consider the skeletal structure shown below:

        N – C – C – N

Draw the Lewis structure and answer the following:

41. How many of the atoms are sp hybridized?

    a) 0

    b) 1

    c) 2

    d) 3

    e) 4

    ANS: e)   4   **PAGE:** 9.1

42. How many pi bonds does the molecule contain?

    a) 0

    b) 2

    c) 4

    d) 6

    e) 7

    ANS: c)   4   **PAGE:** 9.1

43. Which of the following statements about the molecule BN is false?

   a) It is paramagnetic.
   b) Its bond order is 2.
   c) The total number of electrons is 12.
   d) It has two pi bonds.
   e) All of these are true.

   ANS: a)   It is paramagnetic.   **PAGE:** 9.4

44. Which of the following statements about the species CN⁻ is false?

   a) It is paramagnetic.
   b) The total number of electrons is 14.
   c) It has two pi bonds.
   d) All of these are true.

   ANS: a)   It is paramagnetic.   **PAGE:** 9.4

45. Which of the following statements is true?

   a) Electrons are never found in an antibonding MO.
   b) All antibonding MOs are higher in energy than the atomic orbitals of which they are composed.
   c) Antibonding MOs have electron density mainly outside the space between the two nuclei.
   d) None of the above is true.
   e) Two of the above statements are true.

   ANS: e)   Two of the above statements are true.   **PAGE:** 9.2,3

46. Which of the following molecules contains the shortest C — C bond?

   a) C_2H_2
   b) C_2H_4
   c) C_2H_6
   d) C_2Cl_4
   e) b and d

   ANS: a) C_2H_2 **PAGE:** 9.3

47. Which of the nitrogen-containing molecules below is paramagnetic in its lowest energy state?

    a) N_2

    b) NO

    c) NH_3

    d) N_2H_4

    e) none of these

    ANS: b) NO   **PAGE:** 9.3,4

48. If four orbitals on one atom overlap four orbitals on a second atom, how many molecular orbitals will form?

    a) 1

    b) 4

    c) 8

    d) 16

    e) none of these

    ANS: c) 8   **PAGE:** 9.2

49. Which of the following molecules or ions is not paramagnetic in its ground state?

    a) O_2

    b) O_2^+

    c) B_2

    d) NO

    e) F_2

    ANS: e) F_2 **PAGE:** 9.3,4

50. For which of the following diatomic molecules would the bond order become greater if an electron is removed, i.e., if the molecule is converted to the positive ion in its ground state?

    a) B_2

    b) C_2

    c) P_2

    d) F_2

    e) Na_2

    ANS: d) F_2 **PAGE:** 9.3

51. The configuration $(\sigma 2s)^2(\sigma 2s^*)^2(\pi 2py)^1 (\pi 2px)1$

    is the molecular orbital description for the ground state of

    a) Li_2^+

    b) Be_2

    c) B_2

    d) B_2^{2-}

    e) C_2

    ANS: c) B_2 **PAGE:** 9.3

52. Which of the following species is paramagnetic?

    a) C_2

    b) B_2

    c) N_2

    d) H_2

    e) none of these

    ANS: b) B_2 **PAGE:** 9.2,3

53. Which of the following species has the largest dissociation energy?

    a) O_2

    b) O_2^-

    c) O_2^{2-}

    d) O_2^+

    e) O_2^{2+}

    ANS: e) O_2^{2+} **PAGE:** 9.3

54. The fact that O_2 is paramagnetic can be explained by

    a) the Lewis structure of O_2.

    b) resonance.

    c) a violation of the octet rule.

    d) the molecular orbital diagram for O_2.

    e) hybridization of atomic orbitals in O_2.

    ANS: d) the molecular orbital diagram for O_2.   **PAGE:** 9.3

55. For how many of the following does the bond order decrease if you add one electron to the neutral molecule?

B_2, C_2, P_2, F_2

a) 0
b) 1
c) 2
d) 3
e) 4

ANS: c)   2   **PAGE:** 9.3

56. The hybridization of a molecule is measured to determine the shape of the molecule.

ANS: False   **PAGE:** 9.1

57. As the bond order of a bond increases, the bond energy _____ and the bond length _____.

a) increases, increases
b) decreases, decreases
c) increases, decreases
d) decreases, increases
e) More information is needed to answer this question.

ANS: c)   increases. decreases   **PAGE:** 9.2, 9.3

58. Which of the following diatomic molecules has a bond order of 2?

a) B_2
b) C_2
c) P_2
d) F_2
e) Na_2

ANS: b) C_2 **PAGE:** 9.3

59. Which of the following has the largest bond order?

a) N_2
b) N_2^-
c) N_2^{2-}
d) N_2^+
e) N_2^{2+}

ANS: a) N_2 **PAGE:** 9.3

60. Consider the molecular orbital energy level diagrams for O_2 and NO. Which of the following is true?

    I. Both molecules are paramagnetic.

    II. The bond strength of O_2 is greater than the bond strength of NO.

    III. NO is an example of a homonuclear diatomic molecule.

    IV. The ionization energy of NO is smaller than the ionization energy of NO^+.

    a) I only

    b) I and II

    c) I and IV

    d) II and III

    e) I, II, and IV

ANS: c) I and IV   **PAGE:** 9.3,4

61. How many of the following: F_2, B_2, O_2, N_2 , are paramagnetic?

    a) 0

    b) 1

    c) 2

    d) 3

    e) 4

ANS: c) 2   **PAGE:** 9.3

62. Order the following from shortest to longest bond:

    C_2, B_2, H_2, N_2

    a) H_2, N_2, C_2, B_2

    b) N_2, C_2, B_2, H_2

    c) C_2, N_2, H_2, B_2

    d) C_2, B_2, H_2, N_2

    e) none of these

ANS: a) H_2, N_2, C_2, B_2 **PAGE:** 9.2,3

63. Which charge(s) of O_2 would give a bond order of 2.5?

    a) –2

    b) –1

    c) +1

    d) two of these

    e) none of these

ANS: c) +1   **PAGE:** 9.3

64. For how many of the following does bond order decrease if you take away one electron from the neutral molecule?

   B_2, C_2, P_2, F_2

   a) 0
   b) 1
   c) 2
   d) 3
   e) 4

ANS: d) 3   PAGE: 9.3

65. Which of the following electron distributions among the molecular orbitals best describes the NO molecule?

	σ^{2s}	σ^{2s*}	$\pi^{2py}=\pi^{2px}$	σ^{2pz}	$\pi^{2py*}=\pi^{2px*}$	σ^{2pz*}
a)	2	2	4	2	4	2
b)	2	2	4	2	4	1
c)	2	2	4	1	3	0
d)	2	2	4	2	2	0
e)	2	2	4	2	1	0

	σ^{2s}	σ^{2s*}	$\pi^{2py}=\pi^{2px}$	σ^{2pz}	$\pi^{2py*}=\pi^{2px*}$	σ^{2pz*}
ANS: e)	2	2	4	2	1	0

PAGE: 9.4

66. In the molecular orbital description of CO,

   a) the highest energy electrons occupy antibonding orbitals.
   b) six molecular orbitals contain electrons.
   c) there are two unpaired electrons.
   d) the bond order is 3.
   e) All of the above are false.

ANS: d) the bond order is 3.   PAGE: 9.4

67. Consider the molecular orbital description of the NO^- anion. Which of the following statements is false?

   a) NO^- is paramagnetic.
   b) NO^- is isoelectronic with CO.
   c) The bond energy in NO^+ is greater than the bond energy in NO^-.
   d) The bond order in NO^- is 2.
   e) Statements a through d are false.

ANS: b) NO^- is isoelectronic with CO.   PAGE: 9.4

68. The bond order in the NO molecule is

    a) 1.
    b) 1.5.
    c) 2.
    d) 2.5.
    e) 3.

    ANS: d) 2.5.   **PAGE:** 9.4

69. The CO molecule has the bond order:

    a) 0
    b) 1
    c) 2
    d) 3
    e) 4

    ANS: d) 3   **PAGE:** 9.4

70. Which of the following statements (a–d) about the CO_3^{2-} ion is false?

    a) The orbitals on the carbon atom are sp^2 hybridized.
    b) The ion is expected to be diamagnetic.
    c) One C–O bond is shorter than the other.
    d) The ion has a total of 24 electrons.
    e) All the above statements are true.

    ANS: c)   One C — O bond is shorter than the other.   **PAGE:** 9.5

71. The C—C—H bond angles in ethylene, C_2H_4, are 120Á. What is the hybridization of the carbon orbitals?

    ANS: sp^2 **PAGE:** 9.1

72. Which of the following has the shortest bond length?

    a) O_2^{2-}
    b) O_2
    c) O_2^-
    d) O_2^+

    ANS: d) O_2^+ **PAGE:** 9.3

73. Consider the structure of glycine, the simplest amino acid:

$$
\begin{array}{cc}
\text{H} & \text{O} \\
| & \| \\
\text{H}_2\text{N}-\text{C}-\text{C}-\text{OH} \\
| \\
\text{H}
\end{array}
$$

   a) Indicate the hybridizations at each N and C atom in the molecule.
   b) What is the total number of bonds in the molecule?
   c) What is the total number of π bonds in the molecule?

   ANS: a) N sp^3
               C_1 sp^3
               C_2 sp^2
          b) 10 bonds
          c) 1 π bond   **PAGE:** 9.1

74. Draw a molecular orbital diagram for O_2 and N_2. Using molecular orbital theory, explain why the removal of one electron in O_2 strengthens bonding, while the removal of one electron in N_2 weakens bonding.

   ANS: See Sec. 9.3 of Zumdahl, *Chemistry*.   **PAGE:** 9.3

75. What is the bond order of He_2^+?

   a) 0
   b) 1/2
   c) 1
   d) 1 1/2
   e) 2

   ANS: b) 1/2   **PAGE:** 9.2

76. The following statements concern molecules that require resonance. Which is true?

   a) The pi bonding is most clearly delocalized.
   b) The sigma bonding is most clearly delocalized.
   c) Both the sigma and pi bonding are delocalized.
   d) The benzene molecule is best described by the MO theory.
   e) The benzene molecule is best described by the localized electron model.

   ANS: a) The pi bonding is most clearly delocalized.   **PAGE:** 9.5

77. Consider the benzene molecule. Which of the following statements about the molecule is false?

   a) All six C—C bonds are known to be equivalent.
   b) Each carbon atom is sp^2 hybridized.
   c) The localized electron model must invoke resonance to account for the six equal C—C bonds.
   d) It has delocalized pi bonding in the molecule.
   e) The pi bonds of carbon involve sp^2 orbitals.

   ANS: e)   The pi bonds of carbon involve sp^2 orbitals.   **PAGE:** 9.5

78. Give the bond order for each of the following:

   a) H_2
   b) H_2^+
   c) H_2^-
   d) CN^-
   e) CN
   f) CN^+

   ANS: a) 1   b) 0.5   c) 0.5   d) 3   e) 2.5   f) 2   **PAGE:** 9.2,4

79. Which of the following are paramagnetic?

   O_2 O_2^- O_2^{2-} B_2 C_2 N_2 F_2 CN^- P_2

   ANS: O_2 O_2^{2-} B_2 **PAGE:** 9.3,4

80. Explain the concept of delocalization of electrons in SO_3. Indicate how this idea relates to resonance.

   ANS: See Sec. 9.5 of Zumdahl, *Chemistry.*   **PAGE:** 9.5

81. Whenever a set of equivalent tetrahedral atomic orbitals is required it will adopt a set of sp^3 orbitals.

   ANS: True   **PAGE:** 9.1

82. The hybridization of the B in BH_3 is sp^3.

   Ans: False   **PAGE:** 9.1

83. The H_2^- ion is more stable than H_2 since it has an additional electron to produce a net lowering of energy.

   ANS: False   **PAGE:** 9.2

84. Larger bond order means greater bond strength.

    ANS: True   **PAGE:** 9.2

85. When an electron pair is shared in the area centered on a line joining the atoms a σ bond is formed.

    ANS: True   **PAGE:** 9.2

86. According to MO theory, F_2 should be diamagnetic.

    ANS: True   **PAGE:** 9.3

87. Paramagnetism is associated with paired electrons.

    ANS: False   **PAGE:** 9.3

88. The bond order for CN^- is 2.

    ANS: False   **PAGE:** 9.4

89. The mixing of native atomic orbitals to form special orbitals for bonding is called _____.

    ANS: hybridization   **PAGE:** 9.1

90. A(n) _____ molecular orbital is lower in energy than the atomic orbital of which it is composed.

    ANS: bonding   **PAGE:** 9.2

91. _____ is the difference between the number of bonding electrons and the number of antibonding electrons divided by two.

    ANS: Bond order   **PAGE:** 9.2

92. _____ causes a substance to be attracted into the inducing magnetic field.

    ANS: Paramagnetism   **PAGE:** 9.3

93. The concept of _____ is required for certain molecules because the localized electron model assumes electrons are located between a given pair of atoms in a molecule.

    ANS: resonance   **PAGE:** 9.5

94. The number of molecular orbitals formed is always _____ the number of atomic orbitals combined.

    ANS: the same as   **PAGE:** 9.2

209

CHAPTER 10   Liquids and Solids

1. Which one of the following decreases as the strength of the attractive intermolecular forces increases?

   a) The heat of vaporization.
   b) The normal boiling temperature.
   c) The extent of deviations from the ideal gas law.
   d) The sublimation temperature of a solid.
   e) The vapor pressure of a liquid.

   ANS: e)   The vapor pressure of a liquid.   **PAGE:** 10.1,8

2. Order the intermolecular forces (dipole-dipole, London Dispersion, ionic, and hydrogen-bonding) from weakest to strongest .

   a) dipole-dipole, London Dispersion, ionic, and hydrogen-bonding
   b) London Dispersion, dipole-dipole, hydrogen-bonding, ionic
   c) hydrogen-bonding, dipole-dipole, London Dispersion, and ionic
   d) dipole-dipole, ionic, London Dispersion, and hydrogen-bonding
   e) London Dispersion, ionic, dipole-dipole, and hydrogen-bonding

   ANS: b)   London Dispersion, dipole-dipole, hydrogen-bonding,
              ionic   **PAGE:** 10.1

3. Hydrogen bonds account for which of the following observation?

   a) Hydrogen naturally exists as a diatomic molecule.
   b) Hydrogen is easily combustible with oxygen.
   c) Water molecules are bent or "V-shaped".
   d) Air is more dense than hydrogen gas.
   e) For its molar mass, water has a high boiling point.

   ANS: e)   For its molar mass, water has a high boiling point.   **PAGE:** 10.1

4. Which of the following would you expect to have the highest boiling point?

   a) F_2
   b) Cl_2
   c) Br_2
   d) I_2
   e) All of the above have the same boiling point.

   ANS: d) I_2 **PAGE:** 10.1

5. Which of the following is most likely to be a solid at room temperature?

    a) Na_2S
    b) HF
    c) NH_3
    d) N_2
    e) H_2O

    ANS: a) Na_2S **PAGE:** 10.1, 7

6. Which of the following should have the lowest boiling point?

    a) Na_2S
    b) HF
    c) NH_3
    d) N_2
    e) H_2O

    ANS: d) N_2 **PAGE:** 10.1, 7

7. On a relative basis, the weaker the intermolecular forces in a substance,

    a) the greater its heat of vaporization.
    b) the more it deviates from ideal gas behavior.
    c) the greater its vapor pressure at a particular temperature.
    d) the higher its melting point.
    e) none of these

    ANS: c)   the greater its vapor pressure at a particular temperature.   **PAGE:** 10.1, 8

8. Which of the species below would you expect to show the least hydrogen bonding?

    a) NH_3
    b) H_2O
    c) HF
    d) CH_4
    e) all the same

    ANS: d) CH_4 **PAGE:** 10.1

9. The molecules in a sample of solid SO_2 are attracted to each other by a combination of

    a) London forces and H-bonding.
    b) H-bonding and ionic bonding.
    c) covalent bonding and dipole-dipole interactions.
    d) London forces and dipole-dipole interactions.
    e) none of these

    ANS: d)   London forces and dipole-dipole interactions.   **PAGE:** 10.1

10. Which of the following is the correct order of boiling points for KNO_3, CH_3OH, C_2H_6, Ne?

   a) $Ne < CH_3OH < C_2H_6 < KNO_3$

   b) $KNO_3 < CH_3OH < C_2H_6 < Ne$

   c) $Ne < C_2H_6 < KNO_3 < CH_3OH$

   d) $Ne < C_2H_6 < CH_3OH < KNO_3$

   e) $C_2H_6 < Ne < CH_3OH < KNO_3$

   ANS: d) $Ne < C_2H_6 < CH_3OH < KNO_3$ **PAGE:** 10.1,7

11. Which of the following statements about liquids is true?

   a) Droplet formation occurs because of the higher stability associated with increased surface area.

   b) Substances that can form hydrogen bonds will display lower melting points than predicted from periodic trends.

   c) London dispersion forces arise from a distortion of the electron clouds within a molecule or atom.

   d) Liquid rise within a capillary tube because of the small size lowers the effective atmospheric pressure over the surface of the liquid.

   e) The boiling point of a solution is dependent solely on the atmospheric pressure over the solution.

   ANS: c)   London dispersion forces arise from a distortion of the electron clouds within a molecule or atom.   **PAGE:** 10.1,2

12. Which statement regarding water is true?

   a) Energy must be given off in order to break down the crystal lattice of ice to a liquid.

   b) Hydrogen bonds are stronger than covalent bonds.

   c) Liquid water is less dense than solid water.

   d) Only covalent bonds are broken when ice melts.

   e) All of the statements (a–d) are false.

   ANS: e)   All of the statements (a–d) are false.   **PAGE:** 10.1,6,8,9

13. In which of the following groups of substances would dispersion forces be the only significant factors in determining boiling points?

       I. Cl_2 II. HF   III. Ne   IV. KNO_2 V. CCl_4

   a) I, III, V

   b) I, II, III

   c) II, IV

   d) II, V

   e) III, IV, V

   ANS: a)   I, III, V   **PAGE:** 10.1,7

14. The elements of group 5A, the nitrogen family, form compounds with hydrogen having the boiling points listed below:

$$SbH_3 -17°C, AsH_3 -55°C, PH_3 -87°C, NH_3 -33°C$$

The first three elements illustrate a trend where the boiling point decreases as the mass decreases; however, ammonia (NH_3) does not follow the trend because of

   a)   dipole-dipole attraction.
   b)   metallic bonding.
   c)   hydrogen bonding.
   d)   London dispersion forces.
   e)   ionic bonding.

ANS: c) hydrogen bonding.   **PAGE:** 10.1

15. Which substance involves no bonding forces except London dispersion forces?

   a) $NaCl(l)$
   b) $HF(l)$
   c) $N_2(s)$
   d) $H_2O(l)$
   e) $K(s)$

ANS: c) $N_2(s)$ **PAGE:** 10.1

16. On the basis of your knowledge of bonding in liquids and solids, arrange the following substances in order of highest to lowest melting temperature:

$$NaCl, Na, Cl_2, SiO_2$$

   a) $Cl_2, Na, NaCl, SiO_2$
   b) $Na, NaCl, Cl_2, SiO_2$
   c) $SiO_2, NaCl, Na, Cl_2$
   d) $NaCl, SiO_2, Na, Cl_2$
   e) $SiO_2, Na, NaCl, Cl_2$

ANS: c) $SiO_2, NaCl, Na, Cl_2$ **PAGE:** 10.1,7

17. Which of the following substances would you expect to have the lowest boiling point?

   a)   diamond
   b)   methane, CH_4
   c)   sodium nitrate, $NaNO_3$
   d)   glycerine, $C_3H_5(OH)_3$
   e)   copper

ANS: b) methane, CH_4 **PAGE:** 10.4–7

18. The unit cell in this two-dimensional crystal contains _____ Xs and _____ Os.

X   X   X   X
  O   O   O   O
X   X   X   X
  O   O   O   O
X   X   X   X
  O   O   O   O

a) 1,1
b) 2,1
c) 1,2
d) 4,1
e) 1,4

ANS: a)   1,1   **PAGE:** 10.3

19. In general, the density of a compound as a gas is closer in value to that of the compound as a liquid, than the density of the compound as a liquid is closer in value to that of the compound as a solid.

   ANS: False   **PAGE:** 10.1

20. Second row hydrides generally have higher than expected boiling points for their position on the periodic table.

   ANS: True   **PAGE:** 10.1

21. Knowing that ΔH_{vap} for water is 40.7 kJ/mol, calculate P_{vap} of water at 37°C.

   a)   6.90 torr
   b)   12.4 torr
   c)   18.7 torr
   d)   25.4 torr
   e)   52.6 torr

   ANS: e)   52.6 torr   **PAGE:** 10.8

22–24. The molar volume of a certain form of solid lead is 18 cm^3/mol. Assuming cubic closest packed structure, determine the following:

22. The number of Pb atoms per unit cell.

   a)   3
   b)   4
   c)   10
   d)   12
   e)   14

   ANS: b)   4   **PAGE:** 10.4

23. The volume of a single cell.

    a) 1.20×10^2 pm^3
    b) 1.20×10^4 pm^3
    c) 1.20×10^6 pm^3
    d) 1.20×10^8 pm^3
    e) none of these

    ANS: d) 1.20×10^8 pm^3 **PAGE:** 10.4

24. The radius of a Pb atom.

    a) 1.74 pm
    b) 17.4 pm
    c) 174 pm
    d) 1740 pm
    e) none of these

    ANS: c)   174 pm   **PAGE:** 10.4

25. Water sits in an open beaker. Assuming constant temperature and pressure, the rate of evaporation decreases as the water evaporates.

    ANS: False   **PAGE:** 10.8

26. Water sits in an open beaker. Assuming constant temperature and pressure, the vapor pressure of the water decreases as the water evaporates.

    ANS: False   **PAGE:** 10.8

27. Generally the vapor pressure of a liquid is related to

    I. the amount of liquid
    II. atmospheric pressure
    III. temperature
    IV. intermolecular forces
    a) I, III
    b) II, III, IV
    c) I, III, IV
    d) III, IV
    e) all information is needed

    ANS: d)   III, IV   **PAGE:** 10.8

28. A certain solid substance that is very hard, has a high melting point, and is nonconducting unless melted is most likely to be:

   a) I_2

   b) NaCl

   c) CO_2

   d) H_2O

   e) Cu

   ANS: b) NaCl   **PAGE:** 10.4–7

29. Which of the statements a through d is false?

   a) Diamond is a covalent crystal.

   b) The size of the unit cell of Li and Cs is the same.

   c) Molecular crystals usually have low melting points.

   d) Metallic crystals are usually good electrical conductors.

   e) All of the statements a through d are correct.

   ANS: b)   The size of the unit cell of Li and Cs is the same.   **PAGE:** 10.4–7

30. In the unit cell of sphalerite, Zn^{2+} ions occupy half the tetrahedral holes in a face-centered cubic lattice of S^{2-} ions. The number of formula units of ZnS in the unit cell is:

   a) 5

   b) 4

   c) 3

   d) 2

   e) 1

   ANS: b)   4   **PAGE:** 10.4,7

31. The unit cell in a certain lattice consists of a cube formed by an anion at each corner, an anion in the center, and a cation at the center of each face. The unit cell contains a net:

   a) 5 anions and 6 cations.

   b) 5 anions and 3 cations.

   c) 2 anions and 3 cations.

   d) 3 anions and 4 cations.

   e) 2 anions and 2 cations.

   ANS: c)   2 anions and 3 cations.   **PAGE:** 10.4,7

32. Which one of the following statements about solid Cu (face-centered cubic unit cell) is incorrect?

    a) It will conduct electricity.
    b) There are two atoms per unit cell.
    c) The number of atoms surrounding each Cu atom is 12.
    d) The solid has a cubic closest-packed structure.
    e) The length of a face diagonal is four times the Cu radius.

    ANS: b)   There are two atoms per unit cell.   **PAGE:** 10.4

33. In any cubic lattice an atom lying at the corner of a unit cell is shared equally by how many unit cells?

    a) 1
    b) 2
    c) 8
    d) 4
    e) 16

    ANS: c)   8   **PAGE:** 10.4

34. At normal atmospheric pressure and a temperature of 0ÁC, which phase(s) of H_2O can exist?

    a) ice and water
    b) ice and water vapor
    c) water only
    d) water vapor only
    e) ice only

    ANS: a)   ice and water   **PAGE:** 10.8

35. The bonds between hydrogen and oxygen in a water molecule can be characterized as _____.

    a) hydrogen bonds
    b) London dispersion forces
    c) intermolecular forces
    d) intramolecular forces
    e) dispersion forces

    ANS: d)   intramolecular forces   **PAGE:** 10.1

217

36. Assume 12,500 J of energy is added to 2.0 moles (36 grams) of H_2O as an ice sample at 0°C. The molar heat of fusion is 6.02 kJ/mol. The specific heat of liquid water is 4.18 J/mol K. The molar heat of vaporization is 40.6 kJ/mol. The resulting sample contains which of the following?

    a)   only ice
    b)   ice and water
    c)   only water
    d)   water and water vapor
    e)   only water vapor

    ANS: c)   only water   **PAGE:** 10.8

37. When a water molecule forms a hydrogen bond with another water molecule, which atoms are involved in the interaction?

    a)   A hydrogen from one molecule and a hydrogen from the other molecule.
    b)   A hydrogen from one molecule and an oxygen from the other molecule.
    c)   An oxygen from one molecule and an oxygen from the other molecule.
    d)   Two hydrogens from one molecule and one oxygen from the other molecule.
    e)   Two hydrogens from one molecule and one hydrogen from the other molecule.

    ANS: b)   A hydrogen from one molecule and an oxygen from the
    other molecule.   **PAGE:** 10.1

38. Sodium oxide (Na_2O) crystallizes in a structure in which the O^{2-} ions are in a face-centered cubic lattice and the Na^+ ions are in tetrahedral holes. The number of Na^+ ions in the unit cell is:

    a)   2
    b)   4
    c)   6
    d)   8
    e)   none of these

    ANS: d)   8   **PAGE:** 10.4,7

39. A certain metal fluoride crystallizes in such a way that the fluoride ions occupy simple cubic lattice sites, while the metal atoms occupy the body centers of half the cubes. The formula for the metal fluoride is:

    a) MF_2
    b) M_2F
    c)   MF
    d) MF_8
    e)   none of these

    ANS: a) MF_2 **PAGE:** 10.4,7

40. Which of the following statements is (are) false?

    I.   The hexagonal closest-packed structure is ABAB – – –.

    II. A body-centered cubic unit cell has four atoms per unit cell.

    III. For unit cells having the same edge length, a simple cubic structure would have a smaller density than a body-centered cube.

    IV. Atoms in a solid consisting of only one element would have six nearest neighbors if the crystal structure were a simple cubic array.

    a) I

    b) II

    c) II, III

    d) I, IV

    e) II, III, IV

ANS: b) II   **PAGE:** 10.4

41. Aluminum metal crystallizes in a face-centered cubic structure. The relationship between the radius of an Al atom (r) and the length of an edge of the unit cell (E) is:

    a) $r = E/2$

    b) $r = \left(\sqrt{2}/4\right) E$

    c) $r = \left(\sqrt{3}/4\right) E$

    d) $r = 2E$

    e) $r = 4E$

ANS: b) $r = \left(\sqrt{2}/4\right) E$ **PAGE:** 10.4

42. Chromium metal crystallizes as a body-centered cubic lattice. If the atomic radius of Cr is 1.25 angstroms, what is the density of Cr metal in g/cm^3?

    a) 5.52

    b) 7.18

    c) 7.81

    d) 2.76

    e) 3.59

ANS: b) 7.18   **PAGE:** 10.4

43. You are given a small bar of an unknown metal, X. You find the density of the metal to be 10.5 g/cm^3. An X-ray diffraction experiment measures the edge of the unit cell as 409 pm. Assuming that the metal crystallizes in a face-centered cubic lattice, what is X most likely to be?

    a) Ag
    b) Rh
    c) Pt
    d) Pb
    e) none of these

ANS: a)   Ag   **PAGE:** 10.4

44. Silver chloride crystallizes with the sodium chloride (rock salt) structure. The length of a unit cell edge is 555 pm. What is the density of AgCl?

    a) 5.57 g/cm^3
    b) 4.19 g/cm^3
    c) 2.79 g/cm^3
    d) 2.10 g/cm^3
    e) 1.39 g/cm^3

ANS: a)   5.57 g/cm^3 **PAGE:** 10.4

45. The freezing point of helium is –270°C. The freezing point of xenon is –112°C. Both of these are in the noble gas family. Which of the following statements is supported by these data?

    a) Helium and xenon form highly polar molecules.
    b) As the molecular weight of the noble gas increases, the freezing point decreases.
    c) The London dispersion forces between the helium molecules are greater than the London dispersion between the xenon molecules.
    d) The London dispersion forces between the helium molecules are less than the London dispersion forces between the xenon molecules.
    e) none of these

ANS: d)   The London dispersion forces between the helium
              molecules are less than the London dispersion forces
              between the xenon molecules.   **PAGE:** 10.1

46. The process of evaporation happens when which of the following occurs?

    a) A solid becomes a liquid.
    b) A liquid becomes a solid.
    c) A liquid becomes a gas.
    d) A gas becomes a liquid.
    e) A solid becomes a gas.

ANS: c)   A liquid becomes a gas.   **PAGE:** 10.8

47. Which of the following processes must exist in equilibrium with the evaporation process when a measurement of vapor pressure is made?

    a) fusion
    b) vaporization
    c) sublimation
    d) boiling
    e) condensation

    ANS: e)   condensation   **PAGE:** 10.8

48. Which of the following statements about the closest packing of spheres in ionic solids is false?

    a) The packing is done in a way that minimizes repulsions among ions with like charges.
    b) The packing arrangement maximizes electrostatic attractions among oppositely charged ions.
    c) For spheres of a given diameter, tetrahedral holes are larger than octahedral holes.
    d) Trigonal holes are so small that they are never occupied.
    e) None of these.

    ANS: c)   For spheres of a given diameter, tetrahedral holes are
                  larger than octahedral holes.   **PAGE:** 10.7

49. A metal crystallizes in a body-centered unit cell with an edge length of 2.00×10^2 pm. Assume the atoms in the cell touch along the cube diagonal. The percentage of empty volume in the unit cell will be:

    a) 0%
    b) 26.0%
    c) 32.0%
    d) 68.0%
    e) none of these

    ANS: c)   32.0%   **PAGE:** 10.4

50. A metal crystallizes with a face-centered cubic lattice. The edge of the unit cell is 408 pm. The diameter of the metal atom is:

    a) 144 pm
    b) 204 pm
    c) 288 pm
    d) 408 pm
    e) none of these

    ANS: c)   288 pm   **PAGE:** 10.4

221

51. If equal, rigid spheres are arranged in a simple cubic lattice in the usual way, i.e., in such a way that they touch each other, what fraction of the corresponding solid will be empty space? [The volume of a sphere is $(4/3)\pi r^3$, with $\pi = 3.14$.]

   a) 0.52
   b) 0.32
   c) 0.68
   d) 0.48
   e) none of these

   ANS: c) 0.48   **PAGE:** 10.4

52. A salt, MY, crystallizes in a body-centered cubic structure with a Y^- anion at each cube corner and an M^+ cation at the cube center. Assuming that the Y^- anions touch each other and the M^+ cation at the center, and the radius of 6– is 1.50×10^2 pm, the radius of m+ is:

   a) 62.0 pm
   b) 110. pm
   c) 124 pm
   d) 220. pm
   e) none of these

   ANS: b) 110 pm   **PAGE:** 10.4,7

53. Which substance can be described as cations bonded together by mobile electrons?

   a) $Ag(s)$
   b) $S_8(s)$
   c) $Kr(l)$
   d) $KCl(s)$
   e) $HCl(l)$

   ANS: a) $Ag(s)$ **PAGE:** 10.4

54. Which of the following statements is true about p-type silicon?

   a) It is produced by doping Si with P or As.
   b) Electrons are the mobile charge carriers.
   c) It does not conduct electricity as well as pure Si.
   d) All are true.
   e) None is true.

   ANS: e) None is true.   **PAGE:** 10.5

55. Doping Se with As would produce a(n) _____ semiconductor with _____ conductivity compared to pure Se.

    a) n-type, increased
    b) n-type, decreased
    c) p-type, increased
    d) p-type, decreased
    e) intrinsic, identical

    ANS: c) p-type, increased   **PAGE:** 10.5

56. A material is made from Al, Ga, and As. The mole fraction of each element is 0.25, 0.26, and 0.49, respectively. This material would be

    a) a metallic conductor because Al is present.
    b) an insulator.
    c) a p-type semiconductor.
    d) an n-type semiconductor.
    e) none of the above

    ANS: c) a p-type semiconductor.   **PAGE:** 10.5

57. Which of the compounds below is an example of a network solid?

    a) $S_8(s)$
    b) $SiO_2(s)$
    c) $MgO(s)$
    d) $NaCl(s)$
    e) $C_{25}H_{52}(s)$

    ANS: b) $SiO_2(s)$ **PAGE:** 10.5

58. Which of the statements a through d is incorrect?

    a) Molecular solids have high melting points.
    b) The binding forces in a molecular solid include London dispersion forces.
    c) Ionic solids have high melting points.
    d) Ionic solids are insulators.
    e) All of the statements a through d are correct.

    ANS: a) Molecular solids have high melting points.   **PAGE:** 10.6,7

59. At room temperature, CsF is expected to be

    a) a gas.

    b) a conducting solid.

    c) a liquid.

    d) a brittle solid.

    e) a soft solid.

    ANS: d)   a brittle solid.   **PAGE:** 10.7

60. A crystal of NaCl is

    a) soft, low melting, a good electrical conductor.

    b) hard, high melting, a good electrical conductor.

    c) soft, low melting, a poor electrical conductor.

    d) hard, high melting, a poor electrical conductor.

    e) soft, high melting, a poor electrical conductor.

    ANS: d)   hard, high melting, a poor electrical conductor.   **PAGE:** 10.7

61. Solid MgO has the same crystal structure as NaCl. How many oxide ions surround each Mg^{2+} ion as nearest neighbors in MgO?

    a) 4

    b) 6

    c) 8

    d) 12

    e) none of these

    ANS: b)   6   **PAGE:** 10.7

62. Which of the following has the highest melting temperature?

    a) H_2O

    b) CO_2

    c) S_8

    d) MgF_2

    e) P_4

    ANS: d) MgF_2 **PAGE:** 10.6,7

63. Steel is considered to be a(n) _____.

    a) interstitial alloy

    b) ionic solid

    c) molecular solid

    d) substitutional alloy

    e) two of these

    ANS: a)   interstitial alloy   **PAGE:** 10.4

64. Which of the following statements about steel is false?

   a) It contains carbon atoms in the holes of its iron crystals.
   b) The presence of carbon-iron bonds in the alloy make steel harder and stronger than pure iron.
   c) Pure iron is relatively soft and ductile because it lacks directional bonding.
   d) The amount of carbon directly affects the properties of steel.
   e) All of these are true.

   ANS: e)   All of these are true.   **PAGE:** 10.4

65. What is responsible for capillary action, a property of liquids?

   a) surface tension
   b) cohesive forces
   c) adhesive forces
   d) viscosity
   e) two of these

   ANS: e)   two of these   **PAGE:** 10.2

66. When a nonpolar liquid displays a convex meniscus, which of the following explains this behavior?

   a) It has a low surface tension, and therefore clings to the glass.
   b) The cohesive forces are stronger than the adhesive forces toward the glass.
   c) The adhesive forces toward the glass are stronger than the cohesive forces.
   d) The liquid's viscosity is low.
   e) none of these

   ANS: b)   The cohesive forces are stronger than the adhesive forces
                   toward the glass.   **PAGE:** 10.2

67. You are given the following boiling point data:

   a) water, H_2O 100°ÁC
   b) methanol, CH_3OH 64.96°C
   c) ethanol, CH_3CH_2OH 78.5°C
   d) diethyl ether, CH_3OH_2–O–CH_2CH_3 34.5°C
   e) ethylene glycol, HO–CH_2–CH_2–OH   198°C

   Which one of the above liquids would you expect to have the highest vapor pressure at room temperature?

   ANS: d)   diethyl ether, CH_3CH_2–O–CH_2CH_3 **PAGE:** 10.8

68. Given below are the temperatures at which two different liquid compounds with the same empirical formula have a vapor pressure of 400 torr.

Compound	T (°C)
dimethyl ether, CH_3-O-CH_3	–37.8
ethanol, CH_3CH_2OH	63.5

Which of the following statements (a–d) is false?

a) Increasing the temperature will increase the vapor pressure of both liquids.

b) Intermolecular attractive forces are stronger in (liquid) ethanol than in (liquid) dimethyl ether.

c) The normal boiling point of dimethyl ether will be higher than the normal boiling point of ethanol.

d) The reason that the temperature at which the vapor pressure is 400 torr is higher for ethanol (than for dimethyl ether) is that there is strong hydrogen bonding in ethanol.

e) None of these is false.

ANS: c) The normal boiling point of dimethyl ether will be higher than the normal boiling point of ethanol.

PAGE: 10.8

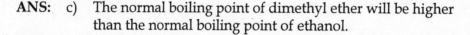

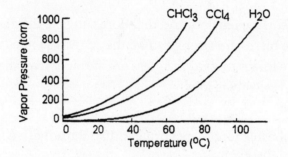

69. Given the graph above, what is the boiling point of carbon tetrachloride at standard pressure?

a) 60°ÁC

b) 34°C

c) 98°C

d) 77°C

e) graph does not give that information

ANS: c) 77°C

PAGE: 10.8

70. A liquid placed in a closed container will evaporate until equilibrium is reached. At equilibrium, which of the statements a through d is not true?

    a) The partial pressure exerted by the vapor molecules is called the vapor pressure of the liquid.

    b) Liquid molecules are still evaporating.

    c) The number of vapor molecules remains essentially constant.

    d) The boundary (meniscus) between liquid and vapor disappears.

    e) All of these are true.

    ANS: d)   The boundary (meniscus) between liquid and vapor disappears.   **PAGE:** 10.8

71. Which best explains the following trend?

Element	b.p. (K)
He	4
Ne	25
Ar	95
Kr	125
Xe	170

    a) London dispersion forces
    b) dipole-dipole interaction
    c) hydrogen bonding
    d) Le Chatelier's principle
    e) none of these

    ANS: a)   London dispersion forces   **PAGE:** 10.1

72. In which of the following processes will energy by evolved as heat?

    a) sublimation
    b) crystallization
    c) vaporization
    d) melting
    e) none of these

    ANS: b)   crystallization   **PAGE:** 10.8

73. When one mole of benzene is vaporized at a constant pressure of 1.00 atm and at its boiling point of 353.0 K, 30.79 kJ of energy (heat) is absorbed and the volume change is +28.90 L. What is ΔE for this process? (1 L-atm = 101.3 J)

    a) 30.79 kJ
    b) –89.87 kJ
    c) 25.80 kJ
    d) 133.71 kJ
    e) 27.86 kJ

    ANS: a)   27.86 kJ   **PAGE:** 10.8

74. When one mole of benzene is vaporized at a constant pressure of 1.00 atm and at its boiling point of 353.0 K, 30.79 kJ of energy (heat) is absorbed and the volume change is +28.90 L. What is ΔH for this process? (1 L-atm = 101.3 J)

    a) 24.95 kJ
    b) 36.63 kJ
    c) 28.72 kJ
    d) 30.79 kJ
    e) 27.87 kJ

    ANS: c)   30.79 kJ   **PAGE:** 10.8

75. Which of the following is paired incorrectly?

    a) crystalline solids – highly regular arrangement of their components
    b) amorphous solids – considerable disorder in their structures
    c) unit cell – the smallest repeating unit of the lattice
    d) gold metal – simple cubic unit cell
    e) glass – amorphous solid

    ANS: d)   gold metal – simple cubic unit cell   **PAGE:** 10.3

76. The normal boiling point of liquid X is less than that of Y, which is less than that of Z. Which of the following is the correct order of increasing vapor pressure of the three liquids at STP?

    a) X, Y, Z
    b) Z, Y, X
    c) Y, X, Z
    d) X, Z, Y
    e) Y, Z, X

    ANS: b)   Z, Y, X   **PAGE:** 10.8

77. The vapor pressure of water at 100.0°C is

   a)   85 torr
   b)   760 torr
   c)   175 torr
   d)   1 torr
   e)   More information is needed.

   ANS: b)   760 torr   **PAGE:** 10.8

78. How much energy is needed to convert 64.0 grams of ice at 0.00°C to water at 75.0°C?

         specific heat (ice) = 2.10 J/(g°C)

         specific heat (water) = 4.18 J/g(g°C)

         heat of fusion = 333 J/g

         heat of vaporization = 2258 J/g

   a)   10.1 kJ
   b)   20.7 kJ
   c)   31.4 kJ
   d)   41.4 kJ
   e)   65.8 kJ

   ANS: d)   41.4 kJ   **PAGE:** 10.8

79. The vapor pressure of water at 80°C is

   a)   0.48 atm
   b)   1.00 atm
   c)   1.20 atm
   d)   2.00 atm
   e)   5.00 atm

   ANS: a)   0.48 atm   **PAGE:** 10.8

80. A certain substance, X, has a triple-point temperature of 20°C at a pressure of 2.0 atm. Which one of the statements a through d cannot possibly be true?

   a)   X can exist as a liquid above 20°C.
   b)   X can exist as a solid above 20°C.
   c)   Liquid X can exist as a stable phase at 25°C, 1 atm.
   d)   Both liquid and solid X have the same vapor pressure at 20°C.
   e)   All of the statements a through d could be true.

   ANS: c)   Liquid X can exist as a stable phase at 25°C, 1 atm.   **PAGE:** 10.9

81. The triple point of iodine is at 90 torr and 115°C. This means that liquid I_2

   a)   is more dense than $I_2(s)$.

   b)   cannot exist above 115°C.

   c)   cannot exist at 1 atmosphere pressure.

   d)   cannot have a vapor pressure less than 90 torr.

   e)   can exist at pressure of 10 torr.

   ANS: d)   cannot have a vapor pressure less than 90 torr.   **PAGE:** 10.9

82. The triple point of CO_2 is at 5.2 atm and –57°C. Under atmospheric conditions present in a typical Boulder, Colorado, laboratory ($P = 630$ torr, $T = 23$°C), solid CO_2 will:

   a)   remain solid.

   b)   boil.

   c)   melt.

   d)   sublime.

   e)   none of these

   ANS: d)   sublime.   **PAGE:** 10.9

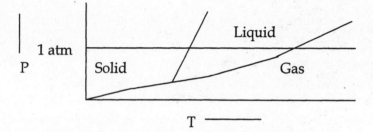

83. Choose the correct statement about the diagram above.

   a)   The diagram is qualitatively correct for water.

   b)   The diagram shows that the melting point of the solid increases with increasing pressure.

   c)   The diagram shows the triple point above 1 atm pressure.

   d)   The diagram could represent the phase diagram of CO_2.

   e)   None of the above statements is correct.

   ANS: b)   The diagram shows that the melting point of the solid increases with increasing pressure.   **PAGE:** 10.9

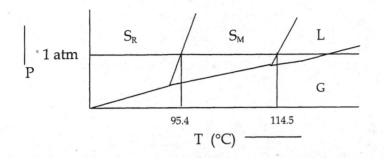

84. Shown above is a phase diagram for sulfur (not drawn to scale). Sulfur can exist in solid modifications, rhombic and monoclinic, denoted by Sr and SM, respectively. Which of the following statements is incorrect?

    a) This system has two triple points.
    b) Under ordinary atmospheric conditions (at sea level), sulfur does not sublime.
    c) At pressures close to 1 atm, rhombic sulfur can be in stable equilibrium with liquid sulfur.
    d) At a given pressure, there is (at most) one temperature at which rhombic sulfur can exist in equilibrium with monoclinic sulfur.
    e) None of the above statements is incorrect.

    ANS: c)   At pressure close to 1 atm, rhombic sulfur can be in stable
            equilibrium with liquid sulfur.   **PAGE:** 10.9

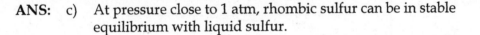
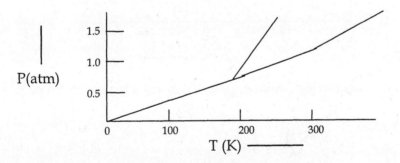

85. Above is a phase diagram for compound X.
    You wish to purify a sample of X which was collected at $P = 1.0$ atm and $T = 100$ by subliming it. In order to sublime the sample, you should:

    a) increase P to 1.5 atm and then increase T to 300 K.
    b) increase T to 300 K, keeping $P = 1.0$ atm.
    c) lower P to 0.5 atm and then increase T to 200 K.
    d) increase T to 300 K and then lower P to 0.5 atm.
    e) abandon the attempt to sublime X.

    ANS: c)   lower P to 0.5 atm and then increase T to 200 K.   **PAGE:** 10.9

231

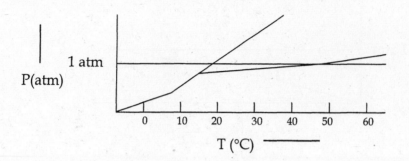

86. Shown above is a phase diagram for compound X. At 25°C and 1 atm X will exist as a:

    a) solid.
    b) liquid.
    c) gas.
    d) gas/liquid at equilibrium.
    e) gas/solid at equilibrium.

    ANS: b)   liquid.   **PAGE:** 10.9

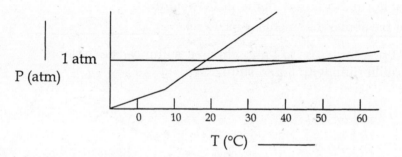

87. Above is a phase diagram for compound X. The normal boiling point of X is most likely:

    a) 21°C
    b) 47°C
    c) 73°C
    d) 18°C
    e) 0°C

    ANS: b)   47°C   **PAGE:** 10.9

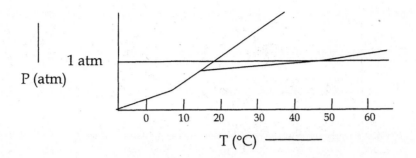

88. Shown above is a phase diagram for compound X.
How will the melting point of X change with increased pressure?

   a) increase
   b) decrease
   c) remain the same
   d) there is not enough information given
   e) increase and then decrease

   ANS: a) increase   **PAGE:** 10.9

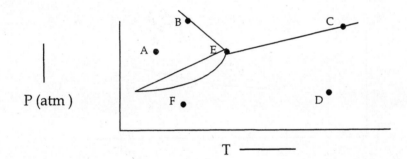

89. Based on the phase diagram shown above, which of the following statements are correct?

   I. Sublimation occurs at a point in the transformation that occurs along a straight line from point A to point F.
   II. C and E represent points where the gas and liquid phases are in equilibrium.
   III. ΔH_{vap} can be measured at point B.
   IV. Molecules at point D have a greater average kinetic energy tan those at point F.
   V. The temperature at point E is called the critical temperature of the compound.
   a) II, V
   b) I, III, IV
   c) I, II, III
   d) II, IV, V
   e) I, II, IV

   ANS: e) I, II, IV   **PAGE:** 10.9

233

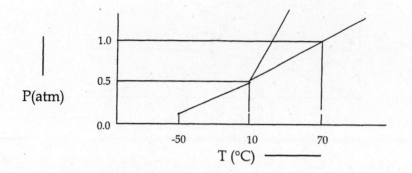

90. A certain substance has the phase diagram shown above. At which of the following
     values of T and P is the substance a pure liquid?

     a) $T = 8°C, P = 1$ atm
     b) $T = 10°ÁC, P = 0.5$ atm
     c) $T = 70°C, P = 1.2$ atm
     d) $T = 80°C, P = 1$ atm
     e) $T = 10°C, P = 1$ atm

     ANS: c) $T = 70°C, P = 1.2$ atm   **PAGE:** 10.9

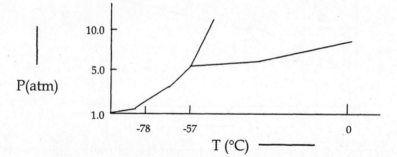

91. A sample consisting of CO_2 (g) and CO_2(s) at equilibrium at $-78°C$ and 1 atm pressure is
     heated to $-30°C$ and the pressure is increased to 8 atm. Based on the phase diagram
     above, what will happen?

     a)   At equilibrium, only CO_2(g) will be present.
     b)   All the CO_2 will be converted to CO_2(l).
     c)   At equilibrium, CO_2(g) and CO_2(l) will be present.
     d)   The melting point of the CO_2(s) will decrease.
     e)   none of these

     ANS: b)   All the CO_2 will be converted to CO_2(l).   **PAGE:** 10.9

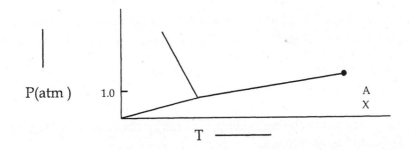

92. Given the above phase diagram, which of the following statements (a–d) is false?

    a) The solid has a higher density than the liquid.
    b) At some (constant) temperature, the gaseous substance can be compressed into a solid and then into a liquid in this order.
    c) When phase A is compressed at constant temperature at point X, no change is observed.
    d) When heated at 1 atm, this substance will first melt, then boil.
    e) None of the above statements is false.

    ANS: a) The solid has a higher density than the liquid.   **PAGE:** 10.9

93. The density of the solid phase of a substance is 0.90 g/cm3 and the density of the liquid phase is 1.0 g/cm^3. A large increase in pressure will

    a) lower the freezing point.
    b) raise the freezing point.
    c) lower the boiling point.
    d) raise the triple point.
    e) lower the triple point.

    ANS: a) lower the freezing point.   **PAGE:** 10.9

94. Make a sketch to show the hydrogen bonding between two acetic acid molecules ($HC_2H_3O_2$).

    PAGE: 10.1

    ANS:

95. The meniscus of mercury curves downward at the edges. Explain using the concepts of cohesion and adhesion.

    ANS: See Sec. 10.2 of Zumdahl, *Chemistry*.   **PAGE:** 10.2

96. 100. g of ice at 0° is added to 300.0 g of water at 60°C. Assuming no transfer of heat to the surroundings, what is the temperature of the liquid water after all the ice has melted?

   ANS: 25.0°C   **PAGE:** 10.8

97. How many grams of ice would be melted by the energy obtained as 18.0 g of steam is condensed at 100°C and cooled to 0°C?

   ANS: 144 g   **PAGE:** 10.8

98. The heat of combustion of bituminous coal is 2.5×10^4 J/g. What quantity of the coal is required to produce the energy to convert 100. pounds of ice at 0°C to steam at 100°C?

   ANS: 5.46 kg   **PAGE:** 10.8

99. Intermolecular forces are weaker than intramolecular bonds.

   ANS: True   **PAGE:** 10.1

100. Hydrogen bonding is a type of London dispersion force.

   ANS: False   **PAGE:** 10.1

101. Methane (CH_4) exhibits stronger hydrogen bond interactions than ammonia (NH_3).

   ANS: False   **PAGE:** 10.1

102. Liquids with large intermolecular forces tend to have high surface tension.

   ANS: True   **PAGE:** 10.2

103. Table salt and table sugar are both crystalline solids.

   ANS: True   **PAGE:** 10.3

104. Atomic solids generally have low melting points.

   ANS: False   **PAGE:** 10.3

105. Ice is a molecular solid.

   ANS: True   **PAGE:** 10.3

106. The net number of spheres in the face-centered cubic unit cell is 4.

   ANS: True   **PAGE:** 10.4

107. Steel is a substitutional alloy.

ANS: False   **PAGE:** 10.4

108. The process of changing from a vapor to a liquid is vaporization.

ANS: False   **PAGE:** 10.8

109. The particularly strong dipole-dipole interaction between hydrogen and nitrogen is known as a _____.

ANS: hydrogen bond   **PAGE:** 10.1

110. The relatively weak forces that exist among noble gas atoms are _____.

ANS: London dispersion forces   **PAGE:** 10.1

111. The resistance of a liquid to an increase in its surface area is the _____ of the liquid.

ANS: surface tension   **PAGE:** 10.2

112. The structures of crystalline solids are most commonly determined by _____.

ANS: X-ray diffraction   **PAGE:** 10.3

113. In a(n) _____ alloy some of the host metal atoms are replaced by other metal atoms of similar size.

ANS: substitutional   **PAGE:** 10.4

114. Iodine moves directly from solid to gas in a process called _____.

ANS: sublimation   **PAGE:** 10.8

1. A solution of hydrogen peroxide is 30.0% H_2O_2 by mass and has a density of 1.11 g/cm^3. The molarity of the solution is:

    a)   7.94 M
    b)   8.82 M
    c)   9.79 M
    d)   0.980 M
    e)   none of these

    ANS: c)   9.79 M   **PAGE:** 11.1

2. The term "proof" is defined as twice the percent by volume of pure ethanol in solution. Thus, a solution that is 95% (by volume) ethanol is 190 proof. What is the molarity of ethanol in a 92 proof ethanol/water solution?

    density of ethanol   = $0.80 \ g/cm^3$
    density of water   = $1.0 \ g/cm^3$
    mol. wt. of ethanol =   46

    a)   0.46 M
    b)   0.80 M
    c)   0.92 M
    d)   8.0 M
    e)   17 M

    ANS: d)   8.0 M   **PAGE:** 11.1

3. In a 0.1 molar solution of NaCl in water, which one of the following will be closest to 0.1?

    a)   the mole fraction of NaCl
    b)   the mass fraction of NaCl
    c)   the mass percent of NaCl
    d)   The molality of NaCl
    e)   all of these are about 0.1

    ANS: d)   the molality of NaCl   **PAGE:** 11.1

4. Calculate the molality of C_2H_5OH in a water solution that is prepared by mixing 50.0 mL of C_2H_5OH with 100.0 mL of H_2O at 20°C. The density of the C_2H_5OH is 0.789 g/mL at 20°C.

    a)   0.086 m
    b)   0.094 m
    c)   1.24 m
    d)   8.56 m
    e)   none of these

    ANS: d)   8.56 m   **PAGE:** 11.1

5. What is the molality of a solution of 50.0 g of propanol ($CH_3CH_2CH_2OH$) in 152 mL water, if the density of water is 1.0 g/mL?

    a)   5.47 m

    b)   0.00547 m

    c)   0.833 m

    d)   0.183 m

    e)   none of these

ANS: a)   5.47 m   **PAGE: 11.1**

6. A solution containing 296.6 g of $Mg(NO_3)_2$ per liter has a density of 1.114 g/mL. The molarity of the solution is:

    a)   2.000 M

    b)   2.446 M

    c)   6.001 M

    d)   1.805 M

    e)   none of these

ANS: a)   2.000 M   **PAGE: 11.1**

7. A solution containing 292 g of $Mg(NO_3)_2$ per liter has a density of 1.108 g/mL. The molality of the solution is:

    a)   2.00 m

    b)   2.41 m

    c)   5.50 m

    d)   6.39 m

    e)   none of these

ANS: b)   2.41 m   **PAGE: 11.1**

8. How many milliliters of 18.4 M H_2SO_4 are needed to prepare 600.0 mL of 0.10 M H_2SO_4?

    a)   1.8 mL

    b)   2.7 mL

    c)   3.3 mL

    d)   4.0 mL

    e)   4.6 mL

ANS: c)   3.3 mL   **PAGE: 11.1**

9. A 20.0-g sample of methyl alcohol (CH_3OH, molar mass = 32.0 g/mol) was dissolved in 30.0 g of water. The mole fraction of CH_3OH is:

    a) 0.400

    b) 0.625

    c) 0.728

    d) 0.667

    e) none of these

    ANS: e)   none of these   **PAGE:** 11.1

10. Which of the following concentration measures will change in value as the temperature of a solution changes?

    a) mass percent

    b) mole fraction

    c) molality

    d) molarity

    e) all of these

    ANS: d)   molarity   **PAGE:** 11.1

11. What is the mole percent of ethanol (C_2H_5OH) in 180 proof vodka, which consists of 71.0 g of ethanol for every 10.0 g of water present?

    a) 73.5%

    b) 71.0%

    c) 87.7%

    d) 26.5%

    e) 22.1%

    ANS: a)   73.5%   **PAGE:** 11.1

12. If 2.00 g of helium gas and 4.00 g of oxygen gas are mixed together what is the mole fraction of helium in the solution?

    a) 0.500

    b) 0.333

    c) 0.800

    d) 0.200

    e) 0.666

    ANS: c)   0.800   **PAGE:** 11.1

13. 3.2 L of an aqueous solution containing 25.00 g of KCl dissolved in pure water is prepared. The molarity of the solution is:

    a) 010 M
    b) 0.46 M
    c) 0.93 M
    d) 1.0 M
    e) 7.8 M

    ANS: a)   0.10 M   **PAGE:** 11.1

14. What volume of a 0.580 M solution of $CaCl_2$ contains 1.28 g of solute?

    a) 2.21 mL
    b) 19.9 mL
    c) 82.3 mL
    d) 100.4 mL
    e) 2.21 L

    ANS: b)   19.9 mL   **PAGE:** 11.1

15. A 3.140 molal solution of NaCl is prepared. How many grams of NaCl are present in a sample containing 3.000 kg of water?

    a) 942.0 g
    b) 755.0 g
    c) 314.0 g
    d) 550.5 g
    e) none of these (a-d)

    ANS: d)   550.5 g   **PAGE:** 11.1

16. Find the mass percent of $CuSO_4$ in a solution whose density is 1.30 g/mL and whose molarity is 1.22 M.

    a) 22.1%
    b) 31.6%
    c) 15.0%
    d) 12.4%
    e) none of these

    ANS: c)   15.0%   **PAGE:** 11.1

17. Rank the following compounds according to increasing solubility in water.

  I. $CH_3-CH_2-CH_2-CH_3$
  II. $CH_3-CH_2-O-CH_2-CH_3$
  III. CH_3-CH_2-OH
  IV. CH_3-OH
  a) I < III < IV < II
  b) I < II < IV < III
  c) III < IV < II < I
  d) I < II < III < IV
  e) No order is correct.

 ANS: d) I < II < III < IV   **PAGE:** 11.2,3

18. Which of the following favors the solubility of an ionic solid in a liquid solvent?

  a) a large magnitude of the solvation energy of the ions
  b) a small magnitude of the lattice energy of the solute
  c) a large polarity of the solvent
  d) all of the above
  e) none of the above

 ANS: d) all of the above   **PAGE:** 11.2

19. When 0.800 g of NH_4NO_3 was added to 150.0 g of water in a Styrofoam cup, the temperature dropped by 0.413°C. The heat capacity of H_2O is 4.18 J/g°C. Assume the specific heat of the solution equals that of pure H_2O and that the calorimeter neither absorbs nor leaks heat. The molar heat of solution of solid NH_4NO_3 is:

  a) +260. J/mol
  b) 26.0 kJ/mol
  c) +2.60 kJ/mol
  d) –2.60 kJ/mol
  e) none of these

 ANS: b) 26.0 kJ/mol   **PAGE:** 11.2

20. Which of the following chemical or physical changes is an endothermic process?

  a) the evaporation of water
  b) the combustion of gasoline
  c) the mixing of sulfuric acid and water
  d) the freezing of water
  e) none of these

 ANS: a) the evaporation of water   **PAGE:** 11.2

21. Which statement about hydrogen bonding is true?

   a) Hydrogen bonding is the intermolecular attractive forces between two hydrogen atoms in solution.

   b) The hydrogen bonding capabilities of water molecules cause $CH_3CH_2CH_2CH_3$ to be more soluble in water than CH_3OH.

   c) Hydrogen bonding of solvent molecules with a solute will not affect the solubility of the solute.

   d) Hydrogen bonding interactions between molecules are stronger than the covalent bonds within the molecule.

   e) Hydrogen bonding arises from the dipole moment created by the unequal sharing of electrons within certain covalent bonds within a molecule.

   ANS: e)   Hydrogen bonding arises from the dipole moment created by the unequal sharing of electrons within certain covalent bonds within a molecule.   **PAGE:** 11.2,3

22. Solid KF has a lattice energy of 804 kJ/mol and a heat of solution (in water) of –15 kJ/mol. RbF has a lattice energy of 768 kJ/mol and a heat of solution (in water) of –24 kJ/mol. Which salt forms stronger attractions with water?

   a) KF, since it has a larger lattice energy

   b) RbF, since it has a smaller lattice energy

   c) KF, since it has a more negative heat of hydration

   d) RbF, since it has a more negative heat of hydration

   e) They form equally strong attractions with water, since they both have negative heats of mixing.

   ANS: d)   RbF, since it has a more negative heat of hydration   **PAGE:** 11.2

23. The lattice energy of NaI is 686 kJ/mol and its heat of solution is –7.6 kJ/mol. Calculate the hydration of energy of NaI(s).

   a) +15.2

   b) –678

   c) –694

   d) +678

   e) +694

   ANS: c)   –694   **PAGE:** 11.2

24. When a substance dissolves in water, heat energy is released if:

   a) the lattice energy is positive.

   b) the hydration energy is positive.

   c) the hydration energy is greater than the lattice energy.

   d) the hydration energy is negative.

   e) none of these (a-d)

   ANS: c)   the hydration energy is greater than the lattice energy.   **PAGE:** 11.2

25. A correct statement of Henry's law is:

   a) the concentration of a gas in solution is inversely proportional to temperature.
   b) the concentration of a gas in solution is directly proportional to the mole fraction of solvent.
   c) the concentration of a gas in solution is independent of pressure.
   d) the concentration of a gas in a solution is inversely proportional to pressure.
   e) none of these

   ANS: e) none of these   **PAGE:** 11.3

26. The solubility of O_2 in water is 0.590 g/L at an oxygen pressure of 15 atm. What is the Henry's law constant for O_2 (in units of L-atm/mol)?

   a) 3.93×10^{-3}
   b) 1.23×10^{-3}
   c) 8.14×10^{2}
   d) 1.26
   e) None of the above are within 5% of the correct answer.

   ANS: c) 8.14×10^{2} **PAGE:** 11.3

27-29. For each of the following solutions, describe the deviation with respect to Raoult's Law. Use the following choices

   a) relatively ideal
   b) positive deviation
   c) negative deviation
   d) More information is needed.
   e) none of these

27. hexane (C_6H_{14}) and chloroform ($CHCl_3$)

   ANS: b) positive deviation   **PAGE:** 11.4

28. acetone (C_3H_6O) and water

   ANS: c) negative deviation   **PAGE:** 11.4

29. hexane (C_6H_{14}) and octane (C_8H_{18})

   ANS: a) relatively ideal   **PAGE:** 11.4

30. At a given temperature, you have a mixture of benzene (vapor pressure of pure benzene = 745 torr) and toluene (vapor pressure of pure toluene = 290. torr). The mole fraction of benzene in the solution is 0.590. Assuming ideal behavior, calculate the mole fraction of toluene in the vapor above the solution.

    a)   0.213
    b)   0.778
    c)   0.641
    d)   0.359
    e)   0.590

    ANS: a)   0.213   **PAGE:** 11.4

31. The vapor pressure of water at 25.0°C is 23.8 torr. Determine the mass of glucose (molar mass = 180 g/mol) needed to add to 500.0 g of water to change the vapor pressure to 23.1 torr.

    a)   72 g
    b)   152 g
    c)   103 g
    d)   115 g
    e)   36 g

    ANS: b)   152 g   **PAGE:** 11.4

32. 150 g of NaCl completely dissolves (producing Na+ and Cl– ions) in 1.00 kg of water at 25.0□C. The vapor pressure of pure water at this temperature is 23.8 torr. Determine the vapor pressure of the solution.

    a)   21.8 torr
    b)   22.5 torr
    c)   20.6 torr
    d)   19.7 torr
    e)   23.1 torr

    ANS: a)   21.8 torr   **PAGE:** 11.4

33. At a given temperature, you have a mixture of benzene (vapor pressure of pure benzene = 745 torr) and toluene (vapor pressure of pure toluene = 290 torr). The mole fraction of benzene in the vapor above the solution is 0.590. Assuming ideal behavior, calculate the mole fraction of toluene in the solution.

    a)   0.213
    b)   0.778
    c)   0.641
    d)   0.359
    e)   0.590

    ANS: c)   0.641   **PAGE:** 11.4

34. At 40°C, heptane has a vapor pressure of 92.0 torr and octane has a vapor pressure of 31.2 torr. Assuming ideal behavior, what is the vapor pressure of a solution that contains twice as many moles of heptane as octane?

    a)   61.6 torr

    b)   51.5 torr

    c)   71.7 torr

    d)   76.8 torr

    e)   none of these

    ANS: c)   71.7 torr   **PAGE:** 11.4

35. A solution is prepared from 31.4 g of a nonvolatile, nondissociating solute and 85.0 g of water. The vapor pressure of the solution at 60□C is (142 torr). The vapor pressure of water at 60°C is 150. torr. What is the molar mass of the solute?

    ANS: 118 g/mol   **PAGE:** 11.4

36. A solution contains 1 mole of liquid A and 3 mol of liquid B. This solution has a vapor pressure of 314 torr at 25°C. At 25°C, liquid A has a vapor pressure of 265 torr and liquid B has a vapor pressure of 355 torr. Which of the following is true?

    a)   This solution exhibits a positive deviation from Raoult's Law.

    b)   This solution exhibits a negative deviation from Raoult's Law.

    c)   This solution is ideal.

    d)   More information is needed to answer this question.

    e)   None of these (a-d)

    ANS: b)   This solution exhibits a negative deviation from Raoult's
            Law.   **PAGE:** 11.4

37.
                               Vapor pressure at 25°C

    benzene (C_6H_6)   94.4 torr
    chloroform ($CHCl_3$)   172.0 torr

    Using the above data, calculate the vapor pressure of chloroform over a chloroform-benzene solution at 25°C, which contains 50.0 g $CHCl_3$ and 50.0 g C_6H_6. Assume the solution behaves ideally.

    a)   68.0 torr

    b)   125 torr

    c)   148 torr

    d)   172 torr

    e)   none of these

    ANS: a)   68.0 torr   **PAGE:** 11.4

38–40. Solutions of benzene and toluene obey Raoult's law. The vapor pressures at 20°C are: benzene, 76 torr; toluene, 21 torr.

38. What is the mole fraction of benzene in a solution whose vapor pressure is 50 torr at 20°C?

    a)   0.28
    b)   0.47
    c)   0.53
    d)   0.72
    e)   0.76

    ANS: c)   0.53   **PAGE:** 11.4

39. If the mole fraction of benzene in a particular solution is 0.53, what is the mole fraction of benzene in the vapor phase in equilibrium with that solution?

    a)   0.28
    b)   0.47
    c)   0.50
    d)   0.53
    e)   0.80

    ANS: e)   0.80   **PAGE:** 11.4

40. The vapor pressure of water at 90°C is 0.692 atm. What is the vapor pressure (in atm) of a solution made by dissolving 1.00 mole of CsF(s) in 1.00 kg of water? Assume that Raoult's law applies.

    a)   0.692 atm
    b)   0.680 atm
    c)   0.668 atm
    d)   0.656 atm
    e)   none of these

    ANS: c)   0.668 atm   **PAGE:** 11.4,7

41. A solution consists of a mixture of benzene and toluene and is allowed to come to equilibrium with its vapor. The vapor is then condensed and found to contain 50.0 mole percent of each component. Calculate the composition (mole percent) of the original solution. The vapor pressures of pure benzene and toluene at this temperature are 750. torr and 300. torr, respectively.

    a)   50.2% benzene
    b)   28.6% benzene
    c)   71.0% benzene
    d)   40.0% benzene
    e)   none of these

    ANS: b)   28.6% benzene   **PAGE:** 11.4

42. A solution is made by adding 0.100 mole of ethyl ether to 0.500 mole of ethyl alcohol. If the vapor pressure of ethyl ether and ethyl alcohol at 20°C are 375 torr and 20.0 torr, respectively, the vapor pressure of the solution at 20°C (assuming ideal behavior) is:

    a) 79.2 torr
    b) 316 torr
    c) 47.5 torr
    d) 395 torr
    e) none of these

    ANS: a)   79.2 torr   **PAGE:** 11.4

43. A salt solution sits in an open beaker. Assuming constant temperature and pressure, the vapor pressure of the solution

    a) increases over time.
    b) decreases over time.
    c) stays the same over time.
    d) Need to know which salt is in the solution to answer this.
    e) Need to know the temperature and pressure to answer this.

    ANS: b)   decreases over time.   **PAGE:** 11.4

44. You dissolve 2.0 g of solid MX in 250. g of water. You find the freezing point to be –0.028°C. Calculate the K_{sp} of the solid.

    a) 5.6×10^{-5}
    b) 7.1×10^{-7}
    c) 2.2×10^{-4}
    d) 6.3×10^{-5}
    e) none of these

    ANS: a) 5.6×10^{-5} **PAGE:** 11.5,7

45. You have a 10.40-g mixture of table sugar ($C_{12}H_{22}O_{11}$) and table salt (NaCl). When this mixture is dissolved in 150. g of water, the freezing point is found to be –2.24°C. Calculate the percent by mass of sugar in the original mixture.

    a) 39.0%
    b) 43.8%
    c) 56.2%
    d) 61.0%
    e) none of these

    ANS: c)   56.2%   **PAGE:** 11.5,7

46. We can predict the solubility of a compound by looking at the sign of the enthalpy of solution.

    ANS: False   **PAGE:** 11.2

47. Adding salt to water decreases the freezing point of the water since it lowers the vapor pressure of the ice.

    ANS: False   **PAGE:** 11.5

48. A solution of two liquids, A and B, shows negative deviation from Raoult's law. This means that

    a) the molecules of A interact strongly with other A-type molecules.
    b) the two liquids have a positive heat of solution.
    c) molecules of A interact weakly, if at all, with B molecules.
    d) the molecules of A hinder the strong interaction between B molecules.
    e) molecules of A interact more strongly with B than A with A or B with B.

    ANS: e)   molecules of A interact more strongly with B with
                    A or B with B.   **PAGE:** 11.4

49. Benzene and toluene form an ideal solution. At 298 K, what is the mole fraction of benzene in the liquid that is in equilibrium with a vapor that has equal partial pressures of benzene and toluene? At 298 K, the vapor pressures of pure benzene and pure toluene are 95 and 28 torr, respectively.

    a) 0.50
    b) 0.77
    c) 0.23
    d) 0.30
    e) none of these

    ANS: c)   0.23   **PAGE:** 11.4

50. A solution of CF_3H in H_2CO would most likely

    a) be ideal.
    b) show positive deviations from Raoult's law.
    c) show negative deviations from Raoult's law.
    d) not be ideal, but the deviations cannot be predicted.
    e) obey Raoult's law.

    ANS: c)   show negative deviations from Raoult's law.   **PAGE:** 11.4

51. A 5.50-gram sample of a compound as dissolved in 250. grams of benzene. The freezing point of this solution is 1.02°C below that of pure benzene. What is the molar mass of this compound? (*Note:* K_f for benzene = 5.12°C/m.)

    a) 22.0 g/mol
    b) 110. g/mol
    c) 220. g/mol
    d) 44.0 g/mol
    e) none of these

    ANS: b)   110. g/mol   **PAGE:** 11.5

52. What is the boiling point change for a solution containing 0.328 moles of naphthalene (a nonvolatile, nonionizing compound) in 250. g of liquid benzene? ($K_b = 2.53°C/m$ for benzene)

    a)   3.32°C
    b)   7.41°C
    c)   1.93°C
    d)   4.31°C
    e)   10.7°C

    ANS: a)   3.32°C   **PAGE:** 11.5

53. Thyroxine, an important hormone that controls the rate of metabolism in the body, can be isolated from the thyroid gland. If 0.455 g of thyroxine is dissolved in 10.0 g of benzene, the freezing point of the solution is 5.144°C. Pure benzene freezes at 5.444°C and has a value for the molal freezing point depression constant of K_f of 5.12°C/m. What is the molar mass of thyroxine?

    a)   777,000 g/mol
    b)   777 g/mol
    c)   2330 g/mol
    d)   285 g/mol
    e)   3760 g/mol

    ANS: b)   777 g/mol   **PAGE:** 11.5

54. When a 20.0-g sample of an unknown compound is dissolved in 500. g of benzene, the freezing point of the resulting solution of 3.77°C. The freezing point of pure benzene is 5.48°C and K_f for benzene is 5.12°C/m. Calculate the molar mass of the unknown compound.

    a)   160. g/mol
    b)   80.0 g/mol
    c)   100. g/mol
    d)   140. g/mol
    e)   120. g/mol

    ANS: e)   120. g/mol   **PAGE:** 11.5

55. To calculate the freezing point of an ideal dilute solution of a single, nondissociating solute of a solvent, the minimum information one must know is:

    a)   the molality (of the solute).
    b)   the molality (of the solute) and the freezing point depression constant of the solvent.
    c)   the same quantities as in b plus the freezing point of the pure solvent.
    d)   all of the quantities in c plus the molecular weight of the solute.
    e)   all of the quantities in c plus the weight of the solvent.

    ANS: c)   the same quantities as in b plus the freezing point of the
                 pure solvent.   **PAGE:** 11.5

56. A liquid-liquid solution is called an ideal solution if

   I.   it obeys $PV = nRT$.
   II. it obeys Raoult's law.
   III. solute-solute, solvent-solvent, and solute-solvent interactions are very similar.
   IV. solute-solute, solvent-solvent, and solute-solvent interactions are quite different.
   a) I, II, III
   b) I, II, IV
   c) II, III
   d) II, IV
   e) I, II, III

   ANS: c) II, III   **PAGE:** 11.4

57. Liquid A and liquid B form a solution that behaves ideally according to Raoult's law. The vapor pressures of the pure substances A and B are 205 torr and 135 torr, respectively. Determine the vapor pressure over the solution if 1.20 moles of liquid A is added to 5.30 moles of liquid B.

   a) 148 torr
   b) 193 torr
   c) 167 torr
   d) 139 torr
   e) 151 torr

   ANS: a) 148 torr   **PAGE:** 11.4

58. Two liquids form a solution and release a quantity of heat. How does the pressure above the solution compare to that predicted by Raoult's law?

   a) It will be greater.
   b) It will be less.
   c) It will be the same.
   d) It will show positive deviation.
   e) none of these.

   ANS: b) It will be less.   **PAGE:** 11.4

59. Determine the change in boiling point for 300.0 g of carbon disulfide (K_b = 2.34°C kg/mol) if 35 g of a nonvolatile, nonionizing compound is dissolved in it. The molar mass of the compound is 70.0 g/mol and the boiling point of the pure carbon disulfide is 46.2°C.

   a) 13.4°C
   b) 10.9°C
   c) 7.7°C
   d) 15.6°C
   e) 3.9°C

   ANS: e) 3.9°C   **PAGE:** 11.5

60. All of the following are colligative properties except:

    a) osmotic pressure
    b) boiling point elevation
    c) freezing point depression
    d) density elevation
    e) none of these

    ANS: d)   density elevation   **PAGE:** 11.5,6

61. Determine the mass of a nonvolatile, nonionizing compound that must be added to 3.00 kg of water to lower the freezing point to 98.7°C. The molar mass of the compound is 50.0 g/mol and the K_f for water is 1.86°C kg/mol.

    a) 162 g
    b) 105 g
    c) 22 g
    d) 72 g
    e) 14 g

    ANS: b)   105 g   **PAGE:** 11.5

62. The freezing point (T_f) for t-butanol is 25.50°C and K_f is 9.1°C/m. Usually t-butanol absorbs water on exposure to the air. If the freezing point of a 10.0-g sample t-butanol is measured as 24.59°C, how many grams of water are present in the sample?

    a) 0.10 g
    b) 0.018 g
    c) 10 g
    d) 1.8 g
    e) 18. g

    ANS: b)   0.018 g   **PAGE:** 11.5

63. The molar mass of a solid as determined by freezing point depression is 10% higher than the true molar mass. Which of the following experimental errors could not account for this discrepancy?

    a) Not all the solid was dissolved.
    b) More than the recorded amount of solvent was pipetted into the solution.
    c) The solid dissociated slightly into two particles when it dissolved.
    d) Some solid was left on the weighing paper.
    e) Before the solution was prepared, the container was rinsed with solvent and not dried.

    ANS: c)   The solid dissociated slightly into two particles when it
                      dissolved.   **PAGE:** 11.5,7

64. Which of the following will cause the calculated molar mass of a compound determined by the freezing point depression method to be greater than the true molar mass?

    a) Water gets into the solvent after the freezing point of the pure solvent is determined.
    b) Some of the solute molecules break apart.
    c) The mass of solvent is smaller than determined from the weighing.
    d) While adding the solute, some was spilled on the lab bench.
    e) all of the above

    ANS: d)   While adding the solute, some was spilled on the lab bench.   **PAGE:** 11.5

65. When a nonvolatile solute is added to a volatile solvent, the solution vapor pressure _____, the boiling point _____, the freezing point _____, and the osmotic pressure across a semipermeable membrane _____.

    a) decreases, increases, decreases, decreases
    b) increases, increases, decreases, increases
    c) increases, decreases, increases, decreases
    d) decreases, decreases, increases, decreases
    e) decreases, increases, decreases, increases

    ANS: e)   decreases, increases, decreases, increases   **PAGE:** 11.5,6

66. A solute added to a solvent raises the boiling point of the solution because

    a) the temperature to cause boiling must be great enough to boil not only the solvent but also the solute.
    b) the solute particles lower the solvent's vapor pressure, thus requiring a higher temperature to cause boiling.
    c) the solute particles raise the solvent's vapor pressure, thus requiring a higher temperature to cause boiling.
    d) the solute increases the volume of the solution, and an increase in volume requires an increase in the temperature to reach the boiling point (derived from $PV = nRT$).
    e) two of the above are correct.

    ANS: b)   the solute particles lower the solvent's vapor pressure, thus requiring a higher temperature to cause boiling.   **PAGE:** 11.5

67. A cucumber is placed in a concentrated salt solution. What will most likely happen?

    a) Water will flow from the cucumber to the solution.
    b) Water will flow from the solution to the cucumber.
    c) Salt will flow into the cucumber.
    d) Salt will precipitate out.
    e) No change will occur.

    ANS: a)   Water will flow from the cucumber to the solution.   **PAGE:** 11.6

68. Polyethylene is a synthetic polymer or plastic with many uses. 1.40 g of a polyethylene sample was dissolved in enough benzene to make 100. mL of solution, and the osmotic pressure was found to be 1.86 torr at 25°C. What is the molar mass of the polyethylene?

    a) 1.06×10^8 g/mol
    b) 1.19×10^4 g/mol
    c) 5720 g/mol
    d) 3.39×10^6 g/mol
    e) 1.40×10^5 g/mol

    ANS: e) 1.40×10^5 g/mol   **PAGE:** 11.6

69. A 0.2 molar solution of a solute, X, in benzene, displays an osmotic pressure given by the formula $\pi = (0.1)RT$. Which of the following is most likely to be the case?

    a) X exists in benzene as X.
    b) X exists in benzene as X_2.
    c) X exists in benzene dissociated into two particles.
    d) This solution strongly deviates from ideal behavior.
    e) None of these is plausible.

    ANS: b)   X exists in benzene as X_2.   **PAGE:** 11.6

70. Osmotic pressure depends on all but which of the following?

    a) atmospheric pressure
    b) the molarity of the solution
    c) temperature
    d) the ratio of moles of solute to solution volume
    e) none of these

    ANS: a)   atmospheric pressure   **PAGE:** 11.6

71. A solution of water and a nonvolatile, nonionizing compound is placed in a tube with a semipermeable membrane on one side. The tube is placed in a beaker of pure water. What initial net effect will occur?

    a) Water will flow from the beaker to the tube.
    b) Water will flow from the tube to the beaker.
    c) The compound will pass through the membrane into the solution.
    d) Nothing will move through the membrane either way.
    e) Equilibrium is immediately established.

    ANS: a)   Water will flow from the beaker to the tube.   **PAGE:** 11.6

72. Determine the osmotic pressure of a solution that contains 0.025 g of a hydrocarbon solute (molar mass = 340 g/mole) dissolved in benzene to make a 350-mL solution. The temperature is 20.0°C.

    a) 1.1 torr
    b) 1.6 torr
    c) 2.2 torr
    d) 3.8 torr
    e) 4.4 torr

    ANS: d)   3.8 torr   **PAGE:** 11.6

73. Solutions that have identical osmotic pressures are called _____ solutions.

    a) hypertonic
    b) isotonic
    c) hypotonic
    d) hemolytic
    e) dyalitic

    ANS: b)   isotonic   **PAGE:** 11.6

74. Calculate the molarity of a solution containing KCl and water whose osmotic pressure at 21°C is 100 torr. Assume complete dissociation of the salt.

    a) 0.005 M
    b) 0.01 M
    c) 0.08 M
    d) 0.0025 M
    e) 0.0002 M

    ANS: d)   0.0025 M   **PAGE:** 11.7

75. Consider pure water separated from an aqueous sugar solution by a semipermeable membrane, which allows water to pass freely but not sugar. After some time has passed, the concentration of sugar solution:

    a) will have increased.
    b) will have decreased.
    c) will not have changed.
    d) might have increased or decreased depending on other factors.
    e) will be the same on both sides of the membrane.

    ANS: b)   will have decreased.   **PAGE:** 11.6

76. A 5.00-gram sample of a compound is dissolved in enough water to form 100.0 mL of solution. This solution has an osmotic pressure of 25 torr at 25°C. If it is assumed that each molecule of the solute dissociates into two particles (in this solvent), what is the molar mass of this solute?

    a) 1560 g/mol
    b) 18,600 g/mol
    c) 37,200 g/mol
    d) 74,400 g/mol
    e) none of these

ANS: d)   74,400 g/mol   **PAGE:** 11.7

77. Calculate the osmotic pressure (in torr) of 6.00 L of an aqueous 0.108 M solution at 30. °C, if the solute concerned is totally ionized into three ions (e.g., it could be Na_2SO_4 or $MgCl_2$).

    a) 8.05
    b) 6.12×10^3
    c) 2.04×10^3
    d) 3.68×10^4
    e) none of these

ANS: b) 6.12×10^3 **PAGE:** 11.7

78. A 0.20 M solution of $MgSO_4$ has an observed osmotic pressure of 7.8 atm at 25°C. Determine the observed van't Hoff factor for this experiment.

    a) 1.2
    b) 1.4
    c) 1.6
    d) 1.8
    e) 2.0

ANS: c)   1.6   **PAGE:** 11.7

79. The observed van't Hoff factor for an electrolyte is less than the expected factor because of _____.

    a) electrolytic repulsion
    b) complete dissociation
    c) coagulation
    d) ion pairing
    e) gelation

ANS: d)   ion pairing   **PAGE:** 11.7

80. Shaving cream is an example of which colloid type?

   a)   aerosol
   b)   foam
   c)   emulsion
   d)   sol
   e)   coagulate

   ANS: b)   foam   **PAGE:** 11.8

81. The most likely reason for colloidal dispersion is _____.

   a)   the Tyndall effect
   b)   coagulation
   c)   precipitation
   d)   emulsion formation
   e)   electrostatic repulsion

   ANS: e)   electrostatic repulsion   **PAGE:** 11.8

82. The osmotic pressure of a 0.0100 M solution of NaCl in water at 25°C is found to be different from 372 torr because:

   a)   osmotic pressures are hard to measure.
   b) Na^+ and Cl^- ions are strongly hydrated.
   c) Na^+ and Cl^- ions can form ion pairs.
   d)   NaCl does not dissociate in water.
   e)   none of these

   ANS: c) Na^+ and Cl^- ions can form ion pairs.   **PAGE:** 11.7

83. How many molecules of sucrose (table sugar), $C_{12}H_{22}O_{11}$, dissolved in 450.0 g of water are needed to make a 1.75-m solution?

   ANS: 4.74×10^{23} molecules   **PAGE:** 11.1

84. What is the percentage by mass of ethanol (C_2H_5OH) in a 1.5-m solution?

   ANS: 6.5%   **PAGE:** 11.1

85. Calculate the molarity of a solution of magnesium chloride with a concentration of 25.0 mg/mL.

   ANS: 0.263 M   **PAGE:** 11.1

86. What is the molarity of a HNO_3 solution prepared by adding 250.0 mL of water to 350.0 mL of 12.3 M HNO_3?

   ANS: 7.18 M   **PAGE:** 11.1

257

87. Determine the molarity of a solution containing 4.56 g $BaCl_2$ in 750.0 mL of solution.

   ANS: 2.92×10^{-2} M   **PAGE:** 11.1

88. Calculate the mole fraction of solvent and solute in a solution prepared by dissolving 117 g NaCl in 3.00 kg H_2O.

   ANS: NaCl = 1.18×10^{-2} H_2O = 9.9×10^{-1} **PAGE:** 11.1

89. Calculate the mole fraction of H_2SO_4 in 9.61 M H_2SO_4. The density of the solution is 1.520 g/L.

   ANS: 0.230   **PAGE:** 11.1

90. Diagram and label a vapor pressure diagram for an ideal solution of two volatile liquids. Indicate the deviation predicted by an endothermic heat of solution.

   ANS: positive deviation; see Sec. 11.4 of Zumdahl, *Chemistry*.   **PAGE:** 11.4

91. Consider a solution containing liquids A and B where the mole fraction of B is 0.60. Assuming ideality, calculate the mole fractions of A and B in the vapor at equilibrium with this solution at 25°C. (The vapor pressures of pure liquid A and B at 25°C are 200. torr and 400. torr, respectively.)

   ANS: P_{total} $= X_a P\square_a + X_b P\square_b$

   $= (0.40) (200.) + (0.60) (400.)$

   $= 80. + 240 = 320$

   $X_a = 80./320 = 0.25$

   $X_b = 240/320 = 0.75$ **PAGE:** 11.4

92. Assuming ideality, calculate the vapor pressure of a 1.00 molal solution of a nonvolatile solute in water at 50°C. (The vapor pressure of water at 50°C is 92.5 torr.)

   ANS: mole fraction of water = $X_{H_2O} = \dfrac{55.5}{(55.5 + 1.0)} = 0.982$

   $0.982 \times 92.5 = 90.8$ torr   **PAGE:** 11.4

93. A chemist is given a white solid that is suspected of being pure cocaine. When 1.22 g of the solid is dissolved in 15.60 g of benzene the freezing point is lowered by 1.32°C. Calculate the molar mass of the solid. The molal freezing point constant (K_f) for benzene is 5.12°C/m.

ANS: $\Delta T = K_f m = 1.32 = 5.12\ m$

$$m = \frac{1.32}{5.12} = 0.2578 \text{ mol/kg benzene}$$

$$\frac{.2578 \text{ mol}}{1 \text{ kg}} = \frac{X \text{ mol}}{.01560 \text{ kg}} ; X = 4.022 \times 10^{-3}$$

1.22 g = 4.022×10^{-3} mol

1 mol = 303 g   **PAGE: 11.5**

94. A chemist is given a white solid that is suspected of being pure cocaine (molar mass = 303.35 g/mol). When 1.22 g of the solid is dissolved in 15.60 g of benzene the freezing point is lowered by 1.32°C. The molar mass is calculated from these data to be 303 g. Assuming the following uncertainties, can the chemist be sure the substance is not codeine (molar mass 299.36)? K_f for benzene is 5.12°C/m.

        Uncertainties

        Mass of solid = ±0.01 g

        Mass of benzene = ±0.01 g

        ΔT (freezing point lowering) = ±0.04°C

        K_f = ±0.01

        Support your answer with calculations.

ANS: We want to find the minimum molar mass given these errors.
        First we want the largest possible m value.

$$m = \frac{\Delta T}{K_f} = \frac{1.36}{5.11} = .2661$$

        max mol present = $.2661 \times .01561 = 4.154 \times 10^{-3}$

$$\text{molar mass} = \frac{1.21 \text{g (min value)}}{4.154 \times 10^{-3}} = 291 \text{ g}$$

        Clearly, the solid could be codeine.   **PAGE: 11.5**

95. What is the molar mass of glucose if 22.5 g gives a freezing point of –0.930°C when dissolved in 250.0 g of water? If the empirical formula is CH_2O, what is the molecular formula?

ANS: 180. g/mol, $C_6H_{12}O_6$ **PAGE: 11.5**

96. Calculate both the boiling point and the freezing point if 46.0 g of glycerol, $C_3H_5(OH)_3$, is dissolved in 500.0 g of H_2O.

    ANS: freezing point = –1.86°C   boiling point = 101°C   **PAGE:** 11.5

97. When 92.0 g of a compound is dissolved in 1000. g of water, the freezing point of the solution is lowered to –3.72°C. Determine the molar mass of the compound.

    ANS: 46.0 g/mol   **PAGE:** 11.5

98. The solubility of a gas usually increases with increasing temperature.

    ANS: False   **PAGE:** 11.3

99. A solution with a positive enthalpy of solution (ΔH_{soln}) is expected to show positive deviations from Raoult's law.

    ANS: True   **PAGE:** 11.4

1. The average rate of disappearance of ozone in the reaction $2O_3(g) \rightarrow 3O_2(g)$ is found to be 9.0×10^{-3} atm over a certain interval of time. What is the rate of appearance of O_2 during this interval?

    a) 1.3×10^{-2} atm/s
    b) 9.0×10^{-3} atm/s
    c) 6.0×10^{-3} atm/s
    d) 3.0×10^{-5} atm/s
    e) 2.7×10^{-5} atm/s

    ANS: a) 1.3×10^{-2} atm/s   **PAGE:** 12.1

2. The balanced equation for the reaction of bromate ion with bromide in acidic solution is given by:

    $$BrO_3^- + 5Br^- + 6H^+ \rightarrow 3Br_2 + 3H_2O$$

    At a particular instant in time, the value of $-\Delta[Br^-]/\Delta t$ is 2.0×10^{-3} mol/L $\cdot$ s. What is the value of $\Delta[Br_2]/\Delta t$ in the same units?

    a) 1.2×10^{-3}
    b) 6.0×10^{-3}
    c) 3.3×10^{-3}
    d) 3.3×10^{-5}
    e) 2.0×10^{-3}

    ANS: a) 1.2×10^{-3} **PAGE:** 12.1

3. Consider the reaction $2H_2 + O_2 \rightarrow 2H_2O$

    What is the ratio of the initial rate of the appearance of water to the initial rate of disappearance of oxygen?

    a) $1:1$
    b) $2:1$
    c) $1:2$
    d) $2:2$
    e) $3:2$

    ANS: b) $2:1$ **PAGE:** 12.1

4. Consider the reaction: $4NH_3 + 7O_2 \rightarrow 4NO_2 + 6H_2O$

At a certain instant the initial rate of disappearance of the oxygen gas is X. What is the value of the appearance of water at the same instant?

a) 1.2 X
b) 1.1 X
c) 0.86 X
d) 0.58 X
e) cannot be determined from the data

ANS: c)   0.86 X   **PAGE:** 12.1

5. Consider the reaction $X \rightarrow Y + Z$

Which of the following is a possible rate law?

a) Rate = $k[X]$
b) Rate = $k[Y]$
c) Rate = $k[Y][Z]$
d) Rate = $k[X][Y]$
e) Rate = $k[Z]$

ANS: a)   Rate = $k[X]$ **PAGE:** 12.2

6. Consider the following rate law: Rate = $k[A]^n[B]^m$

How are the exponents n and m determined?

a) By using the balanced chemical equation
b) By using the subscripts for the chemical formulas
c) By using the coefficients of the chemical formulas
d) By educated guess
e) By experiment

ANS: e)   By experiment   **PAGE:** 12.2

7. The following data were obtained for the reaction of NO with O_2. Concentrations are in molecules/cm^3 and rates are in molecules/$cm^3 \cdot$ s.

$[NO]_0$	$[O_2]_0$	Initial Rate
1×10^{18}	1×10^{18}	2.0×10^{16}
2×10^{18}	1×10^{18}	8.0×10^{16}
3×10^{18}	1×10^{18}	18.0×10^{16}
1×10^{18}	2×10^{18}	4.0×10^{16}
1×10^{18}	3×10^{18}	6.0×10^{16}

Which of the following is the correct rate law?

a) Rate = $k[NO][O_2]$
b) Rate = $k[NO][O_2]^2$
c) Rate = $k[NO]^2[O_2]$
d) Rate = $k[NO]^2$
e) Rate = $k[NO]^2[O_2]^2$

ANS: c) Rate = $k[NO]^2[O_2]$ **PAGE:** 12.3

8. The reaction of $(CH_3)_3CBr$ with hydroxide ion proceeds with the formation of $(CH_3)_3COH$.

$$(CH_3)_3CBr(aq) + OH^-(aq) \rightarrow (CH_3)_3COH(aq) + Br^-(aq)$$

The following data were obtained at 55□C.

Exp.	$[(CH_3)_3CBr]_0$ (mol/L)	$[OH^-]_0$ (mol/L)	Initial Rate (mol/L s)
1	0.10	0.10	1.0×10^{-3}
2	0.20	0.10	2.0×10^{-3}
3	0.10	0.20	1.0×10^{-3}
4	0.30	0.20	?

What will the initial rate (in mol/L $\cdot$ s) be in Experiment 4?

a) 3.0×10^{-3}
b) 6.0×10^{-3}
c) 9.0×10^{-3}
d) 18×10^{-3}
e) none of these

ANS: a) 3.0×10^{-3} **PAGE:** 12.3

9. For a reaction in which A and B react to form C, the following initial rate data were obtained:

[A] (mol/L)	[B] (mol/L)	Initial Rate of Formation of C (mol/L · s)
0.10	0.10	1.00
0.10	0.20	4.00
0.20	0.20	8.00

What is the rate law for the reaction?

a) Rate = $k[A][B]$

b) Rate = $k[A]^2[B]$

c) Rate = $k[A][B]^2$

d) Rate = $k[A]^2[B]^2$

e) Rate = $k[A]^3$

ANS: c)   Rate = $k[A][B]^2$ **PAGE:** 12.3

10. Tabulated below are initial rate data for the reaction

$$2Fe(CN)_6^{3-} + 2I^- \rightarrow 2Fe(CN)_6^{4-} + I_2$$

Run	$[Fe(CN)_6^{3-}]_0$	$[I^-]_0$	$[Fe(CN)_6^{4-}]_0$	$[I_2]_0$	Initial Rate (M/s)
1	0.01	0.01	0.01	0.01	1×10^{-5}
2	0.01	0.02	0.01	0.01	2×10^{-5}
3	0.02	0.02	0.01	0.01	8×10^{-5}
4	0.02	0.02	0.02	0.01	8×10^{-5}
5	0.02	0.02	0.02	0.02	8×10^{-5}

The experimental rate law is:

a) $\dfrac{\Delta[I_2]}{\Delta t} = k[Fe(CN)_6^{3-}]^2[I^-]^2[Fe(CN)_6^{4-}]^2[I_2]$

b) $\dfrac{\Delta[I_2]}{\Delta t} = k[Fe(CN)_6^{3-}]^2[I^-][Fe(CN)_6^{4-}][I_2]$

c) $\dfrac{\Delta[I_2]}{\Delta t} = k[Fe(CN)_6^{3-})]^2[I^-]$

d) $\dfrac{\Delta[I_2]}{\Delta t} = k[Fe(CN)_6^{3-}][I^-]^2$

e) $\dfrac{\Delta[I_2]}{\Delta t} = k[Fe(CN)_6^{3-}][I^-] [Fe(CN)_6^{4-}]$

ANS: c) $\dfrac{\Delta[I_2]}{\Delta t} = k[Fe(CN)_6^{3-}]^2[I^-]$ **PAGE:** 12.3

11. Tabulated below are initial rate data for the reaction

$$2Fe(CN)_6^{3-} + 2I^- \rightarrow 2Fe(CN)_6^{4-} + I_2$$

Run	$[Fe(CN)_6^{3-}]_0$	$[I^-]_0$	$[Fe(CN)_6^{4-}]_0$	$[I_2]_0$	Initial Rate (M/s)
1	0.01	0.01	0.01	0.01	1×10^{-5}
2	0.01	0.02	0.01	0.01	2×10^{-5}
3	0.02	0.02	0.01	0.01	8×10^{-5}
4	0.02	0.02	0.02	0.01	8×10^{-5}
5	0.02	0.02	0.02	0.02	8×10^{-5}

The value of k is:

a) $10^7 \, M^{-5} \, s^{-1}$
b) $10^3 \, M^{-3} \, s^{-1}$
c) $10 \, M^{-2} \, s^{-1}$
d) $50 \, M^{-2} \, s^{-1}$
e) none of these

ANS: c) $10 \, M^{-2} \, s^{-1}$ **PAGE:** 12.3

12-17. A general reaction written as $1A + 2B \rightarrow C + 2D$ is studied and yields the following data:

$[A]_0$	$[B]_0$	Initial $\Delta[C]/\Delta t$
0.150 M	0.150 M	8.00×10^{-3} mol/L $\cdot$ s
0.150 M	0.300 M	1.60×10^{-2} mol/L $\cdot$ s
0.300 M	0.150 M	3.20×10^{-2} mol/L $\cdot$ s

12. What is the order of the reaction with respect to B?

a) 0
b) 1
c) 2
d) 3
e) 4

ANS: b)   1   **PAGE:** 12.3

13. What is the order of the reaction with respect to A?

a) 0
b) 1
c) 2
d) 3
e) 4

ANS: c)   2   **PAGE:** 12.3

265

14. What is the overall order of the reaction?

   a) 0
   b) 1
   c) 2
   d) 3
   e) 4

ANS: d)   3   **PAGE:** 12.3

15. What is the numerical value of the rate constant?

   a) 0.053
   b) 1.19
   c) 2.37
   d) 5.63
   e) none of these (a-d)

ANS: c)   2.37   **PAGE:** 12.3

16. Determine the initial rate of B consumption ($\Delta[B]/\Delta t$) for the first trial?

   a) 8.00×10^{-3} mol/L $\cdot$ s
   b) 1.60×10^{-2} mol/L $\cdot$ s
   c) 3.20×10^{-2} mol/L $\cdot$ s
   d) 4.00×10^{-3} mol/L $\cdot$ s
   e) none of these (a-d)

ANS: b) 1.60×10^{-2} mol/L $\cdot$ s   **PAGE:** 12.3

17. Determine the initial rate of C production ($\Delta[C]/\Delta t$) if [A] = 0.200 M and [B] = 0.500 M ?

   a) 4.74×10^{-2} mol/L $\cdot$ s
   b) 2.37×10^{-1} mol/L $\cdot$ s
   c) 1.19×10^{-1} mol/L $\cdot$ s
   d) 8.23×10^{-2} mol/L $\cdot$ s
   e) none of these (a-d)

ANS: a) 4.74×10^{-2} mol/L $\cdot$ s   **PAGE:** 12.3,4

18-20. Consider the following data concerning the equation:

$$H_2O_2 + 3I^- + 2H^+ \rightarrow I_3^- + 2H_2O$$

	$[H_2O_2]$	$[I^-]$	$[H^+]$	rate
I	0.100 M	5.00×10^{-4} M	1.00×10^{-2} M	0.137 M/sec
II.	0.100 M	1.00×10^{-3} M	1.00×10^{-2} M	0.268 M/sec
III.	0.200 M	1.00×10^{-3} M	1.00×10^{-2} M	0.542 M/sec
IV.	0.400 M	1.00×10^{-3} M	2.00×10^{-2} M	1.084 M/sec

18. The rate law for this reaction is

    a)   rate = $k[H_2O_2][I^-][H^+]$
    b)   rate = $k[H_2O_2]^2[I^-]^2[H^+]^2$
    c)   rate = $k[I^-][H^+]$
    d)   rate = $k[H_2O_2][H^+]$
    e)   rate = $k[H_2O_2][I^-]$

    ANS: e)   rate = $k[H_2O_2][I^-]$ **PAGE:** 12.3

19. The average value for the rate constant k (without units) is

    a)   2710
    b) 2.74×10^4
    c)   137
    d)   108
    e)   none of these

    ANS: a)   2710   **PAGE:** 12.3

20. Two mechanisms are proposed:

    I. $H_2O_2 + I^- \rightarrow H_2O + OI^-$
         $OI^- + H^+ \rightarrow HOI$
         $HOI + I^- + H^+ \rightarrow I_2 + H_2O$
         $I_2 + I^- \rightarrow I_3^-$
    II. $H_2O_2 + I^- + H^+ \rightarrow H_2O + HOI$
         $HOI + I^- + H^+ \rightarrow I_2 + H_2O$
         $I_2 + I^- \rightarrow I_3^-$

Which of the following describes a potentially correct mechanism?

    a)   Mechanism I with the first step the rate determining step.
    b)   Mechanism I with the second step the rate determining step.
    c)   Mechanism II with the first step rate determining.
    d)   Mechanism II with the second step rate determining.
    e)   None of the above could be correct.

    ANS: a)   Mechanism I with the first step the rate determining step.   **PAGE:** 12.6

267

21. A first-order reaction is 45% complete at the end of 35 minutes. What is the length of the half-life of this reaction?

    a) 41 min
    b) 39 min
    c) 30. min
    d) 27 min
    e) none of these

    ANS: a)   41 min

    PAGE: 12.4

22–23. The following initial rate data were found for the reaction

$$2MnO_4^- + 5H_2C_2O_4 + 6H^+ \rightarrow 2Mn^{2+} + 10CO_2 + 8H_2O$$

$[MnO_4^-]_0$	$[H_2C_2O_4]_0$	$[H^+]_0$	Initial Rate (M/s)
1×10^{-3}	1×10^{-3}	1.0	2×10^{-4}
2×10^{-3}	1×10^{-3}	1.0	8×10^{-4}
2×10^{-3}	2×10^{-3}	1.0	1.6×10^{-3}
2×10^{-3}	2×10^{-3}	2.0	1.6×10^{-3}

22. Which of the following is the correct rate law?

    a) Rate $= k[MnO_4^-]^2[H_2C_2O_4]^5[H^+]^6$
    b) Rate $= k[MnO_4^-]^2[H_2C_2O_4][H^+]$
    c) Rate $= k[MnO_4^-][H_2C_2O_4][H^+]$
    d) Rate $= k[MnO_4^-]^2[H_2C_2O_4]$
    e) Rate $= k[MnO_4^-]^2[H_2C_2O_4]^2$

    ANS: d)   Rate $= k[MnO_4^-]^2[H_2C_2O_4]$

    PAGE: 12.3

23. What is the value of the rate constant?

    a) $2 \times 10^5 \, M \cdot s^{-1}$
    b) $2 \times 10^5 \, M^{-2} \cdot s^{-1}$
    c) $200 \, M^{-1} \cdot s^{-1}$
    d) $200 \, M^{-2} \cdot s^{-1}$
    e) $2 \times 10^{-4} \, M \cdot s^{-1}$

    ANS: b) $2 \times 10^5 \, M^{-2} \cdot s^{-1}$

    PAGE: 12.3

24–27. The following questions refer to the reaction between nitric oxide and hydrogen

$$2NO + H_2 \rightarrow N_2O + H_2O$$

Experiment	Initial [NO] (mol/L)	Initial [H$_2$] (mol/L)	Initial Rate of Disappearance of NO (mol/L · s)
1	6.4×10^{-3}	2.2×10^{-3}	2.6×10^{-5}
2	12.8×10^{-3}	2.2×10^{-3}	1.0×10^{-4}
3	6.4×10^{-3}	4.5×10^{-3}	5.1×10^{-5}

24. What is the rate law for this reaction?

    a) Rate = $k[NO]$
    b) Rate = $k[NO]^2$
    c) Rate = $k[NO]^2[H_2]$
    d) Rate = $k[NO][H_2]$
    e) Rate = $k[N_2O][H_2O]$

    ANS: c)   Rate = $k[NO]^2[H_2]$ **PAGE:** 12.3

25. What is the magnitude of the rate constant for this reaction?

    a) 1150
    b) 98
    c) 542
    d) 112
    e) 289

    ANS: e)   289   **PAGE:** 12.3

26. What are the units for the rate constant for this reaction?

    a) $L/mol \cdot s$
    b) $L^2/mol^2 \cdot s$
    c) $mol/L \cdot s$
    d) s^{-2}
    e) L^{-2}

    ANS: b) $L^2/mol^2 \cdot s$ **PAGE:** 12.3

27. What is the order of this reaction?

    a) 3
    b) 2
    c) 1
    d) 0
    e) cannot be determined from the data

    ANS: a)   3   **PAGE:** 12.3

28–29. The reaction

    $$H_2SeO_3(aq)\ 6I^-(aq) + 4H^+(aq) \rightarrow 2I_3^-(aq) + 3H_2O(l) + Se(s)$$

    was studied at 0°C by the method of initial rates:

$[H_2SeO_3]_0$	$[H^+]_0$	$[I^-]_0$	Rate (mol/L s)
1.0×10^{-4}	2.0×10^{-2}	2.0×10^{-2}	1.66×10^{-7}
2.0×10^{-4}	2.0×10^{-2}	2.0×10^{-2}	3.33×10^{-7}
3.0×10^{-4}	2.0×10^{-2}	2.0×10^{-2}	4.99×10^{-7}
1.0×10^{-4}	4.0×10^{-2}	2.0×10^{-2}	6.66×10^{-7}
1.0×10^{-4}	1.0×10^{-2}	2.0×10^{-2}	0.42×10^{-7}
1.0×10^{-4}	2.0×10^{-2}	4.0×10^{-2}	13.4×10^{-7}
1.0×10^{-4}	1.0×10^{-2}	4.0×10^{-2}	3.36×10^{-7}

28. The rate law is

    a) Rate = $k[H_2SeO_3][H^+][I^-]$
    b) Rate = $k[H_2SeO_3][H^+]^2[I^-]$
    c) Rate = $k[H_2SeO_3][H^+][I^-]^2$
    d) Rate = $k[H_2SeO_3]^2[H^+][I^-]$
    e) Rate = $k[H_2SeO_3][H^+]^2[I^-]^3$

    ANS: e)   Rate = $k[H_2SeO_3][H^+]^2[I^-]^3$ **PAGE:** 12.3

29. The numerical value of the rate constant is

    a) 5.2×10^5
    b) 2.1×10^2
    c) 4.2
    d) 1.9×10^{-6}
    e) none of these

    ANS: a) 5.2×10^5 **PAGE:** 12.3

30–33. The following questions refer to the reaction shown below:

   $A + 2B \rightarrow 2AB$

Experiment	Initial [A] (mol/L)	Initial [B] (mol/L)	Initial Rate of Disappearance of A (mol/L · s)
1	0.16	0.15	0.08
2	0.16	0.30	0.30
3	0.08	0.30	0.08

30. What is the rate law for this reaction?

    a) Rate = $k[A][B]$
    b) Rate = $k[A]^2[B]$
    c) Rate = $k[A][B]^2$
    d) Rate = $k[A]^2[B]^2$
    e) Rate = $k[B]$

    ANS: d)   Rate = $k[A]^2[B]^2$ **PAGE:** 12.3

31. What is the magnitude of the rate constant for the reaction?

    a) 140
    b) 79
    c) 119
    d) 164
    e) 21

    ANS: a)   140   **PAGE:** 12.3

32. What are the units for the rate constant for this reaction?

   a) $L/mol \cdot s$
   b) $L^2/mol^2 \cdot s$
   c) $mol/L \cdot s$
   d) $L^3/mol^3 \cdot s$
   e) mol^3/L

   ANS: d) $L^3/mol^3 \cdot s$ **PAGE:** 12.3

33. What is the order of this reaction?

   a) 4
   b) 3
   c) 2
   d) 1
   e) 0

   ANS: a)   4   **PAGE:** 12.3

34. Initial rate data have been determined at a certain temperature for the gaseous reaction
    $2NO + 2H_2 \rightarrow N_2 + 2H_2O$.

$[NO]_0$	$[H_2]_0$	Initial Rate (M/s)
0.10	0.20	0.0150
0.10	0.30	0.0225
0.20	0.20	0.0600

   The numerical value of the rate constant is:

   a) 7.5
   b) 3.0×10^{-3}
   c) 380
   d) 0.75
   e) 3.0×10^{-4}

   ANS: a)   7.5   **PAGE:** 12.3

271

35. The following data were obtained at 25°C:

$[A]_0$	$[B]_0$	$[C]_0$	Rate
0.1	0.2	0.3	0.063
0.3	0.4	0.2	0.084
0.6	0.4	0.2	0.168
0.3	0.4	0.1	0.021
0.6	0.2	0.2	0.168

What is the correct rate law?

a) Rate = $k[A][B][C]$
b) Rate = $k[A][B][C]^2$
c) Rate = $k[A][C]$
d) Rate = $k[A]^3[B]^2[C]$
e) Rate = $k[A][C]^2$

ANS: e)   Rate = $k[A][C]^2$ **PAGE:** 12.3

36–38. The oxidation of Cr^{3+} to CrO_4^{2-} can be accomplished using Ce^{4+} in a buffered solution. The following data were obtained:

Relative Initial Rate	$[Ce^{4+}]_0$	$[Ce^{3+}]_0$	$[Cr^{3+}]_0$
1	2.0×10^{-3}	1.0×10^{-2}	3.0×10^{-2}
2	4.0×10^{-3}	2.0×10^{-2}	3.0×10^{-2}
4	4.0×10^{-3}	1.0×10^{-2}	3.0×10^{-2}
16	8.0×10^{-3}	2.0×10^{-2}	6.0×10^{-2}

36. Determine the order in the rate law of the species Ce^{4+}.

a) 1
b) 2
c) 3
d) –1
e) –2

ANS: b)   2   **PAGE:** 12.3

37. Determine the order in the rate law of the species Ce^{3+}.

a) 1
b) 2
c) 3
d) –1
e) –2

ANS: d)   –1   **PAGE:** 12.3

38. Determine the order in the rate law of the species Cr^{3+}.

    a) 1
    b) 2
    c) 3
    d) –1
    e) –2

    ANS: a)   1   **PAGE:** 12.3

39. The rate expression for a particular reaction is rate = $k[A][B]^2$. If the initial concentration of B is increased from 0.1 M to 0.3 M, the initial rate will increase by which of the following factors?

    a) 2
    b) 6
    c) 12
    d) 3
    e) 9

    ANS: e)   9   **PAGE:** 12.3

40. The reaction $2NO \rightarrow N_2 + O_2$ has the following rate law:

    $$-\frac{\Delta[NO]}{\Delta t} = 2k[NO]^2.$$

    After a period of 2.0×10^3 s, the concentration of NO falls from an initial value of 2.8×10^{-3} mol/L to 2.0×10^{-3} mol/L. What is the rate constant, k?

    a) 7.2×10^{-2} M^{-1}/s
    b) 1.7×10^{-4} M^{-1}/s
    c) 4.0×10^{-4} M^{-1}/s
    d) 4.0×10^{-7} M^{-1}/s
    e) 3.6×10^{-2} M^{-1}/s

    ANS: e) 3.6×10^{-2} M^{-1}/s   **PAGE:** 12.4

41. The following data were collected for the decay of HO_2 radicals:

Time	$[HO_2]$	Time	$[HO_2]$
0 s	1.0×10^{11} molec/cm^3	14 s	1.25×10^{10} molec/cm^3
2 s	5.0×10^{10} molec/cm^3	30 s	6.225×10^{9} molec/cm^3
6 s	2.5×10^{10} molec/cm^3		

    Which of the following statements is true?

    a)   The decay of HO_2 occurs by a first-order process.
    b)   The half-life of the reaction is 2 ms.
    c)   A plot of ln $[HO_2]$ versus time is linear with a slope of $-k$.
    d)   The rate of the reaction increases with time.
    e)   A plot of $1/[HO_2]$ versus time gives a straight line.

    ANS: e)   A plot of $1/[HO_2]$ versus time gives a straight line.   **PAGE:** 12.4

273

42–45. The following questions refer to the gas-phase decomposition of ethylene chloride.

$C_2H_5Cl \rightarrow$ products

Experiment shows that the decomposition is first order.

The following data show kinetics information for this reaction:

Time (s)	ln $[C_2H_5Cl]$ (M)
1.0	–1.625
2.0	–1.735

42. What is the rate constant for this decomposition?

   a)   0.29/s
   b)   0.35/s
   c)   0.11/s
   d)   0.02/s
   e)   0.22/s

   ANS: c)   0.11/s   **PAGE:** 12.4

43. What was the initial concentration of the ethylene chloride?

   a)   0.29 M
   b)   0.35 M
   c)   0.11 M
   d)   0.02 M
   e)   0.22 M

   ANS: e)   0.22 M   **PAGE:** 12.4

44. What would the concentration be after 5.0 seconds?

   a)   0.13 M
   b)   0.08 M
   c)   0.02 M
   d)   0.19 M
   e)   0.12 M

   ANS: a)   0.13 M   **PAGE:** 12.4

45. What is the time to half-life?

   a)   0.7 s
   b)   1.3 s
   c)   8.9 s
   d)   6.3 s
   e)   2.2 s

   ANS: d)   6.3 s   **PAGE:** 12.4

46-47. For a reaction: aA → Products, $[A]_0$ = 6.0 M, and the first two half-lives are 56 and 28 minutes, respectively.

46. Calculate k (without units)

   a) 1.2×10^{-2}
   b) 3.0×10^{-3}
   c) 5.4×10^{-2}
   d) 1.0×10^{-2}
   e)   none of these

   ANS: c) 5.4×10^{-2} **PAGE:** 12.4

47. Calculate [A] at t= 99 minutes.

   a)   2.15 M
   b)   1.83 M
   c)   0.95 M
   d)   0.65 M
   e)   none of these

   ANS: d)   0.65 M   **PAGE:** 12.4

48. For which order reaction is the half life of the reaction proportional to 1/k (k is the rate constant)?

   a)   zero order
   b)   first order
   c)   second order
   d)   all of the above
   e)   none of the above

   ANS: d)   all of the above   **PAGE:** 12.4

49-51. The kinetics of the reaction A + 3B → C + 2D were studied and the following results obtained, where the rate law is

$$-\frac{\Delta[A]}{\Delta t} = k[A]^n[B]^m$$

For a run where $[A]_0 = 1.0 \times 10^{-3}$ M and $[B]_0$ = 5.0 M, a plot of ln [A] versus t was found to give a straight line with slope = -5.0×10^{-2} s^{-1}.

For a run where $[A]_0 = 1.0 \times 10^{-3}$ M and $[B]_0$ = 10.0 M, a plot of ln [A] versus t was found to give a straight line with slope = -7.1×10^{-2} s^{-1}.

49. What is the value of *n*?

   a) 0
   b) 0.5
   c) 1
   d) 1.5
   e) 2

   ANS: c)   1   PAGE: 12.4

50. What is the value of *m*?

   a) 0
   b) 0.5
   c) 1
   d) 1.5
   e) 2

   ANS: b)   0.5   PAGE: 12.4

51. Calculate the value of *k* (ignore units).

   a) 2.2×10^{-2}
   b) 1.0×10^{-2}
   c) 5.0×10^{-2}
   d) 1.1×10^{-1}
   e) none of these

   ANS: a) 2.2×10^{-2} PAGE: 12.4

52–56. For the reaction $2N_2O_5(g) \rightarrow 4NO_2(g) + O_2(g)$, the following data were collected:

t (minutes)	$[N_2O_5]$ (mol/L)
0	1.24×10^{-2}
10.	0.92×10^{-2}
20.	0.68×10^{-2}
30.	0.50×10^{-2}
40.	0.37×10^{-2}
50.	0.28×10^{-2}
70.	0.15×10^{-2}

52. The order of this reaction in N_2O_5 is

   a) 0
   b) 1
   c) 2
   d) 3
   e) none of these

   ANS: b)   1   PAGE: 12.4

53. The concentration of O_2 at $t = 10$. minutes is

a) 2.0×10^{-4} mol/L
b) 0.32×10^{-2} mol/L
c) 0.16×10^{-2} mol/L
d) 0.64×10^{-2} mol/L
e) none of these

ANS: c) 0.16×10^{-2} mol/L   PAGE: 12.4

54. The initial rate of production of NO_2 for this reaction is approximately

a) 6.4×10^{-4} mol/L $\cdot$ min
b) 3.2×10^{-4} mol/L $\cdot$ min
c) 1.24×10^{-2} mol/L $\cdot$ min
d) 1.6×10^{-4} mol/L $\cdot$ min
e) none of these

ANS: a) 6.4×10^{-4} mol/L $\cdot$ min   PAGE: 12.1

55. The half-life of this reaction is approximately

a) 15 minutes
b) 18 minutes
c) 23 minutes
d) 36 minutes
e) 45 minutes

ANS: c)   23 minutes   PAGE: 12.4

56. The concentration N_2O_5 at 100 minutes will be approximately

a) 0.03×10^{-2} mol/L
b) 0.06×10^{-2} mol/L
c) 0.10×10^{-2} mol/L
d) 0.01×10^{-2} mol/L
e) none of these

ANS: b) 0.06×10^{-2} mol/L   PAGE: 12.4

57–59. The following questions refer to the hypothetical reaction A + B → products. The kinetics data given can be analyzed to answer the questions.

$[A]_0$ (mol/L)	$[B]_0$ (mol/L)	Rate of decrease of [A] (M/s)
5.0	5.0	X
10.0	5.0	2X
5.0	10.0	2X

Time (s)	[B] (mol/L)
10.0	100
20.0	100
30.0	100

57.   The rate law for the reaction is Rate = $k[A]^x[B]^y$. What are the values of x and y?

   a) $x = 0$ $y = 1$
   b) $x = 1$ $y = 0$
   c) $x = 1$ $y = 1$
   d) $x = 2$ $y = 1$
   e) $x = 1$ $y = 2$

   ANS: c) $x = 1$ $y = 1$ **PAGE:** 12.3

58.   What form will the pseudo-rate law have?

   a)   Rate = $k'[A]^x$
   b)   Rate = $k'[B]^y$
   c)   Rate = $k'[A]^x[B]^y$
   d)   Rate = $kk'[A]^x$
   e)   Rate = $kk'[B]^y$

   ANS: a)   Rate = $k'[A]^x$ **PAGE:** 12.4

59.   Determine the magnitude of the pseudo-rate constant (k') if the magnitude of X in the rate data is 0.00905.

   a) 4.3×10^{-3}
   b) 1.2×10^{-2}
   c)   0.86
   d)   0.31
   e) 1.81×10^{-3}

   ANS: e) 1.81×10^{-3} **PAGE:** 12.4

60–63. The reaction $A \rightarrow B + C$ is known to be zero order in A with a rate constant of 5.0×10^{-2} mol/L $\cdot$ s at 25°C. An experiment was run at 25°C where $[A]_0 = 1.0 \times 10^{-3}$ M.

60. The integrated rate law is

   a) $[A] = kt$

   b) $[A] - [A]_0 = kt$

   c) $\dfrac{[A]}{[A]_0} = kt$

   d) $\ln \dfrac{[A]}{[A]_0} = kt$

   e) $[A]_0 - [A] = kt$

   ANS: e) $[A]_0 - [A] = kt$ **PAGE:** 12.4

61. After 5.0 minutes, the rate is

   a) 5.0×10^{-2} mol/L $\cdot$ s
   b) 2.5×10^{-2} mol/L $\cdot$ s
   c) 1.2×10^{-2} mol/L $\cdot$ s
   d) 1.0×10^{-3} mol/L $\cdot$ s
   e) none of these

   ANS: a) 5.0×10^{-2} mol/L $\cdot$ s   **PAGE:** 12.4

62. The half-life for the reaction is

   a) 1.0×10^{-2} s
   b) 1.0×10^{2} s
   c) 5.0×10^{-2} s
   d) 5.0×10^{-4} s
   e) none of these

   ANS: a) 1.0×10^{-2} s   **PAGE:** 12.4

63. What is the concentration of B after 5×10^{-3} sec?

   a) 5.0×10^{-5} M
   b) 5.0×10^{-4} M
   c) 7.5×10^{-4} M
   d) 2.5×10^{-4} M
   e) none of these

   ANS: d) 2.5×10^{-4} M   **PAGE:** 12.4

64–65. The reaction

$$2NOBr \rightarrow 2NO + Br_2$$

exhibits the rate law

$$Rate = k[NOBr]^2 = -\frac{\Delta[NOBr]}{\Delta t}$$

where $k = 1.0 \times 10^{-5}$ M$^{-1} \cdot$ s^{-1} at 25°C. This reaction is run where the initial concentration of NOBr ($[NOBr]_0$) is 1.00×10^{-1} M.

64. What is one half-life for this experiment?

a) 5.0×10^{-1} s
b) 6.9×10^4 s
c) 1.0×10^{-5} s
d) 1.0×10^6 s
e) none of these

ANS: d) 1.0×10^6 s **PAGE:** 12.4

65. The [NO] after 1.00 hour has passed is

a) 3.5×10^{-4} M
b) 9.9×10^{-3} M
c) 9.7×10^{-3} M
d) 1.0×10^{-3} M
e) none of these

ANS: a) 3.5×10^{-4} M **PAGE:** 12.4

66–67. For the reaction A $\rightarrow$ Products, successive half-lives are observed to be 10.0 min and 40.0 min. At the beginning of the reaction, [A] was 0.10 M.

66. The reaction follows the integrated rate law

a) $[A] = -kt + [A]_0$

b) $\ln [A] = -kt + \ln [A]_0$

c) $\frac{1}{[A]} = kt + \frac{1}{[A]_0}$

d) $\frac{1}{[A]^2} = kt + \frac{1}{[A]_0{}^2}$

e) none of these

ANS: c) $\frac{1}{[A]} = kt + \frac{1}{[A]_0}$ **PAGE:** 12.4

67. The numerical value of the rate constant is

    a) 0.069
    b) 1.0
    c) 10.0
    d) 5.0×10^{-3}
    e) none of these

ANS: b)   1.0   **PAGE:** 12.4

68. The reaction

$$2N_2O_5(g) \rightarrow O_2(g) + 4NO_2(g)$$

is first order in N_2O_5. For this reaction at 45°C, the rate constant $k = 1.0 \times 10^{-5}$ s^{-1}, where the rate law is defined as

$$\text{Rate} = -\frac{\Delta[N_2O_5]}{\Delta t} = k[N_2O_5]$$

For a particular experiment ($[N_2O_5]_0 = 1.0 \times 10^{-3}$ M), calculate $[N_2O_5]$ after 1.0×10^5 seconds.

    a) 5.0×10^{-4} M
    b) 1.0×10^{-3} M
    c) 3.7×10^{-4} M
    d) 0
    e) none of these

ANS: c) 3.7×10^{-4} M   **PAGE:** 12.4

69–72. Consider the reaction

$$3A + B + C \rightarrow D + E$$

where the rate law is defined as

$$-\frac{\Delta[A]}{\Delta t} = k[A]^2[B][C]$$

An experiment is carried out where $[B]_0 = [C]_0 = 1.00$ M and $[A]_0 = 1.00 \times 10^{-4}$ M.

69. After 3.00 minutes, $[A] = 3.26 \times 10^{-5}$ M. The value of k is

    a) 6.23×10^{-3} L^3/mol$^3 \cdot$ s
    b) 3.26×10^{-5} L^3/mol$^3 \cdot$ s
    c) 1.15×10^2 L^3/mol$^3 \cdot$ s
    d) 1.00×10^8 L^3/mol$^3 \cdot$ s
    e) none of these

ANS: c) 1.15×10^2 L^3/mol$^3 \cdot$ s   **PAGE:** 12.4

70.   The half-life for this experiment is

    a) 1.11×10^2 s

    b)   87.0 s

    c) 6.03×10^{-3} s

    d)   117 s

    e)   none of these

ANS: b)   87.0 s   **PAGE:** 12.4

71.   The concentration of C after 10.0 minutes is

    a)   1.00 M

    b) 1.10×10^{-5} M

    c)   0.330 M

    d)   0.100 M

    e)   none of these

ANS: a)   1.00 M   **PAGE:** 12.4

72.   The concentration of A after 10.0 minutes is

    a) 1.06×10^{-9} M

    b) 2.38×10^{-6} M

    c) 9.80×10^{-6} M

    d) 1.27×10^{-5} M

    e)   none of these

ANS: d) 1.27×10^{-5} M   **PAGE:** 12.4

73–75.   The reaction

$$A \rightarrow B + C$$

is second order in A. When $[A]_0 = 0.100$ M, the reaction is 20.0% complete in 40.0 minutes.

73.   Calculate the value of the rate constant (in L/min · mol).

    a) 6.25×10^{-2}

    b) 5.58×10^{-3}

    c) 1.60×10^1

    d)   1.00

    e)   none of these

ANS: a) 6.25×10^{-2} **PAGE:** 12.4

74. Calculate the half-life for the reaction.

    a) 1.60×10^2 min
    b) 1.11×10^1 min
    c) 1.00×10^1 min
    d) 1.00×10^2 min
    e)   none of these

    ANS: a) 1.60×10^2 min   **PAGE:** 12.4

75. A first-order reaction is 40.% complete at the end of 50. minutes. What is the value of the rate constant (in min^{-1})?

    a) 1.8×10^{-2}
    b) 1.0×10^{-2}
    c) 1.2×10^{-2}
    d) 8.0×10^{-3}
    e)   none of these

    ANS: b) 1.0×10^{-2} **PAGE:** 12.4

76. The OH radical disproportionates according to the elementary chemical reaction $OH + OH \rightarrow H_2O + O$. This reaction is second order in OH. The rate constant for the reaction is 2.0×10^{-12} cm^3/molecule $\cdot$ s at room temperature. If the initial OH concentration is 1.0×10^{13} molecules/cm^3, what is the first half-life for the reaction?

    a)   20. s
    b) 2.0×10^{-3} s
    c)   0.050 s
    d)   0.035 s
    e)   12 s

    ANS: c)   0.050 s   **PAGE:** 12.4

77. At a particular temperature, N_2O_5 decomposes according to a first-order rate law with a half-life of 3.0 s. If the initial concentration of N_2O_5 is 1.0×10^{16} molecules/cm^3, what will be the concentration in molecules/cm^3 after 10.0 s?

    a) 9.9×10^{14}
    b) 1.8×10^{12}
    c) 7.3×10^9
    d) 6.3×10^3
    e) 9.4×10^2

    ANS: a) 9.9×10^{14} **PAGE:** 12.4

78. The reaction

$$3NO \rightarrow N_2O + NO_2$$

is found to obey the rate law Rate = $k[NO]^2$. If the first half-life of the reaction is found to be 2.0 s, what is the length of the fourth half-life?

a) 2.0 s
b) 4.0 s
c) 8.0 s
d) 12.0 s
e) 16.0 s

ANS: e)   16.0 s   **PAGE:** 12.4

79. In 6 M HCl, the complex ion $Ru(NH_3)_6{}^{3+}$ decomposes to a variety of products. The reaction is first order in $Ru(NH_3)_6{}^{3+}$ and has a half-life of 14 hours at 25°C. Under these conditions, how long will it take for the $[Ru(NH_3)_6{}^{3+}]$ to decrease to 12.5% of its initial value?

a) 28 hours
b) 35 hours
c) 2.7 hours
d) 14 hours
e) 42 hours

ANS: e)   42 hours   **PAGE:** 12.4

80. The elementary chemical reaction

$$O + ClO \rightarrow Cl + O_2$$

is made pseudo-first order in oxygen atoms by using a large excess of ClO radicals. The rate constant for the reaction is 3.5×10^{-11} cm^3/molecule · s. If the initial concentration of ClO is 1.0×10^{11} molecules/cm^3, how long will it take for the oxygen atoms to decrease to 10.% of their initial concentration?

a) 2.4 s
b) 0.017 s
c) 3.2×10^{-3} s
d) 0.66 s
e) 23 s

ANS: d)   0.66 s   **PAGE:** 12.4

81. The following data were obtained for the reaction $2A + B \rightarrow C$ where rate = $d\{A\}/dt$

[A](M)	[B](M)	Initial Rate(M/s)
0.100	0.0500	2.13×10^{-4}
0.200	0.0500	4.26×10^{-4}
0.300	0.100	2.56×10^{-3}

Determine the value of the rate constant.

a) 0.426
b) 0.852
c) 0.0426
d) 0.284
e) none of these

ANS: b)   0.852   **PAGE:** 12.3

82. Determine the molecularity of the following elementary reaction: $O_3 \rightarrow O_2 + O$.

a) unimolecular
b) bimolecular
c) termolecular
d) quadmolecular
e) the molecularity cannot be determined

ANS: a)   unimolecular   **PAGE:** 12.6

83. The decomposition of ozone may occur through the two-step mechanism shown:

step 1 $O_3 \rightarrow O_2 + O$

step 2 $O_3 + O \rightarrow 2O_2$

The oxygen atom is considered to be a(n)

a) reactant
b) product
c) catalyst
d) reaction intermediate
e) activated complex

ANS: d)   reaction intermediate   **PAGE:** 12.6,7

84–87. The following questions refer to the reaction $2A_2 + B_2 \rightarrow 2C$. The following mechanism has been proposed:

step 1 (very slow) $A_2 + B_2 \rightarrow R + C$

step 2 (slow) $A_2 + R \rightarrow C$

84. What is the molecularity of step 2?

    a) unimolecular
    b) bimolecular
    c) termolecular
    d) quadmolecular
    e) the molecularity cannot be determined

    ANS: b) bimolecular   **PAGE:** 12.6

85. Which step is –rate determiningî?

    a) both steps
    b) step 1
    c) step 2
    d) a step that is intermediate to step 1 and step 2
    e) none of these

    ANS: b) step 1   **PAGE:** 12.6

86. According to collision theory, the activated complex that forms in step 1 should have the following structure. (The dotted lines represent partial bonds)

    a) 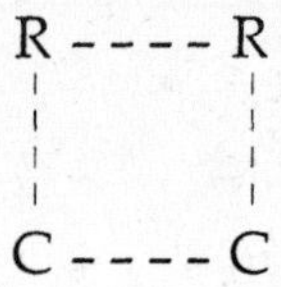 R - - - - R
        | |
        | |
        C - - - - C

    b) A - - - - A
        | |
        | |
        B - - - - B

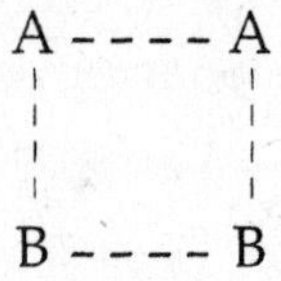

    c) 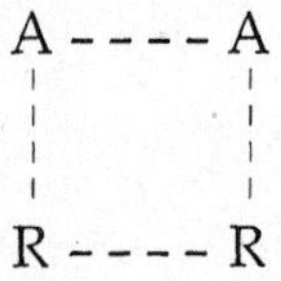 A - - - - A
        | |
        | |
        R - - - - R

    d) 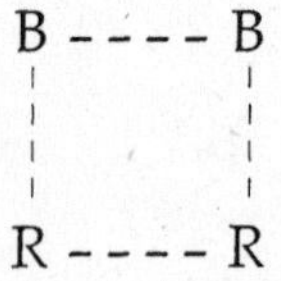 B - - - - B
        | |
        | |
        R - - - - R

    e) 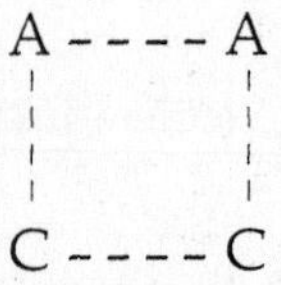 A - - - - A
        | |
        | |
        C - - - - C

    ANS: b)   A - - - - A
                  | |
                  | |
                  B - - - - B 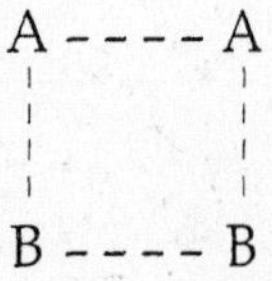   **PAGE:** 12.7

87. According to the proposed mechanism, what should the overall rate law be?

   a)   rate = $k[A_2]^2$
   b)   rate = $k[A_2]$
   c)   rate = $k[A_2][B_2]$
   d)   rate = $k[A_2][R]$
   e)   rate = $k[R]^2$

   ANS: c)   rate = $k[A_2][B_2]$ **PAGE:** 12.6

88–90. Two isomers (A and B) of a given compound dimerize as follows:

$$2A \rightarrow A_2$$

$$2B \rightarrow B_2$$

Both processes are known to be second order in reactant, and k_1 is known to be 0.25 L/mol · s at 25°C, where

$$\text{Rate} = -\frac{\Delta[A]}{\Delta t} = k_1[A]^2$$

In a particular experiment, A and B were placed in separate containers at 25°, where $[A]_0 = 1.0 \times 10^{-2}$ M and $[B]_0 = 2.5 \times 10^{-2}$ M. It was found that $[A] = 3[B]$ after the reactions progressed for 3.0 minutes.

88. Calculate the concentration of A_2 after 3.0 minutes.

   a) 2.8×10^{-22} M
   b) 6.9×10^{-3} M
   c) 3.1×10^{-3} M
   d) 1.6×10^{-3} M
   e)   none of these

   ANS: d) 1.6×10^{-3} M   **PAGE:** 12.4

89. Calculate the value of k_2 where

$$\text{Rate} = -\frac{\Delta[B]}{\Delta t} = k_2[B]^2$$

   a)   2.2 L/mol · s
   b)   0.75 L/mol · s
   c)   1.9 L/mol · s
   d)   0.21 L/mol · s
   e)   none of these

   ANS: a)   2.2 L/mol · s   **PAGE:** 12.4

90. Calculate the half-life for the reaction involving A.

   a) 4.0×10^2 s
   b) 1.7×10^1 s
   c) 2.5×10^3
   d) 1.8×10^2 s
   e)   none of these

   ANS: a) 4.0×10^2 s   **PAGE:** 12.4

91–92. The decomposition of $N_2O_5(g)$ to $NO_2(g)$ and $O_2(g)$ obeys first-order kinetics. Assuming the form of the rate law is

$$\text{Rate} = -\frac{\Delta[N_2O_5]}{\Delta t} = k[N_2O_5]$$

where $k = 3.4 \times 10^{-5}$ s^{-1} at 25°C.

91. What is the initial rate of reaction at 25°C where $[N_2O_5]_0 = 5.0 \times 10^{-2}$ M?

   a) 3.4×10^{-5} mol/L · s
   b) 1.7×10^{-6} mol/L · s
   c) 6.8×10^{-4} mol/L · s
   d) 5.0×10^{-2} mol/L · s
   e)   none of these

   ANS: b) 1.7×10^{-6} mol/L · s   **PAGE:** 12.4

92. What is the half-life for the reaction described?

   a) 5.9×10^5 s
   b) 2.0×10^4 s
   c) 2.4×10^{-5} s
   d) 7.4×10^2 s
   e)   none of these

   ANS: b) 2.0×10^4 s   **PAGE:** 12.4

93. The reaction $2NO_2 \rightarrow 2NO + O_2$ obeys the rate law

$$\frac{\Delta[O_2]}{\Delta t} = 1.40 \times 10^{-2} [NO_2]^2 \text{ at 500. K.}$$

If the initial concentration of NO_2 is 1.00 M, how long will it take for the $[NO_2]$ to decrease to 25.0% of its initial value?

   a)   49.5 s
   b)   71.4 s
   c)   214 s
   d) 1.40×10^{-2} s
   e)   cannot be determined from this data

   ANS: c)   214 s   **PAGE:** 12.4

94. If the reaction $2HI \rightarrow H_2 + I_2$ is second order, which of the following will yield a linear plot?

    a) log [HI] vs time
    b) 1/[HI] vs time
    c) [HI] vs time
    d) ln [HI] vs time

    ANS: b) 1/[HI] vs time **PAGE:** 12.4

95–97. Under certain conditions the reaction $H_2O_2 + 3I^- + 2H^+ \rightarrow I_3^- + 2H_2O$ occurs by the following series of steps:

$$\text{Step 1.} \quad H_2O_2 + H^+ \underset{k_{-1}}{\overset{k_1}{\rightleftharpoons}} H_3O_2^+$$

$$\left(\text{rapid equilibrium constant } K = \frac{k_1}{k_{-1}} \right)$$

Step 2. $H_3O_2^+ + I^- \rightarrow H_2O + HOI$ (slow, rate constant k_2)

Step 3. $HOI + I^- \rightarrow OH^- + I_2$ (fast, rate constant k_3)

Step 4. $OH^- + H^+ \rightarrow H_2O$ (fast, rate constant k_4)

Step 5. $I_2 + I^- \rightarrow I_3^-$ (fast, rate constant k_5)

95. Which of the steps would be called the rate-determining step?

    a) 1
    b) 2
    c) 3
    d) 4
    e) 5

    ANS: b) 2 **PAGE:** 12.6

96. The rate constant k for the reaction would be given by

    a) $k = k_2$
    b) $k = k_2k_3$
    c) $k = k_2K$
    d) $k = k_5$
    e) $k = Kk_2k_3k_4k_5$

    ANS: c) $k = k_2K$ **PAGE:** 12.6

97. The rate law for the reaction would be:

 a) $\Delta[I_3]/\Delta t = k[H_2O_2]$
 b) $\Delta[I_3]/\Delta t = k[H_2O_2][H^+][I^-]$
 c) $\Delta[I_3]/\Delta t = k[H_2O_2][H^+]$
 d) $\Delta[I_3]/\Delta t = k[H_2O_2][I^-]$
 e) $\Delta[I_3]/\Delta t = k[H_2O_2][H^+]^2[I^-]^{-3}$

 ANS: b) $\Delta[I_3]/\Delta t = k[H_2O_2][H^+][I^-]$ **PAGE:** 12.6

98. The reaction

 $$2A + B \rightarrow C$$

 has the following proposed mechanism:

 Step 1: $A + B \rightleftharpoons D$ (fast equilibrium)

 Step 2: $D + B \rightarrow E$

 Step 3: $E + A \rightarrow C + B$

 If step 2 is the rate-determining step, then the rate of formation of C should equal:

 a) $k[A]$
 b) $k[A]^2[B]$
 c) $k[A]^2[B]^2$
 d) $k[A][B]$
 e) $k[A][B]^2$

 ANS: e) $k[A][B]^2$ **PAGE:** 12.6

99. The reaction $2NO + O_2 \rightarrow 2NO_2$ obeys the rate law

 $$-\frac{\Delta[O_2]}{\Delta t} = k_{obsd}[NO]^2[O_2].$$

 Which of the following mechanisms is consistent with the experimental rate law?

 a) $NO + NO \rightarrow N_2O_2$ (slow)
    $N_2O_2 + O_2 \rightarrow 2NO_2$ (fast)

 b) $NO + O_2 \rightleftharpoons NO_3$ (fast equilibrium)
    $NO_3 + NO \rightarrow 2NO_2$ (slow)

 c) $2NO \rightleftharpoons N_2O_2$ (fast equilibrium)
    $N_2O_2 \rightarrow NO_2 + O$ (slow)
    $NO + O \rightarrow NO_2$ (fast)

 d) $O_2 + O_2 \rightarrow O_2 + O_2^*$ (slow)
    $O_2 + NO \rightarrow NO_2 + O$ (fast)
    $O + NO \rightarrow NO_2$ (fast)

 e) none of these

 ANS: b) $NO + O_2 \rightleftharpoons NO_3$ (fast equilibrium)
   $NO_3 + NO \rightarrow 2NO_2$ (slow) **PAGE:** 12.6

100–102.   The questions below refer to the following diagram:

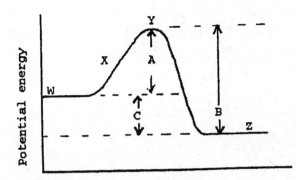

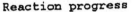

100. Why is this reaction considered to be exothermic?

  a)   Because energy difference B is greater than energy difference C
  b)   Because energy difference B is greater than energy difference A
  c)   Because energy difference A is greater than energy difference C
  d)   Because energy difference B is greater than energy difference C plus energy
       difference A
  e)   Because energy difference A and energy difference C are about equal

  ANS: b)   Because energy difference B is greater than energy
                  difference A   **PAGE:** 12.7

101. At what point on the graph is the activated complex present?

  a)   point W
  b)   point X
  c)   point Y
  d)   point Z
  e)   none of these

  ANS: c)   point Y   **PAGE:** 12.7

102. If the reaction were reversible, would the forward or the reverse reaction have a higher
      activation energy?

  a)   The diagram shows no indication of any activation energy.
  b)   The forward and reverse activation energies are equal.
  c)   The forward activation energy
  d)   The reverse activation energy
  e)   none of these

  ANS: d)   The reverse activation energy   **PAGE:** 12.7

103. What would happen if the kinetic energy of the reactants was not enough to provide the needed activation energy?

    a) The products would be produced at a lower energy state.
    b) The rate of the reaction would tend to increase.
    c) The activated complex would convert into products.
    d) The reactants would re-form.
    e) The products would form at an unstable energy state.

    ANS: d)   The reactants would re-form.   **PAGE:** 12.7

104–106. The questions below refer to the following information:

    The rate constant k for the reaction shown below is 2.6×10^{-8} L/mol · s when the reaction proceeds at 300.0 K. The activation energy is 98000 J/mol. (The universal gas constant (R) is 8.314 J/mol · K)

    $$2NOCl \rightarrow 2NO + Cl_2$$

104. Determine the magnitude of the frequency factor for the reaction.

    a) 1.2×10^{-8}
    b) 4.6×10^{-9}
    c) 3.2×10^{-9}
    d) 2.7×10^{-8}
    e) 9.1×10^{-9}

    ANS: c) 3.2×10^{-9} **PAGE:** 12.7

105. If the temperature changed to 310 K the rate constant k would change. The ratio of k at 310 K to k at 300.0 K is closest to what whole number?

    a) 1
    b) 2
    c) 3
    d) 4
    e) 5

    ANS: d)   4   **PAGE:** 12.7

106. Using the following information determine the activation energy for the reaction shown here:

$$2NO \rightarrow N_2 + O_2$$

Temperature (K)	Rate Constant (L/mol · s)
1400	0.143
1500	0.659

a) 3.2×10^4 J/mol
b) 9.5×10^6 J/mol
c) 2.8×10^4 J/mol
d) 6.8×10^5 J/mol
e) 2.7×10^5 J/mol

ANS: e) 2.7×10^5 J/mol   **PAGE:** 12.7

107. The reaction $2H_2O_2 \rightarrow 2H_2O + O_2$ has the following mechanism?

$$H_2O_2 + I^- \rightarrow H_2O + IO^-$$

$$H_2O_2 + IO^- \rightarrow H_2O + O_2 + I^-$$

The catalyst in the reaction is:

a) H_2O
b) I^-
c) H_2O_2
d) IO^-

ANS: b) I^- **PAGE:** 12.6,8

108. When ethyl chloride, CH_3CH_2Cl, is dissolved in 1.0 M NaOH, it is converted into ethanol, CH_3CH_2OH, by the reaction

$$CH_3CH_2Cl + OH^- \rightarrow CH_3CH_2OH + Cl^-$$

At 25°C the reaction is first order in CH_3CH_2Cl, and the rate constant is 1.0×10^{-3} s^{-1}. If the activation parameters are $A = 3.4 \times 10^{14}$ s^{-1} and $E_a = 100.0$ kJ/mol, what will the rate constant be at 40°C?

a) 6.9×10^{-3} s^{-1}
b) 1.7×10^2 s^{-1}
c) 5.0×10^{-3} s^{-1}
d) 2.0×10^{-3} s^{-1}
e) 5.0×10^{14} s^{-1}

ANS: a) 6.9×10^{-3} s^{-1} **PAGE:** 12.7

109. Which of the following statements best describes the condition(s) needed for a successful formation for a product according to the collision model?

    a) The collision must involve a sufficient amount of energy, provided from the motion of the particles, to overcome the activation energy.

    b) The relative orientation of the particles has little or no effect on the formation of the product.

    c) The relative orientation of the particles has an effect only if the kinetic energy of the particles is below some minimum value.

    d) The relative orientation of the particles must allow for formation of the new bonds in the product.

    e) The energy of the incoming particles must be above a certain minimum value and the relative orientation of the particles must allow for formation of new bonds in the product.

ANS: e) The energy of the incoming particles must be above a certain minimum value and the relative orientation of the particles must allow for formation of new bonds in the product.   **PAGE:** 12.7

110. Which of the following statements is typically true for a catalyst?

    a) The concentration of the catalyst will go down as a reaction proceeds.

    b) The catalyst provides a new pathway in the reaction mechanism.

    c) The catalyst speeds up the reaction.

    d) Two of these.

    e) None of these.

ANS: d) Two of these   **PAGE:** 12.8

111. The catalyzed pathway in a reaction mechanism has a _____ activation energy and thus causes a _____ reaction rate.

    a) higher, lower

    b) higher, higher

    c) lower, higher

    d) lower, steady

    e) higher, steady

ANS: c) lower, higher   **PAGE:** 12.8

112. The rate constant k is dependent on
    I. the concentration of the reactant.
    II. the nature of the reactants.
    III. the temperature.
    IV. the order of the reaction.
    a) none of these
    b) one of these
    c) two of these
    d) three of these
    e) all of these

    ANS: c) two of these   **PAGE:** 12.2,7

113. The rate law for a reaction is found to be Rate = $k[A]^2[B]$. Which of the following mechanisms gives this rate law?
    I. A + B $\rightleftharpoons$ E (fast)
        E + B → C + D (slow)
    II. A + B $\rightleftharpoons$ E (fast)
        E + A → C + D (slow)
    III. A + A → E (slow)
        E + B → C + D (fast)
    a) I
    b) II
    c) III
    d) two of these
    e) none of these

    ANS: b) II   **PAGE:** 12.6

114-116. A reaction represented by the equation

    $3O_2 (g) \rightarrow 2O_3 (g)$

    was studied at a specific temperature and the following data were collected:

time (seconds)	total pressure (atm)
0	1.000
46.89	0.9500
98.82	0.9033
137.9	0.8733
200.0	0.8333
286.9	0.7900
337.9	0.7700
511.3	0.7233

114. Which is the rate law for this reaction?:

    ANS: rate =$k[O_2]$ **PAGE:** 12.4

115. Which is the value of the rate constant?:

ANS: k = 3.47 x 10^{-3} sec^{-1} **PAGE:** 12.4

116. How many seconds would it take for the total pressure to be 0.7133 atm?

ANS: 567 sec   **PAGE:** 12.4

117. The rate constant for a reaction at 40.0°C is exactly three times that at 20.0°C. Calculate the Arrhenius energy of activation for the reaction.

    a)   3.00 kJ/mol
    b)   366 kJ/mol
    c)   41.9 kJ/mol
    d)   3.20 kJ/mol
    e)   none of these

ANS: c)   41.9 kJ/mol   **PAGE:** 12.7

118. Determine (a) the rate equation and (b) the rate constant for the hypothetical reaction A + B → C given the following initial concentrations and initial rate data.

Run #	$[A]_0$ (mol/L)	$[B]_0$ (mol/L)	Initial Rate (mol/L · s)
(1)	0.100	0.100	0.18
(2)	0.100	0.200	0.36
(3)	0.200	0.200	1.44

ANS: a)   rate = $k[A]^2[B]$ (b) 1.8×10^2 L^2/mol^{2}s   **PAGE:** 12.3

119–121. Use the potential energy diagram shown to answer the following:

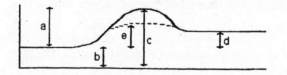

119. Which letter shows the activation energy?

ANS: a   **PAGE:** 12.7

120. Which letter shows the change in energy for the overall reaction?

ANS: d   **PAGE:** 12.7

121. Which letter shows the activation energy using a catalyst?

ANS: e   **PAGE:** 12.7,8

CHAPTER 13   Chemical Equilibrium

1. Which of the following statements concerning equilibrium is not true?

   a) A system that is disturbed from an equilibrium condition responds in a manner to restore equilibrium.
   b) Equilibrium in molecular systems is dynamic, with two opposing processes balancing one another.
   c) The value of the equilibrium constant for a given reaction mixture is the same regardless of the direction from which equilibrium is attained.
   d) A system moves spontaneously toward a state of equilibrium.
   e) The equilibrium constant is independent of temperature.

   ANS: e)   The equilibrium constant is independent of temperature.   **PAGE:** 13.1,2

2. Which of the following statements is true?

   a) When two opposing processes are proceeding at identical rates, the system is at equilibrium.
   b) Catalysts are an effective means of changing the position of an equilibrium.
   c) The concentration of the products equals that of reactants and is constant at equilibrium.
   d) An endothermic reaction shifts toward reactants when heat is added to the reaction.
   e) None of the above statements is true.

   ANS: a)   When two opposing processes are proceeding at identical
                    rates, the system is at equilibrium.   **PAGE:** 13.1,7

3. Indicate the mass action expression for the following reaction:

   $$2X(g) + Y(g) \rightleftharpoons 3W(g) + V(g)$$

   a) $[X]^2[Y][W]^3[V]$

   b) $\dfrac{[W]^3[V]}{[X]^2[Y]}$

   c) $\dfrac{[3W][V]}{[2X][Y]}$

   d) $\dfrac{[X]^2[Y]}{[W]^3[V]}$

   ANS: b) $\dfrac{[W]^3[V]}{[X]^2[Y]}$ **PAGE:** 13.2

4. If, at a given temperature, the equilibrium constant for the reaction

$$H_2(g) + Cl_2(g) \rightleftharpoons 2HCl(g)$$

is K_p, then the equilibrium constant for the reaction

$$HCl(g) \rightleftharpoons (1/2)\, H_2(g) + (1/2)Cl_2\,(g)$$

can be represented as:

a) $\dfrac{1}{K_p{}^2}$

b) $K_p{}^2$

c) $\dfrac{1}{\sqrt{K_p}}$

d) $\sqrt{K_p}$

ANS: c) $\dfrac{1}{\sqrt{K_p}}$ **PAGE:** 13.2,3

5. The value of the equilibrium constant , K, is dependent on

   I.   The temperature of the system.
   II. The nature of the reactants and products.
   III. The concentration of the reactants.
   IV. The concentration of the products.
   a) I, II
   b) II, III
   c) III, IV
   d) It is dependent on three of the above choices.
   e) It is not dependent on any of the above choices.

ANS: a)   I, II   **PAGE:** 13.2

6. Apply the law of mass action to determine the equilibrium expression for
$2NO_2Cl \rightleftharpoons 2NO_2 + Cl_2$

   a) $2[NO_2][Cl_2]/2[NO_2Cl]$
   b) $2[NO_2Cl]/2[NO_2][Cl_2]$
   c) $[NO_2Cl]^2/[NO_2]^2[Cl_2]$
   d) $[NO_2]^2[Cl_2]/[NO_2Cl]^2$
   e) $[NO_2Cl]^2[NO_2]^2[Cl_2]$

ANS: d) $[NO_2]^2[Cl_2]/[NO_2Cl]^2$ **PAGE:** 13.2

7–9.   Consider the chemical system $CO + Cl_2 \rightleftharpoons COCl_2$; $K = 4.6 \times 10^9$ L/mol.

7. How do the equilibrium concentrations of the reactants compare to the equilibrium concentration of the product?

    a) They are much smaller.
    b) They are much bigger.
    c) They are about the same.
    d) They have to be exactly equal.
    e) You can't tell from the information given.

    Ans: a)   They are much smaller.   **PAGE:** 13.2

8. If the concentration of the product were to double, what would happen to the equilibrium constant?

    a) It would double its value.
    b) It would become half its current value.
    c) It would quadruple its value.
    d) It would not change its value.
    e) It would depend on the initial conditions of the product.

    Ans: d)   It would not change its value.   **PAGE:** 13.2

9. Determine the equilibrium constant for the system $N_2O_4 \rightleftharpoons 2NO_2$ at 25°C. The concentrations are shown here: $[N_2O_4] = 4.27 \times 10^{-2}$ M, $[NO_2] = 1.41 \times 10^{-2}$ M

    a) 0.33
    b) 3.0
    c) 0.66
    d) 0.05
    e) 0.0047

    Ans: e)   0.0047   **PAGE:** 13.2

10. At 500.0 K, one mole of gaseous ONCl is placed in a one-liter container. At equilibrium it is 9.0% dissociated according to the equation shown here: $2ONCl \rightleftharpoons 2NO + Cl_2$

    Determine the equilibrium constant.

    a) 4.4×10^{-4}
    b) 2.2×10^2
    c) 1.1×10^2
    d) 2.2×10^{-4}
    e) 9.1×10^{-1}

    ANS: a) 4.4×10^{-4} **PAGE:** 13.5

11. Consider the reaction $H_2 + I_2 \rightleftharpoons 2HI$ whose $K = 54.8$ at 425°C. If an equimolar mixture of reactants gives the concentration of the product to be 0.50 M at equilibrium, determine the concentration of the hydrogen.

   a) 4.6×10^{-3} M
   b) 6.8×10^{-2} M
   c) 1.2×10^{-3} M
   d) 9.6×10^{-2} M
   e) 1.6×10^{-4} M

   ANS: b) 6.8×10^{-2} M   **PAGE:** 13.5

12. Consider the gaseous reaction $CO(g) + Cl_2(g) \rightleftharpoons COCl_2(g)$. What is the expression for K_p in terms of K?

   a) $K(RT)$
   b) $K/(RT)$
   c) $K(RT)^2$
   d) $K/(RT)^2$
   e) $1/K(RT)$

   ANS: b) $K/(RT)$ **PAGE:** 13.3

13. Find the value of the equilibrium constant (K) (at 500 K) for

   $$N_2(g) + 3H_2(g) \rightleftharpoons 2NH_3(g)$$

   The value for K_p at 500 K is 1.5×10^{-5}/atm^2.

   a) 7.5×10^{-2}
   b) 1.3×10^{-2}
   c) 9.6×10^{-2}
   d) 2.5×10^{-2}
   e) 6.0×10^{-2}

   ANS: e) 6.0×10^{-2} **PAGE:** 13.3

14. Consider the following reaction: $CS_2(g) \; 4H_2(g) \rightleftharpoons CH_4(g) + 2H_2S(g)$
   The equilibrium constant K is 0.28 at 900°C. What is K_p at this temperature?

   a) 5.0×10^{-5}
   b) 4.0×10^{-5}
   c) 3.0×10^{-5}
   d) 2.0×10^{-5}
   e) 1.0×10^{-5}

   ANS: c) 3.0×10^{-5} **PAGE:** 13.3

15. Consider the following system at equilibrium:

$$N_2(g) + 3H_2(g) \rightleftharpoons 2NH_3(g) + 92.94 \text{ kJ}$$

Which of the following changes will shift the equilibrium to the right?

I. increasing the temperature
II. decreasing the temperature
III. increasing the volume
IV. decreasing the volume
V. removing some NH_3
VI. adding some NH_3
VII. removing some N_2
VIII. adding some N_2
a) I, IV, VI, VII
b) II, III, V, VIII
c) I, VI, VIII
d) I, III, V, VII
e) II, IV, V, VIII

ANS: e)   II, IV, V, VIII   **PAGE:** 13.7

16. If the equilibrium constant for A + B $\rightleftharpoons$ C is 0.123, then the equilibrium constant for 2C $\rightleftharpoons$ 2A + 2B is _____.

a) 1.00 –2(0.123)
b) 8.13
c) 0.123
d) 66.1
e) 16.3

ANS: d)   66.1   **PAGE:** 13.2

17. Calculate K_p for $H_2O(g) + \frac{1}{2} O_2(g) \rightleftharpoons H_2O_2(g)$ at 600 K, using the following data:

$$H_2(g) + O_2(g) \rightleftharpoons H_2O_2(g) \quad K_p = 2.3 \times 10^6 \text{ at 600 K}$$

$$2H_2(g) + O_2(g) \rightleftharpoons 2H_2O(g) \quad K_p = 1.8 \times 10^{37} \text{ at 600 K}$$

a) 4.4×10^{43}
b) 9.8×10^{24}
c) 1.2×10^{-4}
d) 5.4×10^{-13}
e) 2.6×10^{-31}

ANS: d) 5.4×10^{-13} **PAGE:** 13.2,3

18. Given the equation: $2NOCl_2(g) \rightleftharpoons 2NO(g) + Cl_2(g)$. The equilibrium constant is 0.0150 at 115°C. Calculate K_p.

    a) 0.0150
    b) 0.478
    c) 0.142
    d) 1.41×10^{-4}
    e) none of these

    ANS: b)   0.478   **PAGE:** 13.3

19. For the reaction below, K_p = 1.16 at 800°C.

    $$CaCO_3(s) \rightleftharpoons CaO(s) + CO_2(g)$$

    If a 20.0-gram sample of $CaCO_3$ is put into a 10.0-liter container and heated to 800°C, what percent of the $CaCO_3$ will react to reach equilibrium?

    a) 14.6%
    b) 65.9%
    c) 34.1%
    d) 100.0%
    e) none of these

    ANS: b)   65.9%   **PAGE:** 13.3-5

20. At –80°C, K for the reaction

    $$N_2O_4(g) \rightleftharpoons 2NO_2(g)$$

    is 4.66×10^{-8}. We introduce 0.050 mole of N_2O_4 into a 1.0-L vessel at –80°C and let equilibrium be established. The total pressure in the system at equilibrium will be:

    a) 0.23 atm
    b) 0.79 atm
    c) 1.3 atm
    d) 2.3 atm
    e) none of these

    ANS: b)   0.79 atm   **PAGE:** 13.3,6

302

21. The reaction

$$H_2(g) + I_2(g) \rightleftharpoons 2HI(g)$$

has $K_p = 45.9$ at 763 K. A particular equilibrium mixture at that temperature contains gaseous HI at a partial pressure of 4.00 atm and hydrogen gas at a partial pressure of 0.200 atm. What is the partial pressure of I_2?

   a)   0.200 atm
   b)   0.436 atm
   c)   1.74 atm
   d)   0.574 atm
   e)   14.3 atm

ANS: c) 1.74 atm   **PAGE:** 13.3

22. Consider the reaction:

$$CaCl_2(s) + 2H_2O(g) \rightleftharpoons CaCl_2 \cdot 2H_2O(s)$$

The equilibrium constant for the reaction as written is

   a) $K = \dfrac{[CaCl_2 \bullet 2H_2O]}{[CaCl_2][H_2O]^2}$

   b) $K = \dfrac{1}{[H_2O]^2}$

   c) $K = \dfrac{1}{2[H_2O]}$

   d) $K = [H_2O]^2$

   e) $K = \dfrac{[CaCl_2 \bullet 2H_2O]}{[H_2O]^2}$

ANS: b) $K = \dfrac{1}{[H_2O]^2}$ **PAGE:** 13.4

23–24. Consider the following equilibrium:

$$H_2(g) + I_2(s) \rightleftharpoons 2HI(g) \qquad \Delta H = +68.0 \text{ kJ/mol}$$

23. The proper K_{eq} expression is:

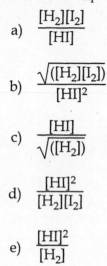

a) $\dfrac{[H_2][I_2]}{[HI]}$

b) $\dfrac{\sqrt{([H_2][I_2])}}{[HI]^2}$

c) $\dfrac{[HI]}{\sqrt{([H_2])}}$

d) $\dfrac{[HI]^2}{[H_2][I_2]}$

e) $\dfrac{[HI]^2}{[H_2]}$

ANS: e) $\dfrac{[HI]^2}{[H_2]}$ **PAGE:** 13.4

24. Which of the following statements about the equilibrium is false?

   a) If the system is heated, the right side is favored.
   b) This is a heterogeneous equilibrium.
   c) If the pressure on the system is increased by changing the volume, the left side is favored.
   d) Adding more $H_2(g)$ increases the equilibrium constant.
   e) Removing HI as it forms forces the equilibrium to the right.

   ANS: d)   Adding more $H_2(g)$ increases the equilibrium constant.   **PAGE:** 13.7

25. Consider the reaction:

$$2SO_2(g) + O_2(g) \rightleftharpoons 2SO_3(g)$$

at constant temperature. Initially a container is filled with pure $SO_3(g)$ at a pressure of 2 atm, after which equilibrium is reached. If y is the partial pressure of O_2 at equilibrium, the value of K_p is:

a) $\dfrac{(2 - 2y)^2}{(y^2)\,(2y)}$

b) $\dfrac{(2 - y)^2}{(y^2)\,(y/2)}$

c) $\dfrac{(2 - y)^2}{(2y)^2\,(y)}$

d) $\dfrac{(2 - 2y)^2}{(2y)^2\,(y)}$

e) none of these

ANS: d) $\dfrac{(2 - 2y)^2}{(2y)^2\,(y)}$ **PAGE:** 13.5

26–27. For the reaction given below, 2.00 moles of A and 3.00 moles of B are placed in a 6.00-L container.

$$A(g) + 2B(g) \rightleftharpoons C(g)$$

26. At equilibrium, the concentration of A is 0.300 mol/L. What is the concentration of B at equilibrium?

   a) 0.300 mol/L
   b) 0.433 mol/L
   c) 0.500 mol/L
   d) 0600 mol/L
   e) none of these

ANS: b)   0.433 mol/L   **PAGE:** 13.2

27. At equilibrium, the concentration of A is 0.300 mol/L. What is the value of K?

   a) 0.146
   b) 0.253
   c) 0.300
   d) 0.589
   e) 1.043

ANS: d)   0.589   **PAGE:** 13.5

28. A 10.0-g sample of solid NH_4Cl is heated in a 5.00-L container to 900°C. At equilibrium the pressure of $NH_3(g)$ is 1.20 atm.

$$NH_4Cl(s) \rightleftharpoons NH_3(g) + HCl(g)$$

The equilibrium constant, K_p, for the reaction is:

a) 1.20

b) 1.44

c) 2.40

d) 31.0

e) none of these

ANS: b)   1.44   **PAGE:** 13.5

29. The following reaction is investigated (assume an ideal gas mixture):

$$2N_2O(g) + N_2H_4(g) \rightleftharpoons 3N_2(g) + 2H_2O(g)$$

Initially there are 0.10 moles of N_2O and 0.25 moles of N_2H_4, in a 10.0-L container. If there are 0.06 moles of N_2O at equilibrium, how many moles of N_2 are present at equilibrium?

a) 0.9

b) 0.04

c) 0.06

d) 0.02

e) none of these

ANS: c)   0.06   **PAGE:** 13.5

30. At a certain temperature K for the reaction

$$2NO_2 \rightleftharpoons N_2O_4$$

is 7.5 liters/mole. If 2.0 moles of NO_2 are placed in a 2.0-liter container and permitted to react at this temperature, calculate the concentration of N_2O_4 at equilibrium.

a) 0.39 moles/liter

b) 0.65 moles/liter

c) 0.82 moles/liter

d) 7.5 moles/liter

e) none of these

ANS: a)   0.39 moles/liter   **PAGE:** 13.5,6

31. Initially 2.0 moles of $N_2(g)$ and 4.0 moles of $H_2(g)$ were added to a 1.0-liter container and the following reaction then occurred:

$$3H_2(g) + N_2(g) \rightleftharpoons 2NH_3(g)$$

The equilibrium concentration of $NH_3(g)$ = 0.68 moles/liter at 700°C. The value for K at 700°C for the formation of ammonia is:

   a) 3.6×10^{-3}
   b) 1.4×10^{-1}
   c) 1.1×10^{-2}
   d) 5.0×10^{-2}
   e)   none of these

   ANS: c) 1.1×10^{-2} **PAGE:** 13.5

32. Consider the reaction $C(s) + CO_2(g) \rightleftharpoons 2CO(g)$. At 1273 K the K_p value is 167.5. What is the P_{CO} at equilibrium if the P_{CO_2} is 0.10 atm at this temperature?

   a)   16.7 atm
   b)   2.0 atm
   c)   1.4 atm
   d)   4.1 atm
   e)   250 atm

   ANS: c)   4.1 atm   **PAGE:** 13.4

33. Which of the following is true for a system whose equilibrium constant is relatively small?

   a)   It will take a short time to reach equilibrium.
   b)   It will take a long time to reach equilibrium.
   c)   The equilibrium lies to the left.
   d)   The equilibrium lies to the right.
   e)   Two of these.

   ANS: c)   The equilibrium lies to the left.   **PAGE:** 13.5

34. The reaction quotient for a system is 7.2×10^2. If the equilibrium constant for the system is 36, what will happen as equilibrium is approached?

   a)   There will be a net gain in product.
   b)   There will be a net gain in reactant.
   c)   There will be a net gain in both product and reactant.
   d)   There will be no net gain in either product or reactant.
   e)   The equilibrium constant will decrease until it equals the reaction quotient.

   ANS: b)   There will be a net gain in reactant.   **PAGE:** 13.5

35. Consider the following equilibrated system: $2NO_2(g) \rightleftharpoons 2NO(g) + O_2(g)$. If the K_p value is 0.860, find the equilibrium pressure of the O_2 gas if the NO_2 gas pressure is 0.520 atm and the P_{NO} is 0.300 atm at equilibrium.

    a)   1.49 atm
    b)   0.78 atm
    c)   0.40 atm
    d)   0.99 atm
    e)   2.58 atm

ANS: e) 2.58 atm   **PAGE:** 13.5

36–37. Consider the following reaction (assume an ideal gas mixture):

$$2NOBr(g) \rightleftharpoons 2NO(g) + Br_2(g)$$

A 1.0-liter vessel was initially filled with pure NOBr, at a pressure of 4.0 atm, at 300 K.

36. After equilibrium was established, the partial pressure of NOBr was 2.5 atm. What is K_p for the reaction?

    a)   0.45
    b)   0.27
    c)   0.18
    d)   0.75
    e)   none of these

ANS: b) 0.27   **PAGE:** 13.5,6

37. After equilibrium was reached, the volume was increased to 2.0 liters, while the temperature was kept at 300 K. This will result in:

    a)   an increase in K_p.
    b)   a decrease in K_p.
    c)   a shift in the equilibrium position to the right.
    d)   a shift in the equilibrium position to the left.
    e)   none of these

ANS: c)   a shift in the equilibrium position to the right.   **PAGE:** 13.7

38–39. Nitric oxide, an important pollutant in air, is formed from the elements nitrogen and oxygen at high temperatures, such as those obtained when gasoline burns in an automobile engine. At 2000°C, K for the reaction

$$N2(g) + O_2(g) \rightleftharpoons 2NO(g)$$

is 0.01.

38. Predict the direction in which the system will move to reach equilibrium at 2000°C if 0.4 moles of N_2, 0.1 moles of O_2, and 0.08 moles of NO are placed in a 1.0-liter container.

    a) The system remains unchanged.
    b) The concentration of NO will decrease; the concentrations of N_2 and O_2 will increase.
    c) The concentration of NO will increase; the concentrations of N_2 and O_2 will decrease.
    d) The concentration of NO will decrease; the concentrations of N_2 and O_2 will remain unchanged.
    e) More information is necessary.

    ANS: b) The concentration of NO will decrease; the concentrations of N_2 and O_2 will increase.   **PAGE:** 13.5

39. A 1-L container originally holds 0.4 mol of N_2, 0.1 mol of O_2, and 0.08 mole of NO. If the volume of the container holding the equilibrium mixture of N_2, O_2, and NO is decreased to 0.5 L without changing the quantities of the gases present, how will their concentrations change?

    a) The concentration of NO will increase; the concentrations of N_2 and O_2 will decrease.
    b) The concentrations of N_2 and O_2 will increase; and the concentration of NO will decrease.
    c) The concentrations of N_2, O_2, and NO will increase.
    d) The concentrations of N_2, O_2, and NO will decrease.
    e) There will be no change in the concentrations of N_2, O_2, and NO.

    ANS: c) The concentrations of N_2, O_2, and NO will increase.   **PAGE:** 13.5,7

40. A sample of solid NH_4NO_3 was placed in an evacuated container and then heated so that it decomposed explosively according to the following equation:

    $$NH_4NO_3(s) \rightleftharpoons N_2O(g) + 2H_2O(g)$$

    At equilibrium the total pressure in the container was found to be 3.20 atm at a temperature of 500°C. Calculate K_p.

    a) 4.10
    b) 1.23
    c) 2.56
    d) 4.85
    e) 1.14

    ANS: d) 4.85   **PAGE:** 13.5

41.   Consider the following reaction:

$$2HF(g) \rightleftharpoons H_2(g) + F_2(g) \ (K = 1.00 \times 10^{-2})$$

Given 1.00 mole of HF(g), 0.500 mole of $H_2(g)$, and 0.750 mole of $F_2(g)$ are mixed in a 5.00-L flask, determine the reaction quotient, Q, and the net direction to achieve equilibrium.

   a) $Q = 0.150$; the equilibrium shifts to the right.
   b) $Q = 0.375$; the equilibrium shifts to the left.
   c) $Q = 0.150$; the equilibrium shifts to the left.
   d) $Q = 0.375$; the equilibrium shifts to the right.
   e) $Q = 0.150$; the system is at equilibrium.

   ANS: b) $Q = 0.375$; the equilibrium shifts to the left.   **PAGE:** 13.5

42.   Equilibrium is reached in chemical reactions when:

   a)   the rates of the forward and reverse reactions become equal.
   b)   the concentrations of reactants and products become equal.
   c)   the temperature shows a sharp rise.
   d)   all chemical reactions stop.
   e)   the forward reaction stops.

   ANS: a)   the rates of the forward and reverse reactions become
             equal.   **PAGE:** 13.1

43–46.   Consider the following equilibrium:

$$2NOCl(g) \rightleftharpoons 2NO(g) + Cl_2(g)$$

with $K = 1.6 \times 10^{-5}$. 1.00 mole of pure NOCl and 1.00 mole of pure Cl_2 are replaced in a 1.00-L container.

43.   If x moles of NOCl react, what is the equilibrium concentration of NO?

   a) $+x$
   b) $+2x$
   c) $-x$
   d) $-2x$
   e) x^2

   ANS: a) $+x$ **PAGE:** 13.6

44. If x moles of NOCl react, what is the equilibrium concentration of Cl_2?

    a) $+x$

    b) $+\dfrac{x}{2}$

    c) $1 + x$

    d) $1 + \dfrac{x}{2}$

    e) $1 + 2x$

    ANS: d) $1 + \dfrac{x}{2}$ **PAGE:** 13.6

45. Calculate the equilibrium concentration of NO(g).

    a) 1.0 M
    b) 1.6×10^{-5} M
    c) 0.50 M
    d) 6.2×10^{-4} M
    e) 4.0×10^{-3} M
    ANS: e) 4.0×10^{-3} M   **PAGE:** 13.6

46. Calculate the equilibrium concentration of Cl_2(g).

    a) 1.6×10^{-5} M
    b) 1.0 M
    c) 0.50 M
    d) 6.2×10^{-4} M
    e) 4.0×10^{-3} M
    ANS: b)   1.0 M   **PAGE:** 13.6

47–49. The questions below refer to the following system:

    A 3.00-liter flask initially contains 1.50 mol of gas A and 0.450 mol of gas B. Gas A decomposes according to the following reaction:

    $$3A \rightleftharpoons 2B + C$$

    The equilibrium concentration of gas C is 0.100 mol/L.

47. Determine the equilibrium concentration of gas A.

    a) 0.100 M
    b) 0.200 M
    c) 0.300 M
    d) 0.500 M
    e) none of these
    ANS: b)   0.200 M   **PAGE:** 13.5

48. Determine the equilibrium concentration of gas B.

    a) 0.150 M
    b) 0.200 M
    c) 0.350 M
    d) 0.450 M
    e) none of these

    ANS: c)   0.350 M **PAGE:** 13.5

49. Determine the value of the equilibrium constant, K.

    a) 0.117
    b) 0.175
    c) 0.227
    d) 1.53
    e) none of these

    ANS: d)   1.53 **PAGE:** 13.5

50. Nitrogen gas (N_2) reacts with hydrogen gas (H_2) to form ammonia (NH_3). At 200°C in a closed container, 1.0 atm of nitrogen gas is mixed with 2.0 atm of hydrogen gas. At equilibrium, the total pressure is 2.0 atm. Calculate the partial pressure of hydrogen gas at equilbrium.

    a) 2.0 atm
    b) 0.50 atm
    c) 1.5 atm
    d) 0.0 atm
    e) none of these

    ANS: b)   0.50 atm **PAGE:** 13.6

51. Given the equation A(aq) + 2B(aq) $\rightleftharpoons$ 3C(aq) + 2D(aq). 45.0 mL of 0.050 M A is mixed with 25.0 mL 0.100 M B. At equilibrium the concentration of C is 0.0410 M. Calculate K.

    a) 7.3
    b) 0.34
    c) 0.040
    d) 0.14
    e) none of these

    ANS: c)   0.040 **PAGE:** 13.5

52. Given the reaction $A(g) + B(g) \rightleftharpoons C(g) + D(g)$. You have the gases A, B, C, and D at equilibrium. Upon adding gas A, the value of K:

    a) increases because by adding A, more products are made, increasing the product to reactant ratio.

    b) decreases because A is a reactant o the product to reactant ratio decreases.

    c) does not change because A does not figure into the product to reactant ratio.

    d) does not change as long as the temperature is constant.

    e) depends on whether the reaction is endothermic or exothermic.

    ANS: d) does not change as long as the temperature is constant.   **PAGE:** 13.2, 7

53. The equilibrium system $2A \rightleftharpoons 2B + C$ has a very small equilibrium constant: $K = 2.6 \times 10^{-6}$. Initially 3 moles of A are placed in a 1.5-L flask. Determine the concentration of C at equilibrium.

    a) 0.011 M

    b) 0.022 M

    c) 0.033 M

    d) 0.044 M

    e) 2.0 M

    ANS: a) 0.011 M   **PAGE:** 13.6

54–57. The questions below refer to the following system:

Cobalt chloride is added to pure water. The Co^{2+} ions hydrate. The hydrated form then reacts with the Cl^- ions to set up the equilibrium shown here:

$$Co(H_2O)_6{}^{2+} + 4\,Cl^- \rightleftharpoons CoCl_4{}^{2-} + 6H_2O$$
$$\text{(pink)} \qquad\qquad \text{(blue)}$$

54. Which statement below describes the change that the system will undergo if hydrochloric acid is added?

    a) It should become more blue.

    b) It should become more pink.

    c) The equilibrium will shift to the right.

    d) The equilibrium will shift to the left.

    e) Two of these.

    ANS: e) Two of these.   **PAGE:** 13.7

55. Which statement below describes the change that the system will undergo if water is added?

    a) More chlorine ions will be produced.

    b) More water will be produced.

    c) The equilibrium will shift to the right.

    d) The color will become more blue.

    e) There will be less of the hydrated cobalt ion at the new equilibrium position.

    ANS: a) More chlorine ions will be produced.   **PAGE:** 13.7

56. Which statement below describes the change that the system will undergo if silver nitrate is added?

    a) It should become more blue.
    b) It should become more pink.
    c) Water will be produced.
    d) The silver ion will react with the $CoCl_4^{2-}$.
    e) Nothing will change.

    ANS: b)   It should become more pink.   **PAGE:** 13.7

57. Which statement below describes the change that the system will undergo if acetone (whose density is lower than water and is insoluble in water) is added?

    a) The system will become pink on the top and blue on the bottom.
    b) The system will become blue on the top and pink on the bottom.
    c) The system will become intensely pink in the middle.
    d) The system will become intensely blue on the top and clear on the bottom.
    e) The system will become intensely pink on the top and clear on the bottom.

    ANS: b) . The system will become blue on the top and pink on the
    bottom.   **PAGE:** 13.7

58–60. The following questions refer to the equilibrium shown here:

$$4NH_3(g) + 5O_2(g) \rightleftharpoons 4NO(g) + 6H_2O(g)$$

58. What would happen to the system if oxygen were added?

    a) More ammonia would be produced.
    b) More oxygen would be produced.
    c) The equilibrium would shift to the right.
    d) The equilibrium would shift to the left.
    e) Nothing would happen.

    ANS: c)   The equilibrium would shift to the right.   **PAGE:** 13.7

59. What would happen to the system if the pressure were decreased?

    a) Nothing would happen.
    b) More oxygen would be produced.
    c) The water vapor would become liquid water.
    d) The ammonia concentration would increase.
    e) The NO concentration would increase.

    ANS: e)   The NO concentration would increase.   **PAGE:** 13.7

60. For a certain reaction at 25.0°C, the value of K is 1.2×10^{-3}. At 50.0°C the value of K is 3.4×10^{-1}. This means that the reaction is

   a)   exothermic.
   b)   endothermic.
   c)   never favorable.
   d)   More information is needed.
   e)   None of these (a-d)

   ANS: a)   Endothermic   **PAGE:** 13.7

61. Ammonia is prepared industrially by the reaction:

$$N_2(g) + 3H_2(g) \rightleftharpoons 2NH_3(g)$$

   For the reaction, $\Delta H° = -92.2$ kJ and K (at 25°C) $= 4.0 \times 10^8$. When the temperature of the reaction is increased to 500°C, which of the following is true?

   a) K for the reaction will be larger at 500°C than at 25°C.
   b)   At equilibrium, more NH_3 is present at 500°C than at 25°C.
   c)   Product formation (at equilibrium) is not favored as the temperature is raised.
   d)   The reaction of N_2 with H_2 to form ammonia is endothermic.
   e)   None of the above is true.

   ANS: c)   Product formation (at equilibrium) is not favored as the
                  temperature is raised.   **PAGE:** 13.7

62-65. Consider the following equilibrium:

$$2H_2(g) + X_2(g) \rightleftharpoons 2H_2X(g) + energy$$

62. Addition of X_2 to a system described by the above equilibrium

   a)   will cause $[H_2]$ to decrease.
   b)   will cause $[X_2]$ to decrease.
   c)   will cause $[H_2X]$ to decrease.
   d)   will have no effect.
   e)   cannot possibly be carried out.

   ANS: a)   will cause $[H_2]$ to decrease.   **PAGE:** 13.7

63. Addition of argon to the above equilibrium

   a)   will cause $[H_2]$ to decrease.
   b)   will cause $[X_2]$ to increase.
   c)   will cause $[H_2X]$ to increase.
   d)   will have no effect.
   e)   cannot possibly be carried out.

   ANS: d)   will have no effect.   **PAGE:** 13.7

64. Increasing the pressure by decreasing the volume will cause

   a)   the reaction to occur to produce H_2X.
   b)   the reaction to occur to produce H_2 and X_2.
   c)   the reaction to occur to produce H_2 but no more X_2.
   d)   no reaction to occur.
   e) X_2 to dissociate.

   ANS: a)   the reaction to occur to produce H_2X.   **PAGE:** 13.7

65. Increasing the temperature will cause

   a)   the reaction to occur to produce H_2X.
   b)   the reaction to occur to produce H_2 and X_2.
   c)   the reaction to occur to produce H_2 but no more X_2.
   d)   no reaction to occur.
   e)   an explosion.

   ANS: b)   the reaction to occur to produce H_2 and X_2.   **PAGE:** 13.7

66. The value of equilibrium constant K is dependent on

   I.   the initial concentrations of the reactants.
   II. the initial concentrations of the products.
   III. the temperature of the system.
   IV. the nature of the reactants and products.
   a)   I, II
   b)   II, III
   c)   III, IV
   d)   It is dependent on three of the above choices.
   e)   It is not dependent on any of the above choices.

   ANS: c)   III, IV   **PAGE:** 13.2

67–72. Given the equation $2A(g) \rightleftharpoons 2B(g) + C(g)$. At a particular temperature, $K = 1.6 \times 10^4$.

67. If you start with 2.0 M of chemical A, calculate the equilibrium concentration of chemical C.

   a) 8.3×10^{-3} M
   b) 6.25×10^{-5} M
   c)   2.0 M
   d)   0.99 M
   e)   none of these

   ANS: d)   0.99 M   **PAGE:** 13.6

68. If you mixed 5.0 mol B, 0.10 mol C, and 0.0010 mol A in a one-liter container, which direction would the reaction initially proceed?

    a)   To the left.
    b)   To the right.
    c)   The above mixture is the equilibrium mixture.
    d)   Cannot tell from the information given.
    e)   None of these (a-d)

    ANS: a)   To the left.   **PAGE:** 13.5

69. At a higher temperature, $K = 1.8 \times 10^{-5}$. If you start with 2.0 M of chemical A, calculate the equilibrium concentration of chemical C.

    a) 6.0×10^{-3} M
    b) 2.6×10^{-2} M
    c)   1.0 M
    d) 2.1×10^{-2} M
    e)   none of these

    ANS: b) 2.6×10^{-2} M   **PAGE:** 13.6

70. Addition of chemical B to an equilibrium mixture of the above will

    a)   cause [A] to increase.
    b)   cause [C] to increase.
    c)   have no effect.
    d)   cannot be determined.
    e)   none of the above.

    ANS: a)   cause [A] to increase.   **PAGE:** 13.7

71. Placing the equilibrium mixture in an ice bath (thus lowering the temperature) will

    a)   cause [A] to increase.
    b)   cause [B] to increase.
    c)   have no effect.
    d)   cannot be determined.
    e)   none of the above.

    ANS: b)   cause [B] to increase.   **PAGE:** 13.7

72. Raising the pressure by lowering the volume of the container will

    a)   cause [A] to increase.
    b)   cause [B] to increase.
    c)   have no effect.
    d)   cannot be determined.
    e)   none of the above.

    ANS: a)   cause [A] to increase.   **PAGE:** 13.7

1. For the equilibrium that exists in an aqueous solution of nitrous acid (HNO_2, a weak acid), the equilibrium constant expression is:

    a) $K = \dfrac{[H^+][NO_2^-]}{[HNO_2]}$

    b) $K = \dfrac{[H^+][N][O]^2}{[HNO_2]}$

    c) $K = [H^+][NO_2^-]$

    d) $K = \dfrac{[H^+]^2[NO_2^-]}{[HNO_2]}$

    e) none of these

    ANS: a) $K = \dfrac{[H^+][NO_2^-]}{[HNO_2]}$ **PAGE:** 14.1

2. Which of the following is a conjugate acid/base pair?

    a) HCl/OCl^-
    b) H_2SO_4/SO_4^{2-}
    c) NH_4^+/NH_3
    d) H_3O^+/OH^-
    e) none of these

    ANS: c) NH_4^+/NH_3 **PAGE:** 14.1

3. The equilibrium constant for the reaction

    $$A^- + H^+ \rightleftharpoons HA$$

    is called:

    a) K_a

    b) K_b

    c) $\dfrac{1}{K_a}$

    d) $\dfrac{K_w}{K_b}$

    e) $K_w K_a$

    ANS: c) $\dfrac{1}{K_a}$ **PAGE:** 14.1

318

4. For the stepwise dissociation of aqueous H_3PO_4, which of the following is not a conjugate acid–base pair?

    a) HPO_4^{2-} and PO_4^{3-}

    b) H_3PO_4 and $H_2PO_4^-$

    c) $H_2PO_4^-$ and HPO_4^{2-}

    d) $H_2PO_4^-$ and PO_4^{3-}

    e) H_3O^+ and H_2O

    ANS: d) $H_2PO_4^-$ and PO_4^{3-} **PAGE:** 14.1,7

5. What is the equilibrium constant for the following reaction?

    $$N_3^- + H_3O^+ \rightleftharpoons HN_3 + H_2O$$

    The K_a value for $HN_3 = 1.9 \times 10^{-5}$.

    a) 5.3×10^{-10}

    b) 1.9×10^{-9}

    c) 1.9×10^{-5}

    d) 5.3×10^4

    e) 1.9×10^9

    ANS: d) 5.3×10^4 **PAGE:** 14.1

6. The hydrogen sulfate or bisulfate ion HSO_4^- can act as either an acid or a base in water solution. In which of the following equations does HSO_4^- act as an acid?

    a) $HSO_4^- + H_2O \rightarrow H_2SO_4 + OH^-$

    b) $HSO_4^- + H_3O^+ \rightarrow SO_3 + 2H_2O$

    c) $HSO_4^- + OH^- \rightarrow H_2SO_4 + O^{2-}$

    d) $HSO_4^- + H_2O \rightarrow SO_4^{2-} + H_3O^+$

    e)   none of these

    ANS: d) $HSO_4^- + H_2O \rightarrow SO_4^{2-} + H_3O^+$ **PAGE:** 14.1,2

7. Using the following K_a values, indicate the correct order of base strength.

    $\quad$ HNO_2 $\qquad$ $K_a = 4.0 \times 10^{-4}$

    $\quad$ HF $\qquad\quad$ $K_a = 7.2 \times 10^{-4}$

    $\quad$ HCN $\qquad$ $K_a = 6.2 \times 10^{-10}$

    a) $CN^- > NO_2^- > F^- > H_2O > Cl^-$

    b) $Cl^- > H_2O > F^- > NO_2^- > CN^-$

    c) $CN^- > F^- > NO_2^- > Cl^- > H_2O$

    d) $H_2O > CN^- > NO_2^- > F^- > Cl^-$

    e)   none of these

    ANS: a) $CN^- > NO_2^- > F^- > H_2O > Cl^-$ **PAGE:** 14.2

8. At 0°C, the ion-product constant of water, K_w, is 1.2×10^{-15}. The pH of pure water at 0°C is:

   a) 7.00
   b) 6.88
   c) 7.56
   d) 7.46
   e) none of these

   ANS: d)   7.46   **PAGE: 14.2,3**

9. The equilibrium constants (K_a) for HCN and HF in H_2O at 25°C are 6.2×10^{-10} and 7.2×10^{-4}, respectively. The relative order of base strengths is:

   a) $F^- > H_2O > CN^-$
   b) $H_2O > F^- > CN^-$
   c) $CN^- > F^- > H_2O$
   d) $F^- > CN^- > H_2O$
   e) none of these

   ANS: c) $CN^- > F^- > H_2O$ **PAGE: 14.2**

10. Given the following acids and Ka values:

$HClO_4$	HOAc	HCN	HF
1×10^7	1.76×10^{-5}	4.93×10^{-10}	3.53×10^{-4}

   which shows the conjugate bases listed by increasing strength?

   a) CN^-, F^-, OAc^-, ClO_4^-
   b) CN^-, OAc^-, F^-, ClO_4^-
   c) CN^-, ClO_4^-, F^-, OAc^-
   d) ClO_4^-, OAc^-, CN^-, F^-
   e) ClO_4^-, F^-, OAc^-, CN^-

   ANS: e) ClO_4^-, F^-, OAc^-, CN^-   **PAGE: 14.2**

11. The conjugate base of a weak acid is

   a) a strong base
   b) a weak base
   c) a strong acid
   d) a weak acid
   e) none of these

   ANS: b)   a weak base   **PAGE: 14.2**

12. Which of the following is the equilibrium constant expression for the dissociation of the weak acid HOCl?

    a) $K = \dfrac{[H^+][OCl^-]}{[HOCl]}$

    b) $K = [H^+][OCl^-]$

    c) $K = \dfrac{[HOCl]}{[H^+][OCl^-]}$

    d) $K = \dfrac{[H^+][O^{2-}][Cl^-]}{[HOCl]}$

    e) none of these

    ANS: a) $K = \dfrac{[H^+][OCl^-]}{[HOCl]}$ **PAGE:** 14.1,2

13–14. The following three equations represent equilibria that lie far to the right.

$$HNO_3(aq) + CN^-(aq) \rightleftharpoons HCN(aq) + NO_3^-(aq)$$

$$HCN(aq) + OH^-(aq) \rightleftharpoons H_2O(l) + CN^-(aq)$$

$$H_2O(l) + CH_3O^-(aq) \rightleftharpoons CH_2OH(aq) + OH^-(aq)$$

13. Identify the strongest acid.

    a) HCN
    b) HNO_3
    c) H_2O
    d) OH^-
    e) CH_3OH

    ANS: b) HNO_3 **PAGE:** 14.2

14. Identify the strongest base.

    a) CH_3O^-
    b) CH_3OH
    c) CN^-
    d) H_2O
    e) NO_3^-

    ANS: a) CH_3O^- **PAGE:** 14.2

15. Given that the K_a for HOCl is 3.5×10^{-8}, calculate the K value for the reaction of HOCl with OH^-.

    a) 3.5×10^6
    b) 3.5×10^{-8}
    c) 3.5×10^{-22}
    d) 2.9×10^{-7}
    e)   none of these

    ANS: a) 3.5×10^6   **PAGE:** 14.2,6,8

16. Calculate the $[H^+]$ in a solution that has a pH of 11.70.

    a)   2.3 M
    b)   11.7 M
    c) 5.0×10^{-3} M
    d) 2.0×10^{-12} M
    e)   none of these

    ANS: d) 2.0×10^{-12} M   **PAGE:** 14.3

17. Calculate the $[H^+]$ in a solution that has a pH of 2.30.

    a)   2.3 M
    b)   11.7 M
    c) 5.0×10^{-3} M
    d) 2.0×10^{-12} M
    e)   none of these

    ANS: c) 5.0×10^{-3} M   **PAGE:** 14.3

18. The pH of a solution at 25°C in which $[OH^-] = 3.4 \times 10^{-5}$ M is:

    a)   4.5
    b)   10.5
    c)   9.5
    d)   6.3
    e)   none of these

    ANS: c)   9.5   **PAGE:** 14.3

19. Consider the reaction $HNO_2(aq) + H_2O(l) \rightleftharpoons H_3O^+(aq) + NO^-(aq)$. Which species is the conjugate base?

    a) $HNO_2(aq)$
    b) $H_2O(l)$
    c) $H_3O^+(aq)$
    d) $NO^-(aq)$
    e)   Two of these

    ANS: e)   Two of these   **PAGE:** 14.1

20. In which of the following reactions does the $H_2PO_4^-$ ion act as an acid?

   a) $H_3PO_4 + H_2O \rightarrow H_3O^+ + H_2PO_4^-$
   b) $H_2PO_4^- + H_2O \rightarrow H_3O^+ + HPO_4^{2-}$
   c) $H_2PO_4^- + OH^- \rightarrow H_3PO_4 + O^{2-}$
   d) The ion cannot act as an acid.
   e) Two of these

   ANS: b) $H_2PO_4^- + H_2O \rightarrow H_3O^+ + HPO_4^{2-}$ **PAGE:** 14.1

21. In deciding which of two acids is the stronger, one must know:

   a) the concentration of each acid solution
   b) the pH of each acid solution
   c) the equilibrium constant of each acid
   d) all of the above
   e) both a and c must be known

   ANS: c) the equilibrium constant of each acid   **PAGE:** 14.2

22. Which of the following is not true for a solution at 25°C that has a hydroxide concentration of 2.5×10^{-6} M?

   a) $K_w = 1 \times 10^{-14}$
   b) The solution is acidic.
   c) The solution is basic.
   d) The [H] is 4×10^{-9} M.
   e) The K_w is independent of what the solution contains.

   ANS: c) The solution is basic.   **PAGE:** 14.2

23. Calculate the $[H^+]$ in a solution that has a pH of 9.7.

   a) 2.0×10^{-10} M
   b) 5.0×10^{-5} M
   c) 3.6×10^{-9} M
   d) 9.7×10^{-9} M
   e) 6.3×10^{-10} M

   ANS: a) 2.0×10^{-10} M   **PAGE:** 14.3

24. Calculate the pH of 0.250 M HNO_3(aq).

   a) 0.600
   b) 2.50
   c) 12.0
   d) 1.20
   e) 13.4

   ANS: a) 0.600   **PAGE:** 14.4

25. Solid calcium hydroxide is dissolved in water until the pH of the solution is 10.94. The hydroxide ion concentration [OH⁻] of the solution is:

    a) 1.1×10^{-11} M

    b)   3.06 M

    c) 8.7×10^{-4} M

    d) 1.0×10^{-14} M

    e)   none of these

ANS: c) 8.7×10^{-4} M   **PAGE:** 14.3

26. As water is heated, its pH decreases. This means that

    a)   the water is no longer neutral

    b) $[H^+] > [OH^-]$

    c) $[OH^-] > [H^+]$

    d)   a and b are correct

    e)   none of these

ANS: e) none of these   **PAGE:** 14.3

27. Which of the following indicates the most basic solution?

    a) $[H^+] = 1 \times 10^{-10}$ M

    b)   pOH =6.7

    c) $[OH^-] = 7 \times 10^{-5}$ M

    d)   pH = 4.2

    e)   At least two of the solutions are equally basic.

ANS: a) $[H^+] = 1 \times 10^{-10}$ M   **PAGE:** 14.3

28. Calculate the pOH of a 5.0 M solution of HCl.

    a)   -0.70

    b)   0.70

    c)   14.70

    d)   13.30

    e)   none of these

ANS: c) 14.70   **PAGE:** 14.4

29. Calculate the pH of a 0.050 M strong acid solution.

    a)   -1.30

    b)   1.30

    c)   12.70

    d)   15.30

    e)   none of these

ANS: b) 1.30   **PAGE:** 14.4

30. For nitrous acid, HNO_2, $K_a = 4.0 \times 10^{-4}$. Calculate the pH of 0.25 M HNO_2.

    a)   2.00
    b)   2.30
    c)   2.70
    d)   3.70
    e)   none of these

    ANS: a)   2.00   **PAGE:** 14.5

31. For weak acid, HX, $K_a = 1.0 \times 10^{-6}$. Calculate the pH of a 0.10 M solution of HX.

    a)   6.00
    b)   3.50
    c)   3.00
    d)   2.50
    e)   none of these

    ANS: b)   3.50   **PAGE:** 14.5

32. Acetic acid ($HC_2H_3O_2$) is a weak acid ($K_a = 1.8 \times 10^{-5}$). Calculate the pH of a 17.6 M $HC_2H_3O_2$ solution.

    a)   4.3
    b)   6.4
    c)   1.7
    d)   0.97
    e)   7.4

    ANS: c)   1.7   **PAGE:** 14.5

33. Determine the molarity of a solution of the weak acid $HClO_2$ ($K_a = 1.10 \times 10^{-2}$) if it has a pH of 1.25.

    a)   0.287 M
    b)   1.23 M
    c)   0.819 M
    d)   3.17 M
    e)   1.52 M

    ANS: a)   0.287 M   **PAGE:** 14.5

325

34–35. The following questions refer to a solution that contains 1.00 M hydrofluoric acid, HF ($K_a = 7.2 \times 10^{-4}$), and 3.00 M hydrocyanic acid, HCN ($K_a = 6.2 \times 10^{-10}$).

34. What is the pH of this mixture of weak acids?

   a) 0.00
   b) 1.57
   c) 3.14
   d) 4.37
   e) 9.21

   ANS: b)   1.57   **PAGE:** 14.5

35. Determine the [CN⁻] at equilibrium.

   a) 4.31×10^{-5} M
   b) 4.28×10^{-7} M
   c) 6.9×10^{-8} M
   d) 6.2×10^{-10} M
   e) none of these

   ANS: c) 6.9×10^{-8} M   **PAGE:** 14.5

36. How many moles of benzoic acid, a monoprotic acid with $K_a = 6.4 \times 10^{-5}$, must be dissolved in 500. mL of H_2O to produce a solution with pH = 2.50?

   a) 1.6×10^{-1}
   b) 2.0×10^{-2}
   c) 7.8×10^{-2}
   d) 0.50
   e) none of these

   ANS: c) 7.8×10^{-2}   **PAGE:** 14.5

37. Calculate the [H⁺] in a 0.010 M solution of HCN, $K_a = 6.2 \times 10^{-10}$.

   a) 1.0×10^{-7} M
   b) 2.5×10^{-6} M
   c) 3.6×10^{-3} M
   d) 6.2×10^{-10} M
   e) none of these

   ANS: b) 2.5×10^{-6} M   **PAGE:** 14.5

38. In a solution prepared by dissolving 0.100 mole of propionic acid in enough water to make 1.00 L of solution, the pH is observed to be 1.35. The K_a for propionic acid ($HC_3H_5O_2$) is:

    a) 2.0×10^{-2}
    b) 3.6×10^{-2}
    c) 4.5×10^{-2}
    d) 5.0×10^{-12}
    e)   none of these

    ANS: b) 3.6×10^{-2} **PAGE:** 14.5

39. A solution of 2.5 M weak acid is 0.52% ionized. What is the K_a value of this acid?

    a) 6.8×10^{-5}
    b) 1.1×10^{-5}
    c) 0.11
    d) 1.3×10^{-2}
    e)   none of these

    ANS: a) 6.8×10^{-5} **PAGE:** 14.5

40. A solution of 8.0 M formic acid (HCOOH) is 0.47% ionized. What is the K_a of formic acid?

    a) 3.4×10^{-8}
    b) 1.8×10^{-4}
    c) 6.9×10^{-6}
    d) 3.8×10^{-2}
    e)   need more data

    ANS: b) 1.8×10^{-4} **PAGE:** 14.5

41. The pH of a 0.100 M solution of an aqueous weak acid (HA) is 3.20. The K_a for the weak acid is:

    a) 6.3×10^{-4}
    b) 7.2×10^{-5}
    c) 4.0×10^{-6}
    d) 3.2
    e)   none of these

    ANS: c) 4.0×10^{-6} **PAGE:** 14.5

42. Saccharin is a monoprotic acid. If the pH of a 1.50×10^{-2} M solution of this acid is 5.53, what is the K_a of saccharin?

    a) 2.0×10^{-4}
    b) 2.9×10^{-6}
    c) 5.8×10^{-10}
    d) 8.4×10^{-12}
    e) none of these

ANS: c) 5.8×10^{-10} **PAGE:** 14.5

43. The pH of a 0.13 M solution of a weak monoprotic acid, HA, is 2.92. Calculate the K_a for this acid.

    a) 0.13
    b) 1.2×10^{-3}
    c) 1.4×10^{-6}
    d) 1.1×10^{-5}
    e) 1.3×10^{-10}

ANS: d) 1.1×10^{-5} **PAGE:** 14.5

44. A monoprotic weak acid when dissolved in water is 0.92% dissociated and produces a solution with a pH of 3.42. Calculate the K_a of the acid.

    a) 1.4×10^{-7}
    b) 2.8×10^{-3}
    c) 3.5×10^{-6}
    d) Need to know the initial concentration of the acid.
    e) None of these.

ANS: c) 3.5×10^{-6} **PAGE:** 14.5

45. If an acid, HA, is 10.0% dissociated in a 1.0 M solution, what is the K_a for this acid?

    a) 9.1×10^{-2}
    b) 1.1×10^{-2}
    c) 8.1×10^{-1}
    d) 6.3×10^{-2}
    e) none of these

ANS: b) 1.1×10^{-2} **PAGE:** 14.5

46. Calculate the pH of a 0.10 M solution of HOCl, $K_a = 3.5 \times 10^{-8}$.

    a) 4.23
    b) 8.46
    c) 3.73
    d) 1.00
    e) 3.23

ANS: a) 4.23   **PAGE:** 14.5

47. Calculate the pOH of a 0.80 M solution of acetic acid ($K_a = 1.8 \times 10^{-5}$).

   a) 9.25
   b) 2.42
   c) 4.74
   d) 11.58
   e) 7.87

   ANS: d)   11.58   **PAGE:** 14.5

48. The pK_a of HOCl is 7.5. Calculate the pH of a 0.5 M solution of HOCl.

   a) 7.5
   b) 6.5
   c) 3.9
   d) 10.1
   e) 0.3

   ANS: c)   3.9   **PAGE:** 14.5

49. When 2.0×10^{-2} mol of nicotinic acid (a monoprotic acid) is dissolved in 350 mL of water, the pH is 3.05. Calculate the K_a of nicotinic acid.

   a) 1.6×10^{-2}
   b) 1.4×10^{-5}
   c) 3.9×10^{-5}
   d) 7.9×10^{-7}
   e) none of these

   ANS: b) 1.4×10^{-5} **PAGE:** 14.5

50. Approximately how much water should be added to 10.0 mL of 12.0 M HCl so that it has the same pH as 0.90 M acetic acid ($K_a = 1.8 \times 10^{-5}$)?

   a) 30 mL
   b) 300 mL
   c) 3 L
   d) 30 L
   e) 300 L

   ANS: d)   30 L   **PAGE:** 14.5

51. As water is heated, its pH decreases. This means that

   a) the water is no longer neutral.
   b) the K_w value is decreasing.
   c) the water has a lower (OH⁻] than cooler water.
   d) the dissociation of water is an endothermic process.
   e) none of these.

   ANS: d)   the dissociation of water is an endothermic process.   **PAGE:** 14.2,3

52. What concentration of acetic acid ($K_a = 1.80 \times 10^{-5}$) has the same pH as that of 5.00×10^{-3} M HCl?

    a) 3.60×10^{-3} M
    b) 5.00×10^{-3} M
    c) 1.39 M
    d) 5.00 M
    e) none of these

    ANS: c) 1.39 M   **PAGE:** 14.4,5

53–54. Consider the reaction HOCl + F$^-$ $\rightleftharpoons$ HF + OCl$^-$

53. Given that K_a for HOCl is 3.5×10^{-8} and the K_a for HF is 7.2×10^{-4} (both at 25°C), which of the following is true concerning K for the above reaction at 25°C?

    a) K is greater than 1.
    b) K is less than 1.
    c) K is equal to 1.
    d) Cannot be determined with the above information.
    e) None of these (a-d)

    ANS: b) K is less than 1   **PAGE:** 13.2,14.5

54. Assuming that the value for K in the above reaction is greater than 1, this means that HF is a stronger acid than HOCl.

    ANS: False   **PAGE:** 13.2,14.5

55–56. Consider the following reactions

    a) $Al^{3+} + 6H_2O \rightleftharpoons Al(OH_2)_6^{3+}$
    b) $Al(OH_2)_6^{3+} \rightleftharpoons Al(OH)(OH_2)_5^{2+} + H^+$
    c) $OCl^- + H_2O \rightleftharpoons HOCl + OH^-$
    d) $CN^- + H^+ \rightleftharpoons HCN$
    e) None of these

55. Which is associated with the definition of K_a?

    ANS: b) $Al(OH_2)_6^{3+} \rightleftharpoons Al(OH)(OH_2)_5^{2+} + H^+$ **PAGE:** 14.1

56. Which is associated with the definition of K_b?

    ANS: c) $OCl^- + H_2O \rightleftharpoons HOCl + OH^-$ **PAGE:** 14.6

57. Which of the following reactions is associated with the definition of K_b?

   a) $Zn(OH_2)_6^{2+} \rightleftharpoons [Zn(OH_2)_5OH]^+ + H^+$

   b) $CN^- + H^+ \rightleftharpoons HCN$

   c) $F^- + H_2O \rightleftharpoons HF + OH^-$

   d) $Cr^{3+} + 6H_2O \rightleftharpoons Cr(OH_2)_6^{3+}$

   e) none of these

   ANS: c) $F^- + H_2O \rightleftharpoons HF + OH^-$ **PAGE:** 14.6

58. Calculate the pH of a 0.10 M solution of $Ca(OH)_2$.

   a) 13.30
   b) 13.00
   c) 0.20
   d) 0.10
   e) none of these

   ANS: a) 13.30   **PAGE:** 14.6

59. Calculate the pH of a 0.02 M solution of KOH.

   a) 1.7
   b) 2.0
   c) 12.0
   d) 12.3
   e) cannot calculate answer unless a volume is given

   ANS: d) 12.3   **PAGE:** 14.6

60. Calculate the pOH of a 0.10 M solution of $Ba(OH)_2$.

   a) 13.30
   b) 0.70
   c) 1.00
   d) 13.00
   e) none of these

   ANS: b) 0.70   **PAGE:** 14.6

61. Calculate the pH of a 0.10 M solution of KOH.

   a) 14.00
   b) 13.00
   c) 1.00
   d) 0.10
   e) none of these

   ANS: b) 13.00   **PAGE:** 14.6

62. A 0.400-g sample of NaOH(s) is added to enough water to make 250.0 mL of solution. The pH of this solution is:

   a)   12.000
   b)   1.398
   c)   2.000
   d)   12.602
   e)   none of these

   ANS: d)   12.602   **PAGE:** 14.6

63. Calculate the pH of a 5.0×10^{-3} M KOH solution.

   a)   2.30
   b)   3.50
   c)   11.70
   d)   5.00
   e)   10.50

   ANS: c)   11.70   **PAGE:** 14.6

64–65. The following questions refer to a 0.70 M solution of hypochlorous acid, HClO.

64. The K_a for the acid is 3.5×10^{-8}. Determine the percent dissociation.

   a)   1.3%
   b)   0.84%
   c)   0.41%
   d)   0.22%
   e)   0.15%

   ANS: d)   0.22%   **PAGE:** 14.5

65. If the molarity was decreased to 0.3 M, which of the following statements would be true?

   a)   The percent dissociation would not change.
   b)   The percent dissociation would increase.
   c)   The percent dissociation would decrease.
   d)   The equilibrium constant would stay the same.
   e)   Two of these.

   ANS: e)   Two of these.   **PAGE:** 14.5

66. Calculate the pH of a 3.40 M solution of NaOH.

   a)   10.4
   b)   20.3
   c)   14.5
   d)   8.50
   e)   none of these

   ANS: c)   14.5   **PAGE:** 14.6

67. The pain killer morphine is a weak base when added to water. The reaction produces one mole of hydroxide ions for every one mole of morphine that dissolves. The K_b is 1.60×10^{-6}. What is the pH of a 5.00×10^{-3} M solution of morphine?

    a) 8.23
    b) 9.95
    c) 11.3
    d) 10.2
    e) none of these

    ANS: b) 9.95   **PAGE:** 14.6

68. Determine the pH of a 0.060 M solution of H_2SO_4. The dissociation occurs in two steps. K_{a1} is extreme large; K_{a2} is 1.2×10^{-2}.

    a) 1.4
    b) 1.3
    c) 1.2
    d) 1.1
    e) 1.0

    ANS: d) 1.1   **PAGE:** 14.7

69. The $[OH^-]$ in a 0.50 M pyridine (C_5H_5N; $K_b = 1.7 \times 10^{-9}$) solution is

    a) 0.50 M
    b) 2.9×10^{-5} M
    c) 1.8×10^{-9} M
    d) 3.3×10^{-10} M
    e) none of these

    ANS: b) 2.9×10^{-5} M   **PAGE:** 14.6

70. Calculate the pH of a 5.0 M solution of aniline ($C_6H_5NH_2$; $K_b = 3.8 \times 10^{-10}$):

    a) 4.36
    b) 9.64
    c) –0.070
    d) 9.30
    e) none of these

    ANS: b) 9.64   **PAGE:** 14.6

71. Calculate the pH of a 0.10 M solution of pyridine (C_5H_5N; $K_b = 1.7 \times 10^{-9}$):

    a) 8.15
    b) 5.88
    c) 9.12
    d) 11.24
    e) none of these

    ANS: c) 9.12   **PAGE:** 14.6

72. Calculate the percentage of pyridine (C_5H_5N) that forms pyridinium ion, $C_5H_5NH^+$, in a 0.10 M aqueous solution of pyridine ($K_b = 1.7 \times 10^{-9}$):

    a)   0.0060%
    b)   1.6%
    c)   0.77%
    d)   0.060%
    e)   0.013%

    ANS: e)   0.013%   PAGE: 14.6

73. Which of the following aqueous solutions will have the highest pH?
    For NH_3, $K_b = 1.8 \times 10^{-5}$; for $C_2H_3O_2^-$, $K_b = 5.6 \times 10^{-10}$.

    a)   2.0 M NaOH
    b)   2.0 M NH_3
    c)   2.0 M $HC_2H_3O_2$
    d)   2.0 M HCl
    e)   all the same

    ANS: a)   2.0 M NaOH   PAGE: 14.6

74. Calculate the pH of a 0.50 M NH_3 ($K_b = 1.8 \times 10^{-5}$) solution.

    a)   13.72
    b)   7.00
    c)   4.78
    d)   2.52
    e)   none of these

    ANS: e)   none of these   PAGE: 14.6

75. The equilibrium constant for the reaction

$$NH_4^+ + OH^- \rightleftharpoons NH_3 + H_2O$$

is:

a) $\dfrac{1}{K_b(NH_3)}$

b) $\dfrac{1}{K_a(NH_4^+)}$

c) $\dfrac{K_w}{K_a(NH_4^+)}$

d) $\dfrac{K_w}{K_b(NH_3)}$

e) $\dfrac{K_b(NH_3)}{K_w}$

ANS: a) $\dfrac{1}{K_b(NH_3)}$ **PAGE:** 14.6

76–81. Calculate the pH of the following aqueous solutions. Choose your answer from the following pH ranges:

a) pH 0.00–2.99
b) pH 3.00–5.99
c) pH 6.00–8.99
d) pH 9.00 –10.99
e) pH 11.00–14.00

76. 0.5 M HOCl ($pK_a = 7.46$)

ANS: b)   pH 3.00–5.99 **PAGE:** 14.5

77. 0.5 M NaF (pK_a for HF = 3.14)

ANS: c)   pH 6.00–8.99 **PAGE:** 14.8

78. 0.5 M aniline ($pK_b = 9.42$)

ANS: d)   pH 9.00–10.99 **PAGE:** 14.6

79. 0.5 m NH_4Cl (pK_b for $NH_3 = 4.74$)

ANS: b)   pH 3.00–5.99 **PAGE:** 14.8

80. 0.5 M H_2S ($pK_{a1} = 7.00$; $pK_{a2} = 12.89$)

ANS: b)   pH 3.00–5.99 **PAGE:** 14.7

81. 0.5 M H_2CO_3 (pK_{a1} = 6.37; pK_{a2} = 10.25)

ANS: b)   pH 3.00–5.99

PAGE: 14.7

82. A 0.10-mol sample of a diprotic acid, H_2A, is dissolved in 250 mL of water. The K_{a1} of this acid is 1.0×10^{-5} and K_{a2} is 1.0×10^{-10}. Calculate the concentration of A^{2-} in this solution.

   a) 1.0×10^{-5} M
   b) 2.0×10^{-3} M
   c) 4.0×10^{-6} M
   d) 1.0×10^{-10} M
   e)   0.40 M

ANS: d) 1.0×10^{-10} M

PAGE: 14.7

83. The pH in a solution of 1.0 M H_2A (K_{a1} = 1.0×10^{-6}; K_{a2} = 1.0×10^{-10}) is:

   a)   8.00
   b)   7.00
   c)   6.00
   d)   3.00
   e)   none of these

ANS: d)   3.00

PAGE: 14.7

84. Calculate the pH of a 0.05 M solution of ascorbic acid (K_{a1} = 7.9×10^{-5}; K_{a2} = 1.6×10^{-12}).

   a)   1.3
   b)   2.7
   c)   3.1
   d)   5.4
   e)   6.5

ANS: b)   2.7

PAGE: 14.7

85. Calculate the $[H^+]$ in 1.0 M solution of Na_2CO_3 (for H_2CO_3, K_{a1} = 4.3×10^{-7}; K_{a2} = 5.6×10^{-11}).

   a) 7.5×10^{-6} M
   b) 6.6×10^{-4} M
   c) 1.3×10^{-2} M
   d) 7.5×10^{-13} M
   e)   none of these

ANS: d) 7.5×10^{-13} M

PAGE: 14.7,8

86. The dihydrogenphosphate ion, $H_2PO_4^-$, has both a conjugate acid and a conjugate base. These are, respectively:

    a) H_3PO_4, PO_4^{3-}

    b) H_3PO_4, HPO_4^{2-}

    c) $H_2PO_4^-$, HPO_4^{2-}

    d) HPO_4^{2-}, PO_4^{3-}

    e) HPO_4^{2-}, H_3PO_4

    ANS: b) H_3PO_4, HPO_4^{2-} **PAGE:** 14.7

87. HOAc $K_a = 1.8 \times 10^{-5}$
    H_2CO_3 $K_{a1} = 4.3 \times 10^{-7}$
                $K_{a2} = 5.6 \times 10^{-11}$

    Which of the following 0.01 M solutions has the highest pH?

    a) HOAc
    b) NaOAc
    c) Na_2CO_3
    d) H_2CO_3
    e) $NaHCO_3$

    ANS: c) Na_2CO_3 **PAGE:** 14.7,8

88. The conjugate acid and conjugate base of bicarbonate ion, HCO_3^-, are, respectively:

    a) H_3O^+ and OH^-

    b) H_3O^+ and CO_3^{2-}

    c) H_2CO_3 and OH^-

    d) H_2CO_3 and CO_3^{2-}

    e) CO_3^{2-} and OH^-

    ANS: d) H_2CO_3 and CO_3^{2-} **PAGE:** 14.7

89. Which of the following species is present in the greatest concentration in a 0.100 M H_2SO_4 solution in H_2O?

    a) H_3O^+

    b) HSO_4^-

    c) H_2SO_4

    d) All species are in equilibrium and therefore have the same concentration.

    e) SO_4^{2-}

    ANS: a) H_3O^+ **PAGE:** 14.7

90. The pH of a 0.150 M solution of a weak base is 10.98. Calculate the pH of a 0.0400 M solution of the base.

    a) 10.5

    b) 10.7

    c) 11.2

    d) 11.5

    e) none of these

    ANS: b)   10.7   **PAGE:** 14.6

91. Which of the following is the correct order for increasing pHs for HNO_3, KCl, NH_4Cl, KOH, and $NaC_2H_3O_2$? (K_a for $HC_2H_3O_2$ is 1.80×10^{-5}, K_a for NH_4^+ is 5.56×10^{-10}).

    a) KCl, NH_4Cl, HNO_3, KOH, $NaC_2H_3O_2$

    b) HNO_3, KCl, NH_4Cl, KOH, $NaC_2H_3O_2$

    c) NH_4Cl, HNO_3, KCl, KOH, $NaC_2H_3O_2$

    d) HNO_3, NH_4Cl, KCl, $NaC_2H_3O_2$, KOH

    e) none of these

    ANS: d) HNO_3, NH_4Cl, KCl, $NaC_2H_3O_2$, KOH   **PAGE:** 14.8

92. Which of the following is the strongest base? (K_b for NH_3 is 1.8×10^{-5}, K_{a2} for H_2SO_4 is 1.2×10^{-2}, K_{a3} for H_3PO_4 is 4.8×10^{-13})

    $$NH_3,\ HSO_4^-,\ PO_4^{3-},\ \text{or}\ NO_3^-$$

    a) NH_3

    b) HSO_4^-

    c) NO_3^-

    d) PO_4^{3-}

    e) Two of these are equally strong.

    ANS: d) PO_4^{3-} **PAGE:** 14.6-8

93. The salt BX, when dissolved in water, produces an acidic solution. Which of the following could be true?

    a) HX is a weak acid.

    b) HX is a strong acid.

    c) The cation B^+ is a weak acid.

    d) All of the above could be true.

    e) Only two of the above (a and c) could be true.

    ANS: d)   All of the above could be true.   **PAGE:** 14.8

94. Calculate the K_a for an unknown monoprotic acid HX, given that a solution of 0.10 M LiX has a pH of 8.90.

    a) 7.9×10^{-6}
    b) 4.3×10^{-8}
    c) 6.2×10^{-10}
    d) 2.6×10^{-10}
    e) 1.6×10^{-5}

    ANS: e) 1.6×10^{-5} **PAGE:** 14.8

95. The sodium salt, NaA, of a weak acid is dissolved in water; no other substance is added. Which of these statements (to a close approximation) is true?

    a) $[H^+] = [A^-]$
    b) $[H^+] = [OH^-]$
    c) $[A^-] = [OH^-]$
    d) $[HA] = [OH^-]$
    e)   none of these

    ANS: d) $[HA] = [OH^-]$ **PAGE:** 14.8

96. The $[H_3O^+]$ of a 0.15 M solution of NH_4Cl in H_2O at 25°C is (K_b for $NH_3 = 1.8 \times 10^{-5}$):

    a) 3.6×10^{-3} M
    b) 4.9×10^{-5} M
    c) 9.1×10^{-6} M
    d) 8.2×10^{-10} M

    ANS: c) 9.1×10^{-6} M   **PAGE:** 14.8

97. Calculate the pH of a 0.30 M solution of NH_4Cl. (K_b for $NH_3 = 1.8 \times 10^{-5}$)

    a)   3.33
    b)   4.89
    c)   9.11
    d)   7.00
    e)   11.67

    ANS: b)   4.89   **PAGE:** 14.8

98. If K_a for HCN is 6.2×10^{-10}, what is K_b for CN^-?

    Note: $CN^- + H_2O \rightleftharpoons HCN + OH^-$ $K_b = \dfrac{[HCN][OH^-]}{[CN^-]}$

    a) 6.2×10^{-24}
    b) 6.2×10^4
    c) 1.6×10^{-5}
    d) 1.6×10^{23}
    e)   none of these

    ANS: c) 1.6×10^{-5} **PAGE:** 14.8

99. If you know K_b for ammonia, NH_3, you can calculate the equilibrium constant, K_a, for the following reaction:

$$NH_4^+ \rightleftharpoons NH_3 + H^+$$

by the equation:

   a) $K_a = K_w K_b$
   b) $K_a = K_w / K_b$
   c) $K_a = 1 / K_b$
   d) $K_a = K_b / K_w$

ANS: b) $K_a = K_w / K_b$ **PAGE:** 14.8

100. Which of the following would give the highest pH when dissolved in water to form a 0.10 M solution?

   a) a strong acid
   b) a weak acid
   c) the potassium salt of a weak acid
   d) the potassium salt of a strong acid
   e) the ammonium salt of a strong acid

   ANS: c)   the potassium salt of a weak acid   **PAGE:** 14.8

101. Which of the following is true about the pH of a solution of sulfuric acid?

   a) If the solution is dilute the pH is not able to be calculated.
   b) If the solution is dilute the pH is completely controlled by the first dissociation.
   c) If the solution is dilute the pH is completely controlled by the second dissociation.
   d) If the solution is concentrated the pH is partially controlled by the second dissociation.
   e) If the solution is dilute the pH is partially controlled by the second dissociation.

   ANS: e)   If the solution is dilute the pH is partially controlled by the second dissociation.   **PAGE:** 14.7

102. What is the pH of a 0.45 M KCl solution?

   a) 10.5
   b) 7.0
   c) 9.2
   d) 1.4
   e) 4.5

   ANS: b)   7.0   **PAGE:** 14.8

103. A 0.240 M solution of the salt NaA has a pH of 8.40. Calculate the K_a value of the acid HA.

    a) 6.60×10^{-17}
    b) 1.05×10^{-5}
    c) 3.80×10^{-4}
    d) 2.63×10^{-11}
    e) none of these

    ANS: c) 3.80×10^{-4} **PAGE:** 14.8

104. The hydrogen halides (HF, HCl, HBr, and HI) are all polar molecules. The strength of the acid each forms in water is based on which of the following?

    a) the polarity of the molecule
    b) the size of the molecule
    c) the strength of the bond
    d) two of these
    e) none of these

    ANS: d)   two of these   **PAGE:** 14.9

105. Which factor listed below is most important in determining the strength of an oxyacid?

    a) the size of the molecule
    b) the ability of the molecule to change atomic orientation
    c) the identity of the central atom in the molecule
    d) the number of oxygen atoms present in the molecule
    e) none of these

    ANS: d)   the number of oxygen atoms present in the molecule   **PAGE:** 14.9

106–110. Use the following choices to describe an aqueous solution made from each of the following substances.
    a) acidic
    b) neutral
    c) basic
    d) cannot tell
    e) None of these (a-d)

106. solid sodium nitrate ($NaNO_3$)

    ANS: b)   neutral   **PAGE:** 14.8

107. solid silver chloride (AgCl)

    ANS: b)   neutral   **PAGE:** 14.8

108. solid sodium carbonate (Na_2CO_3)

    ANS: c)   basic   **PAGE:** 14.8

109. solid ammonium acetate ($NH_4C_2H_3O_2$)

For NH_4^+, $K_a = 5.6 \times 10^{-10}$; for $C_2H_3O_2^-$, $K_b = 5.6 \times 10^{-10}$.

ANS: b)   neutral   **PAGE:** 14.8

110. solid ammonium perchlorate (NH_4ClO_4)

For NH_4^+, $K_a = 5.6 \times 10^{-10}$; for ClO_4^-, $K_b \approx 10^{-21}$.

ANS: a)   acidic   **PAGE:** 14.8

111. The pH of a 1.0 M aqueous solution of NaCl is:

    a)   7.0
    b)   greater than 7.0
    c)   less than 7.0
    d)   not enough information is given
    e)   none of these (a-d)

ANS: a)   7.0   **PAGE:** 14.8

112. The pH of a 1.0 M sodium acetate solution is:

    a)   7.0
    b)   greater than 7.0
    c)   less than 7.0
    d)   not enough information is given
    e)   none of these (a-d)

ANS: b)   greater than 7.0   **PAGE:** 14.8

113. Which of the following would produce a basic aqueous solution?

    a) P_4O_{10}
    b)   KCl
    c) CO_2
    d) NH_4Cl
    e)   none of these

ANS: e)   none of these   **PAGE:** 14.8,10

114. Calculate the pH of a 0.20 M solution of $NaC_2H_3O_2$ (for $HC_2H_3O_2$ $K_a = 1.8 \times 10^{-5}$).

    a)   4.98
    b)   9.02
    c)   5.44
    d)   8.56
    e)   none of these

ANS: b)   9.02   **PAGE:** 14.8

115. Which of the following would produce the most acidic solution?

    a) $HOCl_2$
    b) $HOCl$
    c) $HOBr$
    d) HOI
    e) $HOAt$

    ANS: a) $HOCl_2$ **PAGE:** 14.9

116. Calculate the pH of a 0.005 M solution of potassium oxide, K_2O.

    a) 12.0
    b) 11.7
    c) 7.0
    d) 2.3
    e) 2.0

    ANS: a)   12.0   **PAGE:** 14.10

117. Which of the species below, when dissolved in H_2O, will not produce a basic solution?

    a) SO_2
    b) NH_3
    c) BaO
    d) $Ba(OH)_2$
    e) none of these

    ANS: a) SO_2 **PAGE:** 14.10

118. Define amphoteric substance.

    ANS: See Sec. 14.2 of Zumdahl, *Chemistry*.   **PAGE:** 14.2

119–123. Determine whether the following oxides produce an acidic, basic, or neutral solution when dissolved in water:

119. K_2O

    ANS: basic   **PAGE:** 14.10

120. NO_2

    ANS: acidic   **PAGE:** 14.10

121. Cl_2O

    ANS: acidic   **PAGE:** 14.10

122. CaO

    ANS: basic   **PAGE:** 14.10

123. SO_2

   ANS: acidic   **PAGE:** 14.10

124. Explain why 0.1 M NaCN is basic while 0.1 M $NaNO_3$ is neutral.

   ANS: See Sec. 14.8 of Zumdahl, *Chemistry*.   **PAGE:** 14.8

125. Explain why $Al_2(SO_4)_3$ produces an acidic solution when it is dissolved in water.

   ANS: See Sec. 14.8 of Zumdahl, *Chemistry*.   **PAGE:** 14.8

1. What combination of substances will give a buffered solution that has a pH of 5.05? (Assume each pair of substances is dissolved in 5.0 L of water.)

    (K_b for $NH_3 = 1.8 \times 10^{-5}$; K_b for $C_5H_5N = 1.7 \times 10^{-9}$)

    a) 1.0 mole NH_3 and 1.5 mole NH_4Cl
    b) 1.5 mole NH_3 and 1.0 mole NH_4Cl
    c) 1.0 mole C_5H_5N and 1.5 mole C_5H_5NHCl
    d) 1.5 mole C_5H_5N and 1.0 mole C_5H_5NHCl
    e) none of these

    ANS: c) 1.0 mole C_5H_5N and 1.5 mole C_5H_5NHCl **PAGE:** 15.2

2. You have solutions of 0.200 M HNO_2 and 0.200 M KNO_2 (K_a for $HNO_2 = 4.00 \times 10^{-4}$). A buffer of pH 3.000 is needed. What volumes of HNO_2 and KNO_2 are required to make 1 liter of buffered solution?

    a) 500 mL of each
    b) 286 mL HNO_2; 714 mL KNO_2
    c) 413 mL HNO_2; 587 mL KNO_2
    d) 714 mL HNO_2; 286 mL KNO_2
    e) 587 mL HNO_2; 413 mL KNO_2

    ANS: d) 714 mL HNO_2; 286 mL KNO_2 **PAGE:** 15.2

3. 15.0 mL of 0.50 M HCl is added to a 100.-mL sample of 0.200 M HNO_2 (K_a for $HNO_2 = 4.0 \times 10^{-14}$). What is the equilibrium concentration of NO_2^- ions?

    a) 1.1×10^{-13} M
    b) 6.5×10^{-12} M
    c) 7.5×10^{-14} M
    d) 1.7×10^{-11} M
    e) none of these

    ANS: a) 1.1×10^{-13} M   **PAGE:** 15.2

4. A solution contains 0.250 M HA ($K_a = 1.0 \times 10^{-6}$) and 0.45 M NaA. What is the pH after 0.10 mole of HCl is added to 1.00 L of this solution?

    a) 3.17
    b) 3.23
    c) 6.00
    d) 10.77
    e) 10.83

    ANS: c) 6.00   **PAGE:** 15.2

5. A weak acid, HF, is in solution with dissolved sodium fluoride, NaF. If HCl is added, which ion will react with the extra hydrogen ions from the HCl to keep the pH from changing?

    a) OH⁻
    b) Na⁺
    c) F⁻
    d) Na⁻
    e) none of these

    ANS: c) F⁻   **PAGE:** 15.2

6. Which of the following is true for a buffered solution?

    a) The solution resists change in its [H⁺].
    b) The solution will not change its pH very much even if a concentrated acid is added.
    c) The solution will not change its pH very much even if a strong base is added.
    d) Any H⁺ ions will react with a conjugate base of a weak acid already in solution.
    e) all of these

    ANS: e)   all of these   **PAGE:** 15.2

7–8. The following questions refer to the following system: A 1.0-liter solution contains 0.25 M HF and 0.60 M NaF (K_a for HF is 7.2×10^{-4})

7. What is the pH of this solution?

    a) 1.4
    b) 3.5
    c) 4.6
    d) 2.8
    e) 0.94

    ANS: b)   3.5   **PAGE:** 15.1,2

8. If one adds 0.30 liters of 0.020 M KOH to the solution what will be the change in pH?

    a) 0.0
    b) 0.2
    c) 0.4
    d) 0.5
    e) none of these

    ANS: a)   0.0   **PAGE:** 15.2

9. Calculate the [H^+] in a solution that is 0.10 M in NaF and 0.20 in HF. ($K_a = 7.2 \times 10^{-4}$)

    a) 0.20 M
    b) 7.0×10^{-4} M
    c) 1.4×10^{-3} M
    d) 3.5×10^{-4} M
    e) none of these

    ANS: c) 1.4×10^{-3} M   **PAGE:** 15.2

10. Which of the following will not produce a buffered solution?

    a) 100 mL of 0.1 M Na_2CO_3 and 50 mL of 0.1 M HCl
    b) 100 mL of 0.1 M $NaHCO_3$ and 25 mL of 0.2 M HCl
    c) 100 mL of 0.1 M Na_2CO_3 and 75 mL of 0.2 M HCl
    d) 50 mL of 0.2 M Na_2CO_3 and 5 mL of 1.0 M HCl
    e) 100 mL of 0.1 M Na_2CO_3 and 50 mL of 0.1 M NaOH

    ANS: e)   100 mL of 0.1 M Na_2CO_3 and 50 mL of 0.1 M NaOH   **PAGE:** 15.2

11. How many moles of HCl need to be added to 150.0 mL of 0.50M NaZ to have a solution with a pH of 6.50? (K_a of HZ is 2.3×10^{-5}). Assume negligible volume of the HCl.

    a) 6.8×10^{-3}
    b) 7.5×10^{-2}
    c) 5.0×10^{-1}
    d) 1.0×10^{-3}
    e) none of these

    ANS: d) 1.0×10^{-3} **PAGE:** 15.2

12. Calculate the pH of a solution that is 0.5 M in HF ($K_a = 7.2 \times 10^{-4}$) and 0.6 M in NaF.

    a) 1.72
    b) 3.32
    c) 3.44
    d) 5.53
    e) 8.46

    ANS: b)   3.22   **PAGE:** 15.2

347

13. Consider a solution consisting of the following two buffer systems:

$$H_2CO_3 \rightleftharpoons HCO_3^- + H^+ \quad pK_a = 6.4$$
$$H_2PO_4^- \rightleftharpoons HPO_4^{2-} + H^+ \quad pK_a = 7.2$$

At pH 6.4, which one of the following is true of the relative amounts of acid and conjugate base present?

   a) $[H_2CO_3] > [HCO_3^-]$ and $[H_2PO_4^-] > [HPO_4^{2-}]$

   b) $[H_2CO_3] = [HCO_3^-]$ and $[H_2PO_4^-] > [HPO_4^{2-}]$

   c) $[H_2CO_3] = [HCO_3^-]$ and $[HPO_4^{2-}] > [H_2PO_4^-]$

   d) $[HCO_3^-] > [H_2CO_3]$ and $[HPO_4^{2-}] > [H_2PO_4^-]$

   e) $[H_2CO_3] > [HCO_3^-]$ and $[HPO_4^{2-}] > [H_2PO_4^-]$

   ANS: b) $[H_2CO_3] = [HCO_3^-]$ and $[H_2PO_4^-] > [HPO_4^{2-}]$ **PAGE:** 15.2

14. For a solution equimolar in HCN and NaCN, which statement is false?

   a) This is an example of the common ion effect.
   b) The $[H^+]$ is larger than it would be if only the HCN was in solution.
   c) The $[H^+]$ is equal to the K_a.
   d) Addition of more NaCN will shift the acid dissociation equilibrium of HCN to the left.
   e) Addition of NaOH will increase $[CN^-]$ and decrease $[HCN]$.

   ANS: b)   The $[H^+]$ is larger than it would be if only the HCN was in
              solution.   **PAGE:** 15.2

15. Calculate the pH of a solution that is 2.00 M HF, 1.00 M NaOH, and 0.500 M NaF. (K_a is 7.2×10^{-4})

   a) 3.14
   b) 3.32
   c) 3.02
   d) 2.84
   e) none of these

   ANS: b)   3.32   **PAGE:** 15.2

16. Given 100.0 mL of a buffer that is 0.50 M in HOCl and 0.40 M in NaOCl, what is the pH after 10.0 mL of 1.0 M NaOH has been added? (K_a for HOCl = 3.5×10^{-8})

   a) 6.45
   b) 6.64
   c) 7.36
   d) 7.45
   e) 7.55

   ANS: e)   7.55   **PAGE:** 15.2

17. How many moles of solid NaF would have to be added to 1.0 L of 1.90 M HF solution to achieve a buffer of pH 3.35? Assume there is no volume change. (K_a for HF = 7.2×10^{-4})

    a) 3.1
    b) 2.3
    c) 1.6
    d) 1.0
    e) 4.9

ANS: a) 3.1   **PAGE:** 15.2

18. What is the pH of a solution that results when 0.010 mol HNO_3 is added to 500. mL of a solution that is 0.10 M in aqueous ammonia and 0.20 M in ammonium nitrate. Assume no volume change. (The K_b for NH_3 = 1.8×10^{-5}.)

    a) 8.00
    b) 8.95
    c) 5.05
    d) 8.82
    e) 2.00

ANS: d) 8.82   **PAGE:** 15.2

19. How many mmoles of HCl must be added to 100 mL of a 0.100 M solution of methylamine (pK_b = 3.36) to give a buffer having a pH of 10.0?

    a) 8.1
    b) 18.7
    c) 20.0
    d) 41.5
    e) 12.7

ANS: a) 8.1   **PAGE:** 15.2

20. Calculate the pH of a solution made by mixing 100.0 mL of 0.300 M NH_3 with 100.0 mL of 0.100 M HCl. (K_b for NH_3 is 1.8×10^{-5}).

    a) 9.56
    b) 4.44
    c) 10.6
    d) 3.40
    e) none of these

ANS: a) 9.56   **PAGE:** 15.2

21. Consider a solution of 2.0 M HCN and 1.0 M NaCN (K_a for HCN = 6.2 x 10⁻¹⁰). Which of the following statements is true?

    a) The solution is not a buffer because [HCN] is not equal to [CN⁻].

    b) The pH will be below 7.00 because the concentration of the acid is greater than that of the base.

    c) [OH⁻] > [H⁺]

    d) The buffer will be more resistant to pH changes from addition of strong acid than of strong base.

    e) All of the above are false.

    ANS: c)   [OH⁻] > [H⁺]   **PAGE:** 15.1, 2

22. A solution contains 0.500 M HA (K_a = 1.0 × 10⁻⁸) and 0.250 M NaA. What is the [H⁺] after 0.10 mole of HCl(g) is added to 1.00 L of this solution?

    a) 1.4 × 10⁻⁸ M

    b) 2.0 × 10⁻⁸ M

    c) 2.5 × 10⁻⁹ M

    d) 4.0 × 10⁻⁸ M

    e) none of these

    ANS: d)   4.0 × 10⁻⁸ M   **PAGE:** 15.2

23. Which of the following solutions will be the best buffer at a pH of 9.26? (K_a for $HC_2H_3O_2$ is 1.8 x 10⁻⁵, K_b for NH_3 is 1.8 x 10⁻⁵).

    a) 0.10 M $HC_2H_3O_2$ and 0.10 M Na $C_2H_3O_2$

    b) 5.0 M $HC_2H_3O_2$ and 5.0 M Na $C_2H_3O_2$

    c) 0.10 M NH_3 and 0.10 M NH_4Cl

    d) 5.0 M NH_3 and 5.0 M NH_4Cl

    e) 5.0 M $HC_2H_3O_2$ and 5.0 M NH_3

    ANS: d)   5.0 M NH_3 and 5.0 M NH_4Cl **PAGE:** 15.2, 15.3

24. One milliliter (1.00 mL) of acid taken from a lead storage battery is pipetted into a flask. Water and phenolphthalein indicator are added, and the solution is titrated with 0.50 M NaOH until a pink color appears; 12.0 mL are required. The number of grams of H_2SO_4 (formula weight = 98) present in one liter of the battery acid is (to within 5%):

    a) 240

    b) 290

    c) 480

    d) 580

    e) 750

    ANS: b)   290   **PAGE:** 15.4

25. You are given 5.00 mL of an H_2SO_4 solution of unknown concentration. You divide the 5.00-mL sample into five 1.00-mL samples and titrate each separately with 0.1000 M NaOH. In each titration the H_2SO_4 is completely neutralized. The average volume of NaOH solution used to reach the endpoint is 15.3 mL. What was the concentration of H_2SO_4 in the 5.00-mL sample?

    a)   1.53 M

    b)   0.306 M

    c)   0.765 M

    d) 1.53×10^{-3} M

    e)   3.06 M

ANS: c)   0.765 M   **PAGE:** 15.4

26. What is the molarity of a sodium hydroxide solution if 25.0 mL of this solution reacts exactly with 22.30 mL of 0.253 M sulfuric acid?

    a)   0.113 M

    b)   0.226 M

    c)   0.284 M

    d)   0.451 M

    e)   0.567 M

ANS: d)   0.451 M   **PAGE:** 15.4

27. If 25.0 mL of 0.451 M NaOH solution is titrated with 0.253 M H_2SO_4, the flask at the endpoint will contain (besides the indicator phenolphthalein) as the principal components:

    a)   sodium hydroxide, sulfuric acid, and water

    b)   dissolved sodium sulfate and water

    c)   sodium hydroxide, sodium sulfate, and water

    d)   dissolved sodium sulfate, sulfuric acid, and water

    e)   precipitated sodium sulfate and water

ANS: b)   dissolved sodium sulfate and water   **PAGE:** 15.4

28. A 10-mL sample of tartaric acid is titrated to a phenolphthalein endpoint with 20. mL of 1.0 M NaOH. Assuming tartaric acid is diprotic, what is the molarity of the acid?

    a)   2.0

    b)   1.0

    c)   4.0

    d)   10.

    e)   impossible to determine

ANS: b)   1.0   **PAGE:** 15.4

29. What volume of water must be added to 10. mL of a pH 2.0 solution of HNO_3 in order to change the pH to 4.0?

    a) 10 mL
    b) 90 mL
    c) 1.0×10^2 mL
    d) 990 mL
    e) 99 mL

    ANS: d)   990 mL   **PAGE:** 15.4

30. If 25 mL of 0.75 M HCl are added to 100 mL of 0.25 NaOH, what is the final pH?

    a) 12.70
    b) 12.80
    c) 1.30
    d) 1.20
    e) 7.00

    ANS: a)   12.70   **PAGE:** 15.4

31. A 50.00-mL sample of 0.100 M KOH is titrated with 0.100 M HNO_3. Calculate the pH of the solution after the 52.00 mL of HNO_3 is added.

    a) 6.50
    b) 3.01
    c) 2.71
    d) 2.41
    e) none of these

    ANS: c)   2.71   **PAGE:** 15.4

32. A solution of hydrochloric acid of unknown concentration was titrated with 0.10 M NaOH. If a 100.-mL sample of the HCl solution required exactly 10. mL of the NaOH solution to reach the equivalence point, what was the pH of the HCl solution?

    a) 1.0
    b) 2.0
    c) 0.0
    d) 12.0
    e) –1.0

    ANS: b)   2.0   **PAGE:** 15.4

33–35. A titration of 200.0 mL of 1.00 M H_2A was done with 1.00 M NaOH. For the diprotic acid H_2A, $K_{a1} = 2.5 \times 10^{-5}$, $K_{a2} = 3.1 \times 10^{-9}$.

33. Calculate the pH before any 1.00 M NaOH has been added.

   a) 8.51
   b) 6.56
   c) 4.60
   d) 2.65
   e) 2.30

   ANS: e)   2.30   **PAGE:** 15.4

34. Calculate the pH after 100.0 mL of 1.00 M NaOH have been added.

   a) 13.4
   b) 11.0
   c) 8.51
   d) 6.56
   e) 4.60

   ANS: e)   4.60   **PAGE:** 15.4

35. Calculate the pH after 600.0 mL of 1.00 M NaOH have been added.

   a) 13.4
   b) 11.0
   c) 8.51
   d) 6.56
   e) 4.60

   ANS: a)   13.4   **PAGE:** 15.4

36–38. Consider the titration of 300.0 mL of 0.500 M NH_3 ($K_b = 1.8 \times 10^{-5}$) with 0.500 M HNO_3.

36. After 150.0 mL of 0.500 M HNO_3 have been added, the pH of the solution is:

   a) 4.74
   b) 11.48
   c) 2.52
   d) 9.26
   e) none of these

   ANS: d)   9.26   **PAGE:** 15.4

353

37. How many milliliters of 0.500 M HNO_3 are required to reach the stoichiometric point of the reaction?

    a) 100. mL
    b) 150. mL
    c) 200. mL
    d) 300. mL
    e) none of these

    ANS: d   300. mL   **PAGE:** 15.4

38. At the stoichiometric point of this titration, the pH is:

    a) 2.67
    b) 11.32
    c) 4.93
    d) 9.07
    e) 7.00

    ANS: c)   4.93   **PAGE:** 15.4

39. Consider the titration of 500.0 mL of 0.200 M NaOH with 0.800 M HCl. How many milliliters of 0.800 M HCl must be added to reach a pH of 13.000?

    a) 55.6 mL
    b) 24.6 mL
    c) 18.5 mL
    d) 12.9 mL
    e) 4.32 mL

    ANS: a)   55.6 mL   **PAGE:** 15.4

40. What quantity of NaOH(s) must be added to 2.00 L of 0.500 M HCl to achieve a pH of 13.00? (Assume no volume change.)

    a) 0.200 mol
    b) 1.200 mol
    c) 1.00×10^{-13} mol
    d) 1.500 mol
    e) none of these

    ANS: b)   1.200 mol   **PAGE:** 15.4

41. A 50.0-mL sample of 0.10 M HNO_2 ($K_a = 4.0 \times 10^{-4}$) is titrated with 0.10 M NaOH. The pH after 25.0 mL of NaOH have been added is

    a) 7.00
    b) 1.00
    c) 12.50
    d) 3.40
    e) none of these

    ANS: d)   3.40   **PAGE:** 15.4

42. The pH at the equivalence point of the titration of a strong acid with a strong base is:

    a)   3.9
    b)   4.5
    c)   7.0
    d)   8.2
    e)   none of these

    ANS: c)   7.0   **PAGE:** 15.4

43. The pH at the equivalence point of a titration of a weak acid with a strong base will be

    a)   less than 7.00.
    b)   equal to 7.00.
    c)   greater than 7.00.
    d)   More data is needed to answer this question.

    ANS: c)   greater than 7.00.   **PAGE:** 15.4

44. A 75.0-mL sample of 0.0500 M HCN ($K_a = 6.2 \times 10^{-10}$) is titrated with 0.500 M NaOH. What volume of 0.500 M NaOH is required to reach the stoichiometric point?

    a)   75.0 mL
    b)   7.50 mL
    c)   750. mL
    d)   cannot determine without knowing the pH at the stoichiometric point
    e)   none of these

    ANS: b)   7.50 mL   **PAGE:** 15.4

45. A 75.0-mL sample of 0.0500 M HCN ($K_a = 6.2 \times 10^{-10}$) is titrated with 0.500 M NaOH. What is the [H$^+$] in the solution after 3.0 mL of 0.50 M NaOH have been added?

    a) 1.0×10^{-7} M
    b) 4.1×10^{-10} M
    c) 5.2×10^{-13} M
    d) 9.3×10^{-10} M
    e)   none of these

    ANS: d) 9.3×10^{-10} M   **PAGE:** 15.4

46. A student titrates an unknown weak acid, HA, to a pale pink phenolphthalein endpoint with 25.0 mL of 0.100 M NaOH. The student then adds 13.0 mL of 0.100 M HCl. The pH of the resulting solution is 4.7. Which of the following is true?

    a) At pH 4.7, half the conjugate base, A⁻, has been converted to HA.
    b) The pK_a of the acid is 4.7.
    c) The pK_a of the acid is less than 4.7.
    d) The pK_a of the acid is greater than 4.7.
    e) More than one of the above is correct.

    ANS: d)   The pK_a of the acid is greater than 4.7.   **PAGE:** 15.4

47. How many moles of HCl(g) must be added to 1.0 L of 2.0 M NaOH to achieve a pH of 0.00? (Neglect any volume change.)

    a) 1.0 moles
    b) 2.0 moles
    c) 3.0 moles
    d) 10. moles
    e) none of these

    ANS: c)   3.0 moles   **PAGE:** 15.4

48. A 50.0-mL sample of a 1.50 M NaOH solution is titrated with a 2.00 M HCl solution. What will be the final volume of solution when the NaOH has been completely neutralized by the HCl?

    a) 87.5 mL
    b) 100.0 mL
    c) 90.0 mL
    d) 97.5 mL
    e) 89.0 mL

    ANS: a)   87.5 mL   **PAGE:** 15.4

49. You have 75.0 mL of 0.10 M HA. After adding 30.0 mL of 0.10 M NaOH, the pH is 5.50. What is the K_a value of HA?

    a) 1.0×10^{-10}
    b) 2.1×10^{-6}
    c) 1.0×10^{-4}
    d) 1.3×10^{-6}
    e) none of these

    ANS: b) 2.1×10^{-6} **PAGE:** 15.4

50–51. Consider the titration of 100.0 mL of 0.10 M H_2A ($K_{a1} = 1.5 \times 10^{-4}$; $K_{a2} = 8.0 \times 10^{-7}$) with 0.20 M NaOH.

50. Calculate the $[H^+]$ after 75.0 mL of 0.20 M NaOH has been added.

    a) 1.5×10^{-4} M
    b) 1.1×10^{-5} M
    c) 1.0×10^{-13} M
    d) 8.0×10^{-7} M
    e) none of these

ANS: d) 8.0×10^{-7} M   **PAGE:** 15.4

51. Calculate the volume of 0.20 M NaOH required to reach an $[H^+]$ of 6.0×10^{-4} M.

    a) 0
    b) 10. mL
    c) 25. mL
    d) 50. mL
    e) 65. mL

ANS: b)   10. mL   **PAGE:** 15.4

52. A 50.00-mL sample of a 1.00 M solution of the diprotic acid H_2A ($K_{a1} = 1.0 \times 10^{-6}$ and $K_{a2} = 1.0 \times 10^{-10}$) is titrated with 2.00 M NaOH. How many mL of 2.00 M NaOH must be added to reach a pH of 10?

    a) 0
    b) 12.5 mL
    c) 25.0 mL
    d) 37.5 mL
    e) none of these

ANS: d)   37.5 mL   **PAGE:** 15.4

53. Consider the titration of 100.0 mL of 0.100 M H_2A ($K_{a1} = 1.50 \times 10^{-4}$; $K_{a2} = 1.00 \times 10^{-8}$). How many milliliters of 0.100 M NaOH must be added to reach a pH of 5.000?

    a) 41.9 mL
    b) 93.8 mL
    c) 100. mL
    d) 200. mL
    e) 60.0 mL

ANS: b)   93.8 mL   **PAGE:** 15.4

54. A 100.0-mL sample of 0.500 M H_2A (diprotic acid) is titrated with 0.200 M NaOH. After 125.0 mL of 0.200 M NaOH has been added, the pH of the solution is 4.50. Calculate K_{a1} for H_2A.

   a) 4.5

   b) 1.0×10^{-7}

   c) 3.2×10^{-5}

   d) not enough information to calculate

   e) none of these

   ANS: c) 3.2×10^{-5} **PAGE:** 15.4

55–58. Consider the following information about the diprotic acid ascorbic acid (H_2As for short) (molar mass = 176.1).

	K_{a1}	pK_a
$H_2As \rightleftharpoons HAs^-$	7.9×10^{-5}	4.10
$HAs \rightleftharpoons H^+ + As^{2-}$	1.6×10^{-12}	11.79

The titration curve for disodium ascorbate, Na_2As, with standard HCl is shown below:

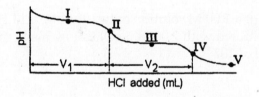

55. What major species is (are) present at point III?

   a) As^{2-} and HAs^-

   b) HAs^- only

   c) HAs^- and H_2As

   d) H_2As only

   e) H_2As and H^+

   ANS: c) HAs^- and H_2As **PAGE:** 15.4

56. What is the pH at point I ($V_1/2$ HCl added)?

   a) 4.10

   b) 7.95

   c) 11.79

   d) 12.39

   e) none of these

   ANS: c)   11.79   **PAGE:** 15.4

57. What is the pH at point III?

   a) 4.10
   b) 7.95
   c) 11.79
   d) 12.39
   e) none of these

   ANS: a)   4.10   **PAGE:** 15.4

58. Which of the following is a major species present at point IV?

   a) H_2As
   b) HAs^-
   c) As^{2-}
   d) H^+
   e) none of these

   ANS: a) H_2As **PAGE:** 15.4

59. A solution contains 10. mmol of H_3PO_4 and 5.0 mmol of NaH_2PO_4. How many milliliters of 0.10 M NaOH must be added to reach the second equivalence point of the titration of the H_3PO_4 with NaOH?

   a) 250
   b) 150
   c) 1.0×10^2
   d) 50
   e) 2.0×10^2

   ANS: a)   250   **PAGE:** 15.4

60. A solution contains 25 mmol of H_3PO_4 and 10. mmol of NaH_2PO_4. What volume of 2.0 M NaOH must be added to reach the second equivalence point of the titration of the H_3PO_4 with NaOH?

   a) 5.0 mL
   b) 12 mL
   c) 25 mL
   d) 30. mL
   e) 60. mL

   ANS: d)   30. mL   **PAGE:** 15.4

61. A 100.-mL sample of a 0.10 M solution of H_3PO_4 is titrated with 0.20 M NaOH. What volume of base must be added to reach the third equivalence point?

    a) 50. mL
    b) 1.0×10^2
    c) 150 mL
    d) 2.0×10^2
    e) 250 mL

    ANS: c)   150 mL   **PAGE:** 15.4

62. For carbonic acid (H_2CO_3), $K_{a1} = 4.30 \times 10^{-7}$ and $K_{a2} = 5.62 \times 10^{-11}$. Calculate the pH of a 0.50 M solution of Na_2CO_3.

    a) 3.33
    b) 2.03
    c) 10.67
    d) 11.97
    e) 8.31

    ANS: d)   11.97   **PAGE:** 15.4

63–64. A solution containing 10. mmol of CO_3^{2-} and 5.0 mmol of HCO_3^- is titrated with 1.0 M HCl.

63. What volume of HCl must be added to reach the first equivalence point?

    a) 5.0 mL
    b) 10. mL
    c) 15 mL
    d) 20. mL
    e) 25 mL

    ANS: b)   10. mL   **PAGE:** 15.4

64. What total volume of HCl must be added to reach the second equivalence point?

    a) 5.0 mL
    b) 10. mL
    c) 20. mL
    d) 25 mL
    e) 30. mL

    ANS: d)   25 mL   **PAGE:** 15.4

65. You dissolve 1.00 gram of an unknown diprotic acid in 200.0 mL of H_2O. This solution is just neutralized by 5.00 mL of a 1.00 M NaOH solution. What is the molar mass of the unknown acid?

  a) 25.0
  b) 50.0
  c) 200.
  d) 400.
  e) none of these

ANS: d) 400.   PAGE: 15.4

66. A 5.95-g sample of an acid, H_2X, requires 45.0 mL of a 0.500 M NaOH solution for complete reaction (removing both protons). The molar mass of the acid is

  a) 132
  b) 178
  c) 264
  d) 529
  e) none of these

ANS: d) 529   PAGE: 15.4

67. A 0.210-g sample of an acid (molar mass = 192 g/mol) is titrated with 30.5 mL of 0.108 M NaOH to a phenolphthalein endpoint. The formula of the acid is:

  a) HA
  b) H_2A
  c) H_3A
  d) H_4A
  e) not enough information given

ANS: c) H_3A PAGE: 15.4

68. Consider the titration of 100.0 mL of 0.250 M aniline ($K_b = 3.8 \times 10^{-10}$) with 0.500 M HCl. Calculate the pH of the solution at the stoichiometric point.

  a) –0.85
  b) 8.70
  c) 2.68
  d) 11.62
  e) none of these

ANS: c) 2.68   PAGE: 15.4

69. Consider the titration of 100.0 mL of 0.250 M aniline ($K_b = 3.8 \times 10^{-10}$) with 0.500 M HCl. For calculating the volume of HCl required to reach a pH of 8.0, which of the following expressions is correct? (x = volume in mL of HCl required to reach a pH of 8.0)

a) $\dfrac{0.5x - (100)(0.25)}{100 + x} = $ [aniline]

b) $[H^+] = x$

c) $\dfrac{0.5x}{100 + x} = $ [aniline]

d) $\dfrac{25 - 0.5x}{100 + x} - 10^{-6} = $ [aniline]

e) none of these

ANS: d) $\dfrac{25 - 0.5x}{100 + x} - 10^{-6} = $ [aniline]   PAGE: 15.4

70. A 100.0-mL sample of 0.2 M $(CH_3)_3N$ ($K_b = 5.3 \times 10^{-5}$) is titrated with 0.2 M HCl. What is the pH at the equivalence point?

a) 9.9
b) 3.1
c) 10.3
d) 5.4
e) 7.0

ANS: d)   5.4   PAGE: 15.4

71. Calculate the pH at the equivalence point for the titration of 1.0 M ethylamine, $C_2H_5NH_2$, by 1.0 M perchloric acid, $HClO_4$. (pK_b for $C_2H_5NH_2 = 3.25$)

a) 6.05
b) 2.24
c) 5.53
d) 2.09
e) 5.38

ANS: c)   5.53   PAGE: 15.4

72. What volume of 0.0100 M NaOH must be added to 1.00 L of 0.0500 M HOCl to achieve a pH of 8.00? The K_a for HOCl is 3.5×10^{-8}.

a) 1.0 L
b) 5.0 L
c) 1.2 L
d) 3.9 L
e) none of these

ANS: d)   3.9 L   PAGE: 15.4

73. Consider the following indicators and their pH ranges:

Methyl orange	3.2–4.4
Methyl red	4.8–6.0
Bromothymol blue	6.0–7.6
Phenolphthalein	8.2–10.0
Alizarin yellow	10.1–12.0

Assume an indicator works best when the equivalence point of a titration comes in the middle of the indicator range. For which of the following titrations would methyl red be the best indicator?

 a)   0.100 M HNO_3 + 0.100 M KOH
 b)   0.100 M aniline (K_b = 3.8 × 10⁻¹⁰) + 0.100 M HCl
 c)   0.100 M NH_3 (K_b = 1.8 × 10⁻⁵) + 0.100 M HCl
 d)   0.100 M HF (K_a = 7.2 × 10⁻⁴) + 0.100 M NaOH
 e)   0.100 M acetic acid (K_a = 1.8 × 10⁻⁵) + 0.100 M NaOH

ANS: c)   0.100 M NH_3 (K_b = 1.8 × 10⁻⁵) + 0.100 M HCl   **PAGE: 15.4,5**

74. Which of the following is the net ionic equation for the reaction that occurs during the titration of nitrous acid with potassium hydroxide?

 a) HNO_2 + K^+ OH^- → KNO_2 + H_2O
 b) HNO_2 + H_2O → NO_2^- + H_3O^+
 c) HNO_2 + KOH → K^+ + NO_2^- + H_2O
 d) HNO_2 + OH^- → NO_2^- + H_2O
 e) H^+ + OH^- → H_2O

ANS: d) HNO_2 + OH^- → NO_2^- + H_2O **PAGE: 15.4**

75. A 100. mL sample of 0.10 M HCl is mixed with 50. mL of 0.10 M NH_3. What is the resulting pH? (K_b for NH_3 = 1.8 × 10⁻⁵)

 a)   12.52
 b)   3.87
 c)   1.30
 d)   7.85
 e)   1.48

ANS: e)   1.48   **PAGE: 15.4**

76. In the titration of a weak acid HA with 0.100 M NaOH the stoichiometric point is known to occur at a pH value of approximately 10. Which of the following indicator acids would be best to use to mark the endpoint of this titration?

    a) indicator A, $K_a = 10^{-14}$
    b) indicator B, $K_a = 10^{-11}$
    c) indicator C, $K_a = 10^{-8}$
    d) indicator D, $K_a = 10^{-6}$
    e) none of these

    ANS: b)   indicator B, $K_a = 10^{-11}$ **PAGE:** 15.5

77. In the titration of a weak acid, HA, with a sodium hydroxide solution the stoichiometric point occurs at pH = 9.5. Which of the following weak acid indicators would be best suited to mark the endpoint of this titration?

    a) HB, $K_a = 10^{-11}$
    b) HC, $K_a = 10^{-13}$
    c) HD, $K_a = 10^{-9}$
    d) HE, $K_a = 10^{-7}$

    ANS: a)   HB, $K_a = 10^{-11}$ **PAGE:** 15.5

78. In the titration of a weak acid HA with 0.100 M NaOH, the stoichiometric point is known to occur at a pH value of approximately 11. Which of the following indicators would be best to use to mark the endpoint of this titration?

    a) an indicator with $K_a = 10^{-10}$
    b) an indicator with $K_a = 10^{-8}$
    c) an indicator with $K_a = 10^{-14}$
    d) an indicator with $K_a = 10^{-11}$
    e) an indicator with $K_a = 10^{-12}$

    ANS: e)   an indicator with $K_a = 10^{-12}$ **PAGE:** 15.5

79. A certain indicator HIn has a pK_a of 9.00 and a color change becomes visible when 7.00% of it is In⁻. At what pH is this color change visible?

    a) 10.2
    b) 3.85
    c) 6.15
    d) 7.88
    e) none of these

    ANS: d)   7.88   **PAGE:** 15.5

80–81. The following questions refer to a 2-liter buffered solution created from 0.31 M NH_3 ($K_b = 1.8 \times 10^{-5}$) and 0.26 M NH_4F.

80. What is the pH of this solution?

    a) 8.4
    b) 9.3
    c) 9.5
    d) 9.2
    e) 9.7

    ANS: b)   9.3   **PAGE:** 15.2

81. When 0.10 mol of H^+ ions is added to the solution what is the pH?

    a) 8.4
    b) 9.6
    c) 9.4
    d) 9.2
    e) 9.7

    ANS: d)   9.2   **PAGE:** 15.2

82. Find the solubility (in mol/L) of lead chloride ($PbCl_2$) at 25°C. $K_{sp} = 1.6 \times 10^{-5}$

    a) 1.6×10^{-2}
    b) 0.020
    c) 7.1×10^{-5}
    d) 2.1
    e) 9.3×10^{-3}

    ANS: a) 1.6×10^{-2} **PAGE:** 15.6

83. Methyl orange is an indicator with a K_a of 1×10^{-4}. Its acid form, HIn, is red, while its base form, In^-, is yellow. At pH 6.0, the indicator will be

    a) red.
    b) orange.
    c) yellow.
    d) blue.
    e) not enough information

    ANS: c)   yellow.   **PAGE:** 15.5

84. The two salts AgX and AgY have very similar solubilities in water. It is known that the salt AgX is much more soluble in acid than is AgY. What can be said about the relative strengths of the acids HX and HY?

    a)   Nothing.

    b)   HY is stronger than HX.

    c)   HX is stronger than HY.

    d)   The acids have equal strengths.

    e)   Cannot be determined.

ANS: b)   HY is stronger than HX.   **PAGE:** 15.6

85. Solubility Products (K_{sp})

    $BaSO_4$ 1.5×10^{-9}

    CoS 5.0×10^{-22}

    $PbSO_4$ 1.3×10^{-8}

    $AgBr$ 5.0×10^{-13}

Which of the following compounds is the most soluble (in moles/liter)?

    a) $BaSO_4$

    b) CoS

    c) $PbSO_4$

    d) $AgBr$

    e) $BaCO_3$

ANS: c) $PbSO_4$ **PAGE:** 15.6

86. How many moles of $Fe(OH)_2$ [$K_{sp} = 1.8 \times 10^{-15}$] will dissolve in one liter of water buffered at pH = 12.00?

    a) 1.8×10^{-11}

    b) 1.8×10^{-9}

    c) 8.0×10^{-6}

    d) 5.0×10^{-12}

    e) 4.0×10^{-8}

ANS: a) 1.8×10^{-11} **PAGE:** 15.6

87. How does the pH of a 0.20 M solution of $NaHCO_3$ compare to that of a 0.10 M solution of $NaHCO_3$?

    a)   It is 2 times as high.

    b)   It is half as much.

    c)   It is the same.

    d)   cannot be determined with the K_a values

    e)   none of these

ANS: c)   It is the same.   **PAGE:** 15.2

88–91.   You have a 250.0-mL sample of 1.00 M acetic acid ($K_a = 1.8 \times 10^{-5}$).

88.   Assuming no volume change, how much NaOH must be added to make the best buffer?

    a)   5.0 g
    b)   10.0 g
    c)   15.0 g
    d)   20.0 g
    e)   none of these

ANS: a)   5.0 g   **PAGE: 15.2**

89.   Calculate the pH of the best buffer.

    a)   7.00
    b)   4.74
    c)   3.14
    d)   2.37
    e)   none of these

ANS: b)   4.74   **PAGE: 15.2**

90.   Calculate the pH after adding 0.0050 mol of NaOH to 1.0 liter of the best buffer.

    a)   7.05
    b)   2.41
    c)   3.54
    d)   4.78
    e)   none of these

ANS: d)   4.78   **PAGE: 15.2**

91.   Calculate the pH after adding 0.0040 mol HCl to 1.0 liter of the best buffer.

    a)   4.72
    b)   2.35
    c)   3.12
    d)   6.98
    e)   none of these

ANS: a)   4.72   **PAGE: 15.2**

92-93. You have two buffered solutions. Buffered solution 1 consists of 5.0 M HOAc and 5.0 M NaOAc; buffered solution 2 is made of 0.050 M HOAc and 0.050 M NaOAc.

92.   How do the pHs of the buffered solutions compare?

   a)   The pH of buffered solution 1 is greater than that of buffered solution 2.
   b)   The pH of buffered solution 2 is greater than that of buffered solution 1.
   c)   The pH of buffered solution 1 is equal to that of buffered solution 2.
   d)   Cannot be determined without the K_a values.
   e)   None of these (a-d).

   ANS: c)   The pH of buffered solution 1 is equal to that of buffered
                  solution 2.   **PAGE:** 15.2

93.   Buffered solution 1 has a greater buffering capacity than buffered solution 2.

   ANS: True   **PAGE:** 15.3

94.   You have two salts, AgX and AgY, with very similar K_{sp} values. You know that K_a for HX is much greater than K_a for HY. Which salt is more soluble in acidic solution?

   a)   AgX
   b)   AgY
   c)   They are equally soluble in acidic solution.
   d)   Cannot be determined by the information given.
   e)   None of these (a-d).

   ANS: b) AgY   **PAGE:** 15.6

95.   You have a solution consisting of 0.10 M Cl^- and 0.10 M CrO_4^{2-}. You add 0.10 M silver nitrate dropwise to this solution. Given that the K_{sp} for Ag_2CrO_4 is 9.0×10^{-12}, and that for AgCl is 1.6×10^{-10}, which of the following will precipitate first?

   a)   silver chloride
   b)   silver chromate
   c)   silver nitrate
   d)   cannot be determined by the information given
   e)   none of these

   ANS: a)   silver chloride   **PAGE:** 15.7

96.   Which of the following compounds has the lowest solubility in mol/L in water?

   a) $Al(OH)_3$ $K_{sp} = 2 \times 10^{-32}$
   b)   CdS $K_{sp} = 1.0 \times 10^{-28}$
   b) $PbSO_4$ $K_{sp} = 1.3 \times 10^{-8}$
   c) $Sn(OH)_2$ $K_{sp} = 3 \times 10^{-27}$
   e) MgC_2O_4 $K_{sp} = 8.6 \times 10^{-5}$

   ANS: b)   CdS $K_{sp} = 1.0 \times 10^{-28}$ **PAGE:** 15.6

97. The solubility of $CaSO_4$ in pure water at 0°C is 1 gram per liter. The value of the solubility product is

   a) 1×10^{-3}
   b) 7×10^{-2}
   c) 1×10^{-4}
   d) 5×10^{-5}

   ANS: d) 5×10^{-5} **PAGE:** 15.6

98. The solubility of AgCl in water is _____ the solubility of AgCl in strong acid at the same temperature.

   a)   greater than
   b)   less than
   c)   about the same as
   d)   cannot be determined
   e)   much different from

   ANS: c)   about the same as   **PAGE:** 15.6

99. The molar solubility of PbI_2 is 1.5×10^{-3} M. Calculate the value of K_{sp} for PbI_2.

   a) 1.5×10^{-3}
   b) 2.3×10^{-6}
   c) 1.4×10^{-8}
   d) 3.4×10^{-9}
   e)   none of these

   ANS: c) 1.4×10^{-8} **PAGE:** 15.6

100. Calculate the concentration of chromate ion, CrO_4^{2-}, in a saturated solution of $CaCrO_4$. ($K_{sp} = 7.1 \times 10^{-4}$)

   a)   0.027 M
   b) 5.0×10^{-7} M
   c) 7.1×10^{-4} M
   d) 3.5×10^{-4} M
   e) 3.5×10^{-2} M

   ANS: a)   0.027 M   **PAGE:** 15.6

101. Calculate the concentration of the silver ion in a saturated solution of silver chloride, AgCl ($K_{sp} = 1.6 \times 10^{-10}$).

   a) 5.4×10^{-4}
   b) 1.3×10^{-5}
   c) 1.6×10^{-10}
   d) 8.0×10^{-11}
   e)   none of these

   ANS: b) 1.3×10^{-5} **PAGE:** 15.6

102. The molar solubility of $BaCO_3$ ($K_{sp} = 1.6 \times 10^{-9}$) in 0.10 M $BaCl_2$ solution is:

    a) 1.6×10^{-10}

    b) 4.0×10^{-5}

    c) 7.4×10^{-4}

    d) 0.10

    e) none of these

    ANS: e)   none of these   **PAGE:** 15.6

103. It is observed that 7.5 mmol of BaF_2 will dissolve in 1.0 L of water. Use these data to calculate the values of K_{sp} for barium fluoride.

    a) 7.5×10^{-3}

    b) 4.2×10^{-7}

    c) 1.7×10^{-6}

    d) 5.6×10^{-5}

    e) 2.1×10^{-12}

    ANS: c) 1.7×10^{-6} **PAGE:** 15.6

104. The K_{sp} of AgI is 1.5×10^{-16}. Calculate the solubility in mol/L of AgI in a 0.30 M NaI solution.

    a) 1.7×10^{-8}

    b) 0.30

    c) 2.6×10^{-17}

    d) 8.5×10^{17}

    e) 5.0×10^{-16}

    ANS: e) 5.0×10^{-16} **PAGE:** 15.6

105. The molar solubility of AgCl ($K_{sp} = 1.6 \times 10^{-10}$) in 0.0020 M sodium chloride at 25□C is:

    a) 0.0020

    b) 1.3×10^{-5}

    c) 8.0×10^{-8}

    d) 1.7×10^{-10}

    e) none of these

    ANS: c) 8.0×10^{-8} **PAGE:** 15.6

106. Silver chromate, Ag_2CrO_4, has a K_{sp} of 9.0×10^{-12}. Calculate the solubility in mol/L of silver chromate.

    a) 1.3×10^{-4} M

    b) 7.8×10^{-5} M

    c) 9.5×10^{-7} M

    d) 1.9×10^{-12} M

    e) 9.8×10^{-5} M

    ANS: a) 1.3×10^{-4} M   **PAGE:** 15.6

107. The solubility of mol/L of Ag_2CrO_4 is 1.3×10^{-4} M at 25°C. Calculate the K_{sp} for this compound.

   a) 8.8×10^{-3}
   b) 6.1×10^{-9}
   c) 8.8×10^{-12}
   d) 4.7×10^{-13}
   e) 2.3×10^{-13}

   ANS: c) 8.8×10^{-12} **PAGE:** 15.6

108. Calculate the concentration of Al^{3+} in a saturated aqueous solution of $Al(OH)_3$ ($K_{sp} = 2 \times 10^{-32}$) at 25°C.

   a) 3×10^{-9}
   b) 7×10^{-9}
   c) 2×10^{-11}
   d) 3×10^{-17}
   e) none of these

   ANS: e)   none of these   **PAGE:** 15.6

109. The solubility in mol/L of $M(OH)_2$ in 0.010 M KOH is 1.0×10^{-5} mol/L. What is the K_{sp} for $M(OH)_2$?

   a) 1.0×10^{-9}
   b) 1.0×10^{-10}
   c) 1.0×10^{-12}
   d) 4.0×10^{-15}
   e) 1.0×10^{-2}

   ANS: a) 1.0×10^{-9} **PAGE:** 15.6

110. The K_{sp} of $PbSO_4(s)$ is 1.3×10^{-8}. Calculate the solubility (in mol/L) of $PbSO_4(s)$ in a 0.0010 M solution of Na_2SO_4.

   a) 1.3×10^{-11} M
   b) 4.5×10^{-6} M
   c) 1.3×10^{-5} M
   d) 1.3×10^{-8} M
   e) 1.4×10^{-4} M

   ANS: c) 1.3×10^{-5} M   **PAGE:** 15.6

111.   The solubility of $Cd(OH)_2$ in water is 1.7×10^{-5} mol/L at 25°C. The K_{sp} value for $Cd(OH)_2$ is:

   a) 2.0×10^{-14}
   b) 4.9×10^{-15}
   c) 5.8×10^{-10}
   d) 2.9×10^{-10}
   e)   none of these

ANS: a) 2.0×10^{-14} **PAGE:** 15.6

112.   The K_{sp} for PbF_2 is 4.0×10^{-8}. If a 0.050 M NaF solution is saturated with PbF_2, what is the $[Pb^{2+}]$ in solution?

   a) 3.8×10^{-3} M
   b) 3.6×10^{-4} M
   c) 5.4×10^{-7} M
   d) 1.6×10^{-5} M
   e) 2.7×10^{-8} M

ANS: d) 1.6×10^{-5} M   **PAGE:** 15.6

113.   Chromate ion is added to a saturated solution of Ag_2CrO_4 to reach 0.10 M CrO_4^{2-}. Calculate the final concentration of silver ion at equilibrium (K_{sp} for Ag_2CrO_4 is 9.0×10^{-12})

   a) 1.7×10^{-6} M
   b) 9.5×10^{-6} M
   c) 6.6×10^{-6} M
   d) 5.5×10^{-11} M
   e) 1.1×10^{-13} M

ANS: b) 9.5×10^{-6} M   **PAGE:** 15.6

114.   The solubility of $La(IO_3)_3$ in a 0.10 M KIO_3 solution is 1.0×10^{-7} mol/L. Calculate the K_{sp} for $La(IO_3)_3$.

   a) 1.0×10^{-8}
   b) 2.7×10^{-9}
   c) 1.0×10^{-10}
   d) 2.7×10^{-27}
   e)   none of these

ANS: c) 1.0×10^{-10} **PAGE:** 15.6

372

115. In a solution prepared by adding excess $PbI_2(s)$ [$K_{sp} = 1.4 \times 10^{-8}$] to water, the [$I^-$] at equilibrium is:

   a) 1.5×10^{-3} mol/L
   b) 2.4×10^{-3} mol/L
   c) 1.2×10^{-3} mol/L
   d) 8.4×10^{-5} mol/L
   e) 3.0×10^{-3} mol/L

   ANS: e) 3.0×10^{-3} mol/L   **PAGE:** 15.6

116. Which of the following salts shows the lowest solubility in water? (K_{sp} values: $Ag_2S = 1.6 \times 10^{-49}$; $Bi_2S_3 = 1.0 \times 10^{-72}$; $HgS = 1.6 \times 10^{-54}$; $Mg(OH)_2 = 8.9 \times 10^{-12}$; $MnS = 2.3 \times 10^{-13}$)

   a) Bi_2S_3
   b) Ag_2S
   c) MnS
   d) HgS
   e) $Mg(OH)_2$

   ANS: d)   HgS   **PAGE:** 15.6

117–118. The next two questions refer to the following: The solubility of silver phosphate (Ag_3PO_4) at 25°C is 1.6×10^{-5} mol/L.

117. Determine the concentration of the Ag^+ ion in a saturated solution.

   a) 1.6×10^{-5} M
   b) 3.2×10^{-5} M
   c) 4.8×10^{-5} M
   d) 6.4×10^{-5} M
   e) 7.6×10^{-5} M

   ANS: c) 4.8×10^{-5} M   **PAGE:** 15.6

118. What is the K_{sp} for the silver phosphate at 25°C?

   a) 7.7×10^{-10}
   b) 1.8×10^{-18}
   c) 8.6×10^{-13}
   d) 3.3×10^{-13}
   e) none of these

   ANS: b) 1.8×10^{-18} **PAGE:** 15.6

119. Barium carbonate has a measured solubility of 4.0×10^{-5} at 25°C. Determine the K_{sp}.

   a) 5.3×10^{-10}
   b) 6.1×10^{-5}
   c) 9.1×10^{-7}
   d) 1.2×10^{-2}
   e) 1.6×10^{-9}

   ANS: e) 1.6×10^{-9} **PAGE:** 15.6

120. A 300.0-mL saturated solution of copper(II) peroidate ($Cu(IO_4)_2$) contains 0.44 grams of dissolved salt. Determine the K_{sp}.

   a) 6.1×10^{-5}
   b) 67.2×10^{-8}
   c) 9.2×10^{-6}
   d) 1.4×10^{-7}
   e) 3.7×10^{-8}

   ANS: d) 1.4×10^{-7} **PAGE:** 15.6

121. The correct mathematical expression for finding the molar solubility (S) of $Sn(OH)_2$ is:

   a) $2S^2 = K_{sp}$
   b) $2S^3 = K_{sp}$
   c) $108S^5 = K_{sp}$
   d) $4S^3 = K_{sp}$
   e) $8S^3 = K_{sp}$

   ANS: d) $4S^3 = K_{sp}$ **PAGE:** 15.6

122. The $[IO_3^-]$ in a saturated solution of $Ce(IO_3)_3$ is 5.55×10^{-3} M. Calculate the K_{sp} for $Ce(IO_3)_3$.

   a) 3.16×10^{-10}
   b) 1.03×10^{-5}
   c) 2.56×10^{-8}
   d) 3.51×10^{-11}
   e) none of these

   ANS: a) 3.16×10^{-10} **PAGE:** 15.6

123. Calculate the solubility of Ag_2CrO_4 [$K_{sp} = 9.0 \times 10^{-12}$] in a 1.0×10^{-2} M $AgNO_3$ solution.

   a) 1.3×10^{-4} mol/L
   b) 2.3×10^{-8} mol/L
   c) 9.0×10^{-8} mol/L
   d) 9.0×10^{-10} mol/L
   e) none of these

   ANS: c) 9.0×10^{-8} mol/L   **PAGE:** 15.6

124. The solubility of $Mg(OH)_2$ ($K_{sp} = 8.9 \times 10^{-12}$) in 1.0 L of a solution buffered (with large capacity) at pH 10.0 is:

    a) 8.9×10^9 moles

    b) 8.9×10^{-4} moles

    c) 8.9×10^{-1} moles

    d) 8.9×10^{-7} moles

    e) none of these

    ANS: b) 8.9×10^{-4} moles   **PAGE:** 15.6

125. Calculate the solubility of $Ca_3(PO_4)_2(s)$ ($K_{sp} = 1.3 \times 10^{-32}$) in a 1.0×10^{-2} M $Ca(NO_3)_2$ solution.

    a) 5.7×10^{-14} mol/L

    b) 6.2×10^{-7} mol/L

    c) 1.6×10^{-14} mol/L

    d) 3.16×10^{-12} mol/L

    e) none of these

    ANS: a) 5.7×10^{-14} mol/L   **PAGE:** 15.6

126. Calculate the solubility of $Cu(OH)_2$ in a solution buffered at pH = 8.50. ($K_{sp} = 1.6 \times 10^{-19}$)

    a) 1.6×10^{-2} M

    b) 1.8×10^{-7} M

    c) 1.6×10^{-8} M

    d) 5.7×10^{-10} M

    e) none of these

    ANS: c) 1.6×10^{-8} M   **PAGE:** 15.6

127. Given the following K_{sp} values

	K_{sp}		K_{sp}
$PbCrO_4$	2.0×10^{-16}	$Pb(OH)_2$	1.2×10^{-15}
$Zn(OH)_2$	4.5×10^{-17}	MnS	2.3×10^{-13}

which statement about solubility in mol/L in water is correct?

    a) $PbCrO_4$, $Zn(OH)_2$, and $Pb(OH)_2$ have equal solubilities in water.

    b) $PbCrO_4$ has the lowest solubility in water.

    c) The solubility of MnS in water will not be pH dependent.

    d) MnS has the highest molar solubility in water.

    e) A saturated $PbCrO_4$ solution will have a higher $[Pb^{2+}]$ than a saturated $Pb(OH)_2$ solution.

    ANS: b) $PbCrO_4$ has the lowest solubility in water.   **PAGE:** 15.6,7

128. The concentration of OH⁻ in a saturated solution of $Mg(OH)_2$ is 3.6×10^{-4} M. The K_{sp} of $Mg(OH)_2$ is

    a) 1.3×10^{-7}

    b) 4.7×10^{-11}

    c) 1.2×10^{-11}

    d) 3.6×10^{-4}

    e)   none of these

ANS: e)   none of these   **PAGE:** 15.6

129. How many moles of CaF_2 will dissolve in 3.0 liters of 0.050 M NaF solution? (K_{sp} for $CaF_2 = 4.0 \times 10^{-11}$)

    a) 8.9×10^{-9}

    b) 8.0×10^{-8}

    c) 4.8×10^{-8}

    d) 2.7×10^{-8}

    e)   none of these

ANS: c) 4.8×10^{-8} **PAGE:** 15.6

130. Which of the following compounds has the lowest solubility in mol/L in water at 25°C?

    a) Ag_3PO_4 $K_{sp} = 1.8 \times 10^{-18}$

    b) $Sn(OH)_2$ $K_{sp} = 5 \times 10^{-26}$

    c) CdS $K_{sp} = 3.6 \times 10^{-29}$

    d) $CaSO_4$ $K_{sp} = 6.1 \times 10^{-5}$

    e) $Al(OH)_3$ $K_{sp} = 2 \times 10^{-33}$

ANS: c) CdS $K_{sp} = 3.6 \times 10^{-29}$ **PAGE:** 15.6

131. A 100.-mL sample of solution contains 10.0 mmol of Ca^{2+} ion. How many mmol of solid Na_2SO_4 must be added in order to cause precipitation of 99.9% of the calcium as $CaSO_4$? The K_{sp} of $CaSO_4$ is 6.1×10^{-5}. Assume the volume remains constant.

    a)   17.4

    b)   10.0

    c)   61.0

    d)   71.0

    e)   2.00

ANS: d)   71.0   **PAGE:** 15.7

132. The K_{sp} of $Al(OH)_3$ is 2×10^{-32}. At what pH will a 0.2 M Al^{3+} solution begin to show precipitation of $Al(OH)_3$?

    a) 3.7

    b) 1.0

    c) 5.6

    d) 10.3

    e) 8.4

ANS: a)   3.7   **PAGE:** 15.7

133–136. The following questions refer to the following system: 3.5×10^2 mL of 3.2 M $Pb(NO_3)_2$ and 2.0×10^2 mL of 0.020 M NaCl are added together. K_{sp} for the lead chloride is 1.6×10^{-5}.

133. Determine the ion product.

    a) 1.1×10^{-4}

    b) 1.5×10^{-2}

    c) 7.8×10^{-3}

    d) 8.1×10^{-4}

    e) none of these

ANS: a) 1.1×10^{-4} **PAGE:** 15.7

134. Will precipitation occur?

    a) Yes

    b) No

    c) Maybe, it depends on the temperature.

    d) Maybe, it depends on the limiting reagent concentration.

    e) None of these.

ANS: a)   Yes   **PAGE:** 15.7

135. What is the limiting reagent in the formation of the lead chloride?

    a) Pb^{2+}

    b) Cl^-

    c) $(NO_3)^-$

    d) $PbCl_2$

    e) $Pb(NO_3)_2$

ANS: b) Cl^- **PAGE:** 15.7

136. Determine the equilibrium concentration of the chloride ion.

    a) 3.9×10^{-4}
    b) 8.0×10^{-6}
    c) 2.8×10^{-3}
    d) 6.1×10^{-2}
    e) none of these

    ANS: c) 2.8×10^{-3} **PAGE:** 15.7

137. The K_{sp} for BaF_2 is 2.4×10^{-5}. When 10 mL of 0.01 M NaF is mixed with 10 mL of 0.01 M $BaNO_3$, will a precipitate form?

    a) No, because Q is 1×10^{-12} and since it is less than K_{sp} no precipitate will form.
    b) Yes, because Q is 1×10^{-12} and since it is less than K_{sp} a precipitate will form.
    c) No, because Q is 1.25×10^{-7} and since it is less than K_{sp} no precipitate will form.
    d) Yes, because Q is 1.25×10^{-7} and since it is less than K_{sp} a precipitate will form.
    e) none of the above

    ANS: c)   No, because Q is 1.25×10^{-7} and since it is less than K_{sp} no
                  precipitate will form.   **PAGE:** 15.7

138. How many moles of $Ca(NO_3)_2$ must be added to 1.0 L of a 0.100 M HF solution to begin precipitation of $CaF_2(s)$? For CaF_2, $K_{sp} = 4.0 \times 10^{-11}$.

    a) 5.8×10^{-7}
    b) 1.6×10^{-9}
    c) 7.0×10^{-11}
    d) 4.0×10^{-9}
    e) 6.3×10^{-7}

    ANS: d) 4.0×10^{-9} **PAGE:** 15.7

139. Which of the following solid salts is more soluble in 1.0 M H^+ than in pure water?

    a) NaCl
    b) $CaCO_3$
    c) KCl
    d) AgCl
    e) KNO_3

    ANS: b) $CaCO_3$ **PAGE:** 15.6

140. A solution contains 0.018 moles each of I^-, Br^-, and Cl^-. When the solution is mixed with 200 mL of 0.24 M $AgNO_3$, how much $AgCl(s)$ precipitates out?

$$K_{sp} \quad AgI \quad = \quad 1.5 \times 10^{-16}$$
$$K_{sp} \quad AgBr \quad = \quad 5.0 \times 10^{-13}$$
$$K_{sp} \quad AgCl \quad = \quad 1.6 \times 10^{-10}$$

a) 0.0 g
b) 1.7 g
c) 2.6 g
d) 3.3 g
e) 5.0 g

ANS: b)   1.7 g   **PAGE:** 15.7

141. A 50.0-mL sample of 0.100 M $Ca(NO_3)_2$ is mixed with 50.00 mL of 0.200 M NaF. When the system has come to equilibrium, which of the following sets of conditions will hold? The K_{sp} for CaF_2 is 4.0×10^{-11}.

	Moles Solid CaF_2 Formed	$[Ca^{2+}]$ (M)	$[F^-]$ (M)
a)	5.0×10^{-3}	3.5×10^{-4} M	7.0×10^{-4} M
b)	5.0×10^{-3}	3.4×10^{-9} M	0.05 M
c)	5.0×10^{-3}	2.2×10^{-4} M	4.3×10^{-4} M
d)	5.0×10^{-3}	3.5×10^{-4} M	4.3×10^{-4} M
e)	10.0×10^{-3}	1.3×10^{-5} M	1.3×10^{-5} M

ANS: c) 5.0×10^{-3} moles $CaF_2(s)$ formed; 2.2×10^{-4} M; 4.3×10^{-4} M   PAGE: 15.7

142. Silver acetate ($AgC_2H_3O_2$) is a sparingly soluble salt with $K_{sp} = 1.9 \times 10^{-3}$. Consider a saturated solution in equilibrium with the solid salt. Compare the effects on the solubility of adding to the solution either the acid HNO_3 or the base NH_3.

a) Either substance would decrease the solubility.
b) NH_3 would increase the solubility, but HNO_3 would decrease it.
c) NH_3 would increase the solubility, but HNO_3 would have virtually no effect.
d) Either substance would increase the solubility.
e) NH_3 would decrease the solubility, but HNO_3 would increase it.

ANS: d)   Either substance would increase the solubility.   **PAGE:** 15.6,8

143. The K_{sp} for $Mn(OH)_2$ is 2.0×10^{-13}. At what pH will $Mn(OH)_2$ begin to precipitate from a solution in which the initial concentration of Mn^{2+} is 0.10 M?

a) 6.47
b) 13.3
c) 5.85
d) 7.03
e) 8.15

ANS: e)   8.15   **PAGE:** 15.7

144. The concentration of Mg^{2+} in seawater is 0.052 M. At what pH will 99% of the Mg^{2+} be precipitated as the hydroxide? (K_{sp} for $Mg(OH)_2 = 8.9 \times 10^{-12}$)

a) 8.35
b) 9.22
c) 6.50
d) 10.12
e) 4.86

ANS: d)   10.12   PAGE: 15.7

145. Sodium chloride is added slowly to a solution that is 0.010 M in Cu^+, Ag^+, and Au^+. The K_{sp} values for the chloride salts are 1.9×10^{-7}, 1.6×10^{-10}, and 2.0×10^{-13}, respectively. Which compound will precipitate first?

a) CuCl(s)
b) AgCl(s)
c) AuCl(s)
d) All will precipitate at the same time.
e) Cannot be determined.

ANS: c)   AuCl(s)   PAGE: 15.7

146. A 0.012-mol sample of Na_2SO_4 is added to 400 mL of each of two solutions. One solution contains 1.5×10^{-3} M $BaCl_2$; the other contains 1.5×10^{-3} M $CaCl_2$. Given that K_{sp} for $BaSO_4 = 1.5 \times 10^{-9}$ and K_{sp} for $CaSO_4 = 6.1 \times 10^{-5}$:

a) $BaSO_4$ would precipitate but $CaSO_4$ would not.
b) $CaSO_4$ would precipitate but $BaSO_4$ would not.
c) Both $BaSO_4$ and $CaSO_4$ would precipitate.
d) Neither $BaSO_4$ nor $CaSO_4$ would precipitate.
e) Not enough information is given to determine if precipitation would occur.

ANS: a) $BaSO_4$ would precipitate but $CaSO_4$ would not.   PAGE: 15.7

147. Which of the following solid salts is more soluble in 1.0 M H^+ than in pure water?

a) NaCl
b) KCl
c) $FePO_4$
d) AgCl
e) KNO_3

ANS: c) $FePO_4$ PAGE: 15.6

148. Which of the following solid salts should be more soluble in 1.0 M NH_3 than in water?

a) Na_2CO_3
b) KCl
c) AgBr
d) KNO_3
e) none of these

ANS: c)   AgBr   PAGE: 15.8

149. The overall K_f for the complex ion $Ag(NH_3)_2^+$ is 1.7×10^7. The K_{sp} for AgI is 1.5×10^{-16}. What is the molar solubility of AgI in a solution that is 2.0 M in NH_3?

    a) 1.5×10^{-9}
    b) 1.3×10^{-3}
    c) 1.0×10^{-4}
    d) 5.8×10^{-12}
    e) 8.4×10^{-5}

    ANS: c) 1.0×10^{-4} **PAGE:** 15.8

150. If 30 mL of 5.0×10^{-4} M $Ca(NO_3)_2$ are added to 70 mL of 2.0×10^{-4} M NaF, will a precipitate occur? (K_{sp} of $CaF_2 = 4.0 \times 10^{-11}$)

    a) No, because the ion product is greater than K_{sp}.
    b) Yes, because the ion product is less than K_{sp}.
    c) No, because the ion product is less than K_{sp}.
    d) Not enough information is given.
    e) Yes, because the ion product is greater than K_{sp}.

    ANS: c) No, because the ion product is less than K_{sp}. **PAGE:** 15.7

151. Given the following values of equilibrium constants:

$$Cu(OH)_2(s) \rightleftharpoons Cu^{2+}(aq) + 2OH^-(aq) \quad K_{sp} = 1.6 \times 19^{-19}$$

$$Cu(NH_3)_4^{2+} \rightleftharpoons Cu^{2+}(aq) + 4NH_3(aq) \quad K = 1.0 \times 10^{-13}$$

What is the value of the equilibrium constant for the reaction:

$$Cu(OH)_2(s) + 4NH_3(aq) \rightleftharpoons Cu(NH_3)_4^{2+}(aq) + 2OH^-(aq)$$

    a) 1.6×10^{-19}
    b) 6.2×10^{31}
    c) 1.6×10^{-6}
    d) 1.6×10^{-32}
    e) 1.0×10^{13}

    ANS: c) 1.6×10^{-6} **PAGE:** 15.8

152–154. A 50.0-mL sample of 2.0×10^{-4} M $CuNO_3$ is added to 50.0 mL of 4.0 M NaCN. Cu^+ reacts with CN^- to form the complex ion $Cu(CN)_3^{2-}$:

$$Cu(CN)_3^{2-} \rightleftharpoons Cu^+ + 3CN^- \quad K = 1.0 \times 10^{-9}$$

152. The concentration of CN^- at equilibrium is

    a) 4.0 M
    b) 2.0 M
    c) 1.0 M
    d) 6.0×10^{-4} M
    e) none of these

    ANS: b) 2.0 M **PAGE:** 15.8

153. The concentration of Cu^+ at equilibrium is

    a) 2.0×10^{-4} M

    b) 1.0×10^{-4} M

    c) 1.2×10^{-14} M

    d) 5.0×10^{-14} M

    e) none of these

ANS: c) 1.2×10^{-14} M   **PAGE:** 15.8

154. Calculate the solubility of $CuBr(s)$ ($K_{sp} = 1.0 \times 10^{-5}$) in 1.0 L of 1.0 M NaCN.

    a) 1.0 mol/L

    b) 1.0×10^{-6} mol/L

    c) 0.33 mol/L

    d) 1.0×10^3 mol/L

    e) none of these

ANS: c)   0.33 mol/L   **PAGE:** 15.8

155–156. Consider a solution made by mixing 500.0 mL of 4.0 M NH_3 and 500.0 mL of 0.40 M $AgNO_3$. Ag^+ reacts with NH_3 to form $AgNH_3^+$ and $Ag(NH_3)_2^+$:

$$Ag^+ + NH_3 \rightleftharpoons AgNH_3^+ \qquad K_1 = 2.1 \times 10^3$$

$$AgNH_3^+ + NH_3 \rightleftharpoons Ag(NH_3)_2^+ \qquad K_2 = 8.2 \times 10^3$$

155. The concentration of $Ag(NH_3)_2^+$ at equilibrium is:

    a) 2.0 M

    b) 0.40 M

    c) 0.20 M

    d) 1.0×10^{-3} M

    e) none of these

ANS: c)   0.20 M   **PAGE:** 15.8

156. The concentration of Ag^+ at equilibrium is:

    a) 2.0 M

    b) 1.2×10^{-8} M

    c) 4.5×10^{-9} M

    d) 1.6 M

    e) none of these

ANS: c) 4.5×10^{-9} M   **PAGE:** 15.8

157–160.   The following questions refer to the following system: 500.0 mL of 0.020 M $Mn(NO_3)_2$ are mixed with 1.0 L of 1.0 M $Na_2C_2O_4$. The oxalate ion, C_2O_4, acts as a ligand to form a complex ion with the Mn^{2+} ion with a coordination number of two.

$$Mn^{2+} + C_2O_4^{2-} \rightleftharpoons MnC_2O_4 \qquad\qquad K_1 = 7.9 \times 10^3$$
$$[Mn(C_2O_4)_2]^{2-} \rightleftharpoons MnC_2O_4 + C_2O_4^{2-} \qquad K_2 = 1.26 \times 10^{-2}$$

157.   What is the equilibrium constant for the following formation:
$Mn^{2+} + 2C_2O_4^{2-} \rightleftharpoons [Mn(C_2O_4)_2]^{2-}$

   a)   1.0
   b) 3.7×10^2
   c) 2.1×10^{-1}
   d) 6.3×10^5
   e)   none of these

   ANS: d) 6.3×10^5 　　　　　　　　　　　　　　　　　　　　　　**PAGE:** 15.8

158.   Find the equilibrium concentration of the $[Mn(C_2O_4)_2]^{2-}$ ion.

   a) 9.2×10^{-5} M
   b)   0.01 M
   c) 2.5×10^{-8}
   d) 1.3×10^{-4}
   e) 6.7×10^{-3}

   ANS: e) 6.7×10^{-3} 　　　　　　　　　　　　　　　　　　　　　　**PAGE:** 15.8

159.   Find the equilibrium concentration of the $Mn(C_2O_4)$ ion.

   a) 9.2×10^{-5} M
   b)   0.01 M
   c) 2.5×10^{-8}
   d) 1.3×10^{-4}
   e) 6.7×10^{-3}

   ANS: d) 1.3×10^{-4} 　　　　　　　　　　　　　　　　　　　　　　**PAGE:** 15.8

160.   Find the equilibrium concentration of the Mn^{2+} ion.

   a) 9.2×10^{-5} M
   b)   0.01 M
   c) 2.5×10^{-8}
   d) 1.3×10^{-4}
   e) 6.7×10^{-3}

   ANS: c) 2.5×10^{-8} 　　　　　　　　　　　　　　　　　　　　　　**PAGE:** 15.8

161. Calculate the molar concentration of uncomplexed Zn^{2+} in a solution that contains 0.20 mole of $Zn(NH_3)_4^{2+}$ per liter and 0.0116 M NH_3 at equilibrium? The overall K_f for $Zn(NH_3)_4^{2+}$ is 3.8×10^9.

   a) 2.9×10^{-3} M

   b) 8.8×10^{-3} M

   c) 6.7×10^{-4} M

   d) 2.0×10^{-13} M

   e)   none of these

   ANS: a) 2.9×10^{-3} M   **PAGE:** 15.8

162. The cation M^{2+} reacts with NH_3 to form a series of complex ions as follows:

   $$M^{2+} + NH_3 \rightleftharpoons M(NH_3)^{2+} \qquad K_1 = 10^2$$

   $$M(NH_3)^{2+} + NH_3 \rightleftharpoons M(NH_3)_2^{2+} \quad K_2 = 10^3$$

   $$M(NH_3)_2^{2+} + NH_3 \rightleftharpoons M(NH_3)_3^{2+} \quad K_3 = 10^2$$

   A 1.0×10^{-3} mol sample of $M(NO_3)_2$ is added to 1.0 L of 15.0 M NH_3 ($K_b = 1.8 \times 10^{-5}$). Choose the dominant species in this solution.

   a) M^{2+}

   b) $M(NH_3)^{2+}$

   c) $M(NH_3)_2^{2+}$

   d) $M(NH_3)_3^{2+}$

   ANS: d) $M(NH_3)_3^{2+}$ **PAGE:** 15.8

163. The K_f for the complex ion $Ag(NH_3)_2^+$ is 1.7×10^7. The K_{sp} for AgCl is 1.6×10^{-10}. Calculate the molar solubility of AgCl in 1.0 M NH_3.

   a) 5.2×10^{-2}

   b) 4.7×10^{-2}

   c) 2.9×10^{-3}

   d) 1.3×10^{-5}

   e) 1.7×10^{-10}

   ANS: b) 4.7×10^{-2} **PAGE:** 15.8

CHAPTER 16   Spontaneity, Entropy, and Free Energy

1. For which process is ΔS negative?

    a)   evaporation of 1 mol of $CCl_4(l)$
    b)   mixing 5 mL ethanol with 25 mL water
    c)   compressing 1 mol Ne at constant temperature from 1.5 atm to 0.5 atm
    d)   raising the temperature of 100 g Cu from 275 K to 295 K
    e)   grinding a large crystal of KCl to powder

    ANS: c)   compressing 1 mol Ne at constant temperature from
                   1.5 atm to 0.5 atm   **PAGE:** 16.1,5

2. In which reaction is $\Delta S°$ expected to be positive?

    a) $I_2(g) \rightarrow I_2(s)$
    b) $H_2O(l) \rightarrow H_2O(s)$
    c) $CH_3OH(g) + (3/2)O_2(g) \rightarrow CO_2(g) + 2H_2O(l)$
    d) $2O_2(g) + 2SO(g) \rightarrow 2SO_3(g)$
    e)   none of these

    ANS: e)   none of these   **PAGE:** 16.1,5

3. Which statement is true?

    a)   All real processes are irreversible.
    b)   A thermodynamically reversible process takes place infinitely fast.
    c)   In a reversible process, the state functions of the system are always much greater than those of the surroundings.
    d)   There is always more heat given off to the surroundings in a reversible process than in an unharnessed one.
    e)   All statements (a–d) are true.

    ANS: a)   All real processes are irreversible.   **PAGE:** 16.9

4. A 100-mL sample of water is placed in a coffee cup calorimeter. When 1.0 g of an ionic solid is added, the temperature decreases from 21.5°C to 20.8°C as the solid dissolves. For the dissolving of the solid

    a) $\Delta H < 0$
    b) $\Delta S_{univ} > 0$
    c) $\Delta S_{sys} < 0$
    d) $\Delta S_{surr} > 0$
    e)   none of these

    ANS: b) $\Delta S_{univ} > 0$ **PAGE:** 16.1–3

385

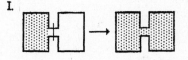

I.

5. Which of the following result(s) in an increase in the entropy of the system?

    I.   (See diagram above.)
    II. $Br_2(g) \rightarrow Br_2(l)$
    III. $NaBr(s) \rightarrow Na^+(aq) + Br^-(aq)$
    IV. $O_2(298\ K) \rightarrow O_2(373\ K)$
    V. $NH_3(1\ atm,\ 298\ K) \rightarrow NH_3(3\ atm,\ 298\ K)$
    a)   I
    b)   II, V
    c)   I, III, IV
    d)   I, II, III, IV
    e)   I, II, III, V

    ANS: c)   I, III, IV   **PAGE:** 16.1,5

6. A mixture of hydrogen and chlorine remains unreacted until it is exposed to ultraviolet light from a burning magnesium strip. Then the following reaction occurs very rapidly:

    $$H_2(g) + Cl_2(g) \rightarrow 2HCl(g) \quad \Delta G = -45.54\ kJ$$

    $$\Delta H = -44.12\ kJ$$

    $$\Delta S = -4.76\ J/K$$

    Select the statement below that best explains this behavior.
    a)   The reactants are thermodynamically more stable than the products.
    b)   The reaction has a small equilibrium constant.
    c)   The ultraviolet light raises the temperature of the system and makes the reaction more favorable.
    d)   The negative value for ΔS slows down the reaction.
    e)   The reaction is spontaneous, but the reactants are kinetically stable.

    ANS: e)   The reaction is spontaneous, but the reactants are
                  kinetically stable.   **PAGE:** 16.1,4

7. Ten identical coins are shaken vigorously in a cup and then poured out onto a table top. Which of the following distributions has the highest probability of occurrence? (T = Tails, H = Heads)

    a) $T_{10}H_0$
    b) T_8H_2
    c) T_7H_3
    d) T_5H_5
    e) T_4H_6

    ANS: d) T_5H_5 **PAGE:** 16.1

8. Which statement below is not upheld by the second law of thermodynamics?

    a)   The change of entropy of the universe is always positive.
    b)   The entropy of a perfect crystal at 0 K is zero.
    c)   Machines always waste some energy.
    d)   A machine is never 100% efficient.
    e)   All of these

    ANS: b)   The entropy of a perfect crystal at 0 K is zero.   **PAGE:** 16.2

9. If two pyramid-shaped dice (with numbers 1 through 4 on the sides) were tossed, which outcome has the highest entropy?

    a)   The sum of the dice is 3.
    b)   The sum of the dice is 4.
    c)   The sum of the dice is 5.
    d)   The sum of the dice is 6.
    e)   The sum of the dice is 7.

    ANS: c)   The sum of the dice is 5.   **PAGE:** 16.1

10. A two-bulbed flask contains seven particles. What is the probability of finding all seven particles on the left side?

    a)   3.1%
    b)   0.32%
    c)   0.78%
    d)   0.93%
    e)   0.13%

    ANS: c)   0.78%   **PAGE:** 16.1

11. Which of the following shows a decrease in entropy?

    a)   precipitation
    b)   gaseous reactants forming a liquid
    c)   a burning piece of wood
    d)   melting ice
    e)   two of these

    ANS: a)   precipitation   **PAGE:** 16.1

12. A chemical reaction is most likely to be spontaneous if it is accompanied by

    a)   increasing energy and increasing entropy.
    b)   lowering energy and increasing entropy.
    c)   increasing energy and decreasing entropy.
    d)   lowering energy and decreasing entropy.
    e)   None of these (a-d)

    ANS: b)   lowering energy and increasing entropy.   **PAGE:** 16.1–3

13. For the dissociation reaction of the acid HF

    $$HF(aq) \rightleftharpoons H^+(aq) + F^-(aq)$$

    ΔS is observed to be negative. The best explanation is:

    a) This is the expected result since each HF molecule produces two ions when it dissociates.

    b) Hydration of the ions produces the negative value of ΔS.

    c) The reaction is expected to be exothermic and thus ΔS should be negative.

    d) The reaction is expected to be endothermic and thus ΔS should be negative.

    e) None of these can explain the negative value of ΔS.

    ANS: b)   Hydration of the ions produces the negative value of ΔS.   **PAGE:** 16.1,5

14. The second law of thermodynamics states that

    a) the entropy of a perfect crystal is zero at 0 K.

    b) the entropy of the universe is constant.

    c) the energy of the universe is increasing.

    d) the entropy of the universe is increasing.

    e) the energy of the universe is constant.

    ANS: d)   the entropy of the universe is increasing.   **PAGE:** 16.2

15. Which of the following statements is (are) always true?

    I. In order for a process to be spontaneous, the entropy of the universe must increase.

    II. A system cannot have both energy disorder and positional disorder.

    III. $\Delta S_{univ} = \dfrac{\Delta G}{T}$

    IV. $S°$ is zero for elements in their standard states.

    a) I

    b) I, IV

    c) I, III, IV

    d) II, IV

    e) II

    ANS: a)   I   **PAGE:** 16.2–5

16. Which of the following statements is always true for a spontaneous process?

    I. $\Delta S_{sys} > 0$
    II. $\Delta S_{surr} > 0$
    III. $\Delta S_{univ} > 0$
    IV. $\Delta G_{sys} > 0$
    a) I
    b) III
    c) IV
    d) I and III
    e) III and IV

ANS: b) III   **PAGE:** 16.2,4

17. Assume that the enthalpy of fusion of ice is 6020 J/mol and does not vary appreciably over the temperature range 270–290 K. If one mole of ice at 0°C is melted by heat supplied from surroundings at 280 K, what is the entropy change in the surroundings, in J/K?

    a) +22.0
    b) +21.5
    c) 0.0
    d) –21.5
    e) –22.0

ANS: d) –21.5   **PAGE:** 16.3

18. If the change in entropy of the surroundings for a process at 451 K and constant pressure is –326 J/K, what is the heat flow absorbed by for the system?

    a) 326 kJ
    b) 24.2 kJ
    c) –147 kJ
    d) 12.1 kJ
    e) 147 kJ

ANS: e) 147 kJ   **PAGE:** 16.3

19. The heat of vaporization for 1.0 mole of water at 100°C and 1.0 atm is 40.6 kJ/mol. Calculate ΔS for the process $H_2O(l) \rightarrow H_2O(g)$ at 100°C.

    a) 109 J/K mol
    b) –109 J/K mol
    c) 406 J/K mol
    d) –406 J/K mol
    e) none of these

ANS: a) 109 J/K mol   **PAGE:** 16.4

20. A change of state that occurs in a system is accompanied by 64.0 kJ of heat, which is transferred to the surroundings at a constant pressure and a constant temperature of 300. K. For this process ΔS_{surr} is:

    a) 64.0 kJ
    b) –64.0 kJ
    c) –213 J/K
    d) 213 J/K
    e) none of these

    ANS: d)   213 J/K   **PAGE:** 16.3

21. For a spontaneous exothermic process, which of the following must be true?

    a) ΔG must be positive.
    b) ΔS must be positive.
    c) ΔS must be negative.
    d) Two of the above must be true.
    e) None of the above (a-c) must be true.

    ANS: e)   None of the above (a-c) must be true.   **PAGE:** 16.4

22-23. The enthalpy of vaporization of ethanol is 38.7 kJ/mol at its boiling point (78°C).

22. Calculate the value of ΔS_{surr} when 1.00 mole of ethanol is vaporized at 78.0°C and 1.00 atm.

    a) 0
    b) 496 J/K mol
    c) 110. J/K mol
    d) –110. J/K mol
    e) –496 J/K mol

    ANS: d)   –110. J/K mol   **PAGE:** 16.3

23. Calculate the value of ΔS when 1.00 mole of ethanol is vaporized at 78.0°C and 1.00 atm.

    a) 0
    b) 496 J/K mol
    c) 110. J/K mol
    d) –110. J/K mol
    e) –496 J/K mol

    ANS: c)   110. J/K mol   **PAGE:** 16.4

24. ΔS_{surr} is _____ for exothermic reactions and _____ for endothermic reactions.

    a)   favorable, unfavorable
    b)   unfavorable, favorable
    c)   favorable, favorable
    d)   unfavorable, unfavorable
    e)   cannot tell

    ANS: a)   favorable, unfavorable   **PAGE:** 16.3

25. ΔS is _____ for exothermic reactions and _____ for endothermic reactions.

    a)   favorable, unfavorable
    b)   unfavorable, favorable
    c)   favorable, favorable
    d)   unfavorable, unfavorable
    e)   cannot tell

    ANS: e)   cannot tell   **PAGE:** 16.3

26. For the vaporization of a liquid at a given pressure: (Note: Answers c and d imply that ΔG is zero at some temperature.)

    a) ΔG is positive at all temperatures.
    b) ΔG is negative at all temperatures.
    c) ΔG is positive at low temperatures, but negative at high temperatures.
    d) ΔG is negative at low temperatures, but positive at high temperatures.
    e)   None of these (a-d)

    ANS: c) ΔG is positive at low temperatures, but negative at high
                     temperatures.   **PAGE:** 16.4

27. For a particular chemical reaction

    $$\Delta H = 5.5 \text{ kJ and } \Delta S = -25 \text{ J/K}$$

    Under what temperature condition is the reaction spontaneous?

    a)   When $T < -220$ K.
    b)   When $T < 220$ K.
    c)   The reaction is spontaneous at all temperatures.
    d)   The reaction is not spontaneous at any temperature.
    e)   When $T > 220$ K.

    ANS: d)   The reaction is not spontaneous at any temperature.   **PAGE:** 16.4

28–30. The following questions refer to the following reaction at constant 25°C and 1 atm.

$$2Fe(s) + (3/2)O_2(g) + 3H_2O(l) \rightarrow 2Fe(OH)_3(s) \ \Delta H = kJ/mol$$

Substance	S° (J/mol K)
$Fe(OH)_3(s)$	107
$Fe(s)$	27
$O_2(g)$	205
$H_2O(l)$	70

28. Determine ΔS_{surr} for the reaction (in kJ/mol K)

  a) 3.14
  b) 0.937
  c) 0.378
  d) 1.31
  e) 2.65

ANS: e)   2.65   **PAGE:** 16.3

29. Determine ΔS_{univ} for the reaction (in kJ/mol K)

  a) 0.22
  b) 2.2
  c) 0.36
  d) 2.8
  e) 3.6

ANS: b)   2.2   **PAGE:** 16.3,5

30. What must be true about ΔG for this reaction?

  a) $\Delta G = \Delta H$
  b) $\Delta G = 0$
  c) $\Delta G > 0$
  d) $\Delta G < 0$
  e) $\Delta G = \Delta S_{univ}$

ANS: d) $\Delta G < 0$ **PAGE:** 16.4

31. Which of the following is true for exothermic processes?

  a) $\Delta S_{surr} < 0$
  b) $\Delta S_{surr} = -\Delta H/T$
  c) $\Delta S_{surr} = 0$
  d) $\Delta S_{surr} > 0$
  e) two of these

ANS: e)   two of these   **PAGE:** 16.3

32. For the reaction $A + B \rightarrow C + D$, $\Delta H° = +40$ kJ and $\Delta S° = +50$ J/K. Therefore, the reaction under standard conditions is

    a)   spontaneous at temperatures less than 10 K.
    b)   spontaneous at temperatures greater than 800 K.
    c)   spontaneous only at temperatures between 10 K and 800 K.
    d)   spontaneous at all temperatures.
    e)   nonspontaneous at all temperatures.

ANS: b)   spontaneous at temperatures greater than 800 K.   **PAGE:** 16.4

33. In which case must a reaction be spontaneous at all temperatures?

    a) ΔH is positive, ΔS is positive.
    b) $\Delta H = 0$, ΔS is negative.
    c) $\Delta S = 0$, ΔH is positive.
    d) ΔH is negative, ΔS is positive.
    e)   none of these

ANS: d) ΔH is negative, ΔS is positive.   **PAGE:** 16.4

34. Consider the dissociation of hydrogen:

$$H_2(g) \rightleftharpoons 2H(g)$$

One would expect that this reaction:

    a)   will be spontaneous at any temperature.
    b)   will be spontaneous at high temperatures.
    c)   will be spontaneous at low temperatures.
    d)   will not be spontaneous at any temperature.
    e)   will never happen.

ANS: b)   will be spontaneous at high temperatures.   **PAGE:** 16.4,5

35. For the process $CHCl_3(s) \rightarrow CHCl_3(l)$, $\Delta H° = 9.2$ kJ/mol and $\Delta S° = 43.9$ J/mol/K. What is the melting point of chloroform?

    a)   –63°C
    b)   210°C
    c)   5°C
    d)   63°C
    e)   –5°C

ANS: a)   –63°C   **PAGE:** 16.4

36. For the process S_8 (rhombic) $\rightarrow$ S_8 (monoclinic) at 110°C, $\Delta H = 3.21$ kJ/mol and $\Delta S = 8.70$ J/K · mol (at 110°C).

    Which of the following is correct?

    a) This reaction is spontaneous at 110°C (S_8 (monoclinic) is stable).
    b) This reaction is spontaneous at 110°C (S_8 (rhombic) is stable).
    c) This reaction is nonspontaneous at 110°C (S_8 (rhombic) is stable).
    d) This reaction is nonspontaneous at 110°C (S_8 (monoclinic) is stable).
    e) Need more data.

    ANS: a) This reaction is spontaneous at 110°C (S_8 (monoclinic) is stable).   **PAGE:** 16.4

37. As O_2(l) is cooled at 1 atm, it freezes at 54.5 K to form Solid I. At a lower temperature, Solid I rearranges to Solid II, which has a different crystal structure. Thermal measurements show that ΔH for the I $\rightarrow$ II phase transition is –743.1 J/mol, and ΔS for the same transition is –17.0 J/K mol. At what temperature are Solids I and II in equilibrium?

    a) 2.06 K
    b) 43.7 K
    c) 31.5 K
    d) 53.4 K
    e) They can never be in equilibrium because they are both solids.

    ANS: b) 43.7 K   **PAGE:** 16.4

38. At constant pressure, the following reaction

    $$2NO_2(g) \rightarrow N_2O_4(g)$$

    is exothermic. The reaction (as written) is

    a) always spontaneous.
    b) spontaneous at low temperatures, but not high temperatures.
    c) spontaneous at high temperatures, but not low temperatures.
    d) never spontaneous.
    e) Cannot tell.

    ANS: b) spontaneous at low temperatures, but not high temperatures.   **PAGE:** 16.4,5

39–41. At 1 atm, liquid water is heated above 100°C.

39. ΔS_{surr} for this process is

    a) greater than zero.
    b) less than zero.
    c) equal to zero.
    d) More information is needed to answer this question.
    e) None of these (a-d)

    ANS: b) less than zero.   **PAGE:** 16.3,4

40. ΔS for this process is

    a) greater than zero.
    b) less than zero.
    c) equal to zero.
    d) More information is needed to answer this question.
    e) None of these (a-d)

    ANS: a)   greater than zero.   **PAGE:** 16.3,4

41. ΔS_{univ} for this process is

    a) greater than zero.
    b) less than zero.
    c) equal to zero.
    d) More information is needed to answer this question.
    e) None of these (a-d)

    ANS: a)   greater than zero.   **PAGE:** 16.3,4

42. Given the following data (ΔH_f, $S°$, respectively) for N_2O_4 (l) –20 kJ/mol, 209 J/K · mol, and N_2O_4(g) 10 kJ/mol, 304 J/K · mol. Above what temperature (in °C) is the vaporization of N_2O_4 liquid spontaneous?

    ANS: Above 43°C.   **PAGE:** 16.4

43–45. Given that ΔH_{vap} is 52.6 kJ/mol, and boiling point is 83.4°C, 1 atm, if one mole of this substance is vaporized at 1 atm, calculate the following:

43. ΔS_{surr}

    a) -148 J/K · mol
    b) 148 J/K · mol
    c) 630 J/K · mol
    d) –630 J/K · mol
    e) 0

    ANS: a)   –148 J/K · mol   **PAGE:** 16.3

44. ΔS

    a) -148 J/K · mol
    b) 148 J/K · mol
    c) 630 J/K · mol
    d) –630 J/K · mol
    e) 0

    ANS: b)   148 J/K · mol   **PAGE:** 16.4

45. ΔG

a)   -148 J/K · mol
b)   148 J/K · mol
c)   630 J/K · mol
d)   –630 J/K · mol
e)   0

ANS: e)   0   PAGE: 16.4

46.   As long as the disorder of the surroundings is increasing, a process will be spontaneous.

ANS: False   PAGE: 16.3,4

47.   For a given process, ΔS_{surr} and ΔS_{sys} have opposite signs.

ANS: False   PAGE: 16.3,4

48.   If $\Delta S_{surr} = -\Delta S_{sys}$, the process is at equilibrium.

ANS: True   PAGE: 16.3,4

49. $\Delta H°$ is zero for a chemical reaction at constant temperature.

ANS: False   PAGE: 16.3

50.   The melting point of water is 0°C at 1 atm pressure because under these conditions

a) ΔS for the process $H_2O(s) \rightarrow H_2O(l)$ is positive.
b) ΔS and ΔS_{surr} for the process $H_2O(s) \rightarrow H_2O(l)$ are both positive.
c) ΔS and ΔS_{surr} for the process $H_2O(s) \rightarrow H_2O(l)$ are equal in magnitude and opposite in sign.
d) ΔG is positive for the process $H_2O(s) \rightarrow H_2O(l)$.
e)   None of these is correct.

ANS: c) ΔS and ΔS_{surr} for the process $H_2O(s) \rightarrow H_2O(l)$ are equal in
            magnitude and opposite in sign.   PAGE: 16.4

51-54.   Substance X has a heat of vaporization of 55.4 kJ/mol at its normal boiling point (423
°C). For the process X (l) $\rightarrow$ X (g) at 1 atm and 423 °C calculate the value of:

51. ΔS_{univ}.

a)   0
b)   79.6 J/K·mol
c)   103 J/K·mol
d)   -79.6 J/K·mol
e)   -103 J/K·mol

ANS: a)   0   PAGE: 16.4

52. ΔS_{surr}

    a)   0
    b)   79.6 J/K·mol
    c)   103 J/K·mol
    d)   -79.6 J/K·mol
    e)   -103 J/K·mol

    ANS: d)   -79.6 J/K·mol   **PAGE:** 16.3

53. ΔS

    a)   0
    b)   79.6 J/K·mol
    c)   103 J/K·mol
    d)   -79.6 J/K·mol
    e)   -103 J/K·mol

    ANS: b)   79.6 J/K·mol   **PAGE:** 16.4

54. ΔG

    a)   0
    b)   79.6 J/K·mol
    c)   103 J/K·mol
    d)   -79.6 J/K·mol
    e)   -103 J/K·mol

    ANS: a)   0   **PAGE:** 16.4

55. For a certain process at 355 K, ΔG = -12.4 kJ and ΔH = -9.2 kJ. Therefore, ΔS for the process is

    a)   0
    b)   9.0 J/K·mol
    c)   -9.0 J/K·mol
    d)   -21.6 J/K·mol
    e)   21.6 J/K·mol

    ANS: b)   9.0 J/K·mol   **PAGE:** 16.4

56. Consider the freezing of liquid water at –10°C. For this process what are the signs for ΔH, ΔS, and ΔG?

	ΔH	ΔS	ΔG
a)	+	–	0
b)	–	+	0
c)	–	+	–
d)	+	–	–
e)	–	–	–

ANS:	ΔH	ΔS	ΔG
e)	–	–	–

    PAGE: 16.4

57. When a stable diatomic molecule spontaneously forms from its atoms, what are the signs of $\Delta H°$, $\Delta S°$, and $\Delta G°$?

	$\Delta H°$	$\Delta S°$	$\Delta G°$
a)	+	+	+
b)	+	–	–
c)	–	+	+
d)	–	–	+
e)	–	–	–

ANS: $\Delta H°$ $\Delta S°$ $\Delta G°$

   e)   –   –   –   PAGE: 16.4,5

58. Elemental sulfur exists in two crystalline forms, rhombic and monoclinic. From the following data, calculate the equilibrium temperature at which monoclinic sulfur and rhombic sulfur are in equilibrium.

	$\Delta H_f°$ (kJ/mol)	$S°$ (J/K · mol)
S (rhombic)	0	31.88
S (monoclinic	0.30	32.55

   a)   +450 K
   b)   +210 K
   c)   –210 K
   d)   –450 K
   e)   0 K

ANS: a)   +450 K   PAGE: 16.4–6

59. The reaction

$$2H_2O(g) \rightarrow 2H_2(g) + O_2(g)$$

has a positive value of $\Delta G°$. Which of the following statements must be true?

   a)   The reaction is slow.
   b)   The reaction will not occur. [When $H_2O(g)$ is introduced into a flask, no O_2 or H_2 will form even over a long period of time.]
   c)   The reaction is exothermic.
   d)   The equilibrium lies far to the right.
   e)   None of these is true.

ANS: e)   None of these is true.   PAGE: 16.4,8

60. For the process of a certain liquid vaporizing at 1 atm, $\Delta H°_{vap}$ = 42.3 kJ/mol and $\Delta S°_{vap}$ = 74.1 J/mol · K. Assuming these values are independent of T, what is the normal boiling point of this liquid?

  a) 571°C
  b) 844°C
  c) 298°C
  d) 0.57°C
  e) none of these

ANS: c)   298°C   **PAGE: 16.4**

61. Consider the following processes:

  I.   Condensation of a liquid.

  II. Increasing the volume of 1.0 mol of an ideal gas at constant temperature.

  III. Dissolving an ionic solid in water.

  IV. Heating 1.0 mol of an ideal gas at constant volume.

  For how many of these is ΔS positive?

  a) 0
  b) 1
  c) 2
  d) 3
  e) 4

ANS: d)   3   **PAGE: 16.5**

62. The third law of thermodynamics states

  a) the entropy of the universe is increasing.
  b) the entropy of the universe is constant.
  c) the entropy is zero at 0 K for a perfect crystal.
  d) the absolute entropy of a substance decreases with increasing temperature.
  e) the entropy of the universe equals the sum of the entropy of system and surroundings.

ANS: c)   the entropy is zero at 0 K for a perfect crystal.   **PAGE: 16.5**

63. Which of the following is not a state function?

  a) q
  b) G
  c) H
  d) E
  e) P

ANS: a) q **PAGE: 16.6**

399

64. The standard free energy of formation of AgCl(s) is –110 kJ/mol. $\Delta G°$ for the reaction $2AgCl(s) \rightarrow 2Ag(s) + Cl_2(g)$ is:

    a)   110 kJ
    b)   220 kJ
    c)   –110 kJ
    d)   –220 kJ
    e)   none of these

    ANS: b)   220 kJ   **PAGE: 16.6**

65. Given the following free energies of formation:

$$\Delta G_f°$$

$C_2H_2(g)$	209.2 kJ/mol
$C_2H_6(g)$	–32.9 kJ/mol

    calculate K_p at 298 K for $C_2H_2(g) + 2H_2(g) \rightleftharpoons C_2H_6(g)$

    a) 9.07×10^{-1}
    b)   97.2
    c) 1.24×10^{31}
    d) 2.72×10^{42}
    e)   None of these is within a factor of 10 of the correct answer.

    ANS: d) 2.72×10^{42}   **PAGE: 16.6,8**

66. Given the following data, calculate the normal boiling point for formic acid (HCOOH).

	$\Delta H_f°$ (kJ/mol)	$S°$ (J/mol K)
HCOOH(l)	–410.	130.
HCOOH(g)	–363	251

    a)   2.57 K
    b)   1730°C
    c)   388°C
    d)   82°C
    e)   115°C

    ANS: e)   115°C   **PAGE: 16.4-6**

400

67. Consider the following hypothetical reaction at 310 K. Standard free energies of formation are given in parentheses.

$$B \longrightarrow C \qquad \Delta G° = -31.4 \text{ kJ/mol}$$
$$(?) \qquad (176.4 \text{ kJ/mol})$$

Calculate the standard free energy of formation of compound B.

   a)   207.8 kJ/mol
   b)   –207.8 kJ/mol
   c)   145.0 kJ/mol
   d)   –145.0 kJ/mol
   e)   none of these

   ANS: a)   207.8 kJ/mol   **PAGE: 16.6**

68. The acid dissociation constant for a weak acid HX at 25°C is 1.60×10^{-8}. Calculate the free energy of formation for $X^-(aq)$ at 25°C. The standard free energies of HX(aq) and $H^+(aq)$ at 25°C are –211.5 kJ/mol and 0, respectively.

   a)   –12.5 kJ/mol
   b)   255 kJ/mol
   c)   0
   d)   –167 kJ/mol
   e)   322 kJ/mol

   ANS: d)   –167 kJ/mol   **PAGE: 16.6,8**

69. The standard molar free energies of formation of $NO_2(g)$ and $N_2O_4(g)$ at 25°C are 51.84 and 98.28 kJ/mol, respectively. What is the value of K_p (in atm) for the reaction written as follows at 25°C?

$$2NO_2 \rightleftharpoons N_2O_4$$

   a) 1.37×10^8
   b) 1.17×10^4
   c)   8.84
   d)   0.113
   e) 7.31×10^{-9}

   ANS: c)   8.84   **PAGE: 16.6,8**

70. For the reaction $Cl_2O(g) + (3/2)O_2(g) \rightarrow 2ClO_2(g)$,

   $\Delta H° = 126.4$ kJ/mol and $\Delta S° = -74.9$ J/K mol. At 377°C, $\Delta G°$ equals:

   a)   98.3 kJ/mol
   b)   77.8 kJ/mol
   c)   175.1 kJ/mol
   d)   51.5 kJ/mol
   e)   none of these

   ANS: c)   175.1 kJ/mol   **PAGE: 16.6**

71. Given that ΔG_f° for NH_3 = –16.67 kJ/mol, calculate the equilibrium constant for the following reaction at 298 K:

$$N_2(g) + 3H_2(g) \rightleftharpoons 2NH_3(g)$$

   a) 6.98×10^5
   b) 8.36×10^2
   c) 8.36×10^{-2}
   d) 1.20×10^{-3}
   e) 1.42×10^{-6}

ANS: a) 6.98×10^5 **PAGE:** 16.6,8

72. The following reaction takes place at 120°C:

$$H_2O(l) \rightarrow H_2O(g) \qquad \Delta H = 44.0 \text{ kJ/mol} \qquad \Delta S = 0.119 \text{ kJ/mol K}$$

Which of the following must be true?

   a)   The reaction is not spontaneous.
   b)   The reaction is spontaneous.
   c) $\Delta G = 0$
   d) $\Delta G < 0$
   e)   two of these

ANS: e)   two of these **PAGE:** 16.4

73. Determine $\Delta G°$ for the following reaction:

$$CH_4(g) + 2O_2(g) \rightarrow CO_2(g) + 2H_2O(l)$$

Substance	ΔG_f° (kJ/mol)
$CH_4(g)$	–50.7
$O_2(g)$	0
$CO_2(g)$	–394.4
$H_2O(l)$	–237.4

   a)   207.7 kJ
   b)   106.3 kJ
   c)   817.9 kJ
   d)   130.4 kJ
   e)   943.1 kJ

ANS: c)   817.9 kJ **PAGE:** 16.6

74–76. The questions below refer to the following:
When ignited, solid ammonium dichromate decomposes in a fiery display. This is the reaction for a "volcano" demonstration. The decomposition produces nitrogen gas, water vapor, and chromium(III) oxide. The temperature is constant at 25°C.

Substance	ΔH_f° (kJ/mol)	S° (kJ/mol · K)
$Cr_2O_3(g)$	–1140	0.0812
$H_2O(l)$	–242	0.1187
$N_2(g)$	0	0.1915
$(NH_4)_2Cr_2O_7$	–22.5	0.1137

74. Determine ΔS° reaction (in kJ/mol · K).

    a) 0.7421
    b) 0.6412
    c) 0.9892
    d) 0.6338
    e) 0.5461

    ANS: d)   0.6338   **PAGE:** 16.5

75. Determine ΔS°_{univ} (in kJ/mol · K).

    a) 7.63
    b) –6.09
    c) –7.91
    d) 6.09
    e) –8.14

    ANS: a)   7.63   **PAGE:** 16.4

76. Determine ΔG° (in kJ/mol).

    a) –6119.7
    b) –2274.7
    c) –3042.6
    d) –5419.3
    e) –1488.8

    ANS: b)   –2274.7   **PAGE:** 16.6

77. Calculate K_{sp} for the salt NaCl at 25°C.

Substance	ΔG_f° (in kJ/mol)
Na^+(aq)	−262
Cl^-(aq)	−131
NaCl(s)	−384

   a)   40
   b)   4
   c)   1
   d)   0.4
   e)   0.04

   ANS: a)   40   **PAGE:** 16.8

78. Determine ΔG° for the weak acid, HF, at 25°C. ($K_a = 7.2 \times 10^{-4}$)

   a)   140 kJ
   b)   0.16 kJ
   c)   53 kJ
   d)   92 kJ
   e)   18 kJ

   ANS: e)   18 kJ   **PAGE:** 16.8

79–83. Consider the reaction

$$2N_2O_5(g) \rightleftharpoons 4NO_2(g) + O_2(g)$$

   at 25°C for which the following data are relevant:

	ΔH_f°	S°
N_2O_5	11.29 kJ/mol	655.3 J/K · mol
NO_2	33.15 kJ/mol	239.9 J/K · mol
O_2	?	204.8 J/K · mol

79. Calculate ΔH° for the reaction.

   a)   110.02 kJ
   b)   21.86 kJ
   c)   −21.86 kJ
   d)   115.20 kJ
   e)   −155.20 kJ

   ANS: a)   110.02 kJ   **PAGE:** 16.6

404

80. Calculate $\Delta S°$ for the reaction.

    a) 89.5 J/K

    b) 249.2 J/K

    c) 453.8 J/K

    d) 249.2 J/K

    e) −115.6 J/K

ANS: c)   453.8 J/K   **PAGE:** 16.5

81. Calculate $\Delta G°$ for the reaction at 25°C.

    a) −135 kJ

    b) 98.7 kJ

    c) −25.2 kJ

    d) −11.2 kJ

    e) 0

ANS: c)   −25.2 kJ   **PAGE:** 16.6

82. Which of the following is true for this reaction?

    a) Both $\Delta H°$ and $\Delta S°$ favor the reaction's spontaneity.

    b) Both $\Delta H°$ and $\Delta S°$ oppose the reaction's spontaneity.

    c) $\Delta H°$ favors the reaction, but $\Delta S°$ opposes it.

    d) $\Delta H°$ opposes the reaction, but $\Delta S°$ favors it.

    e) The reaction cannot occur at room temperature.

ANS: d) $\Delta H°$ opposes the reaction, but $\Delta S°$ favors it.   **PAGE:** 16.4,6

83. The reaction is allowed to proceed until all substances involved have reached their equilibrium concentrations. Under those conditions what is ΔG for the reaction?

    a) −135 kJ

    b) 98.7 kJ

    c) −25.2 kJ

    d) −11.2 kJ

    e) 0

ANS: e)   0   **PAGE:** 16.8

84. At 699 K, $\Delta G° = -23.25$ kJ for the reaction $H_2(g) + I_2(g) \rightleftharpoons 2HI(g)$. Calculate ΔG for this reaction if the reagents are both supplied at 10.0 atm pressure and the product is at 1.00 atm pressure.

    a) −3.5 kJ

    b) −36.6 kJ

    c) +36.6 kJ

    d) −50.0 kJ

    e) +50.0 kJ

ANS: d)   −50.0 kJ   **PAGE:** 16.7

85. Assume that the reaction

$$CO(g) + H_2O(g) \rightleftharpoons CO_2(g) + H_2(g)$$

occurs in an ideal mixture of ideal gases. At 700 K, $K_p = 5.10$. At this temperature, $\Delta G°$ equals:

   a) 0 kJ
   b) 29.7 kJ
   c) 9.48 kJ
   d) −9.48 kJ
   e) −4.12 kJ

ANS: d) −9.48 kJ   **PAGE:** 16.8

86. Consider the reaction

$$2SO_2(g) + O_2(g) \rightleftharpoons 2SO_3(g)$$

for which $\Delta H° = -200.$ kJ and $\Delta S° = -187$ J/K at 25°C. Assuming that $\Delta H°$ and $\Delta S°$ are independent of temperature, calculate the temperature where $K_p = 1$.

   a) 970. K
   b) 2070 K
   c) 200. K
   d) 1070 K
   e) none of these

ANS: d) 1070 K   **PAGE:** 16.8

87. For the following reaction,

$$CO_2(g) + 2H_2O(g) \rightarrow CH_4(g) + 2O_2(g), \Delta H° = 803 \text{ kJ}$$

which of the following will increase K?

   a) decrease number of moles of methane
   b) increase volume of system
   c) increase the temperature of system
   d) all of the above
   e) none of the above

ANS: c)   increase the temperature of system   **PAGE:** 16.8

88. For a particular reaction the equilibrium constant is 1.50×10^{-2} at 370.°C and $\Delta H°$ is +16.0 kJ at 25°C. Assuming $\Delta H°$ and $\Delta S°$ are temperature independent, calculate $\Delta S°$ for the reaction.

   a) −18.8 J/K
   b) +18.8 J/K
   c) −10.0 J/K
   d) +10.0 J/K
   e) none of the these

ANS: c)   −10.0 J/K   **PAGE:** 16.8

89. Calculate $\Delta G°$ for $H_2O(g) + (1/2)O_2(g) \rightleftharpoons H_2O_2(g)$ at 600. K, using the following data:

$$H_2(g) + O_2(g) \rightleftharpoons H_2O_2 \qquad K_p = 2.3 \times 10^6 \text{ at } 600. \text{ K}$$

$$2H_2(g) + O_2(g) \rightleftharpoons 2H_2O(g) \qquad K_p = 1.8 \times 10^{37} \text{ at } 600. \text{ K}$$

   a) +140 kJ
   b) –220 kJ
   c) –290 kJ
   d) –350 kJ
   e) +290 kJ

ANS: a)   +140 kJ   PAGE: 16.8

90. For which of the following processes would $\Delta S°$ be expected to be most positive?

   a) $O_2(g) + 2H_2(g) \rightarrow 2H_2O(g)$
   b) $H_2O(l) \rightarrow H_2O(s)$
   c) $NH_3(g) + HCl(g) \rightarrow NH_4Cl(g)$
   d) $2NH_4NO_3(s) \rightarrow 2N_2(g) + O_2(g) + 4H_2O(g)$
   e) $N_2O_4(g) \rightarrow 2NO_2(g)$

ANS: d) $2NH_4NO_3(s) \rightarrow 2N_2(g) + O_2(g) + 4H_2O(g)$ PAGE: 16.1,5

91. Consider the following hypothetical reaction (at 310. K). Standard free energies in kJ/mol are given in parentheses.

$$\begin{array}{cccccc} A & \rightarrow & B & + & C & \Delta G° = ? \\ (-32.2) & & (207.8) & & (-237.0) & \end{array}$$

What is the value of the equilibrium constant for the reaction at 310. K?

   a) 0.31
   b) 1.9
   c) 1.0
   d) 2.2×10^{10}
   e) 4.5×10^{-11}

ANS: a)   0.31   PAGE: 16.8

92. The equilibrium constant K_p for the dissociation reaction of Cl_2

$$Cl_2(g) \rightleftharpoons 2Cl(g)$$

was measured as a function of temperature (in K). A graph of $\ln K_p$ versus $1/T$ for this reaction gives a straight line with a slope of -1.352×10^4 and an intercept of 14.51. The value of ΔS for this dissociation reaction is:

   a) 26.81 J/K · mol
   b) 112.0 J/K · mol
   c) 120.6 J/K · mol
   d) 53.14 J/K · mol
   e) none of these

ANS: c)   120.6 J/K · mol   PAGE: 16.8

407

93. The following reaction has a $\Delta G°$ value of 42.6 kJ/mol at 25° C.

$$HB(aq) + H_2O(l) \rightleftharpoons H_3O^+(aq) + B^-(aq)$$

Calculate the K_a for the acid HB.

a) 1.63
b) –17.2
c) 3.41×10^{-8}
d) 42,600
e) 14.0

ANS: c) 3.41×10^{-8} **PAGE:** 16.8

94. The standard free energy of formation of nitric oxide, NO, at 1000. K (roughly the temperature in an automobile engine during ignition) is 78 kJ/mol. Calculate the equilibrium constant for the reaction

$$N_2(g) + O_2(g) \rightleftharpoons 2NO(g)$$

at 1000. K.

a) 1.8×10^{-19}
b) 0.99
c) 4.3×10^{-10}
d) 7.1×10^{-9}
e) 8.4×10^{-5}

ANS: d) 7.1×10^{-9} **PAGE:** 16.8

95. Consider the reaction

$$2NO_2(g) \rightleftharpoons N_2O_4(g); \Delta H° = -56.8 \text{ kJ} \qquad \Delta S° = -175 \text{ J/K}$$

In a container (at 298 K) $N_2O_4(g)$ and $NO_2(g)$ are mixed with initial partial pressures of 2.4 atm and 0.42 atm, respectively. Which of the following statements is correct?

a) Some $N_2O_4(g)$ will decompose into $NO_2(g)$.
b) Some $NO_2(g)$ will dimerize to form $N_2O_4(g)$.
c) The system is at equilibrium at these initial pressures.
d) The final total pressure must be known to answer this question.
e) None of these.

ANS: a) Some $N_2O_4(g)$ will decompose into $NO_2(g)$.   **PAGE:** 16.8

96–101. Consider the gas phase reaction

$$NO + (1/2)O_2 \rightleftharpoons NO_2$$

for which $\Delta H° = -57.0$ kJ and $K = 1.5 \times 10^6$ at 25°C.

96. Calculate $\Delta H°$ at 25°C for the following reaction:

$$2NO + O_2 \rightleftharpoons 2NO_2$$

   a) 57.0 kJ
   b) –114 kJ
   c) –28.5 kJ
   d) 778 kJ

ANS: b)   –114 kJ   **PAGE:** 16.6

97. Calculate K for the following reaction at 25°C:

$$2NO + O_2 \rightleftharpoons 2NO_2$$

   a) 3.0×10^6
   b) 2.3×10^{12}
   c) 7.5×10^5
   d) 1.2×10^3
   e) 1.5×10^6

ANS: b) 2.3×10^{12} **PAGE:** 16.8

98. Calculate $\Delta G°$ at 25°C for the following reaction:

$$2NO + O_2 \rightleftharpoons 2NO_2$$

   a) –70.5 kJ
   b) –5.91 kJ
   c) –57.0 kJ
   d) +5.91 kJ
   e) +70.5 kJ

ANS: a)   –70.5 kJ   **PAGE:** 16.8

99. Calculate $\Delta S°$ at 25°C for the following reaction:

$$2NO + O_2 \rightleftharpoons 2NO_2$$

   a) –1740 J/K
   b) –146 J/K
   c) +528 J/K
   d) +146 J/K
   e) +1740 J/K

ANS: b)   –146 J/K   **PAGE:** 16.4,8

100. For this system at equilibrium, how will raising the temperature affect the amount of NO present?

    a)   The amount of NO will increase.

    b)   The amount of NO will decrease.

    c)   The amount of NO will remain the same.

    d)   Cannot be determined.

    e)   Answer depends on the value of K.

ANS: a)   The amount of NO will increase.   **PAGE:** 16.8

101. What would be the effect on the amount of NO present of compressing the equilibrium system to a smaller volume, while keeping the temperature constant?

    a)   The amount of NO will increase.

    b)   The amount of NO will decrease.

    c)   The amount of NO will remain the same.

    d)   Cannot be determined.

    e)   Answer depends on the value of K.

ANS: b)   The amount of NO will decrease.   **PAGE:** 16.8

102–103. Given

$$CH_3CO_2H(aq) \rightleftharpoons H^+(aq) + CH_3CO_2^-(aq)$$

at 25°C, $K_a = 1.8 \times 10^{-5}$

102. What is $\Delta G°$ at 25°C?

    a)   –27,000 J

    b)   +27,000 J

    c)   –2300 J

    d)   +2300 J

    e)   +270 J

ANS: b)   +27,000 J   **PAGE:** 16.8

103. What is ΔG at 25°C for a solution in which the initial concentrations are:

$$[CH_3CO_2H]_o = 0.10 \text{ M}$$

$$[H^+]_o = 2.0 \times 10^{-8} \text{ M}$$

$$[CH_3CO_2^-]_o = 0.010 \text{ M}$$

    a)   +50. kJ

    b)   –50. kJ

    c)   +23 kJ

    d)   –23 kJ

    e)   27 kJ

ANS: d)   –23 kJ   **PAGE:** 16.7,8

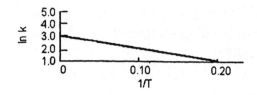

104. The equilibrium constant of a certain reaction was measured at various temperatures to give the plot shown above. What is $\Delta S°$ for the reaction in J/mol · K?

   a) 0.20
   b) 3.0
   c) 25
   d) −50.
   e) −8.3 × 10³

   ANS: c) 25   **PAGE:** 16.8

105. Consider a weak acid, HX. If a 0.10 M solution of HX has a pH of 5.83 at 25°C, what is $\Delta G°$ for the acid's dissociation reaction at 25°C?

   a) −61 kJ
   b) −30. kJ
   c) 0
   d) 30. kJ
   e) 61 kJ

   ANS: e) 61 kJ   **PAGE:** 16.8

106. For the reaction $CO(g) + 2H_2(g) \rightleftharpoons CH_3OH(g)$, $\Delta G°_{700K} = -13.46$ kJ. The K_p for this reaction at 700. K is:

   a) 10.1
   b) 16.7
   c) 22.5
   d) 9.90 × 10⁻²
   e) none of these

   ANS: a) 10.1   **PAGE:** 16.8

107. For the reaction $2HF(g) \rightleftharpoons H_2(g) + F_2(g)$, $\Delta G° = 38.3$ kJ, at 1000 K. If, at this temperature, 5.00 moles of $HF(g)$, 0.500 moles of $H_2(g)$, and 0.75 moles of $F_2(g)$ are mixed in a 1.00-L container:

   a) Some HF will decompose (to yield H_2 and F_2).
   b) The system is at equilibrium.
   c) Some HF will be formed (from H_2 and F_2).
   d) Not enough data are given to answer this question.
   e) None of these (a-d).

   ANS: c) Some HF will be formed (from H_2 and F_2).   **PAGE:** 16.8

108–110.   Consider the following system at equilibrium at 25°C:

   $$PCl_3(g) + Cl_2(g) \rightleftharpoons PCl_5(g)$$

   for which

   $$\Delta H° = -92.5 \text{ kJ at } 25°C.$$

108. If the temperature of the system is raised, the ratio of the partial pressure of PCl_5 to the partial pressure of PCl_3 will

   a) increase.
   b) decrease.
   c) stay the same.
   d) impossible to tell without more information.
   e) none of these

   ANS: b) decrease.   **PAGE:** 16.8

109. When some $Cl_2(g)$ is added at constant volume and temperature, the ratio of the partial pressure of PCl_5 to the partial pressure of PCl_3 will

   a) increase.
   b) decrease.
   c) stay the same.
   d) impossible to tell without more information.
   e) none of these

   ANS: a) increase.   **PAGE:** 16.8

110. When the volume is decreased at constant temperature, the ratio of the partial pressure of PCl_5 to the partial pressure of PCl_3 will

   a) increase.
   b) decrease.
   c) stay the same.
   d) impossible to tell without more information.
   e) none of these

   ANS: a) increase.   **PAGE:** 16.8

111. Water gas, a commercial fuel, is made by the reaction of hot coke carbon with steam.

$$C(s) + H_2O(g) \rightarrow CO(g) + H_2(g)$$

When equilibrium is established at 800°C the concentrations of CO, H_2, and H_2O are 4.00×10^{-2}, 4.00×10^{-2}, and 1.00×10^{-2} mole/liter, respectively. Calculate the value of $\Delta G°$ for this reaction at 800°C.

a) 109 kJ
b) –43.5 kJ
c) 193 kJ
d) 16.3 kJ
e) none of these

ANS: d)   16.3 kJ   **PAGE:** 16.8

112–113.   The equilibrium constant K_p (in atm) for the dissociation reaction of Cl_2

$$Cl_2 \rightleftharpoons 2Cl$$

was measured as a function of temperature (in K).

A graph of ln K_p versus $1/T$ for this reaction gives a straight line with a slope of -1.352×10^4 and an intercept of 14.51.

112. From these data, which of the following statements is true?

a) The reaction is exothermic.
b) The reaction is endothermic.
c) The reaction rate is high
d) The reaction is not spontaneous.
e) None of these.

ANS: b)   The reaction is endothermic.   **PAGE:** 16.8

113. The value of ΔH for this dissociation reaction is:

a) –122.1 kJ
b) 112.4 kJ
c) 26.8 kJ
d) 122.1 kJ
e) none of these

ANS: b)   112.4 kJ   **PAGE:** 16.8

413

114. In which of the following changes is the work done by the system the largest at 25°C?

    a) an isothermal free expansion of an ideal gas from 1 to 10 liters

    b) an isothermal expansion of an ideal gas from 1 to 10 liters against an opposing pressure of 1 atm

    c) an isothermal expansion of an ideal gas from 1 to 10 liters against an opposing pressure of 5 atm

    d) an isothermal reversible expansion of an ideal gas from 1 to 10 liters

    e) the work is the same for processes a–d

    ANS: d)   an isothermal reversible expansion of an ideal gas from 1 to 10 liters   **PAGE:** 16.9

115. For a certain process, at 300. K, $\Delta G = -10.0$ kJ and $\Delta H = -7.0$ kJ. If the process is carried out reversibly, the amount of useful work that can be performed is

    a) –23.0 kJ

    b) –7.0 kJ

    c) –3.0 kJ

    d) –10.0 kJ

    e) –17.0 kJ

    ANS: d)   –10.0 kJ   **PAGE:** 16.9

116. For a certain process, at 300 K, $\Delta G = -10.0$ kJ and $\Delta H = -7.0$ kJ. If the process is carried out so that no useful work is performed, ΔG is

    a) +10.0 kJ

    b) +7.0 kJ

    c) 0

    d) –7.0 kJ

    e) –10.0 kJ

    ANS: e)   –10.0 kJ   **PAGE:** 16.9

117–120. Would you predict an increase or decrease in entropy for each of the following?

117. The freezing of water

    ANS: decrease in entropy   **PAGE:** 16.1,5

118. $2H_2(g) + O_2(g) \rightarrow 2H_2O(g)$

    ANS: decrease in entropy   **PAGE:** 16.1,5

119. $2KClO_3(s) \rightarrow 2KCl(s) + 3O_2(g)$

    ANS: increase in entropy   **PAGE:** 16.1,5

120. $He(g)$ at 3 atm $\rightarrow$ $He(g)$ at 1 atm

    ANS: increase in entropy   **PAGE:** 16.1,5

CHAPTER 17 Electrochemistry

1. Ammonium metavandate reacts with sulfur dioxide in acidic solution as follows (hydrogen ions and H_2O omitted):

   $$xVO_3^- + ySO_2 \rightarrow xVO^{2+} + ySO_4^{2-}$$

   The ratio $x : y$ is:

   a) 1 : 1
   b) 1 : 2
   c) 2 : 1
   d) 1 : 3
   e) 3 : 1

   ANS: c) 2 : 1 **PAGE:** 17.1

2. The following reaction occurs in basic solution:

   $$F_2 + H_2O \rightarrow O_2 + F^-$$

   When the equation is balanced, the sum of the coefficients is:

   a) 10
   b) 11
   c) 12
   d) 13
   e) none of these

   ANS: d) 13 **PAGE:** 17.1

3. When the equation for the following reaction in basic solution is balanced, what is the sum of the coefficients?

   $$MnO_2 + HO_2^- \rightarrow MnO_4^-$$

   a) 11
   b) 31
   c) 14
   d) 9
   e) 18

   ANS: d) 9 **PAGE:** 17.1

4. The reaction below occurs in basic solution. In the balanced equation, what is the sum of the coefficients?

$$Zn + NO_3^- \rightarrow Zn(OH)_4^{2-} + NH_3$$

   a) 12
   b) 15
   c) 19
   d) 23
   e) 27

ANS: d) 23   **PAGE:** 17.1

5. What is the oxidation state of Hg in Hg_2Cl_2?

   a) +2
   b) −1
   c) −2
   d) +1
   e) 0

ANS: d) +1   **PAGE:** 17.1

6. How many electrons are transferred in the following reaction?

$$2ClO_3^- + 12H^+ + 10I^- \rightarrow 5I_2 + Cl_2 + 6H_2O$$

   a) 12
   b) 5
   c) 2
   d) 30
   e) 10

ANS: e) 10   **PAGE:** 17.1

7. Which energy conversion shown below takes place in a galvanic cell?

   a) electrical to chemical
   b) chemical to electrical
   c) mechanical to chemical
   d) chemical to mechanical
   e) mechanical to electrical

ANS: b)   chemical to electrical   **PAGE:** 17.1

8. Which of the following reactions is possible at the anode of a galvanic cell?

    a) $Zn \rightarrow Zn^{2+} + 2e^-$
    b) $Zn^{2+} + 2e^- \rightarrow Zn$
    c) $Zn^{2+} + Cu \rightarrow Zn + Cu^{2+}$
    d) $Zn + Cu^{2+} \rightarrow Zn^{2+} + Cu$
    e) two of these

    ANS: a) $Zn \rightarrow Zn^{2+} + 2e^-$ **PAGE: 17.1**

9. How many electrons are transferred in the following reaction?

    $$Fe + 2HCl \rightarrow FeCl_2 + H_2$$

    a) 0
    b) 1
    c) 2
    d) 4
    e) not enough information given

    ANS: c)   2   **PAGE: 17.1**

10. Which of the following is true for the cell shown here?

    $$Zn(s) \,|\, Zn^{2+}(aq) \,||\, Cr^{3+}(aq) \,|\, Cr(s)$$

    a) The electrons flow from the cathode to the anode.
    b) The electrons flow from the zinc to the chromium.
    c) The electrons flow from the chromium to the zinc.
    d) The chromium is oxidized.
    e) The zinc is reduced.

    ANS: b)   The electrons flow from the zinc to the chromium.   **PAGE: 17.1,2**

11. How many electrons are transferred in the following reaction?

    $$SO_3^{2-}(aq) + MnO_4^-(aq) \rightarrow SO_4^{2-}(aq) + Mn^{2+}(aq)$$

    a) 6
    b) 2
    c) 10
    d) 4
    e) 3

    ANS: c)   10   **PAGE: 17.1**

12. A strip of copper is placed in a 1 M solution of copper nitrate and a strip of silver is placed in a 1 M solution of silver nitrate. The two metal strips are connected to a voltmeter by wires and a salt bridge connects the solutions. The following standard reduction potentials apply:

$$Ag^+(aq) + e^- \rightarrow Ag(s) \qquad E° = +0.80 \text{ V}$$

$$Cu^{2+}(aq) + 2e^- \rightarrow Cu(s) \qquad E° = +0.34 \text{ V}$$

When the voltmeter is removed and the two electrodes are connected by a wire, which of the following does not take place?

   a) Electrons flow in the external circuit from the copper electrode to the silver electrode.
   b) The silver electrode increases in mass as the cell operates.
   c) There is a net general movement of silver ions through the salt bridge to the copper half-cell.
   d) Negative ions pass through the salt bridge from the silver half-cell to the copper half-cell.
   e) Some positive copper ions pass through the salt bridge from the copper half-cell to the silver half-cell.

   ANS: c) There is a net general movement of silver ions through the salt bridge to the copper half-cell.   **PAGE:** 17.1,2

13. Which of the following species cannot function as an oxidizing agent?

   a) $S(s)$
   b) $NO_3^-(ag)$
   c) $Cr_2O_7^{-2}(aq)$
   d) $I^- (aq)$
   e) $MnO_4^-(aq)$

   ANS: d) $I^-(aq)$ **PAGE:** 17.1

14. When the equation for the following reaction in basic solution is balanced, what is the sum of the coefficients?

$$MnO_4^- (aq) + CN^-(aq) \rightarrow MnO_2(s) + CNO^-(aq)$$

   a) 13
   b) 8
   c) 10
   d) 20
   e) 11

   ANS: a) 13   **PAGE:** 17.1

15. Which of the following is the strongest oxidizing agent?

$$MnO_4^- + 4H^+ + 3e^- \rightarrow MnO_2 + 2H_2O \qquad E° = 1.68 \text{ V}$$
$$I_2 + 2e^- \rightarrow 2I^- \qquad E° = 0.54 \text{ V}$$
$$Zn^{2+} + 2e^- \rightarrow Zn \qquad E° = -0.76 \text{ V}$$

    a) MnO_4^-
    b) I_2
    c) Zn^{2+}
    d) Zn
    e) MnO_2

ANS: a) MnO_4^- **PAGE:** 17.2

16. Which metal, Al or Ni could reduce Zn^{2+} to $Zn(s)$ if placed in a Zn^{2+} (aq) solution?

$$Zn^{2+} + 2e^- \rightarrow Zn \qquad E° = -0.76 \text{ V}$$
$$Al^{3+} + 3e^- \rightarrow Al \qquad E° = -1.66 \text{ V}$$
$$Ni^{2+} + 2e^- \rightarrow Ni \qquad E° = -0.23 \text{ V}$$

    a)   Al
    b)   Ni
    c)   Both Al and Ni would work.
    d)   Neither Al nor Ni would work.
    e)   Cannot be determined.

ANS: a)   Al   **PAGE:** 17.2

17. Which of the following is the best reducing agent?

$$Cl_2 + 2e^- \rightarrow 2Cl^- \qquad E° = 1.36 \text{ V}$$
$$Mg^{2+} + 2e^- \rightarrow Mg \qquad E° = -2.37 \text{ V}$$
$$2H^+ + 2e^- \rightarrow H_2 \qquad E° = 0.00 \text{ V}$$

    a) Cl_2
    b) H_2
    c)   Mg
    d) Mg^{2+}
    e) Cl^-

ANS: c)   Mg   **PAGE:** 17.2

18–20. Consider the galvanic cell shown below (the contents of each half-cell are written beneath each compartment):

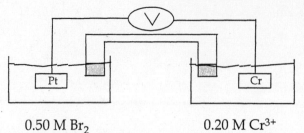

0.50 M Br_2 0.20 M Cr^{3+}
0.10 M Br^-

The standard reduction potentials are as follows:

$$Cr^{3+} + 3e^- \rightarrow Cr(s) \qquad E° = -0.73 \text{ V}$$

$$Br_2(aq) + 2e^- \rightarrow 2Br^- \qquad E° = +1.09 \text{ V}$$

18.   What is $E°$ for this cell?

a)   1.82 V
b)   0.36 V
c)   4.75 V
d)   1.79 V
e)   4.40 V

ANS: a)   1.82 V   **PAGE:** 17.2

19.   What is the value of E for this cell at 25°C?

a)   2.21 V
b)   1.76 V
c)   2.12 V
d)   1.88 V
e)   0.59 V

ANS: d)   1.88 V   **PAGE:** 17.4

20.   Which of the following statements about this cell is false?

a)   This is a galvanic cell.
b)   Electrons flow from the Pt electrode to the Cr electrode.
c)   Reduction occurs at the Pt electrode.
d)   The cell is not at standard conditions.
e)   To complete the circuit, cations migrate into the left half-cell and anions migrate into the right half-cell from the salt bridge.

ANS: b)   Electrons flow from the Pt electrode to the Cr electrode.   **PAGE:** 17.2

21–30. Refer to the galvanic cell below (the contents of each half-cell are written beneath each compartment):

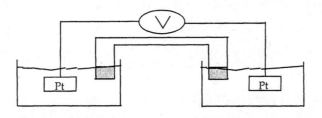

0.10 M MnO_4^-	0.40 M Cr^{3+}
0.20 M Mn^{2+}	0.30 M $Cr_2O_7^{2-}$
0.010 M H^+	0.010 M H^+

The standard reduction potentials are as follows:

$$MnO_4^- + 8H^+ + 5e^- \rightarrow Mn^{2+} + 4H_2O \qquad E° = 1.51 \text{ V}$$

$$Cr_2O_7^{2-} + 14H^+ + 5e^- \rightarrow 2\,Cr^{3+} + 7H_2O \qquad E° = 1.33 \text{ V}$$

21. When current is allowed to flow, which species is oxidized?

 a) $Cr_2O_7^{2-}$

 b) Cr^{3+}

 c) MnO_4^-

 d) Mn^{2+}

 e) H^+

ANS: b) Cr^{3+} **PAGE: 17.2,4**

22. When current is allowed to flow, which species is reduced?

 a) $Cr_2O_7^{2-}$

 b) Cr^{3+}

 c) MnO_4^-

 d) Mn^{2+}

 e) H^+

ANS: c) MnO_4^- **PAGE: 17.2,4**

23. What is the value of $E°_{cell}$?

 a) –0.18 V

 b) 2.84 V

 c) 0.18 V

 d) 1.79 V

 e) 2.29 V

ANS: c)   0.18 V   **PAGE: 17.2**

24. What is the oxidation state of Cr in $Cr_2O_7^{2-}$?

    a) +7
    b) +6
    c) +12
    d) –1
    e) –2

    ANS: b)   +6   **PAGE:** 17.1

25. What is the value of Q, the reaction quotient, for this cell reaction?

    a) 6.7×10^{40}
    b) 1.5×10^{-41}
    c) 1.5×10^{-4}
    d) 6.7×10^{3}

    ANS: b) 1.5×10^{-41} **PAGE:** 17.4

26. In which direction do electrons flow in the external circuit?

    a) left to right
    b) right to left
    c) no current flows; the cell is at equilibrium
    d) Cannot be determined.
    e) none of these

    ANS: b)   right to left   **PAGE:** 17.1,2,4

27. In the balanced cell reaction what is the stoichiometric coefficient for H^+?

    a) 5
    b) 6
    c) 30
    d) 22
    e) 2

    ANS: d)   22   **PAGE:** 17.2

28. How many electrons are transferred in the balanced reaction (i.e., what will be the value of n in the Nernst equation)?

    a) 5
    b) 6
    c) 30
    d) 22
    e) 2

    ANS: c)   30   **PAGE:** 17.2,4

29. What is the cell potential at 25°C as read on the digital voltmeter?

    a) 0.18 V
    b) 2.58 V
    c) 0.10 V
    d) 0.59 V
    e) 0.26 V

    ANS: e)   0.26 V   **PAGE:** 17.4

30. What is the value of the equilibrium constant at 25°C for the net spontaneous cell reaction?

    a) 7.3×10^{-11}
    b) 6.1×10^{-92}
    c) 91
    d) 1.1×10^3
    e) 1.6×10^{91}

    ANS: e) 1.6×10^{91} **PAGE:** 17.4

31. A cell is set up with copper and lead electrodes in contact with $CuSO_4(aq)$ and $Pb(NO_3)_2(aq)$, respectively, at 25°C. The standard reduction potentials are:

    $$Pb^{2+} + 2e^- \rightarrow Pb \qquad E° = -0.13 \text{ V}$$

    $$Cu^{2+} + 2e^- \rightarrow Cu \qquad E° = +0.34 \text{ V}$$

    If the Pb^{2+} and Cu^{2+} are each 1.0 M, the potential of the cell, in volts, is:

    a) 0.46
    b) 0.92
    c) 0.22
    d) 0.58
    e) none of these

    ANS: a)   0.46   **PAGE:** 17.2

32-34. Consider an electrochemical cell with a zinc electrode immersed in 1.0 M Zn^{2+} and a silver electrode immersed in 1.0 M Ag^+.

    $$Zn^{2+} + 2e^- \rightarrow Zn \qquad\qquad E° = -0.76 \text{ V}$$
    $$Ag^+ + e^- \rightarrow Ag \qquad\qquad E° = 0.80 \text{ V}$$

32. Calculate $E°$ for this cell

    a) 0.04 V
    b) -0.04 V
    c) 1.56 V
    d) -1.56 V
    e) none of these

    ANS: c)   1.56 V   **PAGE:** 17.2

33. Which of the electrodes is the anode?

ANS: The zinc electrode.   **PAGE:** 17.2

34. If $[Zn^{2+}]_0$ is 0.050 M and $[Ag^+]_0$ is 10.00 M, calculate E.

   a)   0.137 V
   b)   0.108 V
   c)   1.63 V
   d)   1.66 V
   e)   1.70 V

ANS: d)   1.66 V   **PAGE:** 17.4

35-36. Consider an electrochemical cell with a zinc electrode immersed in 1.0 M Zn^{2+} and a nickel electrode immersed in 0.10 M Ni^{2+}.

$$Zn^{2+} + 2e^- \rightarrow Zn \qquad\qquad\qquad E° = -0.76 \text{ V}$$
$$Ni^{2+} + 2e^- \rightarrow Ni \qquad\qquad\qquad E° = -0.23 \text{ V}$$

35. Calculate E for this cell.

   a)   0.53 V
   b)   0.50 V
   c)   0.56 V
   d)   0.47 V
   e)   0.59 V

ANS: b)   0.50 V   **PAGE:** 17.4

36. Calculate the concentration of Ni^{2+} if the cell is allowed to run to equilibrium at 25°C.

   a)   1.10 M
   b)   0.20 M
   c)   0.10 M
   d)   0 M
   e)   none of these

ANS: e)   none of these   **PAGE:** 17.4

37. The galvanic cell described by $Zn(s) \mid Zn^{2+}(aq) \parallel Cu^{2+}(aq) \mid Cu(s)$ has a standard cell potential of 1.101 volts. Given that $Zn(s) \rightarrow Zn^{2+}(aq) + 2e^-$ has an oxidation potential of 0.762 volts, determine the reduction potential for Cu^{2+}.

 a) –1.863 V
 b) 1.863 V
 c) –0.339 V
 d) 0.339 V
 e) none of these

ANS: d)   0.339 V   **PAGE:** 17.2

38–39. The following questions refer to a galvanic cell that utilizes the following reaction (unbalanced):

$$(AuCl_4)^-(aq) + Cu(s) \rightarrow Au(s) + Cl^-(aq) + Cu^{2+}(aq)$$

38. Given the following information determine the standard cell potential:

Species	Standard Reduction Potential (V)
$Au^{3+}(aq)$	1.498
$Cu^{2+}(aq)$	0.339

 a) 1.159 V
 b) 1.837 V
 c) 1.979 V
 d) 1.462 V
 e) 2.102 V

ANS: a)   1.159 V   **PAGE:** 17.2

39. Determine the number of electrons transferred during the reaction (balanced).

 a) 2
 b) 3
 c) 4
 d) 6
 e) 9

ANS: d)   6   **PAGE:** 17.2

40. Choose the correct statement given the following information:

$$Fe^{3+}(aq) + e^- \rightarrow Fe^{2+}(aq) \qquad E° = 0.77 \text{ volt}$$

$$Fe(CN)_6^{3-} + e^- \rightarrow Fe(CN)_6^{4-} \quad E° = 0.36 \text{ volt}$$

a) $Fe^{2+}(aq)$ is more likely to be oxidized than Fe^{2+} complexed to CN^-.
b) $Fe^{3+}(aq)$ is more likely to be reduced than Fe^{3+} complexed to CN^-.
c) Both a and b are true.
d) Complexation of Fe ions with CN^- has no effect on their tendencies to become oxidized or reduced.
e) None of these is true.

ANS: b) $Fe^{3+}(aq)$ is more likely to be reduced than Fe^{3+} complexed to CN^-. PAGE: 17.2

41. The reduction potentials for Au^{3+} and Ni^{2+} are as follows:

$$Au^{3+} + 3e^- \rightarrow Au \qquad E° = +1.50 \text{ V}$$

$$Ni^{2+} + 2e^- \rightarrow Ni \qquad E° = -0.23 \text{ V}$$

Calculate $\Delta G°$ (at 25°C) for the reaction:

$$2Au^{3+} + 3Ni \rightarrow 3Ni^{2+} + 2Au$$

a) -5.00×10^2 kJ
b) $+5.00 \times 10^2$ kJ
c) -2140 kJ
d) $+1.00 \times 10^3$ kJ
e) -1.00×10^3 kJ

ANS: e) -1.00×10^3 kJ PAGE: 17.3

42. Tables of standard reduction potentials are usually given at 25°C. $E°$ depends on temperature. Which of the following equations describes the temperature dependence of $E°$?

a) $E° = \dfrac{nF}{RT} - \ln k$

b) $E° = \Delta H° - T\Delta S°$

c) $E° = -\dfrac{\Delta H°}{nF} + \dfrac{T\Delta S°}{nF}$

d) $\ln E° = -\dfrac{\Delta H°}{RT} + \dfrac{\Delta S°}{R}$

e) none of these

ANS: c) $E° = -\dfrac{\Delta H°}{nF} + \dfrac{T\Delta S°}{nF}$ PAGE: 17.3

43. For a reaction in a voltaic cell both $\Delta H°$ and $\Delta S°$ are positive. Which of the following statements is true?

    a) $E°_{cell}$ will increase with an increase in temperature.
    b) $E°_{cell}$ will decrease with an increase in temperature.
    c) $E°_{cell}$ will not change when the temperature increases.
    d) $\Delta G° > 0$ for all temperatures.
    e) None of the above statements is true.

    ANS: a) $E°_{cell}$ will increase with an increase in temperature.   **PAGE:** 17.3

44. The standard free energies of formation of several aqueous species are:

	kJ/mol
$H^+(aq)$	0
$H_2O(l)$	–237
$CH_3OH(aq)$	–163
$HCOOH(aq)$	–351
e^-	0

    What is the standard reduction potential of methanoic acid in aqueous solution (i.e., for $HCOOH + 4H^+ + 4e^- \rightarrow CH_3OH + H_2O$)?

    a) +0.13 V
    b) +0.17 V
    c) +0.25 V
    d) –0.13 V
    e) –0.25 V

    ANS: a)   +0.13 V   **PAGE:** 17.3

45. A fuel cell designed to react grain alcohol with oxygen has the following net reaction:

    $$C_2H_5OH(l) + 3O_2(g) \rightarrow 2CO_2(g) + 3H_2O(l)$$

    The maximum work one mole of alcohol can yield by this process is 1320 kJ. What is the theoretical maximum voltage this cell can achieve?

    a) 0.760 V
    b) 1.14 V
    c) 2.01 V
    d) 2.28 V
    e) 13.7 V

    ANS: b)   1.14 V   **PAGE:** 17.3,5

46. Consider the following reduction potentials:

$$Cu^{2+} + 2e^- \rightarrow Cu \qquad E° = +0.34 \text{ V}$$

$$Pb^{2+} + 2e^- \rightarrow Pb \qquad E° = -0.13 \text{ V}$$

For a galvanic cell employing the Cu, Cu^{2+} and Pb, Pb^{2+} couples, calculate the maximum amount of work that would accompany the reaction of one mole of lead under standard conditions.

a) −40.5 kJ

b) −45.3 kJ

c) −90.7 kJ

d) No work can be done. The system is at equilibrium.

e) none of these

ANS: c) −90.7 kJ   **PAGE:** 17.3

47. Consider the hydrogen–oxygen fuel cell where

$$H_2(g) + \frac{1}{2} O_2(g) \rightleftharpoons H_2O(l) \qquad \Delta G° = -237.18 \text{ kJ/mol } H_2$$

Which of the following statements is true?

a) At standard conditions, the maximum work the fuel cell could do on the surroundings is 237.18 kJ/mol.

b) In the real world, the actual amount of useful work the cell can do is less than 237.18 kJ.

c) More energy is dissipated as waste heat in the fuel cell than in the reversible pathway.

d) a, b, and c are all true.

e) a, b, and c are all false.

ANS: d)   a, b, and c are all true.   **PAGE:** 17.3,5

48. Determine $\Delta G°$ for a cell that utilizes the following reaction:

$$Cl_2(g) + 2Br^- (aq) \rightarrow 2Cl^- (aq) + Br_2 (l)$$

The standard reduction for the chlorine gas is 1.360 volts and the standard reduction for the bromine liquid is 1.077 volts.

a) 471 kJ

b) 236 kJ

c) 27.3 kJ

d) 54.6 kJ

e) 82.5 kJ

ANS: d)   54.6 kJ   **PAGE:** 17.3

428

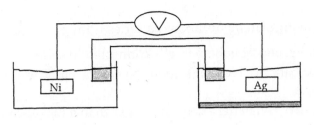

1.0×10^{-3} M Ni^{2+} 1.0 M HCl

1.0 M HCl   AgCl(s)

49. Calculate E at 25°C for the cell shown above, given the following data:

$$Ag^+ + e^- \rightarrow Ag(s) \qquad E° = 0.80 \text{ V}$$

$$Ni^{2+} + 2e^- \rightarrow Ni(s) \qquad E° = -0.23 \text{ V}$$

$$K_{sp} \text{ for AgCl} = 1.6 \times 10^{-10}$$

a) 0.83 V

b) 0.54 V

c) 1.01 V

d) 2.98 V

e) cannot be determined from the data given

ANS: b)   0.54 V   **PAGE:** 17.4

50–51. The following questions refer to the following system:

$$3Ag(s) + NO_3^-(aq) + 4H^+ (aq) \rightarrow 3Ag^+(aq) + NO(g) + 2H_2O(l)$$

Anode reaction: $Ag \rightarrow Ag^+_{(aq)} + 1e^-$ $E° = -0.799$ V

Cathode reaction: $NO_3^-(aq) + 4H^+(aq) + 3e^- \rightarrow NO(g) + 2H_2O(l)$ $E° = 0.964$ V

50. Determine the standard cell potential.

a) 1.763 V

b) 0.165 V

c) 1.422 V

d) –1.433 V

e) 2.403 V

ANS: b)   0.165 V   **PAGE:** 17.2

51. Determine the equilibrium constant at 25°C.

a) 3.21×10^5

b) 6.41×10^2

c) 9.97×10^{12}

d) 2.41×10^8

e) 4.43×10^{15}

ANS: d) 2.41×10^8 **PAGE:** 17.4

52. Which of the following statements about batteries is false?

    a) A battery is a group of galvanic cells connected in series.
    b) Lead storage batteries contain lead at the anode and lead coated with lead dioxide at the cathode.
    c) The alkaline dry cell battery can last longer than a nickel-cadmium battery.
    d) A fuel cell is a galvanic cell for which the reactants are continuously supplied.
    e) Dry cell batteries are used in tape players and portable radios.

    ANS: c)   The alkaline dry cell battery can last longer than a nickel-
              cadmium battery.   PAGE: 17.5

53. A galvanic cell consists of a left compartment with a tin electrode in contact with 0.1 M $Sn(NO_3)_2$(aq) and a right compartment with a lead electrode in contact with 1×10^{-3} M $Pb(NO_3)_2$(aq). The relevant reduction potentials are:

    $$Pb^{2+} + 2e^- \rightarrow Pb \qquad E° = -0.13 \text{ V}$$
    $$Sn^{2+} + 2e^- \rightarrow Sn \qquad E° = -0.14 \text{ V}$$

    When this cell is allowed to discharge spontaneously at 25°C, which of the following statements is true?

    a) Electrons will flow from left to right through the wire.
    b) Pb^{2+} ions will be reduced to Pb metal.
    c) The concentration of Sn^{2+} ions in the left compartment will increase.
    d) The tin electrode will be the cathode.
    e) No noticeable change will occur, because the cell is at equilibrium.

    ANS: d)   The tin electrode will be the cathode.   PAGE: 17.4

54. A cell is set up with copper and lead electrodes in contact with $CuSO_4$(aq) and $Pb(NO_3)_2$(aq), respectively, at 25°C. The standard reduction potentials are:

    $$Pb^{2+} + 2e^- \rightarrow Pb \qquad E° = -0.13 \text{ V}$$
    $$Cu^{2+} + 2e^- \rightarrow Cu \qquad E° = +0.34 \text{ V}$$

    If sulfuric acid is added to the $Pb(NO_3)_2$ solution, forming a precipitate of $PbSO_4$, the cell potential:

    a) increases
    b) decreases
    c) is unchanged
    d) can't tell what will happen
    e) none of these

    ANS: a)   increases   PAGE: 17.4

55. A concentration cell is constructed using two Ni electrodes with Ni^{2+} concentrations of 1.0 M and 1.00×10^{-4} M in the two half-cells. The reduction potential of Ni^{2+} is -0.23 V. Calculate the potential of the cell at 25°C.

    a) -0.368 V
    b) $+0.132$ V
    c) -0.132 V
    d) $+0.118$ V
    e) $+0.0592$ V

ANS: d) $+0.118$ V   **PAGE:** 17.4

56. The standard potential for the reaction $A + B \rightleftharpoons C + D$ is 1.50 volts. The equilibrium constant K for this reaction at 25°C is:

    a) 2.5×10^{25}
    b) 4.0×10^{-26}
    c)   25.4
    d) -25.4
    e)   not enough information given

ANS: e)   not enough information given   **PAGE:** 17.4

57. The reduction potentials for Ni^{2+} and Sn^{2+} are as follows:

$$Ni^{2+} + 2e^- \rightarrow Ni \qquad E° = -0.23 \text{ V}$$
$$SN^{2+} + 2e^- \rightarrow Sn \qquad E° = -0.14 \text{ V}$$

Calculate the equilibrium constant at 25°C for the reaction

$$Sn^{2+} + Ni \rightleftharpoons Sn + Ni^{2+}$$

    a) 1.9×10^{-4}
    b)   1.9
    c)   3.0
    d) 1.5×10^{13}
    e) 1.1×10^{3}

ANS: e) 1.1×10^{3} **PAGE:** 17.4

58–60.

Reaction	$E°$ (volts)
$Na^+ + e^- \rightarrow Na$	–2.71
$Al^{3+} + 3e^- \rightarrow Al$	–1.66
$Fe^{2+} + 2e^- \rightarrow Fe$	–0.44
$Cu^{2+} + 2e^- \rightarrow Cu$	+0.34
$Ag^+ + e^- \rightarrow Ag$	+0.80
$Cl_2 + 2e^- \rightarrow 2Cl^-$	+1.36
$F_2 + 2e^- \rightarrow 2F^-$	+2.87

58. Which of the following would be the best oxidizing agent?

   a) Cl_2
   b) Fe
   c) Na
   d) Na^+
   e) F^-

   ANS: a) Cl_2 **PAGE:** 17.2

59. Copper will spontaneously reduce which of the following?

   a) Fe^{2+} and Ag^+
   b) Fe^{2+}
   c) Ag^+
   d) Al^{3+}
   e) Fe^{2+} and Al^{3+}

   ANS: c) Ag^+ **PAGE:** 17.2

60. Determine the standard potential, $E°$, of a cell that employs the reaction
   $Fe + Cu^{2+} \rightarrow Fe^{2+} + Cu$.

   a) –0.10 V
   b) 0.20 V
   c) 0.10 V
   d) 0.78 V
   e) –0.78 V

   ANS: d) 0.78 V   **PAGE:** 17.2

61. An excess of finely divided iron is stirred up with a solution that contains Cu^{2+} ion, and the system is allowed to come to equilibrium. The solid materials are then filtered off and electrodes of solid copper and solid iron are inserted into the remaining solution. What is the value of the ratio $[Fe^{2+}]/[Cu^{2+}]$ at 25°C?

   a) 1
   b) 0
   c) 2.2×10^{26}
   d) 4.4×10^{-27}
   e) none of these

   ANS: c) 2.2×10^{26} **PAGE:** 17.4

62. An excess of finely divided iron is stirred up with a solution that contains Cu^{2+} ion, and the system is allowed to come to equilibrium. The solid materials are then filtered off and electrodes of solid copper and solid iron are inserted into the remaining solution. What potential develops between these two electrodes at 25°C?

    a)   0

    b)   –0.78 V

    c)   0.592 V

    d)   0.296 V

    e)   not enough information given

    ANS: a) 0   **PAGE:** 17.4

63. The equilibrium constant at 25°C for the reaction

$$2Al + 3Cu^{2+} \rightarrow 2Al^{3+} + 3Cu$$

is approximately

    a) 10^{203}

    b) 10^{34}

    c) 10^{68}

    d) 10^{-203}

    e)   none of these

    ANS: a) 10^{203} **PAGE:** 17.4

64. Of Sn^{2+}, Ag^+, and/or Zn^{2+}, which could be reduced by Cu?

    a) Sn^{2+}

    b) Ag^+

    c) Zn^{2+}

    d)   Two of them could be reduced by Cu.

    e)   All of them could be reduced by Cu.

    ANS: b) Ag^+ **PAGE:** 17.2

65. You wish to plate out zinc metal from a zinc nitrate solution. Which metal, Al or Ni, could you place in the solution to accomplish this?

    a)   Al

    b)   Ni

    c)   Both Al and Ni would work.

    d)   Neither Al nor Ni would work.

    e)   Cannot be determined.

    ANS: a) Al   **PAGE:** 17.2

66. Which of the following is the best reducing agent?

   a) Cl_2
   b) H_2
   c) Mg
   d) Mg^{2+}
   e) Cl^-

   ANS: c)   Mg   PAGE: 17.2

67–68. Consider a galvanic cell based in the reaction $Fe^{2+} + Cr_2O_7^{2-} \rightarrow Fe^{3+} + Cr^{3+}$ in acidic solution.

67. What is the coefficient of Fe^{3+} in the balanced equation?

   a) 1
   b) 2
   c) 3
   d) 4
   e) none of these

   ANS: b)   2   PAGE: 17.1

68. Calculate the voltage of the standard cell carrying out this reaction.

   a) 0
   b) 0.21 V
   c) –0.21 V
   d) 0.56 V
   e) –0.56 V

   ANS: d)   0.56 V   PAGE: 17.2

69. Concentration cells work because standard reduction potentials are dependent on concentration.

   ANS: False   PAGE: 17.4

70–71. You make a cell with an aluminum electrode in a solution of aluminum nitrate and a zinc electrode in a solution of zinc nitrate.

70. If you could increase the concentration of Zn^{2+}, which of the following is true about the cell potential?

   a) It would increase.
   b) It would decrease.
   c) It would remain constant.
   d) Cannot be determined.
   e) None of these (a-d).

   ANS: a)   It would increase.   PAGE: 17.4

71. If you could increase the concentration of Al^{3+}, which of the following is true about the cell potential?

    a) It would increase.
    b) It would decrease.
    c) It would remain constant.
    d) Cannot be determined.
    e) None of these (a-d).

    ANS: b)   It would decrease.   **PAGE:** 17.4

72-73. A common car battery consists of six identical cells each of which carries out the reaction

$$Pb + PbO_2 + 2HSO_4^- + 2H^+ \rightarrow 2PbSO_4 + 2H_2O$$

72. The value of $E°$ for such a cell is 2.04 V. Calculate $\Delta G°$ at 25°C for the reaction.

    a) −787 kJ
    b) −98 kJ
    c) −394 kJ
    d) −197 kJ
    e) −0.121 kJ

    ANS: c)   −394 kJ   **PAGE:** 17.3

73. Suppose that in starting a car on a cold morning a current of 125 amperes is drawn for 15.0 seconds from a cell of the type described above. How many grams of Pb would be consumed? (The atomic weight of Pb is 207.19.)

    a) 8.05
    b) 2.01
    c) 0.0180
    d) 0.0360
    e) 4.02

    ANS: b)   2.01   **PAGE:** 17.7

74. A galvanic cell is constructed with copper electrodes and Cu^{2+} in each compartment. In one compartment, the $[Cu^{2+}] = 1.0 \times 10^{-3}$ M and in the other compartment, the $[Cu^{2+}] = 2.0$ M. Calculate the potential for this cell at 25°C. The standard reduction potential for Cu^{2+} is +0.34 V.

    a) 0.44 V
    b) −0.44 V
    c) 0.098 V
    d) −0.098 V
    e) 0.78 V

    ANS: c)   0.098 V   **PAGE:** 17.4

435

75. Using the following data

$$E°$$

$$PbO_2 + 4H^+ + SO_4{}^{2-} + 2e^- \rightarrow PbSO_4(s) + 2H_2O \qquad +1.69$$

$$PbO_2 + 4H^+ + 2e^- \rightarrow Pb^{2+} + 2H_2O \qquad +1.46$$

calculate the K_{sp} value at 25°C for $PbSO_4(s)$.

 a) 2.57×10^{105}
 b) 3.89×10^{-105}
 c) 5.9×10^7
 d) 1.7×10^{-8}
 e) None of these is within 5% of the correct answer.

ANS: d) 1.7×10^{-8} **PAGE:** 17.4

76. Calculate the solubility product of silver iodide at 25°C given the following data:

$$E° \text{ (V)}$$

$$AgI(s) + e^- \rightarrow Ag(s) + I^- \qquad -0.15$$

$$I_2(s) + 2e^- \rightarrow 2I^- \qquad +0.54$$

$$Ag^+ + e^- \rightarrow Ag(s) \qquad +0.80$$

 a) 2.9×10^{-3}
 b) 1.9×10^{-4}
 c) 2.1×10^{-12}
 d) 9.0×10^{-17}
 e) 2.4×10^{-24}

ANS: d) 9.0×10^{-17} **PAGE:** 17.4

77–78. An antique automobile bumper is to be chrome plated. The bumper, which is dipped into an acidic $Cr_2O_7{}^{2-}$ solution, serves as a cathode of an electrolytic cell. The atomic mass of Cr is 51.996; 1 faraday = 96,485 coulombs.

77. If oxidation of H_2O occurs at the anode, how many moles of oxygen gas will evolve for every 1.00×10^2 grams of Cr(s) deposited?

 a) 2.88
 b) 0.48
 c) 11.5
 d) 7.7
 e) 1.44

ANS: a)   2.88   **PAGE:** 17.7

436

78. If the current is 10.0 amperes, how long will it take to deposit 100×10^2 grams of Cr(s) onto the bumper?

    a) 10.3 h
    b) 1.29 days
    c) 309 min
    d) 76.3 s
    e) 2 mo, 25 days, 14 h, and 6 s

    ANS: b)   1.29 days   **PAGE:** 17.7

79. In which of the following cases can $E°$ be equal to zero?

    a) In any cell at equilibrium.
    b) In a concentration cell.
    c) $E°$ can never be equal to zero.
    d) Choices a and b are both correct.
    e) None of these.

    ANS: b)   In a concentration cell.   **PAGE:** 17.3,4

80. In which of the following cases must E be equal to zero?

    a) In any cell at equilibrium.
    b) In a concentration cell.
    c) E can never be equal to zero.
    d) Choices a and b are both correct.
    e) None of these.

    ANS: a)   In any cell at equilibrium.   **PAGE:** 17.3,4

81. If a reducing agent M reacts with an oxidizing agent N^+ to give M^+ and N, and the equilibrium constant for the reaction is 1.0, then what is the $E°$ value for the oxidation-reduction reaction?

    a) 0.0 volt
    b) –1.0 volt
    c) 1.0 volt
    d) 0.059 volt
    e) 0.030 volt

    ANS: a)   0.0 volt   **PAGE:** 17.4

82. Copper is electroplated from $CuSO_4$ solution. A constant current of 4.00 amp is applied by an external power supply. How long will it take to deposit 1.00×10^2 g of Cu? The atomic mass of copper is 63.546.

    a)   21.1 h
    b)   10.0 min
    c)   1.60 days
    d)   11.2 s
    e)   2.91 h

    ANS: a)   21.1 h   **PAGE:** 17.7

83. What quantity of charge is required to reduce 40.0 g of $CrCl_3$ to chromium metal? (1 faraday = 96,485 coulombs)

    a) 2.45×10^4 C
    b) 7.31×10^4 C
    c) 2.20×10^5 C
    d) 9.65×10^4 C
    e)   none of these

    ANS: b) 7.31×10^4 C   **PAGE:** 17.7

84. Electrolysis of a molten salt with the formula MCl, using a current of 3.86 amp for 16.2 min, deposits 1.52 g of metal. Identify the metal. (1 faraday = 96,485 coulombs)

    a)   Li
    b)   Na
    c)   K
    d)   Rb
    e)   Ca

    ANS: c)   K   **PAGE:** 17.7

85. If a constant current of 5.0 amperes is passed through a cell containing Cr^{3+} for 1.0 hour, how many grams of Cr will plate out onto the cathode? (The atomic mass of Cr is 51.996.)

    a)   0.054 g
    b)   9.7 g
    c)   3.2 g
    d)   1.5 g
    e)   93 g

    ANS: c)   3.2 g   **PAGE:** 17.7

86. If an electrolysis plant operates its electrolytic cells at a total current of 1.0×10^6 amp, how long will it take to produce one metric ton (one million grams) of Mg(s) from seawater containing Mg^{2+}? (1 faraday = 96,485 coulombs)

    a) 2.2 h
    b) 2.4 days
    c) 55 min
    d) 3.7 h
    e) 1 year

    ANS: a)   2.2 h   **PAGE:** 17.7

87. Nickel is electroplated from a $NiSO_4$ solution. A constant current of 5.00 amp is applied by an external power supply. How long will it take to deposit 100. g of Ni? The atomic mass of Ni is 58.69.

    a) 18.3 h
    b) 2.40 days
    c) 63.1 min
    d) 56.7 s
    e) 1.20 s

    ANS: a)   18.3 h   **PAGE:** 17.7

88. Which type of battery has been designed for use in space vehicles?

    a) lead storage
    b) alkaline dry cell
    c) mercury cells
    d) fuel cells
    e) silver cells

    ANS: d)   fuel cells   **PAGE:** 17.5

89. Which of the following statements about corrosion is false?

    a) Patina is the layer of tarnish that gives silver a richer appearance.
    b) The oxidation of most metals by oxygen is spontaneous.
    c) Most metals will develop a thin oxide coating, which protects their internal atoms from oxidation.
    d) A car exposed to the elements will rust faster in the Midwest than in Arizona.
    e) All of these are true.

    ANS: a)   Patina is the layer of tarnish that gives silver a richer
    appearance.   **PAGE:** 17.6

90. Which of the following statements is false?

   a) Stainless steel contains chromium and nickel, which form protective oxide coatings.
   b) Galvanized steel is coated with zinc to form an oxide coating.
   c) Cathodic protection is a method used to protect steel in buried tanks and pipelines.
   d) Chromium and tin are often used to plate steel by forming a durable oxide coating.
   e) All of these are true.

   ANS: b)   Galvanized steel is coated with zinc to form an oxide coating.   PAGE: 17.6

91. Which of the following is incorrectly paired?

   a) alumina – pure aluminum oxide
   b) Downs cell – electrolyzes molten sodium chloride
   c) mercury cell – used in preventing contamination of NaOH by NaCl
   d) Hall-Heroult process – uses cryolite in production of aluminum
   e) All of these are correct.

   ANS: e)   All of these are correct.   PAGE: 17.8

92. A solution of MnO_4^{2-} is electrolytically reduced to Mn^{3+}. A current of 8.64 amp is passed through the solution for 15.0 minutes. What is the number of moles of Mn^{3+} produced in this process? (1 faraday = 96,486 coulombs)

   a) 0.0806
   b) 0.0403
   c) 0.0201
   d) 0.0269
   e) 0.778

   ANS: d)   0.0269   PAGE: 17.7

93. How many seconds would it take to deposit 21.40 g of Ag (atomic mass = 107.87) from a solution of $AgNO_3$ using a current of 10.00 amp?

   a) 9649 s
   b) 4825 s
   c) 3828 s
   d) 1914 s
   e) none of these

   ANS: d)   1914 s   PAGE: 17.7

94. Gold (atomic mass = 197) is plated from a solution of chlorauric acid, $HAuCl_4$; it deposits on the cathode. Calculate the time it takes to deposit 0.50 gram of gold, passing a current of 0.10 amperes. (1 faraday = 96,485 coulombs)

    a) 41 minutes
    b) 2.0 hours
    c) 1.0 hour
    d) 6.0 hours
    e) none of these

    ANS: b)   2.0 hours   **PAGE:** 17.7

95. An unknown metal (M) is electrolyzed. It took 74.1 s for a current of 2.00 amp to plate 0.107 g of the metal from a solution containing $M(NO_3)_3$. Identify the metal.

    a) La
    b) Bi
    c) Ga
    d) Cu
    e) Rh

    ANS: b)   Bi   **PAGE:** 17.7

96. Gold is produced electrochemically from an aqueous solution of $Au(CN)_2^-$ containing an excess of CN^-. Gold metal and oxygen gas are produced at the electrodes. How many moles of O_2 will be produced during the production of 1.00 mole of gold?

    a) 0.25
    b) 0.50
    c) 1.00
    d) 3.56
    e) 4.00

    ANS: a)   0.25   **PAGE:** 17.7

1. In the following nuclear equation, identify the missing product:

$$\begin{matrix} 43 \\ 20 \end{matrix} Ca + \alpha \rightarrow \text{_____} + \begin{matrix} 1 \\ 1 \end{matrix} H$$

   a) $\begin{matrix} 46 \\ 22 \end{matrix} Ti$

   b) $\begin{matrix} 46 \\ 21 \end{matrix} Sc$

   c) $\begin{matrix} 44 \\ 22 \end{matrix} Ti$

   d) $\begin{matrix} 42 \\ 18 \end{matrix} Ar$

   ANS: b) $\begin{matrix} 46 \\ 21 \end{matrix} Sc$ **PAGE:** 18.1,3

2. Identify the missing particle in the following equation:

$$\begin{matrix} 238 \\ 92 \end{matrix} U \rightarrow \begin{matrix} 4 \\ 2 \end{matrix} He + ?$$

   a) $\begin{matrix} 242 \\ 94 \end{matrix} Pu$

   b) $\begin{matrix} 234 \\ 90 \end{matrix} Th$

   c) $\begin{matrix} 242 \\ 90 \end{matrix} Th$

   d) $\begin{matrix} 234 \\ 92 \end{matrix} U$

   e) none of these

   ANS: b) $\begin{matrix} 234 \\ 90 \end{matrix} Th$ **PAGE:** 18.1

3. The ratio of the atomic radius to the nuclear radius is approximately:

   a) 10^{-5}
   b) 10^5
   c) 10^2
   d) 10^{15}
   e) 10^{-15}

   ANS: b) 10^5 **PAGE:** 18.1

4. An unstable isotope of rhenium, ^{191}Re, has a half-life of 9.8 minutes and is a beta producer. What is the other product of the reaction?

   a) ^{191}Os
   b) ^{191}W
   c) ^{192}Pt
   d) ^{190}W
   e) ^{190}Os

   ANS: a) ^{191}Os **PAGE:** 18.1

5. The nuclide $^{232}_{90}$Th is radioactive. When one of these atoms decays, a series of α and β^--particle emissions occurs, taking the atom through many transformations to end up as an atom of $^{208}_{82}$Pb. How many α particles are emitted in converting $^{232}_{90}$Th into $^{208}_{82}$Pb?

 a)   6
 b)   8
 c)   2
 d)   214
 e)   4

ANS: a)   6   **PAGE:** 18.1

6. In the following fission reaction, identify the other product:

$$^{235}_{92}U + ^{1}_{0}n \rightarrow ^{139}_{53}I + 2^{1}_{0}n + \underline{\hspace{1.5cm}}$$

 a) $^{89}_{39}Y$

 b) $^{95}_{39}Y$

 c) $^{95}_{42}Mo$

 d) $^{94}_{42}Mo$

 e) $^{94}_{40}Zr$

ANS: b) $^{95}_{39}Y$ **PAGE:** 18.1,6

7. What nuclide is necessary to balance the following fission reaction?

$$^{235}_{92}U + ^{1}_{0}n \rightarrow 3^{1}_{0}n + ^{139}_{56}Ba + \underline{\hspace{1.5cm}}$$

 a) $^{96}_{35}Br$

 b) $^{96}_{36}Kr$

 c) $^{94}_{37}Rb$

 d) $^{94}_{36}Kr$

 e) $^{90}_{38}Sr$

ANS: d) $^{94}_{36}Kr$ **PAGE:** 18.1,6

8. It is desired to determine the concentration of arsenic in a lake sediment sample by means of neutron activation analysis. The nuclide $^{75}_{33}$As captures a neutron to form $^{76}_{33}$As, which in turn undergoes β decay. The daughter nuclide produces the characteristic γ rays used for the analysis. What is the daughter nuclide?

    a) $^{75}_{34}$Se

    b) $^{76}_{32}$Ge

    c) $^{74}_{31}$Ga

    d) $^{76}_{34}$Se

    e) $^{74}_{34}$Se

    ANS: d) $^{76}_{34}$Se   **PAGE:** 18.1

9. Which of the following is a product of α decay of $^{238}_{92}$U?

    a) $^{234}_{90}$Th

    b) $^{238}_{93}$Np

    c) $^{238}_{91}$Pa

    d) $^{235}_{92}$U

    e) $^{235}_{92}$Pu

    ANS: a) $^{234}_{90}$Th   **PAGE:** 18.1

10. Electron capture transforms $^{40}_{19}$K into what nuclide?

    a) $^{40}_{20}$Ca

    b) $^{40}_{18}$Ar

    c) $^{4}_{2}$He

    d) $^{40}_{19}$K-

    e) $^{39}_{20}$Ca

    ANS: b) $^{40}_{18}$Ar   **PAGE:** 18.1

11. The stable nuclide $^{206}_{82}$Pb is formed from $^{238}_{92}$U by a long series of α and β decays. Which of the following nuclides could not be involved in the decay series?

    a) $^{234}_{90}$Th

    b) $^{234}_{92}$U

    c) $^{212}_{84}$Po

    d) $^{210}_{81}$Tl

    e) $^{226}_{88}$Ra

    ANS: b) $^{234}_{92}$U   **PAGE:** 18.1

12. Identify the missing particle in the following nuclear equation:

    $$^{241}_{95}\text{Am} + ^{4}_{2}\text{He} \rightarrow \text{_____} + 2\,^{1}_{0}\text{n}$$

    a) $^{245}_{97}$Bk

    b) $^{246}_{97}$Bk

    c) $^{247}_{97}$Bk

    d) $^{244}_{97}$Bk

    e) $^{243}_{97}$Bk

    ANS: d) $^{243}_{97}$Bk   **PAGE:** 18.1,3

13. Identify the missing particle in the following nuclear equation:

    $$^{27}_{13}\text{Al} + \text{_____} \rightarrow ^{24}_{11}\text{Na} + \alpha$$

    a) $^{1}_{0}$n

    b) $^{-1}_{0}$n

    c) $^{0}_{-1}$e

    d) $^{0}_{1}$e

    e) $2\,^{1}_{0}$n

    ANS: a) $^{1}_{0}$n   **PAGE:** 18.1,3

14. Which of the following processes decreases the atomic number by 1?

    a) gamma-ray production
    b) electron capture
    c) beta-particle production
    d) positron production
    e) At least two of the above processes decrease the atomic number by 1.

    ANS: e)   At least two of the above processes decrease the atomic
               number by 1.   **PAGE:** 18.1

15. If $^{214}_{82}$Pb undergoes a beta decay and the product of this decay undergoes another beta decay, which nuclide is produced?

    a) $^{212}_{82}$Bi

    b) $^{214}_{82}$Pb

    c) $^{214}_{84}$Po

    d) $^{212}_{83}$Bi

    e) $^{206}_{82}$Pb

ANS: c) $^{214}_{84}$Po   **PAGE:** 18.1

16. The rate constant for the beta decay of thorium-234 is 2.88×10^{-2}/day. What is the half-life of this nuclide?

    a) 53.1 days

    b) 1.22 days

    c) 0.693 days

    d) 24.1 days

    e) 101 days

ANS: d) 24.1 days   **PAGE:** 18.2

17. Which of the following balanced equations is labeled incorrectly?

    a) fission: $^{209}_{83}$Bi + $^{4}_{2}$He → $^{211}_{85}$At + 2^{1}_{0}n

    b) fusion: $^{2}_{1}$H + $^{2}_{1}$H → $^{3}_{1}$H + $^{1}_{1}$H

    c) bombardment: $^{239}_{94}$Pu + $^{1}_{0}$n → $^{240}_{95}$Am + $^{0}_{-1}$e

    d) beta production: $^{239}_{92}$U → $^{239}_{93}$Np + $^{0}_{-1}$e

    e) All are correctly labeled.

ANS: a) fission: $^{209}_{83}$Bi + $^{4}_{2}$He → $^{211}_{85}$At + 2^{1}_{0}n   **PAGE:** 18.1,3,6

18. Electron capture transforms $^{7}_{4}$Be into what nuclide?

    a) $^{6}_{3}$Li

    b) $^{7}_{5}$B

    c) $^{7}_{3}$Li

    d) $^{6}_{5}$B

    e) $^{12}_{6}$C

ANS: c) $^{7}_{3}$Li   **PAGE:** 18.1

19. A radioactive isotope of vanadium, $^{53}_{23}$V, decays by producing β particles and gamma rays. The nuclide formed has the atomic number:

    a) 22

    b) 21

    c) 23

    d) 24

    e) none of these

ANS: d) 24   **PAGE:** 18.1

20. The nuclide $^{208}_{81}$Tl is the daughter nuclide resulting from the α decay of what parent nuclide?

    a) $^{210}_{82}$Pb

    b) $^{204}_{79}$Au

    c) $^{297}_{80}$Hg

    d) $^{212}_{83}$Bi

    e) $^{4}_{2}$He

ANS: d) $^{212}_{83}$Bi   **PAGE:** 18.1

21. The nuclide $^{12}_{7}$N is unstable. What type of radioactive decay would be expected?

    a) β⁻

    b) β⁺

    c) σ

    d) α

    e) $^{1}_{0}$n

ANS: b) β⁺   **PAGE:** 18.1

22. Breeder reactors are used to convert the nonfissionable nuclide $^{238}_{92}$U to a fissionable product. Neutron capture of the $^{238}_{92}$U is followed by two successive beta decays. What is the final fissionable product?

    a) $^{239}_{94}$Pu

    b) $^{235}_{88}$Ra

    c) $^{235}_{92}$U

    d) $^{238}_{94}$Pu

    e) $^{239}_{93}$Np

ANS: a) $^{239}_{94}$Pu   **PAGE:** 18.1,6

23. Nuclides with too many neutrons to be in the band of stability are most likely to decay by what mode?

   a) α
   b) fission
   c) β$^+$
   d) electron capture
   e) β$^-$

   ANS: e)   β$^-$ **PAGE:** 18.1

24. The most likely decay mode (or modes) of the unstable nuclide $^{11}_{6}$C would be:

   a) positron production.
   b) α-particle production.
   c) electron capture.
   d) β$^-$ production.
   e) either positron production or electron capture or both.

   ANS: e)   either positron production or electron capture or both.   **PAGE:** 18.1

25. Which types of processes are likely when the neutron-to-proton ratio in a nucleus is too low?

   I.   α decay
   II. β decay
   III. positron production
   IV. electron capture
   a) I, II
   b) II, III
   c) III, IV
   d) II, III, IV
   e) II, IV

   ANS: c)   III, IV   **PAGE:** 18.1

26. When the Pd-106 nucleus is struck with an alpha particle, a proton is produced along with a new element. What is this new element?

   a) Cd-112
   b) Cd 109
   c) Ag-108
   d) Ag-109
   e) none of these

   ANS: d)   Ag-109   **PAGE:** 18.1, 3

27.   When $^{238}_{93}$Np undergoes β- emission, the products are:

    a) $^{238}_{92}$U + $^{0}_{1}$e

    b) $^{238}_{94}$Pu + $^{0}_{-1}$e

    c) $^{238}_{92}$U + $^{0}_{-1}$e

    d) $^{234}_{91}$Pa + $^{4}_{2}$He

    e) $^{238}_{94}$Np + $^{0}_{-1}$e

    ANS: b) $^{238}_{94}$Pu + $^{0}_{-1}$e   **PAGE:** 18.1

28.   Which reaction will produce an isotope of the parent nuclide?

    a) $^{210}_{84}$Po → $^{4}_{2}$He + ?

    b) $^{88}_{25}$Br → $^{1}_{0}$n + ?

    c) $^{227}_{89}$Ac → $^{0}_{-1}$e + ?

    d) $^{13}_{7}$N → $^{0}_{1}$e + ?

    e) $^{73}_{33}$As + $^{0}_{-1}$e → ?

    ANS: b) $^{88}_{25}$Br → $^{1}_{0}$n + ?   **PAGE:** 18.1

29, 30.   When the U-235 nucleus is struck with a neutron, the Ce-144 and Sr-90 nucleii are produced along with some neutrons and electrons.

29.   How many neutrons are emitted?

    a)   2
    b)   3
    c)   4
    d)   5
    e)   6

    ANS: a)   2   **PAGE:** 18.1,6

30.   How many electrons are emitted?

    a)   2
    b)   3
    c)   4
    d)   5
    e)   6

    ANS: c)   4   **PAGE:** 18.1,6

31. Consider a certain type of nucleus that has a rate constant of 2.50×10^{-2} min^{-1}. Calculate the time required for the sample to decay to one-fourth of its initial value.

    a) 2.50×10^{-2} min
    b) 5.00×10^{-2} min
    c) 23.8 min
    d) 37.4 min
    e) 55.4 min

    ANS: e) 55.4 min   **PAGE:** 18.2

32. Consider a certain type of nucleus that has a half-life of 32 min. Calculate the percent of original sample of nuclides remaining after 3.0 hours have passed.

    a) 98.0%
    b) 67%
    c) 3.2%
    d) 2.0%
    e) 1.4%

    ANS: d) 2.0%   **PAGE:** 18.2

33. Consider a certain type of nucleus that has a half-life of 32 min. Calculate the time required for 65% of the nuclides to decompose.

    a) 20 min
    b) 27 min
    c) 32 min
    d) 39 min
    e) 48 min

    ANS: c) 48 min   **PAGE:** 18.2

34. The number of a certain radioactive nuclide present in a sample decays from 160 to 20 in 30 minutes. What is the half-life of this radioactive species?

    a) 5 minutes
    b) 10 minutes
    c) 15 minutes
    d) 20 minutes
    e) 30 minutes

    ANS: b) 10 minutes   **PAGE:** 18.2

35. The half-life of ^{90}Sr is 28 years. How long will it take for a given sample of ^{90}Sr to be 90.% decomposed?

   a)   9 half-lives
   b)   4.3 years
   c)   93 years
   d)   5.7 × 10^{-3} years
   e)   none of these

   ANS: c)   93 years   **PAGE:** 18.2

36. The number of half-lives needed for a radioactive element to decay to about 6% of its original activity is (choose nearest number):

   a)   2
   b)   3
   c)   4
   d)   5
   e)   6

   ANS: c)   4   **PAGE:** 18.2

37. The Br-82 nucleus has a half-life of about 1.0 x 10^3 minutes. If you wanted 1.0 g of Br-82 and the delivery time was three days, about how much NaBr should you order (assuming all of the Br in the NaBr was Br-82)?

   a)   2.0 g
   b)   18 g
   c)   21 g
   d)   26 g
   e)   42 g

   ANS: d)   26 g   **PAGE:** 18.2

38. When the U-235 nucleus is struck with a neutron, the Zn-72 and Sm-160 nuclei are produced along with some neutrons. How many neutrons are emitted?

   a)   2
   b)   3
   c)   4
   d)   5
   e)   6

   ANS: c)   4   **PAGE:** 18.1,6

39–40. The questions below refer to the following:

An archaeological sample contains 0.743 g of lead-206 and 2.145 g of uranium-238. Assume that all the lead now present in the rock came from the radioactive decay of the uranium and that no appreciable amounts of other radioactive nuclides are present in the sample

39. The decay rate constant for the uranium is 1.54×10^{-10}/year. Determine the half-life of the uranium.

   a) 4.51×10^9/year
   b) 6.21×10^6/year
   c) depends on the age of the sample
   d) depends on the organic content of the sample
   e) two of these

   ANS: a) 4.51×10^9/year   **PAGE:** 18.2

40. What is the age of the sample?

   a) 2.93×10^7 years
   b) 3.67×10^{10} years
   c) 2.18×10^9 years
   d) 8.96×10^{12} years
   e) none of these

   ANS: c) 2.18×10^9 years   **PAGE:** 18.4

41. Use the following data to determine the expected ^{14}C activity in the Shroud of Turin. The atmospheric activity of ^{14}C is 15 cpm/gC (counts per minute per gram of carbon). Assume that the cloth was made in the year 24 A.D. The half-life of ^{14}C is 5730 years.

   a) 28 cpm/gC
   b) 7.3 cpm/gC
   c) 5.1 cpm/gC
   d) 11 cpm/gC
   e) 12 cpm/gC

   ANS: e)   12 cpm/gC   **PAGE:** 18.4

42. A radioactive sample has an initial activity of 2.00×10^6 cpm (counts per minute), and after 4 days, its activity is 9.0×10^5 cpm. What is its activity after 40 days?

   a) 4.5 cpm
   b) 6.8×10^2 cpm
   c) 9.0×10^4 cpm
   d) 5.5×10^3 cpm
   e) none of these

   ANS: b) 6.8×10^2 cpm   **PAGE:** 18.2

43.   A sample of wood from an Egyptian mummy case gives a ^{14}C count of 9.4 cpm/gC (counts per minute per gram of carbon). How old is the wood? (The initial decay rate of ^{14}C is 15.3 cpm/gC, and its half-life is 5730 years.)

   a)   6400 yr
   b)   4570 yr
   c)   4030 yr
   d)   3420 yr
   e)   none of these

   ANS: c)   4030 yr   **PAGE:** 18.4

44.   If a tree dies and the trunk remains undisturbed for 13,750 years, what percentage of original ^{14}C is still present? (half-life of ^{14}C = 5730 years)

   a)   5.20%
   b)   19.0%
   c)   2.20%
   d)   45.0%

   ANS: b)   19.0%   **PAGE:** 18.4

45–46.   A certain radioactive sample contains 2.4×10^3 nuclides at a certain time ($t = 0$); 3.0 h later the sample contains 6.0×10^2 nuclides.

45.   For this sample the ratio of the decay rates at $t = 0$ to $t = 3.0$ h is:

   a)   1.0
   b)   8.0
   c)   4.0
   d)   16
   e)   none of these

   ANS: c)   4.0   **PAGE:** 18.2

46.   The ratio of the decay rates at $t = 0$ to $t = 3.0$ h is 4.0. The value of the rate constant for this process is:

   a)   2.2 h^{-1}
   b) 4.6×10^{-1} h^{-1}
   c) $1.6 \times$ h^{-1}
   d)   3.0 h^{-1}
   e)   none of these

   ANS: b) 4.6×10^{-1} h^{-1} **PAGE:** 18.2

47. The half-life of ^{90}Sr is 28.1 years. How long will it take a 10.0-g sample of ^{90}Sr to decompose to 0.10 g?

    a) 80. years
    b) 140 years
    c) 190 years
    d) 2800 years

    ANS: c)   190 years   **PAGE:** 18.2

48. The half-life for electron capture for $^{40}_{19}$K is 1.3 billion years. What will be the $^{40}_{19}$K / $^{40}_{18}$Ar ratio in a rock that is 4.5 billion years old?

    a) 0.091
    b) 11.
    c) 0.10
    d) 10.
    e) 0.36

    ANS: c)   0.10   **PAGE:** 18.2

49. The half-life for electron capture for $^{40}_{19}$K is 1.30×10^9 years. What percent of the original $^{40}_{19}$K remains after 3.90×10^9 years?

    a) 33.3%
    b) 12.5%
    c) 50.0%
    d) 25.0%
    e) 75.0%

    ANS: b)   12.5%   **PAGE:** 18.2

50. Fresh rainwater or surface water contains enough tritium ($^3_1$H) to show 5.5 decompositions per minute per 100. g of water. Tritium has a half-life of 12.3 years. You are asked to check a vintage wine claimed to have been produced in 1946. How many decompositions per minute should you expect to observe in 100. g of that wine?

    a) 0.35
    b) 0.49
    c) 1.7
    d) 0.035
    e) 49

    ANS: b)   0.49   **PAGE:** 18.2

51. The rate constant for the decay of $^{45}_{20}$Ca is 4.23×10^{-3}/day. What is the half-life of ^{45}Ca?

   a) 118 days
   b) 164 days
   c) 211 days
   d) 236 days
   e) none of these

ANS: b) 164 days   **PAGE:** 18.2

52. A radioactive element has a half-life of 1.0 hour. How many hours will it take for the number of atoms present to decay to 1/16th of the initial value?

   a) 16
   b) 8
   c) 4
   d) 15
   e) 2.77

ANS: c) 4   **PAGE:** 18.2

53. It is desired to determine the blood volume of a live mouse. To do this, 0.10 mL of a saline suspension of red blood cells labeled with $^{59}_{26}$Fe is injected into the tail vein. Before injection the gamma rays were counted for this 0.10-mL solution and the count rate found to be 1.0×10^4 cpm. After a sufficient time for the blood to be thoroughly mixed, 0.10 mL of blood is removed and counted. The sample is found to have a count rate of 476 cpm. What is the approximate blood volume of the mouse?

   a) 0.48 mL
   b) 21 mL
   c) 4.8 mL
   d) 4.7 mL
   e) 2.1 mL

ANS: e) 2.1 mL   **PAGE:** 18.2

54. A 0.20-mL sample of a solution containing $^3_1$H that produces 3.7×10^3 cps is injected into the bloodstream of an animal. After allowing circulatory equilibrium to be established, a 0.20-mL sample of blood is found to have an activity of 20 cps. Calculate the blood volume of the animal.

   a) 18 mL
   b) 37 mL
   c) 11 mL
   d) 180 mL
   e) none of these

ANS: b) 37 mL   **PAGE:** 18.2

55. Radioactive tracers are useful in studying very low concentrations of chemical species. A chemist has a sample of HgI_2 in which part of the iodine is the radioactive nuclide of mass 131, so that the count rate is 5.0×10^{11} counts per minute per mole of I. The solid mercuric iodide is placed in water and allowed to come to equilibrium. Then 100 mL of the solution is withdrawn, and its radioactivity is measured and found to give 22 counts per minute. What is the molar concentration of iodide ion in the solution?

   a) 1.1×10^{-9}
   b) 4.4×10^{-10}
   c) 1.1×10^{-10}
   d) 1.1×10^{-11}
   e) 4.4×10^{-11}

   ANS: b) 4.4×10^{-10} **PAGE:** 18.2

56. The half-life of a sample has been defined as the time it takes for half of a sample to decay. The fifth-life can be defined as the time it takes for one-fifth of a sample to decay. Given these definitions, calculate the fifth-life of a sample that has a half-life of 20 years.

   a)   6.8 years
   b)   8.0 years
   c)   49 years
   d)   50 years
   e)   none of these

   ANS: a)   6.8 years   **PAGE:** 18.2

57–58. The Fe-56 nucleus is known to be stable. Answer the following questions.

57. What is the most likely decay for the Fe-53 nucleus?

   a)   β decay
   b)   positron emission
   c)   α decay
   d)   γ-ray emission
   e)   two of these

   ANS: e)   two of these   **PAGE:** 18.1

58. What is the most likely decay for the Fe-59 nucleus?

   a)   β decay
   b)   positron emission
   c)   α decay
   d)   γ-ray emission
   e)   two of these

   ANS a)   β decay   **PAGE:** 18.1

59–60. The U-238 nucleus decays to form Pb-206 by α and β decays.

59. Calculate the number of α decays.

    a) 2
    b) 4
    c) 6
    d) 8
    e) none of these

ANS: d)   8   **PAGE:** 18.1

60. Calculate the number of β decays.

    a) 2
    b) 4
    c) 6
    d) 8
    e) none of these

ANS: c)   6   **PAGE:** 18.1

61. The Cs-131 nuclide has a half-life of 30 years. After 120 years, about 3 grams remain. The original mass of the Cs-131 sample is closest to

    a) 30 g
    b) 40 g
    c) 50 g
    d) 60 g
    e) 70 g

ANS: c)   50 g   **PAGE:** 18.2

62. The I-131 nuclide has a half-life of 8 days. If you originally have a 1.8-kg sample, after 2 months you will have approximately

    a) 40 g
    b) 30 g
    c) 20 g
    d) 10 g
    e) less than 1 g

ANS: d)   10 g   **PAGE:** 18.2

63. The so-called "magic numbers" of protons and neutrons produce special chemical stability.

ANS: False   **PAGE:** 18.1

64. As atomic mass increases, the proton/neutron ratio of stable nuclides decreases.

ANS: True   PAGE: 18.1

65. The mass defect arises because the sum of masses of the component nucleons is less than that of the nucleus.

ANS: False   PAGE: 18.5

66. Which statement is true about the following reaction?

$$\underset{7}{^{14}}\text{N} + \underset{2}{^{4}}\text{He} \rightarrow \underset{8}{^{17}}\text{O} + \underset{1}{^{1}}\text{H}$$

| 13.992 | 4.0015 | 16.9986 | 1.0073 |
| amu | amu | amu | amu |

   a) Energy is absorbed in the reaction.
   b) Energy is released in the reaction.
   c) No energy change is associated with the reaction.
   d) Not enough information is given to determine the energy change.
   e) None of these.

ANS: a) Energy is absorbed in the reaction.   PAGE: 18.5

67. One of the hopes for solving the world's energy problem is to make use of the fusion reaction:

$$\underset{1}{^{2}}\text{H} + \underset{1}{^{3}}\text{H} \rightarrow \underset{2}{^{4}}\text{He} + \underset{0}{^{1}}\text{n} + \text{energy}$$

How much energy is released when one mole of deuterium is fused with one mole of tritium according to the above reaction? The masses of the atoms and the neutrons are:

$\underset{1}{^{2}}\text{H} = 2.0140$ amu $\underset{1}{^{3}}\text{H} = 3.01605$ amu

$\underset{2}{^{4}}\text{He} = 4.002603$ amu $\underset{0}{^{1}}\text{n} = 1.008665$ amu

The speed of light is 2.9979×10^8 m/s

   a) 5.63×10^8 J
   b) 56.3 J
   c) 1.69×10^{12} J
   d) 7.84×10^{44} J
   e) 8.44×10^{11} J

ANS: c) 1.69×10^{12} J   PAGE: 18.5

68. Consider the following process:

$$^{14}_{7}N + ^{4}_{2}He \rightarrow ^{17}_{8}O + ^{1}_{1}H$$

Masses (amu): 14.003074   4.002603   16.999133   1.007825

Which statement describes ΔE for the process?

a) 1.15×10^{11} J are released.
b) 1.15×10^{14} J are released.
c) 1.15×10^{18} J are absorbed.
d) 1.15×10^{11} J are absorbed.
e) none of these

ANS: d) 1.15×10^{11} J are absorbed.   **PAGE:** 18.5

69. Calculate ΔE in kilojoules per mole for the following reaction:

$$^{230}_{90}Th \rightarrow ^{4}_{2}He + ^{226}_{88}Ra$$

Atomic masses: ^{230}Th = 230.0332, ^{4}He = 4.00260, ^{226}Ra = 226.02544.

a) -4.6×10^8 kJ/mol
b) -2.4×10^6 kJ/mol
c) 0
d) $+2.4 \times 10^6$ kJ/mol
e) $+4.6 \times 10^8$ kJ/mol

ANS: a) -4.6×10^8 kJ/mol   **PAGE:** 18.5

70. Calculate the change in energy in kJ/mol for the transmutation of radium from the given molar masses:

$$^{226}_{88}Ra \rightarrow ^{4}_{2}He + ^{222}_{86}Rn$$

g/mol 226.0254   4.0026   222.0176

a) -5.2 kJ/mol
b) -1.6 kJ/mol
c) -4.7×10^{14} kJ/mol
d) -4.7×10^8 kJ/mol
e) $+1.6 \times 10^8$ kJ/mol

ANS: d) -4.7×10^8 kJ/mol   **PAGE:** 18.5

71. The smallest amount of radioactive material that will support a self-sustained reaction is called the

a) molar mass.
b) moderator.
c) supercritical mass.
d) subcritical mass.
e) critical mass.

ANS: e) critical mass   **PAGE:** 18.6

459

72–73.   The questions below refer to the following:

Iron-56 ($^{56}_{26}$Fe) has a binding energy per nucleon of 8.79 MeV.
(1 MeV is 1.60×10^{-13} J)

72.   Determine the amount of energy needed to "decompose" one mole of iron-56 nuclei.

a) 3.47×10^{11} J
b) 8.47×10^{11} J
c) 8.90×10^{11} J
d) 1.13×10^{14} J
e) 7.75×10^{13} J

ANS: b) 8.47×10^{11} J   **PAGE: 18.5**

73.   Determine the difference in mass between one mole of iron-56 nuclei and the component nucleons of which it is made.

a) 9.41×10^{-6} kg
b) 2.43×10^{-5} kg
c) 6.65×10^{-5} kg
d) 5.27×10^{-4} kg
e) 7.21×10^{-4} kg

ANS: a) 9.41×10^{-6} kg   **PAGE: 18.5**

74.   Which of the following is true for the fission of uranium-235?

a)   The electron is captured by the nucleus, which becomes unstable.
b)   The products include neutrons.
c)   The nuclides produced are individually heavier than the uranium nuclide.
d)   The nuclides produced are more stable than the uranium nuclide.
e)   Two of these

ANS: e)   Two of these   **PAGE: 18.6**

75.   If more than one neutron from each fission event causes another fission event, the fission situation is described as

a)   critical.
b)   subcritical.
c)   supercritical.
d)   moderated.
e)   none of these

ANS: c)   supercritical.   **PAGE: 18.6**

76. Which of the following is not a factor in determining the biological effects of radiation exposure?

    a)   the energy of the radiation
    b)   the age of the organism at which the exposure occurs
    c)   the penetrating ability of the radiation
    d)   the chemical properties of the radiation source
    e)   the ionizing ability of the radiation

    ANS: b)   the age of the organism at which the exposure occurs   **PAGE:** 18.7

77. The greatest radiation exposure for Americans comes from which of the following?

    a)   medical x rays
    b)   nuclear power plants
    c)   electrical transmission wires
    d)   industrial waste
    e)   the combination of the natural causes of radiation including cosmic rays

    ANS: e)   the combination of the natural causes of radiation
    including cosmic rays   **PAGE:** 18.7

1–4.   Choose the group from the given list.

    a) Group 1A
    b) Group 2A
    c) Group 3A
    d) Group 4A
    e) Group 5A

1. Reacts with H_2 to form compounds with the general formula MH_2.

    ANS: b)   Group 2A   **PAGE:** 19.1,4

2. Reacts with F_2 to form compounds with the general formula MF_2.

    ANS: b)   Group 2A   **PAGE:** 19.1,4

3. This group contains two of the most important elements found on earth.

    ANS: d)   Group 4A   **PAGE:** 19.1,6

4. The elements in this group are termed alkali metals.

    ANS: a)   Group 1A   **PAGE:** 19.1,2

5. In a given period this group has the element with the largest atomic radius.

    a) Group 1A
    b) Group 2A
    c) Group 3A
    d) Group 4A
    e) Group 5A

    ANS: e)   Group 1A   **PAGE:** 19.1

6. Elements in this group lose two valence electrons to non-metals to form ionic compounds.

    a) Group 1A
    b) Group 2A
    c) Group 3A
    d) Group 4A
    e) Group 5A

    ANS: b)   Group 2A   **PAGE:** 19.1

7. Which of the following is a metalloid?

    a) carbon
    b) oxygen
    c) hydrogen
    d) copper
    e) silicon·

    ANS: e) silicon   PAGE: 19.1

8. Which group contains two elements that exhibit +2 and +4 oxidation states?

    a) Group 1A
    b) Group 3A
    c) Group 4A
    d) Group 5A
    e) Group 7A

    ANS: c) Group 4A   PAGE: 19.1,6

9. Which of the following exhibits the greatest metallic character?

    a) Cs
    b) Rb
    c) K
    d) Na
    e) all are equally metallic

    ANS: a) Cs   PAGE: 19.1

10. What is the most abundant element found in the human body?

    a) carbon
    b) hydrogen
    c) calcium
    d) oxygen
    e) water

    ANS: d) oxygen   PAGE: 19.1

11. Hydrogen and lithium react very differently, although they are both members of Group 1. What is the primary reason for this difference?

    a) The metallic character increases going down a group.
    b) The ionization energy increases going down a group.
    c) Electron affinity increases going down a group.
    d) Electronegativity increases going down a group.
    e) There is a very large difference in the atomic radii of H and Li.

    ANS: e)   There is a very large difference in the atomic radii of H and Li.   PAGE: 19.1

12. All of the following are semimetals except

    a) B
    b) Ge
    c) Al
    d) Sb
    e) Si

    ANS: c) Al   **PAGE:** 19.1

13. Which oxide of a Group 2A element is amphoteric?

    a) Be
    b) Mg
    c) Ca
    d) Sr
    e) Ba

    ANS: a) Be   **PAGE:** 19.1

14. Which oxide of a Group 2A element is not highly ionic?

    a) Be
    b) Mg
    c) Ca
    d) Sr
    e) Ba

    ANS: a) Be   **PAGE:** 19.1

15. Choose the metal with the largest first ionization energy.

    a) Na
    b) Mg
    c) Al
    d) K
    e) Ca

    ANS: c) Al   **PAGE:** 19.1

16. Which group shows the correct order of first ionization energy?

    a) Na > P > Cl
    b) Cs > Na > K
    c) K > Ca > Ge
    d) Cs < Rb < Na
    e) Al > Si > P

    ANS: d) Cs < Rb < Na   **PAGE:** 19.1

17. The ion that aluminum is most likely to form is isoelectronic with:

    a) Ar
    b) Na
    c) Ne
    d) Mg
    e) none of these

    ANS: c) Ne   **PAGE:** 19.5

18. Which element of Group 3A behaves as a nonmetal or semimetal?

    a) B
    b) Al
    c) Ga
    d) In
    e) B and Al

    ANS: a) B   **PAGE:** 19.1

19. What reason is given for the stability of C—C, N—N, and O—O bonds, compared to the instability of Si—Si, P—P, and S—S bonds?

    a) Their metallic character varies greatly.
    b) Large differences in their ionization energies.
    c) Large differences in their electronegativities.
    d) Large differences in their abilities to form strong pi bonds.
    e) None of these.

    ANS: d)   Large differences in their abilities to form strong pi bonds.   **PAGE:** 19.1

20. What are the most abundant metals in the earth's crust, oceans, and atmosphere?

    a) titanium and silicon
    b) aluminum and iron
    c) manganese and nickel
    d) tin and lead
    e) iron and lead

    ANS: b)   aluminum and iron   **PAGE:** 19.1

21. Which of the following oxides is amphoteric?

    a) BeO
    b) MgO
    c) CaO
    d) SrO
    e) BaO

    ANS: a) BeO   **PAGE:** 19.1

22. True or false: Hydrogen is a nonmetal while lithium is an active metal even though they are in the same group.

    a) True. Such differences are common for elements in the same group.
    b) False. Because the elements are in the same group, they have similar metallic qualities.
    c) True. This can be explained because of the very large difference in atomic radii between hydrogen and lithium.
    d) False. Both hydrogen and lithium are non-metals
    e) none of these

    ANS: c) True. This can be explained because of the very large difference in atomic radii between hydrogen and lithium.   **PAGE:** 19.1

23. Choose the metal with the smallest radius.

    a) Li(s)
    b) Na(s)
    c) K(s)
    d) Mg(s)
    e) Al(s)

    ANS: e) Al(s)   **PAGE:** 19.1

24. Within a group, as the atomic numbers of the elements increase, the

    a) ionization energies decrease.
    b) atomic masses decrease.
    c) elements become less metallic.
    d) atomic radii decrease.

    ANS: a) ionization energies decrease.   **PAGE:** 19.1

25. Which group contains the most active metals?

    a) Group 1A
    b) Group 3A
    c) Group 2A
    d) Group 4A

    ANS: a) Group 1A   **PAGE:** 19.1

26. Which of the following metals has the highest melting point?

    a) Na
    b) Mg
    c) Al
    d) Ca
    e) K

    ANS: c) Al   **PAGE:** 19.2,5

27. Choose the element with the largest atomic radius.

     a) Li
     b) B
     c) N
     d) O
     e) Ne

     ANS: a)   Li   **PAGE:** 19.1

28. Choose the element with the smallest atomic radius.

     a) Li
     b) Na
     c) K
     d) Rb
     e) Cs

     ANS: a)   Li   **PAGE:** 19.1

29. Choose the element that is the strongest reducing agent in the gas phase.

     a) Li
     b) Na
     c) K
     d) Rb
     e) Cs

     ANS: e)   Cs   **PAGE:** 19.2

30. Choose the element that is the strongest reducing agent in aqueous solution.

     a) Li
     b) Na
     c) K
     d) Rb
     e) Cs

     ANS: a)   Li   **PAGE:** 19.2

31. Choose the element with the highest melting point.

     a) Li
     b) Na
     c) K
     d) Rb
     e) Cs

     ANS: a)   Li   **PAGE:** 19.2

32. Choose the only element that forms a regular oxide in the presence of an excess of oxygen gas.

    a) Li
    b) Na
    c) K
    d) Rb
    e) Cs

ANS: a) Li   PAGE: 19.2

33. Choose the element whose ion has the largest concentration inside a human cell.

    a) Li
    b) Na
    c) K
    d) Rb
    e) Cs

ANS: c) K   PAGE: 19.2

34. Choose the metal with the lowest melting point.

    a) Li
    b) Na
    c) K
    d) Rb
    e) Cs

ANS: e) Cs   PAGE: 19.2

35. Which of the following is the second most abundant (by mass) element in the earth's crust, oceans, and atmosphere?

    a) hydrogen
    b) oxygen
    c) carbon
    d) aluminum
    e) silicon

ANS: e) silicon   PAGE: 19.1

36. Superoxides have the general formula of:

    a) MO_2
    b) M_2O_2
    c) M_2O
    d) M_2O_3
    e) MO

ANS: a) MO_2 PAGE: 19.2

37. What compounds are useful in breathing apparatus and air supply packs?

    a) oxides
    b) peroxides
    c) superoxides
    d) alkali metals
    e) none of these

    ANS: c)   superoxides   **PAGE:** 19.2

38. What ions are very important for the proper functioning of biologic systems, such as nerves and muscles?

    a) alkaline earth metal ions
    b) alkali metal ions
    c) oxygen ions
    d) hydrogen ions
    e) nitrogen ions

    ANS: b)   alkali metal ions   **PAGE:** 19.2

39. What ion seems to affect the levels of neurotransmitters, and thus is used in the treatment of depression or mania?

    a) Ca^{2+}
    b) K^+
    c) Na^+
    d) Li^+
    e) Mg^{2+}

    ANS: d) Li^+ **PAGE:** 19.2

40. Ionic hydrides are formed when hydrogen combines with elements from:

    I.   Group 1A
    II. Group 2A
    III. Group 3A
    a) I, II, and III
    b) I and II
    c) I and III
    d) II and III
    e) none of these

    ANS: b)   I and II   **PAGE:** 19.3

41. _____ are formed when hydrogen combines with other nonmetals.

    a) covalent hydrides
    b) nonmetallic hydrides
    c) active hydrides
    d) interstitial hydrides
    e) ionic hydrides

    ANS: a) covalent hydrides   **PAGE:** 19.3

42. _____ are formed when transition metal crystals are treated with hydrogen gas.

    a) Covalent hydrides
    b) Metallic hydrides
    c) Active hydrides
    d) Saltlike hydrides
    e) Ionic hydrides

    ANS: b) metallic hydrides   **PAGE:** 19.3

43. Due to environmental concerns, researchers have been seeking low-cost alternatives to fossil fuels. One such alternative is _____ , which can be liberated from water, using solar energy.

    a) hydrogen
    b) oxygen
    c) carbon
    d) ozone
    e) none of these

    ANS: a) hydrogen   **PAGE:** 19.3

44. What alkaline earth metal is often used to produce the bright light for photographic flash units?

    a) calcium
    b) beryllium
    c) magnesium
    d) barium
    e) strontium

    ANS: c) magnesium   **PAGE:** 19.4

45. The strongest reducing agent in the alkali metals is:

    a) K
    b) Na
    c) Cs
    d) Fr
    e) Li

    ANS: e) Li   **PAGE:** 19.2

46. Choose the metal that reacts least vigorously with water.

    a) Mg
    b) Ca
    c) Sr
    d) Ba
    e) All of these react equally vigorously with water.

    ANS: a) Mg   **PAGE:** 19.4

47. Choose the metal that is produced by electrolysis of its molten chloride salt.

    a) Mg
    b) Ca
    c) Sr
    d) Ba
    e) all of these

    ANS: e)   all of these   **PAGE:** 19.4

48. Which of the following is the best explanation as to why lithium is the strongest reducing agent of the alkali metals?

    a)   The ionization energy of lithium is the highest of the alkali metals.
    b)   The ionization energy of lithium is the lowest of the alkali metals.
    c)   The standard reduction potential of lithium is the most positive of the alkali metals.
    d)   The relatively high charge density of lithium compared to the other alkali metals.
    e)   none of these

    ANS: d)   The relatively high charge density of lithium compared to
                  the other alkali metals.   **PAGE:** 19.2

49. Ionic hydrates are formed with hydrogen combined with elements from

    a)   group 1A
    b)   group 2A
    c)   group 3A
    d)   all of the above
    e)   two of the above

    ANS: e)   two of the above   **PAGE:** 19.3

50. Order the following bonds from highest to lowest bond energy: carbon–carbon, silicon–silicon, silicon–oxygen.

    a) C—C, Si—Si, Si—O
    b) Si—O, C—C, Si—Si
    c) Si—Si, Si—O, C—C
    d) Si—O, Si—Si, C—C
    e) C—C, Si—O, Si—Si

    ANS: b) Si—O, C—C, Si—Si   **PAGE:** 19.6

51. Order the following from lowest to highest boiling point: $SnCl_4$, $SnBr_4$, SnI_4.

    a) $SnCl_4$, $SnBr_4$, SnI_4
    b) $SnBr_4$, SnI_4, $SnCl_4$
    c) $SnCl_4$, SnI_4, $SnBr_4$
    d) SnI_4, $SnBr_4$, $SnCl_4$
    e) $SnCl_4$, SnI_4, $SnBr_4$

    ANS: a) $SnCl_4$, $SnBr_4$, SnI_4 **PAGE:** 19.6

52. The Group 3A elements are all metals.

    ANS: False   **PAGE:** 19.5

53. Choose the solid that has the smallest ionization energy.

    a) Be(s)
    b) Mg(s)
    c) Ca(s)
    d) Sr(s)
    e) Ba(s)

    ANS: e) Ba(s)   **PAGE:** 19.4

54. Which of the following ions interferes with the action of detergents in hard water?

    a) Na^+
    b) Ca^{2+}
    c) Mg^{2+}
    d) Ca^{2+} and Mg^{2+}
    e) Na^+, Ca^{2+}, and Mg^{2+}

    ANS: d) Ca^{2+} and Mg^{2+} **PAGE:** 19.4

55. Alkaline earth metals react less vigorously with water than do the alkali metals.

    ANS: True   **PAGE:** 19.2,4

56. Salts can consist of hydrogen.

    ANS: True   **PAGE:** 19.3

472

57. The compound SiO_2 does not exist as a discrete molecule while CO_2 does. This can be explained because

   a)   the Si—O bond is unstable.
   b)   the Lewis structure of SiO_2 has an even number of electrons.
   c)   the SiO_2 is a solid while CO_2 is a gas.
   d)   the 3p orbital of the Si has little overlap with the 2p of the O.
   e)   none of these

   ANS: d)   the 3p orbital of the Si has little overlap with the 2p of the O.   PAGE: 19.1,6

58. Because Li is the strongest reducing agent of the alkali metals, it reacts most quickly with water of the alkali metals.

   ANS: False   PAGE: 19.2

59. Which of the following has the highest melting point?

   a)   Sr(s)
   b)   Be(s)
   c)   Mg(s)
   d)   Ca(s)
   e)   Ba(s)

   ANS: b)   Be(s)   PAGE: 19.4

60. Which member of Group 2A reacts least vigorously with water?

   a)   Mg
   b)   Sr
   c)   Ca
   d)   Ba
   e)   All of these react in the same manner.

   ANS: a)   Mg   PAGE: 19.4

61. The element with the lowest melting point is:

   a)   B
   b)   Al
   c)   Ga
   d)   Tl
   e)   All have the same melting point.

   ANS: c)   Ga   PAGE: 19.5

62. The element with the widest liquid range is:

a) B
b) Al
c) Ga
d) Tl
e) All are the same.

ANS: c) Ga   **PAGE:** 19.5

63. The element that exhibits the oxidation states +1 and +3 is:

a) B
b) Al
c) Ga
d) Tl
e) all of these

ANS: d) Tl   **PAGE:** 19.5

64. The element with the highest ionization energy is:

a) B
b) Al
c) Ga
d) Tl
e) All are the same.

ANS: a) B   **PAGE:** 19.5

65. The element found in bauxite is:

a) B
b) Al
c) Ga
d) Tl
e) all of these

ANS: b) Al   **PAGE:** 19.5

66. The element that reacts with N_2 to form a compound of the general formula MN is:

a) B
b) Al
c) Ga
d) Tl
e) all of these

ANS: b) Al   **PAGE:** 19.5

67. The solid substance with the empirical formula SiO_2 is commonly called:

    a) silicon
    b) silica
    c) silicate
    d) silicone
    e) none of these

    ANS: b) silica   **PAGE:** 19.1,6

68. What element is found in the structural minerals that make up our bones and teeth?

    a) strontium
    b) barium
    c) calcium
    d) silicon
    e) magnesium

    ANS: c) calcium   **PAGE:** 19.4

69. In cation-exchange resins, what ion replaces Ca^{2+} and Mg^{2+} in the hard water that is passed over the resin?

    a) H^+
    b) Li^+
    c) Na^+
    d) K^+
    e) Ba^{2+}

    ANS: c) Na^+ **PAGE:** 19.4

70. How many of the following statements are false?

    I. The group 3A elements are all metals.
    II. Alkaline earth metals react less vigorously with water than do the alkali metals.
    III. Salts can consist of hydrogen.
    IV. Because Li is the strongest reducing agent of the alkali metals, it reacts most quickly with water of the alkali metals.

    a) 0
    b) 1
    c) 2
    d) 3
    e) 4

    ANS: c) 2   **PAGE:** 19.2-5

71. Which of the following is the most abundant metal on earth?

    a) calcium
    b) iron
    c) copper
    d) aluminum
    e) zinc

    ANS: d) aluminum   **PAGE:** 19.5

72. How many oxides of carbon are there?

    a) 1
    b) 2
    c) 3
    d) 4
    e) 5

    ANS: c) 3   **PAGE:** 19.6

73. Which element is found in the ore galena?

    a) tin
    b) lead
    c) aluminum
    d) silicon
    e) germanium

    ANS: b) lead   **PAGE:** 19.6

74. The largest commercial use of lead is in

    a) gasoline.
    b) protective coatings for steel.
    c) semiconductors.
    d) paints.
    e) batteries used in automobiles.

    ANS: e) batteries used in automobiles.   **PAGE:** 19.6

75. With which of the following elements does silicon form the strongest bonds?

    a) Si
    b) C
    c) H
    d) O
    e) B

    ANS: d) O   **PAGE:** 19.6

76. The chemistry of silicon is dominated by its bonding with

  a) Cl
  b) S
  c) Al
  d) F
  e) none of these

  ANS: e)   none of these   **PAGE:** 19.6

77. Which element in Group 4A has the strongest metallic character?

  a) Pb
  b) C
  c) Si
  d) Ge

  ANS: a)   Pb   **PAGE:** 19.6

78–93. Write a balanced equation for each of the following reactions:

  78. Lithium metal with excess $O_2(g)$.

  ANS: $4Li(s) + O_2(g) \rightarrow 2Li_2O(s)$ **PAGE:** 19.2

  79. Sodium metal with a limited amount of $O_2(g)$.

  ANS: $4Na(s) + O_2(g) \rightarrow 2Na_2O(s)$ **PAGE:** 19.2

  80. Sodium metal with excess $O_2(g)$.

  ANS: $2Na(s) + O_2(g) \rightarrow Na_2O_2(s)$ **PAGE:** 19.2

  81. Rubidium metal with $O_2(g)$.

  ANS: $Rb(s) + O_2(g) \rightarrow RbO_2(s)$ **PAGE:** 19.2

  82. Potassium superoxide with $H_2O(l)$.

  ANS: $KO_2(s) + 2H_2O(l) \rightarrow 2K^+(aq) + 2OH^-(aq) + O_2(g) + H_2O_2(aq)$ **PAGE:** 19.2

  83. Cesium metal with $Cl_2(g)$.

  ANS: $2Cs(s) + Cl_2(g) \rightarrow 2CsCl(s)$ **PAGE:** 19.2

  84. Sodium metal with $H_2(g)$.

  ANS: $2Na(s) + H_2(g) \rightarrow 2NaH(s)$ **PAGE:** 19.2

  85. Lithium metal with $H_2O(l)$.

  ANS: $2Li(s) + 2H_2O(l) \rightarrow 2Li^+(aq) + 2OH^-(aq) + H_2(g)$ **PAGE:** 19.2

86. Lithium metal with $N_2(g)$.

ANS: $6Li(s) + N_2(g) \rightarrow 2Li_3N(s)$ **PAGE:** 19.2

87. Magnesium metal with $O_2(g)$.

ANS: $2Mg(s) + O_2(g) \rightarrow 2MgO(s)$ **PAGE:** 19.4

88. Strontium metal with $Br_2(l)$.

ANS: $Sr(s) + Br_2(l) \rightarrow SrBr_2(s)$ **PAGE:** 19.4

89. Aluminum metal with $O_2(g)$ at high temperatures.

ANS: $2Al + 3O_2 \rightarrow 2Al_2O_3$ **PAGE:** 19.5

90. Gallium metal with $I_2(s)$.

ANS: $2Ga(s) + 3I_2(s) \rightarrow 2GaI_3(s)$ **PAGE:** 19.5

91. Tin metal with $O_2(g)$.

ANS: $Sn(s) + O_2(g) \rightarrow SnO_2(s)$ **PAGE:** 19.6

92. Lead metal with $Br_2(l)$.

ANS: $Pb(s) + Br_2(l) \rightarrow PbBr_2(s)$ **PAGE:** 19.6

93. Thermal decomposition of $PbBr_4(s)$.

ANS: $PbBr_4(s) \rightarrow PbBr_2(s) + Br_2(g)$ **PAGE:** 19.6

94. Which element in group 3A has a high strength-to-weight ratio and thus is highly important as a structural material?

ANS: aluminum **PAGE:** 19.5

1. Choose the element obtained from liquefaction of air.

    a) N
    b) P
    c) As
    d) Sb
    e) Bi

    ANS: a) N   **PAGE:** 20.1

2. Choose the element with the largest electronegativity.

    a) N
    b) P
    c) As
    d) Sb
    e) Bi

    ANS: a) N   **PAGE:** 20.1

3. Choose the most metallic element.

    a) N
    b) P
    c) As
    d) Sb
    e) Bi

    ANS: e) Bi   **PAGE:** 20.1

4. Choose the element with the largest ionization energy.

    a) N
    b) P
    c) As
    d) Sb
    e) Bi

    ANS: a) N   **PAGE:** 20.1

5. Which Group 5A element cannot form molecules with five covalent bonds?

    a) N
    b) P
    c) As
    d) Sb
    e) Bi

    ANS: a) N   **PAGE:** 20.1

479

6. The ability of the Group 5A elements to form _____ greatly decreases after nitrogen.

    a) molecules with five covalent bonds
    b) pi bonds
    c) larger molecules with single bonds
    d) molecules with four covalent bonds
    e) all of these

    ANS: b) pi bonds   **PAGE:** 20.1

7. The strength of the N—N bond in nitrogen is important

    a) because it allows N_2 gas to serve as a medium for experiments involving oxygen or water.
    b) both thermodynamically and kinetically.
    c) in the use of nitrogen-based explosives.
    d) in the exothermic decomposition of binary compounds containing nitrogen.
    e) all of these

    ANS: e) all of these   **PAGE:** 20.2

8. Dynamite was invented by

    a) Haber
    b) Frasch
    c) Nobel
    d) Priestly
    e) Teller

    ANS: c) Nobel   **PAGE:** 20.2

9. The process of transforming N_2 to a form usable by animals and plants is called

    a) nitrogen fixation.
    b) fertilization.
    c) denitrification.
    d) the Ostwald process.
    e) nitrogenation.

    ANS: a) nitrogen fixation.   **PAGE:** 20.2

10. In which of the following compounds does N have its maximum oxidation state?

    a) N_2O_5
    b) N_2O
    c) NO
    d) N_2O_3
    e) NO_2

    ANS: a) N_2O_5 **PAGE:** 20.2

11. The oxidation state of the sulfur atom in $S_2O_3^{2-}$ is:

    a) 0
    b) 1
    c) 2/3
    d) 2
    e) 3

ANS: d) 2   **PAGE:** 20.6

12. The oxidation state of the sulfur atom in $S_4O_6^{2-}$ is:

    a) 0
    b) 1
    c) 3/2
    d) 5/2
    e) 2/5

ANS: d) 5/2   **PAGE:** 20.6

13. Compounds containing bismuth in the +5 oxidation state tend to be _____ and compounds containing bismuth in the +3 oxidation state tend to be _____.

    a) ionic, ionic
    b) ionic, molecular
    c) molecular, molecular
    d) molecular, ionic
    e) none of these

ANS: d) molecular, ionic   **PAGE:** 20.1

14. Pi bonding tends to be important in all elements of Group 5.

ANS: False   **PAGE:** 20.1

15. The strength of the triple bond in the N_2 molecule is important

    a) both kinetically and thermodynamically.
    b) kinetically but not thermodynamically.
    c) thermodynamically but not kinetically.
    d) neither thermodynamically nor kinetically.
    e) none of these

ANS: a) both kinetically and thermodynamically.   **PAGE:** 20.2

16. Which of the following is not a possible oxidation state of nitrogen?

    a) +2

    b) +1

    c) 0

    d) -2

    e) -4

ANS: e) -4   **PAGE:** 20.2

17. The Ostwald process

    a) is used to manufacture ammonia.

    b) transforms nitrogen to other nitrogen-containing compounds.

    c) is used to recover sulfur from underground deposits.

    d) is used to produce nitric acid.

    e) none of these

ANS: d) is used to produce nitric acid.   **PAGE:** 20.2

18. The bond strength of HCl is greater than that of HF.

ANS: False   **PAGE:** 20.7

19. The acid $HClO_4$ is a stronger acid than $HClO_2$.

ANS: True   **PAGE:** 20.7

20. Choose the species with the largest bond strength.

    a) F_2

    b) Cl_2

    c) Br_2

    d) I_2

    e) All are the same.

ANS: b) Cl_2 **PAGE:** 20.7

21. Choose the species with the largest ionization energy.

    a) F

    b) Cl

    c) Br

    d) I

    e) All are the same.

ANS: a) F   **PAGE:** 20.7

22. Choose the species with the largest electron affinity.

     a) F
     b) Cl
     c) Br
     d) I
     e) All are the same.

     ANS: b) Cl   PAGE: 20.7

23. Choose the species with the largest radius.

     a) F
     b) F-
     c) Cl
     d) Cl-
     e) All are the same.

     ANS: d) Cl-   PAGE: 20.7

24. All of the following contribute to nitrogen-fixation except

     a) lightning.
     b) bacteria on the roots of legumes.
     c) the combustion process in car engines.
     d) the Haber process.
     e) the Ostwald process.

     ANS: e)   the Ostwald process.   PAGE: 20.2

25. Recent studies indicate that lightning may be responsible for as much as _____% of the total fixed nitrogen available on earth.

     a) 5
     b) 25
     c) 50
     d) 75
     e) 95

     ANS: c) 50   PAGE: 20.2

26. Fixed nitrogen that accumulates in soil, lakes, and rivers promotes the growth of

     a) legumes.
     b) all plants.
     c) algae and other undesirable organisms.
     d) bacteria.
     e) all of these

     ANS: c)   algae and other undesirable organisms.   PAGE: 20.2

27. The most important hydride of nitrogen is

   a) ammonia.
   b) hydrazine.
   c) styrofoam.
   d) agricultural pesticides.
   e) none of these

   ANS: a)   ammonia.   **PAGE:** 20.2

28. What nitrogen-containing compound is used as rocket fuel?

   a) nitrous oxide
   b) ammonia
   c) nitric oxide
   d) hydrazine
   e) nitrogen dioxide

   ANS: d)   hydrazine   **PAGE:** 20.2

29. Which of the following is not a use of hydrazine?

   a) agricultural pesticides
   b) fungicides
   c) herbicides
   d) insecticides
   e) All are uses of hydrazine.

   ANS: e)   All are uses of hydrazine.   **PAGE:** 20.2

30. Of F, Cl, Br, and I, which of the following correctly lists the largest radius of the anion, the element with the highest electronegativity, and the highest bond energy of the diatomic molecule, respectively?

   a) I^-, Cl, F_2
   b) I^-, F, Br_2
   c) Br^-, Br, I_2
   d) I^-, F, Cl_2
   e) none of these

   ANS: d) I^-, F, Cl_2 **PAGE:** 20.7

31. Of the following, which form compounds?

    I. He
   II. Ar
  III. Xe
  IV. Kr
   a) I, II
   b) II, III
   c) I, II, III
   d) II, III, IV
   e) III, IV

ANS: e) III, IV   **PAGE:** 20.8

32. Choose the species with the smallest hydration energy (absolute value).

   a) F^-
   b) Cl^-
   c) Br^-
   d) I^-
   e) all the same

ANS: d) I^- **PAGE:** 20.7

33. Choose the species that is the most reactive.

   a) F_2
   b) Cl_2
   c) Br_2
   d) I_2
   e) All are the same.

ANS: a) F_2 **PAGE:** 20.7

34. F_2 is a better oxidizing agent than Cl_2 in the gas phase principally because:

   a) F_2 has a weaker bond than Cl_2.
   b) F_2 has a stronger bond than Cl_2.
   c) the electron affinity of F is greater than that of Cl.
   d) the electronegativity of Cl is greater than that of F.
   e) the ionization energy for F is greater than that for Cl.

ANS: a) F_2 has a weaker bond than Cl_2.   **PAGE:** 20.7

35. Choose the group containing the most reactive nonmetals.

   a) Group 1A
   b) Group 3A
   c) Group 5A
   d) Group 7A
   e) Group 8A

   ANS: d)   Group 7A   **PAGE:** 20.7

36. Dinitrogen monoxide is more commonly known as

   a) nitric oxide.
   b) laughing gas.
   c) hydrazine.
   d) nitrous oxide.
   e) two of these

   ANS: e)   two of these   **PAGE:** 20.2

37. What nitrogen-containing compound has a role in controlling the earth's temperature?

   a) N_2O
   b) nitric oxide
   c) nitrogen oxide
   d) ammonia
   e) N_2

   ANS: a) N_2O **PAGE:** 20.2

38. What nitrogen-containing compound is produced commercially in the Ostwald process?

   a) hydrazine
   b) nitric acid
   c) nitrous acid
   d) ammonia
   e) nitrous oxide

   ANS: b)   nitric acid   **PAGE:** 20.2

39. Which is the most reactive form of phosphorus?

   a) black phosphorus
   b) white phosphorus
   c) red phosphorus
   d) Two of these are equally reactive.
   e) All of these (a-c) are equally reactive.

   ANS: b)   White phosphorus   **PAGE:** 20.3

40. Which form of phosphorus is highly toxic?

    a) white phosphorus
    b) red phosphorus
    c) black phosphorus
    d) tetraphosphorus decaoxide
    e) none of these

    ANS: a) white phosphorus   **PAGE:** 20.3

41. Phosphoric acid easily undergoes _____ reactions.

    a) addition
    b) substitution
    c) polymeric
    d) condensation
    e) nucleophilic

    ANS: d) condensation   **PAGE:** 20.3

42. For the process $X^-(g) \rightarrow X^-(aq)$, select the ion with the most negative value of ΔH.

    a) F^-
    b) Cl^-
    c) Br^-
    d) I^-
    e) All the same.

    ANS: a) F^- **PAGE:** 20.7

43. For the process $X^-(g) \rightarrow X^-(aq)$, select the ion with the most negative value of ΔS.

    a) F^-
    b) Cl^-
    c) Br^-
    d) I^-
    e) All the same

    ANS: a) F^- **PAGE:** 20.7

44. Within the halogen family, as atomic number increases,

    a) ionic radius decreases.
    b) covalent atomic radius increases.
    c) melting point decreases.
    d) electronegativity increases.
    e) none of these

    ANS: b) covalent atomic radius increases.   **PAGE:** 20.7

45. Phosphorus is found in nature

   a) as white phosphorus.
   b) as red phosphorus.
   c) as black phosphorus.
   d) usually as the PO_4^{3-} ion in phosphate rock.
   e) in gypsum.

   ANS: d)   usually as the PO_4^{3-} ion in phosphate rock.   **PAGE:** 20.3

46. Why is phosphorus added to soil as a fertilizer?

   a) It is essential for plant growth.
   b) It is often found in an inaccessible form in the soil.
   c) Most soils do not have large amounts of phosphorus.
   d) two of these
   e) all of these

   ANS: d)   two of these   **PAGE:** 20.3

47. What Group 6A element has been studied for its ability to protect against cancer?

   a) sulfur
   b) polonium
   c) selenium
   d) tellurium
   e) oxygen

   ANS: c)   selenium   **PAGE:** 20.4

48. What Group 6A element was discovered in pitchblende by the Curies?

   a) sulfur
   b) polonium
   c) selenium
   d) tellurium
   e) oxygen

   ANS: b)   polonium   **PAGE:** 20.4

49. What Group 6A element has 27 isotopes and is highly toxic and very radioactive?

   a) sulfur
   b) polonium
   c) selenium
   d) tellurium
   e) oxygen

   ANS: b)   polonium   **PAGE:** 20.4

50. What Group 6A elements are semiconductors?

    a) selenium and polonium
    b) tellurium and polonium
    c) sulfur and selenium
    d) selenium and tellurium
    e) sulfur and tellurium

    ANS: d)   selenium and tellurium   **PAGE:** 20.4

51. All of the following are true about ozone except

    a) it causes skin cancer.
    b) it is formed in the pollution from car exhaust.
    c) it can be used to purify water.
    d) it exists naturally in the upper atmosphere.
    e) it prevents UV light from reaching the earth.

    ANS: a)   it causes skin cancer.   **PAGE:** 20.5

52. What process is used to recover sulfur?

    a) the Haber process
    b) the Ostwald process
    c) the Frasch process
    d) the contact process
    e) the wet process

    ANS: c)   the Frasch process   **PAGE:** 20.6

53. The fact that the SO molecule is very unstable while O_2 is stable can be best explained because:

    a) The S-O bond is inherently unstable.
    b) Sulfur lacks the ability to form double bonds.
    c) The difference in electronegativity between the sulfur atom and the oxygen atom makes it unlikely for the S-O bond to form.
    d) There exists much stronger p bonding between oxygen atoms than between a sulfur atom and oxygen atom.
    e) none of these

    ANS: d)   There exists much stronger p bonding between oxygen atoms than between a sulfur atom and oxygen atom.   **PAGE:** 20.6

54. All of the following statements about helium are true except

 a) it forms no compounds.
 b) it is used as a coolant.
 c) the major sources on earth are natural gas deposits.
 d) it is used in luminescent lighting.
 e) it is a component of the sun.

 ANS: d)   it is used in luminescent lighting.   **PAGE:** 20.8

55–65. Choose the correct molecular structure for each compound from the given choices.

 a) trigonal bipyramidal
 b) trigonal planar
 c) tetrahedral
 d) octahedral
 e) none of these

55. $SeBr_4(g)$

 ANS: e)   none of these   **PAGE:** 20.3

56. CO_3^{2-}

 ANS: b)   trigonal planar   **PAGE:** 20.2

57. Cl_2O

 ANS: e)   none of these   **PAGE:** 20.6

58. XeF_5^+

 ANS: e)   none of these   **PAGE:** 20.8

59. CCl_4

 ANS: c)   tetrahedral   **PAGE:** 20.2

60. $AsCl_5(g)$

 ANS: a)   trigonal bipyramidal   **PAGE:** 20.2

61. NO_3^-

 ANS: b)   trigonal planar   **PAGE:** 20.2

62. PCl_3

 ANS: e)   none of these   **PAGE:** 20.3

63. NH_4^+

 ANS: c)   tetrahedral   **PAGE:** 20.2

64. ClO_4^-

ANS: c)   tetrahedral

PAGE: 20.7

65. SeF_6

ANS: d)   octahedral

PAGE: 20.4

66. Which of the following Noble gases have been observed to form compounds?

a)   He and Ar
b)   Kr and Xe
c)   Xe
d)   Ar, Kr, and Xe
e)   The Noble gases never form compounds since they have filled outer shells.

ANS: b)   Kr and Xe

PAGE: 20.8

67-80. Write a balanced equation for each of the following:

67. the reaction of hydrazine with $O_2(g)$

ANS: $N_2H_4(l) + O_2(g) \rightarrow N_2(g) + 2H_2O(g)$

PAGE: 20.2

68. the oxidation of copper metal by 6 M nitric acid

ANS: $8H^+(aq) + 2NO_3^-(aq) + 3Cu(s) \rightarrow 3Cu^{2+}(aq) + 4H_2O(l) + 2NO(g)$

PAGE: 20.2

69. the thermal decomposition of $NO(g)$

ANS: $3NO(g) \rightarrow N_2O(g) + NO_2(g)$

PAGE: 20.2

70. the reaction of sodium phosphide with water

ANS: $2Na_3P(s) + 6H_2O(l) \rightarrow 2PH_3(g) + 6Na^+(aq) + 6OH^-(aq)$

PAGE: 20.3

71. the reaction of $P_4O_{10}(s)$ with water

ANS: $P_4O_{10}(s) + 6H_2O(l) \rightarrow 4H_3PO_4(aq)$

PAGE: 20.3

72. the reaction of phosphorus pentachloride with water

ANS: $PCl_5(s) + 4H_2O(l) \rightarrow H_3PO_4(aq) + 5HCl(aq)$

PAGE: 20.3

73. the reaction of phosphorus trichloride with water

ANS: $PCl_3(l) + 3H_2O(l) \rightarrow H_3PO_3(aq) + 3HCl(aq)$

PAGE: 20.3

74. the reaction of calcium fluoride with sulfuric acid

ANS: $CaF_2(s) + H_2SO_4(aq) \rightarrow CaSO_4(s) + 2HF(g)$

PAGE: 20.7

75. the reaction of chlorine gas with cold water

ANS: $Cl_2(g) + H_2O(l) \rightarrow HOCl(aq) + H^+(aq) + Cl^-(aq)$

PAGE: 20.7

76. the reaction of iodine monochloride with water

   ANS: $ICl(s) + H_2O(l) \rightarrow H^+(aq) + Cl^-(aq) + HOI(aq)$ **PAGE:** 20.7

77. the reaction of xenon hexafluoride with excess water

   ANS: $XeF_6(s) + 3H_2O(l) \rightarrow XeO_3(aq) + 6HF(aq)$ **PAGE:** 20.8

78. the thermal decomposition of ammonium nitrate

   ANS: $NH_4NO_3(s) \rightarrow N_2O(g) + 2H_2O(g)$ **PAGE:** 20.2

79. the decomposition of nitric acid in sunlight

   ANS: $4HNO_3(aq) \rightarrow 4NO_2(aq) + 2H_2O(l) + O_2(g)$ **PAGE:** 20.2

80. the oxidation of sulfur dioxide by oxygen gas

   ANS: $2SO_2(g) + O_2(g) \rightarrow 2SO_3(g)$ **PAGE:** 20.6

1. What are the oxidation numbers of the central metal atom in the following coordination compounds? $K_3[Fe(CN)_6]$, $[Cr(NH_3)_4Br_2]Br$, $[Ni(H_2O)_6]Cl_2$, $Na_2[TaF_7]$ are

    a) 3, 3, 3, 5
    b) 3, 3, 2, 7
    c) −3, 3, 2, 5
    d) −3, 1, 2, 5
    e) 3, 3, 2, 5

    ANS: e) 3, 3, 2, 5   **PAGE:** 21.1,3

2. Which metal ion has a d^5 electron configuration?

    a) Pd^{2+}
    b) Ag^+
    c) Fe^{3+}
    d) Os^{2+}
    e) Co^{2+}

    ANS: c) Fe^{3+} **PAGE:** 21.1

3. Which of the following is a d^7 ion?

    a) Co(II)
    b) Cu(II)
    c) Mn(II)
    d) Mn(IV)
    e) At least two of the above (a-d) are d^7 ions.

    ANS: a) Co(II)   **PAGE:** 21.1

4. What is the electron configuration of the Sc(I) ion?

    a) $[Ar]4s^14d^1$
    b) $[Ar]4s^13d^1$
    c) $[Ar]3s^13d^1$
    d) $[Ar]4s^2$
    e) $[Ar]3d^2$

    ANS: e) $[Ar]3d^2$ **PAGE:** 21.1

5. True or false: Transition metals show great similarities both within a given period and within a given vertical group.

    ANS: True   **PAGE:** 21.1

6. A coordination compound of Cu^{2+} can be described as $Cu(NH_3)_xSO_4$ and is known to contain 29.9% NH_3. The value of x is:

    a) 2

    b) 3

    c) 4

    d) 6

    e) none of these

    ANS: c) 4

PAGE: 21.3

7. The coordination theory was proposed by:

    a) Bailar

    b) Jorgensen

    c) Blomstrand

    d) Werner

    e) none of these

    ANS: d) Werner

PAGE: 21.3

8. Ethylenediamine (en) is a bidentate ligand. What is the coordination number of cobalt in $[Co(en)_2Cl_2]Cl$?

    a) four

    b) five

    c) seven

    d) eight

    e) six

    ANS: e) six

PAGE: 21.3

9. Which of the following coordination compounds will form a precipitate when treated with an aqueous solution of $AgNO_3$?

    a) $[Cr(NH_3)_3Cl_3]$

    b) $[Cr(NH_3)_6]Cl_3$

    c) $[Cr(NH_3)Cl]SO_4$

    d) $Na_3[Cr(CN)_6]$

    e) $Na_3[CrCl_6]$

    ANS: b) $[Cr(NH_3)_6]Cl_3$

PAGE: 21.3

10-13. Suppose you are studying coordination compounds of Co(II) with the ligand pyridine (py, C_5H_5N, molar mass = 79.10). You isolate a crystalline compound, and since the only available anions are Cl^- and NO_3^-, you hypothesize the empirical formula of the coordination compound must be $Co(II)_w(py)_x(Cl)_y(NO_3)_z$.

10. You discover that the complex decomposes in water. You dissolve 0.1000 g of the complex in H_2O and add excess $NaHg(SCN)_4$, which precipitates Co(II) as $CoHg(SCN)_4(s)$. After the precipitate is washed and dried, its mass is 0.1102 g. How many grams of cobalt are contained in 0.100 g of the complex?

   a) 0.1102
   b) 0.0396
   c) 0.0132
   d) 0.437
   e) 0.0548

   ANS: c)   0.0132   PAGE: 21.3

11. You analyze for pyridine (K_b is approximately 10^{-9}) by dissolving 0.1000 g of complex in 10 mL of H_2O and titrating with a 0.01 M HCl solution. Which of the following indicators should be used to detect the endpoint? (Assume that the initial concentration of pyridine is approximately 0.01 M.)

   a) bromophenol blue, pH range of color change = 3.0–4.6
   b) methyl red, pH range of color change = 4.8–6.0
   c) bromothymol blue, pH range of color change = 6.0–7.6
   d) thymol blue, pH range of color change = 8.0 –9.6
   e) alizarin yellow, pH range of color change = 10.1–12.0

   ANS: a)   bromophenol blue, pH range of color change = 3.0–4.6   PAGE: 21.3

12. Addition of $AgNO_3$ to aqueous solutions of the complex results in a cloudy white precipitate, presumably AgCl. You dissolve 0.1000 g of the complex in H_2O and perform a precipitation titration with 0.0500 M $AgNO_3$ as the titrant. Using an electrode that is sensitive to $[Ag^+]$, you reach the endpoint after 9.00 mL of titrant are added. How many grams of chloride ion were present in the 0.1000-g sample?

   a) 4.50×10^{-4}
   b) 5.00×10^{-3}
   c) 1.77×10^{-3}
   d) 6.38×10^{-2}
   e) 1.60×10^{-2}

   ANS: e) 1.60×10^{-2} PAGE: 21.3

13. Analysis of the data from a titration indicates that a 0.1000-g sample of the complex contains 0.708 g of py. Further analysis shows that 0.1000 g of the complex contains a 0.0132 g of cobalt and 0.0160 g of chloride. What is the empirical formula of the complex?

   a) $Co(py)_6(Cl)(NO_3)$
   b) $Co(py)_4Cl_2$
   c) $Co_2(py)_5(Cl)_2(NO_3)_2$
   d) $Co_3(py)_8(Cl)_2(NO_3)_4$
   e) $Co(py)_4(NO_3)_2$

   ANS: b) $Co(py)_4Cl_2$ **PAGE:** 21.3

14. Which of the following complexes shows geometric isomerism?

   a) $[Co(NH_3)_5Cl]SO_4$
   b) $[Co(NH_3)_6]Cl_3$
   c) $[Co(NH_3)_5Cl]Cl_2$
   d) $K[Co(NH_3)_2Cl_4]$
   e) none of these

   ANS: d) $K[Co(NH_3)_2Cl_4]$ **PAGE:** 21.4

15. What is the sum of the geometric and optical isomers that the complex ion $Co(en)_2Cl_2^+$ exhibits?

   a) 0
   b) 1
   c) 2
   d) 3
   e) 4

   ANS: d)   3   **PAGE:** 21.4

16. Which of the following ligands might give linkage isomers?

   a) NO_2^-
   b) SCN^-
   c) $H_2NHC_2CH_2NH_2$
   d) a and b
   e) a, b, and c

   ANS: d)   a and b   **PAGE:** 21.4

17. Give the number of geometrical isomers for the octahedral compound [$Ma_2B_2C_2$], where A, B, and C represent ligands.

    a) 1
    b) 2
    c) 3
    d) 5
    e) none of these

    ANS: d) 5   **PAGE:** 21.4

18. For the process $Co(NH_3)_5Cl^{2+} + Cl^- \rightarrow Co(NH_3)_4Cl_2^+ + NH_3$ what would be the ratio of *cis* to *trans* isomer in the product?

    a) 1 : 1
    b) 1 : 2
    c) 1 : 4
    d) 4 : 1
    e) 2 : 1

    ANS: d) 4 : 1   **PAGE:** 21.4

19. The ____ isomer of the complex $Ni(en)_2Cl_2$ exhibits optical isomers, but the ____ isomer does not.

    a) *cis, trans*
    b) *trans, cis*
    c) Both isomers exhibit optical isomers.
    d) Neither isomers exhibit optical isomers.

    ANS: a) *cis, trans*   **PAGE:** 21.4

20. How many of the following compounds exhibit geometric isomers?
    I. $Pt(NH_3)_2Cl_2$ (square planar)
    II. [$Co(H_2O)_2$]Cl_3
    III. $Ni(NH_3)_4(NO_2)_2$
    IV. $K_2[CoCl_4]$
    a) 0
    b) 1
    c) 2
    d) 3
    e) 4

    ANS: c) 2   **PAGE:** 21.4

497

21. Which of the following transition metals are important to the U.S. economy and defense?

    a) chromium and cobalt
    b) manganese
    c) platinum and palladium
    d) all of these
    e) a and b only

    ANS: d)   all of these

PAGE: 21.1

22. Transition metals display great similarities

    a) within a given period.
    b) within a given vertical group.
    c) with the semimetals.
    d) all of these
    e) a and b only

    ANS: e)   a and b only

PAGE: 21.1

23. Which of the transition metals is the best conductor of heat and electric current?

    a) copper
    b) silver
    c) gold
    d) tungsten
    e) titanium

    ANS: b)   silver

PAGE: 21.1

24. Which metal is most widely used in the electrical systems of homes and factories?

    a) copper
    b) silver
    c) gold
    d) tungsten
    e) titanium

    ANS: a)   copper

PAGE: 21.1

25. A complex ion is a charged species consisting of a metal ion surrounded by

    a) other transition metals.
    b) hydrogen ions.
    c) ligands.
    d) ligands and counter ions.
    e) none of these

    ANS: c)   ligands.

PAGE: 21.1

26. What is the electron configuration of the Ni(II) ion?

    a) $[Ar] 4s^2 3d^6$
    b) $[Ar] 4s^1 3d^7$
    c) $[Ar] 4s^2 3d^8$
    d) $[Ar] 3d^8$
    e) none of these

    ANS: d) $[Ar] 3d^8$ **PAGE:** 21.1

27. What is the electron configuration of the Mn(II) ion?

    a) $[Ar] 4s^2 3d^5$
    b) $[Ar] 4s^1 3d^5$
    c) $[Ar] 4s^2 3d^3$
    d) $[Ar] 3d^5$
    e) none of these

    ANS: d) $[Ar] 3d^5$ **PAGE:** 21.1

28. The reducing abilities of the first-row transition metals generally _____ going from left to right across the period.

    a) decrease
    b) increase
    c) stay the same
    d) none of these
    e) remain at 1.0 V

    ANS: a)   decrease   **PAGE:** 21.1

29. Which of the following transition metals is most likely to form an oxide?

    a) gold
    b) silver
    c) platinum
    d) palladium
    e) copper

    ANS: e)   copper   **PAGE:** 21.1

30. What transition metal is used in stainless steel?

    a) nickel
    b) titanium
    c) chromium
    d) iridium
    e) niobium

    ANS: c)   chromium   **PAGE:** 21.1

31. What transition metal is used in magnets, catalysts, and drill bits?

    a)   nickel

    b)   copper

    c)   platinum

    d)   cobalt

    e)   titanium

ANS: d)   cobalt   **PAGE:** 21.1

32. The phenomenon called the _____ contradiction is responsible for the great similarity in atomic size and chemistry of 4d and 5d elements.

    a)   transition

    b)   coordination

    c)   none of these

    d)   isomeric

    e)   lanthanide

ANS: e)   lanthanide   **PAGE:** 21.1

33. What transition metal has the combination of toughness, stretchability, and resilience that makes it ideal for use in bicycle frames?

    a)   titanium

    b)   platinum

    c)   tungsten

    d)   nickel

    e)   aluminum

ANS: a)   titanium   **PAGE:** 21.2

34. This transition metal is used in the production of a hard steel used for rock crushers and bank vaults, and can be found in nodules on the ocean floor.

    a)   iron

    b)   manganese

    c)   magnesium

    d)   cobalt

    e)   nickel

ANS: b)   manganese   **PAGE:** 21.2

35. What heavy metal is the most abundant and most important to our civilization?

    a) iron
    b) gold
    c) magnesium
    d) cobalt
    e) copper

    ANS: a) iron   **PAGE:** 21.2

36. Which of the following statements concerning the complex ion $Co(en)_2Cl_2^+$ is true?
    (en = ethylenediamine, $NH_2CH_2CH_2NH_2$)?

    a) The complex ion contains Co(I).
    b) The complex ion exhibits *cis* and *trans* geometric isomers, but no optical isomers.
    c) The complex ion exhibits two geometric isomers (*cis* and *trans*) and two optical isomers.
    d) Since en is a strong field ligand (large Δ), the complex ion is paramagnetic.
    e) The geometric isomers of the complex ion have identical chemical properties.

    ANS: c) The complex ion exhibits two geometric isomers (*cis* and
    trans) and two optical isomers.   **PAGE:** 21.4,6

37. Which of the following is true about coordination complexes?

    a) The metal is a Lewis base and the ligands are Lewis acids.
    b) Only complexes with coordination number six are found in nature.
    c) When the ligands approach a transition metal ion in an octahedral field, the d_{xz}, d_{yz}, and d_{xy} atomic orbitals are affected the least by the ligands.
    d) None of the above is true.
    e) All of the above are true.

    ANS: c) When the ligands approach a transition metal ion in an
    octahedral field, the d_{xz}, d_{yz}, and d_{xy} atomic orbitals are
    affected the least by the ligands.   **PAGE:** 21.2,6

38. Which of the following is paramagnetic?

    a) $Zn(H_2O)_6^{2+}$

    b) $Co(NH_3)_6^{3+}$ (strong field)

    c) $Cu(CN)_3^{2-}$

    d) $Mn(CN)_6^{2-}$ (strong field)

    e) none of these

    ANS: d) $Mn(CN)_6^{3-}$ (strong field)   **PAGE:** 21.6

501

39. The complex ions of Zn^{2+} are all colorless. The most likely explanation for this is:

    a) Zn^{2+} is paramagnetic.
    b) Zn^{2+} exhibits –d orbitalî splittings in its complexes such that they absorb all wavelengths in the visible region.
    c) Since Zn^{2+} is a d^{10} ion, it does not absorb visible light even though the –d orbitalî splittings are correct for absorbing visible wavelengths.
    d) Zn^{2+} is not a transition metal ion.
    e) None of these is correct.

    ANS: c)   Since Zn^{2+} is a d^{10} ion, it does not absorb visible light even though the –d orbitalî splittings are correct for absorbing visible wavelengths.   **PAGE:** 21.6

40. Which is lower in energy in transition metal ions, the 3d orbitals or 4s orbitals?

    a)   the 4s orbitals
    b)   the 3d orbitals
    c)   about equal in energy
    d)   cannot be determined

    ANS: b)   the 3d orbitals   **PAGE:** 21.1

41. The expected electron configuration of Cu^+ is $[Ar]3s^13d^9$.

    ANS: False   **PAGE:** 21.1

42. Which of the following is true?

    a)   The first ionization energy for Zn is significantly higher than that of Sc.
    b)   The first ionization energy for Zn is significantly lower than that of Sc.
    c)   The third ionization energy for Zn is significantly higher than that of Sc.
    d)   The third ionization energy for Zn is significantly lower than that of Sc.
    e)   Two of these are correct.

    ANS: c)   The third ionization energy for Zn is significantly higher than that of Sc.   **PAGE:** 21.1

43. Because they have the same atoms, bonds, and formulas, geometric isomers have the same color.

    ANS: False   **PAGE:** 21.4

44. Copper(I) complexes would be expected to be colorless.

    ANS: True   **PAGE:** 21.6

45. Calculate the total number of unpaired electrons in the following complex ions: $Zn(OH_2)_6^{2+}$, $Ni(CN)_4^{2-}$ (square planar), $Co(NH_3)_6^{3+}$ (strong field).

   a) 0
   b) 1
   c) 2
   d) 3
   e) 4

   ANS: a) 0   **PAGE:** 21.6

46. Which of the following crystal field diagrams is correct for $Co(CN)_6^{4-}$ where CN^- is a strong field ligand?

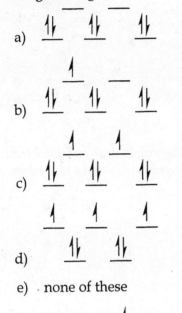

   e) none of these

   ANS: b)   **PAGE:** 21.6

47. Which of the following crystal field diagrams is correct for $Mn(CN)_6^{3-}$ (CN⁻ is a strong field ligand)?

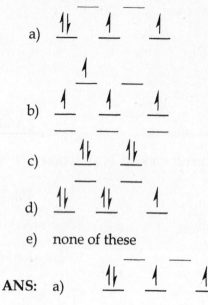

a)

b)

c)

d)

e)   none of these

ANS: a)

PAGE: 21.6

48. Choose the most likely pattern for the crystal field diagram for the complex *trans*-$[Ni(NH_3)_2(CN)_4]^{2-}$ where CN⁻ produces a much stronger crystal field than does NH_3.

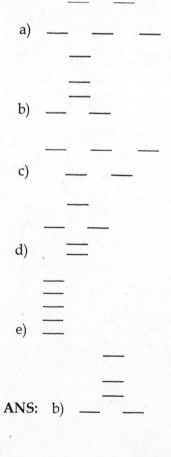

a)

b)

c)

d)

e)

ANS: b)

PAGE: 21.6

49–54. Specify the number of unpaired electrons.

  a) 0
  b) 1
  c) 2
  d) 3
  e) 5

49. $CuCl_2^-$ (linear)

  ANS: a)   0   **PAGE:** 21.6

50. $Ni(NH_3)_6^{2+}$

  ANS: c)   2   **PAGE:** 21.6

51. $NiCl_4^{2-}$ (tetrahedral)

  ANS: c)   2   **PAGE:** 21.6

52. CoF_6^{3-} (weak field)

  ANS: d)   4   **PAGE:** 21.6

53. $Co(en)_3^{3+}$ (strong field)

  ANS: a)   0   **PAGE:** 21.6

54. $Mn(H_2O)_4^{3+}$ (tetrahedral)

  ANS: d)   4   **PAGE:** 21.6

55. The complex FeL_6^{2+}, where L is a neutral ligand, is known to be diamagnetic. The number of d electrons in this complex ion is:

  a) 4
  b) 5
  c) 6
  d) 7
  e) 8

  ANS: c)   6   **PAGE:** 21.6

56. The empirical formula of a compound with a mass percent composition of 6.78% H, 31.43% N, 39.76% Cl, and 22.03% Co is consistent with which of the following complexes?

  a) $[Co(NH_3)_3Cl_3]$
  b) $[Co(NH_3)_4Cl_2]Cl$
  c) $[Co(NH_3)_5Cl]Cl_2$
  d) $[Co(NH_3)_6]Cl_3$
  e)   none of these

  ANS: d) $[Co(NH_3)_6]Cl_3$ **PAGE:** 21.3

505

57. Fluoride ion ranks low in the spectrochemical series and produces a weak crystal field in complex ions. Based on this information, predict the number of unpaired electrons in CoF_6^{3-}.

    a) 0
    b) 1
    c) 2
    d) 3
    e) 4

ANS: e) 4

PAGE: 21.6

58. According to crystal field theory, how many unpaired electrons are present in the complex ion $[Fe(H_2O)_6]^{3+}$? The water molecules are weak field ligands.

    a) 1
    b) 2
    c) 3
    d) 4
    e) 5

ANS: e) 5

PAGE: 21.6

59. How many unpaired electrons are present in the tetrahedral complex $[CoCl_4]^{2-}$?

    a) 1
    b) 2
    c) 3
    d) 4
    e) 5

ANS: c) 3

PAGE: 21.6

60. Which transition metal is valued for its high electrical conductivity and resistance to corrosion, and is widely used for plumbing?

    a) iron
    b) manganese
    c) magnesium
    d) cobalt
    e) copper

ANS: e) copper

PAGE: 21.2

61. What transition metal is mainly used for galvanizing steel?

    a) iron
    b) zinc
    c) copper
    d) cobalt
    e) nickel

ANS: b) zinc

PAGE: 21.2

62. Which has the greatest number of unpaired electrons?

  a) The square planar complex $Ni(CN)_4^{2-}$.
  b) The tetrahedral complex $FeCl_4^-$.
  c) Neither of the above have any unpaired electrons.
  d) Both (a and b) have the same number (non-zero) of unpaired electrons.
  e) More information is needed.

  ANS: b)   The tetrahedral complex $FeCl_4^-$.   **PAGE:** 21.6

63. In the crystal field model, ligands are treated as negative point charges.

  ANS: True   **PAGE:** 21.6

64. Cytochromes consist of two main parts:

  a) myoglobin and heme
  b) heme and porphyrin
  c) heme and a protein
  d) myoglobin and porphyrin
  e) an iron ion and porphyrin

  ANS: c)   heme and a protein   **PAGE:** 21.7

65. A d^6 ion (Fe^{2+}) is complexed with six strong-field ligands (for example, SCN^-). What is the number of unpaired electrons in this complex?

  a) 0
  b) 1
  c) 2
  d) 3
  e) 4

  ANS: a)   0   **PAGE:** 21.6

66. The complex ion $Fe(CN)_6^{4-}$ (no unpaired electrons) is classified as:

  a) weak field
  b) strong field
  c) no way to tell

  ANS: b)   strong field   **PAGE:** 21.6

67. The complex ion $Co(NH_3)_6^{2+}$ (three unpaired electrons) is classified as:

  a) weak field
  b) strong field
  c) no way to tell

  ANS: a)   weak field   **PAGE:** 21.6

68. The complex ion $Ni(NH_3)_6^{2+}$ (two unpaired electrons) is classified as:

    a) weak field
    b) strong field
    c) no way to tell

    ANS: c)   no way to tell

    PAGE: 21.6

69. Which of the following statements is true about the octahedral complexes of Ni^{2+}?

    a) Both strong- and weak-field complexes are diamagnetic.
    b) The strong-field complex is diamagnetic and the weak-field complex is paramagnetic.
    c) The strong-field complex is paramagnetic and the weak-field complex is diamagnetic.
    d) Both strong- and weak-field complexes are paramagnetic.

    ANS: d)   Both strong- and weak-field complexes are paramagnetic.   **PAGE:** 21.6

70. Consider the following complexes:

    I. $Pt(NH_3)_2Cl_2$ (square planar)

    II. $Rh (en)_3^{2+}$ (en = $H_2N—CH_2—CH_2—NH_2$ and is bidentate)

    III. $CoCl_4^{2-}$ (tetrahedral)

    The complex(es) having geometrical (*cis–trans*) isomers, but not optical isomers is (are):

    a) I
    b) II
    c) III
    d) I, II
    e) I, II, III

    ANS: a)   I

    PAGE: 21.4

71. Consider the following complexes:

I. $Pt(NH_3)_2Cl_2$ (square planar)

II. $Rh(en)_3^{2+}$ (en = $H_2N—CH_2—CH_2—NH_2$ and is bidentate)

III. $CoCl_4^{2-}$ (tetrahedral)

The complex(es) having optical isomers, but not optical isomers is (are):

a) I
b) II
c) III
d) I, II
e) I, II, III

ANS: b) II   **PAGE:** 21.4

72. Which of the following complexes can exhibit optical isomerism?
(en = $H_2N—CH_2—CH_2—NH_2$ and is bidentate)

a) *cis*–$Co(NH_3)_4Cl_2$
b) *trans*–$Co(en)_2Br_2$
c) *cis*–$Co(en)_2Cl_2$
d) $Co(NH_3)_3Cl_3$
e) none of these

ANS: c) *cis*–$Co(en)_2Cl_2$ **PAGE:** 21.4

73. How many d electrons are present on the metal ion in the complex ion $PtCl_6^{2-}$?

a) 8
b) 6
c) 4
d) 3
e) 2

ANS: b) 6   **PAGE:** 21.3

74. Which of the metal ions in the following complex ions has a d^5 electron configuration?

   a) $V(H_2O)_6^{2+}$

   b) $Mo(NH_3)_6^{3+}$

   c) $Co(CN)_4^-$

   d) $Fe(CN)_6^{3-}$

   e) $RhCl_6^{4-}$

   ANS: d) $Fe(CN)_6^{3-}$ **PAGE:** 21.3

75. How many unpaired electrons are there in $Ir(Br)_6^{4-}$?
   (Br^- is a weak-field ligand.)

   a) 4

   b) 3

   c) 2

   d) 1

   e) 0

   ANS: b)   3   **PAGE:** 21.6

76. In which of the following complexes does the transition metal have a d^8 configuration?

   a) $PtCl_4^{2-}$

   b) $Cu(H_2O)_6^{2+}$

   c) $Ni(CO)_4$

   d) $Zn(NH_3)_4^{2+}$

   e) $Fe(CN)_6^{3-}$

   ANS: a) $PtCl_4^{2-}$ **PAGE:** 21.3

77. The complex ion $NiCl_4^{2-}$ is tetrahedral. The number of unpaired electrons in the complex is:

   a) 0

   b) 1

   c) 2

   d) 3

   e) 4

   ANS: c)   2   **PAGE:** 21.6

510

78. How many unpaired electrons are there in the tetrahedral complex ion $[FeCl_4]^-$?

   a) 1
   b) 2
   c) 3
   d) 4
   e) 5

   ANS: e) 5

PAGE: 21.6

79. A metal ion in a high-spin octahedral complex has two more unpaired electrons than the same ion does in a low-spin octahedral complex. The metal ion could be:

   a) V^{2+}
   b) Cu^{2+}
   c) Mn^{2+}
   d) Cr^{3+}
   e) Co^{2+}

   ANS: e) Co^{2+}

PAGE: 21.6

80. For which of the following metal ions would there be no low-spin versus high-spin distinction in octahedral complexes?

   a) Cr^{2+}
   b) V^{2+}
   c) Fe^{3+}
   d) Mn^{2+}
   e) Co^{3+}

   ANS: b) V^{2+}

PAGE: 21.6

81. How many unpaired electrons are there in a complex ion having a d^5 electron configuration and an octahedral geometry in the weak field case?

   a) 1
   b) 2
   c) 3
   d) 4
   e) 5

   ANS: e) 5

PAGE: 21.6

82. The spectrochemical series is

$$I^- < Br^- < Cl^- < F^- < OH^- < H_2O < NH_3 < en < NO_2^- < CN^-$$

Which of the following complexes will absorb visible radiation of the highest energy (shortest wavelength)?

a) $[Co(H_2O)_6]^{3+}$
b) $[Co(I)_6]^{3-}$
c) $[Co(OH)_6]^{3-}$
d) $[Co(en)_3]^{3+}$
e) $[Co(NH_3)_6]^{3+}$

ANS: d) $[Co(en)_3]^{3+}$

PAGE: 21.6

83–87. Here are some crystal field representations of d electrons in an octahedral field:

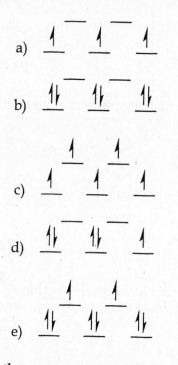

Choose the representation that fits the transition metal atom in the following species:

83. $Fe(OH_2)_6^{3+}$ (assume weak field)

ANS: c)

PAGE: 21.6

84. $[Co(NH_3)_4Br_2]^+$

ANS: b)

PAGE: 21.6

85. $K_4Mn(CN)_6$ (assume strong field)

ANS: d)   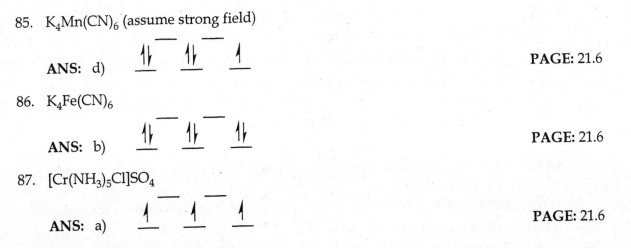   **PAGE:** 21.6

86. $K_4Fe(CN)_6$

ANS: b)   **PAGE:** 21.6

87. $[Cr(NH_3)_5Cl]SO_4$

ANS: a)   **PAGE:** 21.6

88. A complex ion is a square planar complex. It has a d^8 electron configuration. What is the most reasonable d orbital scheme for this complex?

a)

b)

c)

d)

e)

ANS: d)   **PAGE:** 21.6

89. Which of the following is true in describing the crystal field model?

    a) The metal ion and ligand interaction is treated as a Lewis acid–base interaction.
    b) The ligands are treated as negative point charges.
    c) The metal ion–ligand bonds are considered to be completely ionic.
    d) The electrons are assumed to be localized.
    e) None of the above is true.

   ANS: b)   The ligands are treated as negative point charges.   **PAGE:** 21.6

90. Which model(s) accounts for the magnetism and color of coordination compounds?

    I. the localized electron model
    II. the crystal field model
    a) I
    b) II
    c) both I and II
    d) neither I nor II

   ANS: b) II
                                                                          PAGE: 21.5,6

91. Which of the following are structural isomers?

    I. coordination isomers
    II. linkage isomers
    III. geometric isomers
    IV. optical isomers
    a) I, III
    b) II, IV
    c) I, III, IV
    d) II, III
    e) I, II

   ANS: e)   I, II
                                                                          PAGE: 21.4

92. Which of the following complexes would be diamagnetic (all electrons paired)? Assume the strong-field case for all complexes.

    a) $[Ni(CN)_6]^{4-}$
    b) $[Ti(CN)_6]^{3-}$
    c) $[Co(CN)_6]^{3-}$
    d) $[Cr(CN)_6]^{3-}$

   ANS: c) $[Co(CN)_6]^{3-}$
                                                                          PAGE: 21.6

93. How many unpaired electrons are there in the complex ion $[Co(NO_3)_6]^{4-}$? For this ion the nitrate ligands produce a very strong crystal field.

    a) 1
    b) 2
    c) 3
    d) 4
    e) 5

    ANS: a) 1   PAGE: 21.6

94. Hemoglobin is a complex of

    a) Co^{3+}
    b) Mg^{2+}
    c) Fe^{2+}
    d) Sc^{3+}
    e) none of these

    ANS: c) Fe^{2+} PAGE: 21.7

95. A certain complex ion has a distorted octahedral structure in which the ligands along the plus and minus z axes are compressed (pushed in closer to the central metal ion). The d orbital splitting diagram for this complex ion would be:

    a)
    ```
              - - - - -
                d_z2
              - - - - -
               d_x2-y2
    - - - - -           - - - - -
      d_xz                d_yz
              - - - - -
                d_xy
    ```

    b)
    ```
              - - - - -     - - - - -
                d_z2          d_x2-y2
    - - - - -     - - - - -       - - - - -
      d_xz          d_xy            d_xz
    ```

    c)
    ```
              - - - - -
               d_x2-y2
              - - - - -
                d_z2
              - - - - -
                d_xy
    - - - - -           - - - - -
      d_xz                d_yz
    ```

    d)
    ```
    - - - - -     - - - - -     - - - - -
      d_xy          d_xz          d_yz
              - - - - -     - - - - -
                d_z2          d_x2-y2
    ```

e)

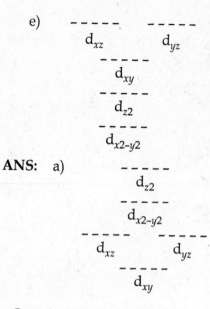

ANS: a)

PAGE: 21.6

96. Cytochrome C contains

    a) cobalt
    b) iron
    c) magnesium
    d) chromium
    e) none of these

    ANS: b) iron

PAGE: 21.7

97. Oxygen is stored in mammalian tissue in which type of molecule?

    a) hemoglobin
    b) myoglobin
    c) chlorophyll
    d) cytochrome
    e) prophyrin

    ANS: b) myoglobin

PAGE: 21.7

98. Pig iron usually contains about 5%:

    a) aluminum
    b) oxygen
    c) sodium
    d) sulfur
    e) carbon

    ANS: e) carbon

PAGE: 21.8

99. Name the careful heat treatment of metals that provides the proper combination of strength without too much brittleness.

    a) tempering
    b) core hardening
    c) fire polishing
    d) blast furnace

    ANS: a) tempering   **PAGE:** 21.8

100. The strength of steel is due to the effect of what substance with the iron?

    a) copper
    b) carbon monoxide
    c) sulfur
    d) carbon
    e) zinc

    ANS: d) carbon   **PAGE:** 21.8

101. Name the process currently most important for making steel.

    a) blast furnace process
    b) open hearth process
    c) tempering process
    d) leaching process

    ANS: b) open hearth process   **PAGE:** 21.8

102. Which of the following materials is added to the blast furnace to produce slag?

    a) sulfur
    b) carbon
    c) silicon
    d) limestone
    e) none of these

    ANS: d) limestone   **PAGE:** 21.8

103. An element common to brass and bronze is:

    a) nickel
    b) tin
    c) copper
    d) iron
    e) zinc

    ANS: c) copper   **PAGE:** 21.2

104. Which 3d transition metal is mixed with concentrated sulfuric acid to give a powerful cleaning solution for removing organic materials from analytical glassware?

a) chromium
b) iron
c) cobalt
d) scandium
e) manganese

ANS: a) chromium

PAGE: 21.2

105. Which complex ion shape is not capable of showing *cis–trans* isomerism?

a) octahedral
b) square planar
c) tetrahedral
d) none of these

ANS: c) tetrahedral

PAGE: 21.4

106. When the body adapts to high altitudes, it makes more _____ to adapt to lower oxygen concentrations in the blood.

a) myoglobin
b) iron
c) protein
d) hemoglobin
e) fatty tissue

ANS: d) hemoglobin

PAGE: 21.7

107. The transition metal _____ assists insulin in the control of blood sugar and may also be involved in the control of cholesterol.

a) scandium
b) titanium
c) iron
d) nickel
e) chromium

ANS: e) chromium

PAGE: 21.7

108. This molecule is toxic because it has about 200 times the affinity for the Fe^{2+} in hemoglobin as oxygen does, causing asphyxiation if enough of it is present in the air.

a) CN^-
b) CO
c) CO_2
d) NH_3
e) CH_4

ANS: b) CO

PAGE: 21.7

109. Carboxyhemoglobin is formed when _____ prevents the normal uptake of oxygen in the blood.

    a) CN^-

    b) CO

    c) CO_2

    d) NH_3

    e) CH_4

    ANS: b) CO **PAGE:** 21.7

110. Which of the following ligands are capable of linkage isomerism?

        N^-

        NO_2^-

        NH_3

        $NH_2CH_2CH_2NH_2$

        OCN^-

        Cl^-

        H_2O

        SCN^-

    ANS: SCN^-, NO_2^-, and OCN^- **PAGE:** 21.4

111. Define stereoisomerism.

    ANS: See Sec. 21.4 of Zumdahl, *Chemistry*.   **PAGE:** 21.4

112. Define optical isomerism.

    ANS: See Sec. 21.4 of Zumdahl, *Chemistry*.   **PAGE:** 21.4

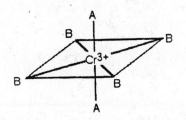

113. Consider the pseudo-octahedral complex of Cr^{3+} shown above, where A and B represent Lewis bases and where A produces a stronger crystal field than B. Draw an appropriate crystal field diagram for this complex (include the electrons).

ANS:

$$d_{z2}\quad - - - - -$$

$$d_{x2-y2}\quad - - - - -$$

$$d_{xz}\quad - - - - -\qquad d_{yz}\quad - - - - -$$

$$d_{xy}\quad - - - - -$$

PAGE: 21.6

114. The 3d electrons in $Co(NH_3)_6^{3+}$ are all paired but $Fe(H_2O)_6^{3+}$ has unpaired electrons (is paramagnetic). Explain.

ANS: Both complex ions have six 3d electrons. $Co(NH_3)_6^{3+}$ is low spin because NH_3 produces a strong field when it coordinates with CO^{3+}. $Fe(H_2O)_6^{2+}$ is high spin because H_2O produces a weak field when it coordinates with Fe^{2+}.

PAGE: 21.6

115. The color of a transition metal complex results from:

   a)   bending vibrations.
   b)   stretching vibrations.
   c)   transition of an electron between d orbitals.
   d)   transition of an electron between an s and a p orbital.
   e)   nuclear magnetic resonance.

   ANS: c)   transition of an electron between d orbitals.

PAGE: 21.6

116–123. How many unpaired electrons are found in each of the following complex ions?

116. $CoBr_4^-$ (tetrahedral)

   ANS: 4

PAGE: 21.6

117. $Fe(CN)_6^{4-}$

   ANS: 0

PAGE: 21.6

118. $[Zn(CN)_6]^{4-}$

   ANS: 0

PAGE: 21.6

119. $NiCl_4^{2-}$

   ANS: 0

PAGE: 21.6

120. $FeCl_4^{2-}$

   ANS: 4

PAGE: 21.6

121. $[Ni(CN)_6]^{4-}$

    ANS: 2

PAGE: 21.6

122. $[Cr(CN)_4]^{2-}$

    ANS: 4

PAGE: 21.6

123. $[Co(NH_3)_4]^{2+}$

    ANS: 3

PAGE: 21.6

124. The metals with the highest ionization energies are most likely to be found in nature in the elemental state.

    ANS: True

PAGE: 21.1

125. Metals usually have higher melting points than nonmetals.

    ANS: True

PAGE: 21.1

126. Co^{2+} in water is blue.

    ANS: False

PAGE: 21.1

127. The coordination theory was proposed by Alfred Packer.

    ANS: False

PAGE: 21.3

128. The election configuration of Mn^{2+} is $[Ar]\ 4s^2 3d^3$.

    ANS: False

PAGE: 21.1

129. All tetrahedral complex ions are high spin.

    ANS: True

PAGE: 21.6

130. The complex ions containing Zn^{2+} are intensely colored.

    ANS: False

PAGE: 21.6

131. The complexes of Zn^{2+} are all diamagnetic.

    ANS: True

PAGE: 21.6

1. Name the following:

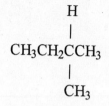

a)   isopropane
b)   methylpentane
c)   methylbutane
d)   *n*-pentane
e)   dodecane

ANS: c)   methylbutane

PAGE: 22.1

2. Name the following:

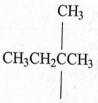

a)   *n*-heptane
b)   2-methyl-2-ethylbutane
c)   3,3-dimethylpentane
d)   2,2-diethylpropane

ANS: c)   3,3-dimethylpentane

PAGE: 22.1

3. Name the following:

$$CH_3 — CH_2 — CH_3$$

a)   ethane
b)   propane
c)   butane
d)   pentane
e)   hexane

ANS: b)   propane

PAGE: 22.1

4. Name the following:

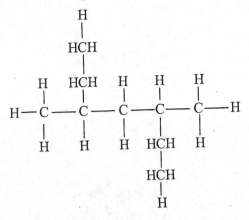

a) 2,4-diethylpentane
b) 3,5-dimethylheptane
c) secondary ethylpentane
d) 2,3-dimethyl-2,3-diethylpropane
e) none of these

ANS: b)   3,5-dimethylheptane

PAGE: 22.1

5. Name the following:

$$CH_3$$
$$|$$
$$CH_3 - C - CH_3$$
$$|$$
$$CH_3 - CH - CH_2 - CH - CH_3$$
$$|$$
$$CH_2$$
$$|$$
$$CH_3 - CH_2 - CH_2 - C - CH_2 - CH_2 - CH_3$$
$$|$$
$$CH_3 - C - CH_3$$
$$|$$
$$CH_3$$

a) 2,2,3,5-tetramethyl-7-propyl-7-t-butyldecane
b) 6-propyl-2,6-di-t-butylnonane
c) 2,2,5,7,8,8-hexamethyl-3,3-dipropylnonane
d) isonanane
e) none of these

ANS: a)   2,2,3,5-tetramethyl-7-propyl-7-t-butyldecane

PAGE: 22.1

523

6. Name the following:

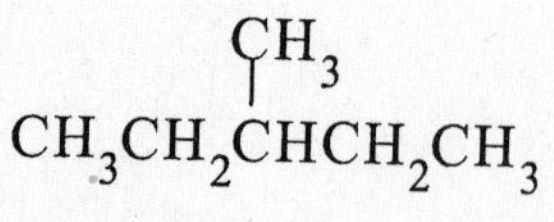

$$CH_3$$
$$CH_3CH_2CHCH_2CH_3$$

a) *n*-hexane
b) isohexane
c) 1,2,3-trimethylpropane
d) methyl-diethylmethane
e) 3-methylpentane

ANS: e) 3-methylpentane

PAGE: 22.1

7. Name the following:

$$CH_3—(CH_2)_7—CH_3$$

a) heptane
b) hexane
c) octane
d) nonane
e) decane

ANS: d) nonane

PAGE: 22.1

8. The compound below is the carbon skeleton (minus any hydrogen atoms) of

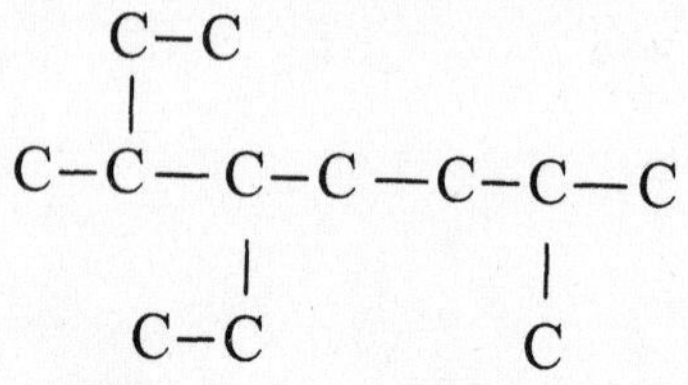

$$C-C$$
$$|$$
$$C-C—C-C—C-C—C$$
$$|\qquad\quad|$$
$$C-C\qquad C$$

I. a $C_{12}H_{26}$
II. a substituted octane
III. a compound with 3 tertiary carbons
IV. a compound with 3 secondary carbons
V. a compound with 2 isopropyl groups

a) I, II, III
b) II, III, IV
c) III, IV, V
d) II, IV, V
e) I, II, III, IV

ANS: a) I, II, III

PAGE: 22.1

9. A student gave a molecule the following name:

2-methyl-4-t-butylpentane

However, the teacher pointed out that, although the molecule could be correctly drawn from this name, the name violates the IUPAC rules. What is the correct (IUPAC) name of the molecule?

   a) 2-t-butyl-4-methylpentane
   b) 2,2,3,5-tetramethylhexane
   c) 2,4,5,5-tetramethylhexane
   d) 1-sec-butyl-1,2,2-trimethylpentane
   e) none of these (a-d)

ANS: b) 2,2,3,5-tetramethylhexane   **PAGE: 22.1**

10. Which of the following names is a correct one?

   a) 3-methyl-4-isopropylpentane
   b) 2-ethyl-4-tertiary-butylpentane
   c) 2,2,3,5-tetramethylheptane
   d) t-butylethane
   e) *trans*-1,2-dimethylethane

ANS: c) 2,2,3,5-tetramethylheptane   **PAGE: 22.1**

11. What is the compound whose carbon skeleton (minus any hydrogen atoms) appears below?

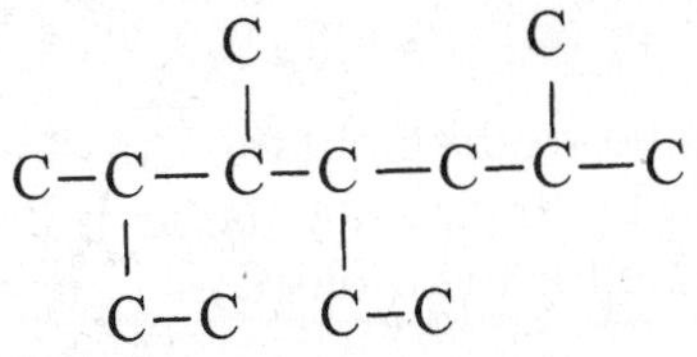

   a) 2,4-diethyl-3,6-dimethylheptane
   b) 2,5-dimethyl-4,6-diethylheptane
   c) 1,4-diethyl-3,6-dimethyl-tridecane
   d) 5-ethyl-3,6-trimethyloctane
   e) 4-ethyl-2,5,6-trimethyloctane

ANS: e)   4-ethyl-2,5,6-trimethyloctane   **PAGE: 22.1**

12. How many isomers of C_3H_8 are there?

   a) 1
   b) 2
   c) 3
   d) 5
   e) 6

ANS: a)   1   **PAGE: 22.1,2**

13. Cyclobutane has 109° bond angles like all alkanes.

ANS: False

PAGE: 22.1

14. A student gave a molecule the following name:

2-ethyl-3-methyl-5-isopropylhexane

However, his TA pointed out that, although the molecule could be correctly drawn from this name, the name violates the systematic rules. What is the correct (systematic) name of the molecule?

a) 3,4-dimethyl-6-isopropylheptane
b) 2-isopropyl-4,5-dimethylheptane
c) 3,4,6,7-tetramethyloctane
d) 1,2-diethyl-3,6,7-trimethylheptane
e) 2,3,5,6-tetramethyloctane

ANS: e)   2,3,5,6-tetramethyloctane

PAGE: 22.1

15. How many isomers are there of "dichloroethene"?

a) 2
b) 3
c) 4
d) 5
e) 6

ANS: b)   3

PAGE: 22.1,2

16. In lecture, the professor named a molecule 4-ethylpentane. An alert student pointed out that although the correct structure could be drawn, the name did not follow systematic rules. What is the correct systematic name for the molecule?

a) 2-ethylpentane
b) 1-methyl-1-propylpropane
c) 3-methylhexane
d) 4-methylhexane
e) none of these (a-d)

ANS: c)   3-methylhexane

PAGE: 22.1

17. Which is a possible product of the chlorination of butane in the presence of light?

a) C_4H_9Cl
b) C_4H_8Cl
c) $C_4H_{10}Cl_2$
d) $C_4H_6Cl_2$
e) $C_4H_9Cl_2$

ANS: a) C_4H_9Cl

PAGE: 22.1

18. One of the ingredients on a margarine container is listed as "polyunsaturated corn oil." This means that

    a)   all the carbon bonds in the oil are single bonds.
    b)   many of the polymer bonds are unsaturated.
    c)   all the carbon–carbon bonds are triple bonds.
    d)   many of the carbon–carbon bonds are multiple bonds.
    e)   none of these

    ANS: d)   many of the carbon-carbon bonds are multiple bonds.   **PAGE: 22.1,2**

19. Which of the following pairs is incorrect?

    a)   ethane – C_2H_4
    b)   pentane – C_5H_{12}
    c)   hexane – C_6H_{14}
    d)   heptane – C_7H_{16}
    e)   octane – C_8H_{18}

    ANS: a)   ethane – C_2H_4 **PAGE: 22.1**

20. Which of the following, upon reacting with oxygen, would form the greatest amount of carbon dioxide?

    a)   *n*-pentane
    b)   isopentane
    c)   neopentane
    d)   Two of the above would form equal amounts.
    e)   All (a-c) of the above would form equal amounts.

    ANS: e)   All (a-c) of the above would form equal amounts.   **PAGE: 22.1**

21. Propane undergoes dehydrogenation. The product of this is

    a)   1-propene
    b)   2-propene
    c)   *cis*-1-propene
    d)   *trans*-1-propene
    e)   *cis*-2-propene

    ANS: a)   1-propene   **PAGE: 22.1, 2**

22. Chemical reactions involving alkanes in which hydrogen atoms are removed and the product is an unsaturated hydrocarbon are called

    a)   combustion reactions.
    b)   dehydrogenation reactions.
    c)   substitution reactions.
    d)   addition reactions.
    e)   polymerization reactions.

    ANS: b)   dehydrogenation reactions.   **PAGE: 22.2**

23. How many of the following molecules exist?

      I.   methene
     II.   cycloethane
    III.   cyclopropyne
   IV.   neobutane

   a)   0
   b)   1
   c)   2
   d)   3
   e)   4

ANS: a)   0

PAGE: 22.1, 2

24. Indicate the total number of isomers in the following compound:

    C_4H_{10}

ANS: 2

PAGE: 22.1

25. Name the following:

$$CH_3-\underset{\underset{H}{|}}{\overset{\overset{CH_2CH_3}{|}}{C}}-C\equiv C-H$$

   a)   1-hexyne
   b)   2-ethynyl butane
   c)   2-ethyl-3-butyne
   d)   3-methyl-1-pentyne
   e)   3-methyl-4-pentyne

ANS: d)   3-methyl-1-pentyne

PAGE: 22.2

26. Name the following:

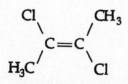

   a)   2-chloro-3-chloro-*cis*-2-butene
   b)   2,3-dichloro-*cis*-2-butene
   c)   2,3-dichloro-*trans*-2-butene
   d)   1-chloro-1-methyl-2-chloro-propene
   e)   2,3-dichloro-1-methyl-propene

ANS: c)   2,3-dichloro-*trans*-2-butene

PAGE: 22.2

27.   Name the following:

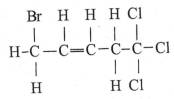

   a)   1,1,1-trichloro-5-bromo-3-pentene
   b)   5,5,5-trichloro-1-bromo-2-pentene
   c)   1,1,1-trichloro-5-bromo-2-pentene
   d)   1,1,1-trichloro-5-bromo-3-pentyne
   e)   none of these

   ANS: b)   5,5,5-trichloro-1-bromo-2-pentene

PAGE: 22.2

28. $CH_3C \equiv CCH_2CH_2Cl$ is named:

   a)   1-chloro-3-pentyne
   b)   5-chloro-2-pentene
   c)   1-acetylenyl-3-chloropropane
   d)   5-chloro-2-pentyne
   e)   1-chloro-3-pentene

   ANS: d)   5-chloro-2-pentyne

PAGE: 22.2

29. $H_2CCHCH_2N(CH_3)_2$ is

   a)   an alkyne and a secondary amine.
   b)   an alkene and a primary amine.
   c)   an alkene and a tertiary amine.
   d)   an alkyne and a tertiary amine.
   e)   none of these

   ANS: c)   an alkene and a tertiary amine.

PAGE: 22.2,4

30. Which of the following compounds can exhibit geometrical isomerism?

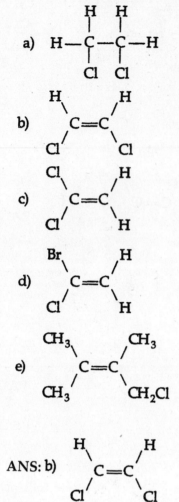

a) H—C—C—H (with H, H on top and Cl, Cl on bottom)

b) C=C (with H, H on top and Cl, Cl on bottom)

c) C=C (with Cl, H on top and Cl, H on bottom)

d) C=C (with Br, H on top and Cl, H on bottom)

e) C=C (with CH$_3$, CH$_3$ on top and CH$_3$, CH$_2$Cl on bottom)

ANS: b)   C=C (with H, H on top and Cl, Cl on bottom)

PAGE: 22.2

31. Consider the following four compounds:

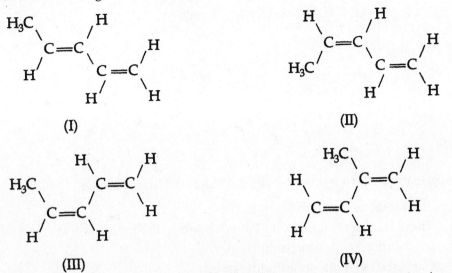

(I)   (II)

(III)   (IV)

Which of the above compounds would have the same physical properties (m.p., b.p., density, etc.)?

a) I and II
b) I and III
c) II and III
d) III and IV
e) I and IV

ANS: c) II and III   **PAGE: 22.2**

32. How many structural and geometrical isomers are there of chloropropene?

a) 2
b) 3
c) 4
d) 5
e) more than 5

ANS: c) 4   **PAGE: 22.2**

33. Which of the following types of compounds must have an sp^2-hybridized carbon center?

a) ethers
b) ketones
c) alcohols
d) alkanes
e) amines

ANS: b) ketones   **PAGE: 22.2,3,4**

34. How many geometric isomers can be drawn for the following compound:

$CH_3CH=CHCH_2CH=C(CH_3)_2$

a) 2
b) 3
c) 4
d) 5
e) 6

ANS: a) 2

PAGE: 22.2

35. Consider the molecule *trans*-2-butene. Which statement is true?

a) The molecule has two ? bonds.
b) There is free rotation around every bond in the molecule.
c) *Cis*-2-butene is its structural isomer.
d) Carbon #2 exhibits sp^2 hybridization.
e) none of the above

ANS: d) Carbon #2 exhibits sp^2 hybridization.

PAGE: 22.2

36. For which of the following compound(s) are *cis* and *trans* isomers possible?

a) 2,3-dimethyl-2-butene
b) 3-methyl-2-pentene
c) 4,4-dimethylcyclohexanol
d) ortho-chlorotoluene
e) All can exhibit *cis/trans* isomers.

ANS: b) 3-methyl-2-pentene

PAGE: 22.2,3,4

37. Which of the following is not a structural isomer of 1-pentene?

a) 2-pentene
b) 2-methyl-2-butene
c) cyclopentane
d) 3-methyl-1-butene
e) 1-methyl-cyclobutene

ANS: e) 1-methyl-cyclobutene

PAGE: 22.1,2

38. How many different possible tetramethylbenzenes exist?

a) 2
b) 3
c) 4
d) 5
e) 6

ANS: b) 3

PAGE: 22.3

39. Hydrocarbons containing a carbon–carbon triple bond are called

   a) alkynes
   b) alkenes
   c) cyclic alkanes
   d) aldehydes
   e) alkanes

   ANS: a) alkynes

PAGE: 22.2

40. Mothballs contain what aromatic hydrocarbon?

   a) naphthalene
   b) benzene
   c) anthracene
   d) phenanthrene
   e) toluene

   ANS: a) naphthalene

PAGE: 22.3

41. What alcohols have the greatest commercial value?

   a) methanol and ethanol
   b) methanol and phenol
   c) ethanol and phenol
   d) 1-propanol and ethanol
   e) 1-propanol and methanol

   ANS: a) methanol and ethanol

PAGE: 22.4

42. Which of the following has an optical isomer?

a) 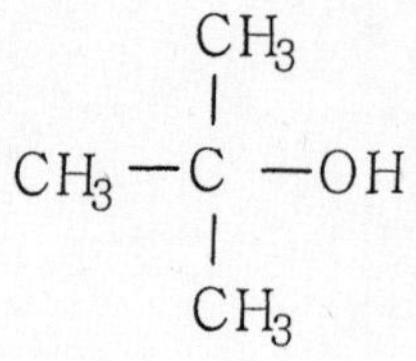
$$CH_3-\underset{\underset{CH_3}{|}}{\overset{\overset{CH_3}{|}}{C}}-OH$$

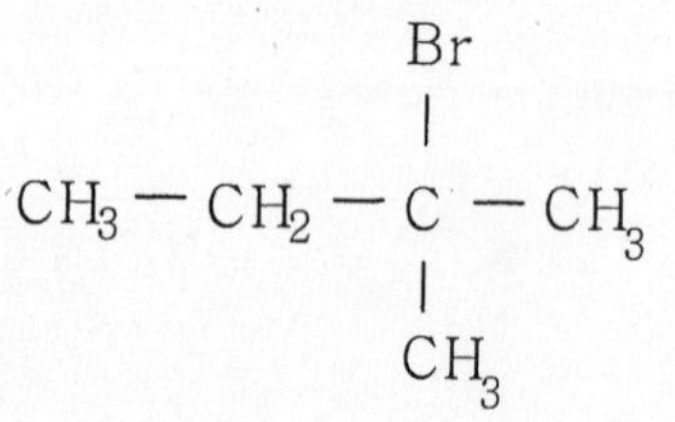

b)
$$CH_3-CH_2-\underset{\underset{CH_3}{|}}{\overset{\overset{Br}{|}}{C}}-CH_3$$

c)
$$CH_3CH_2CH_2\overset{\overset{O}{\|}}{C}OH$$

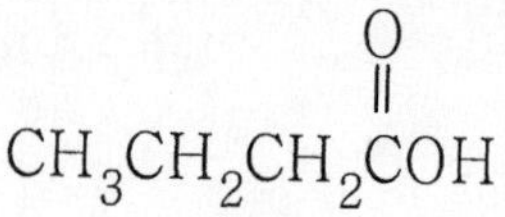

d) 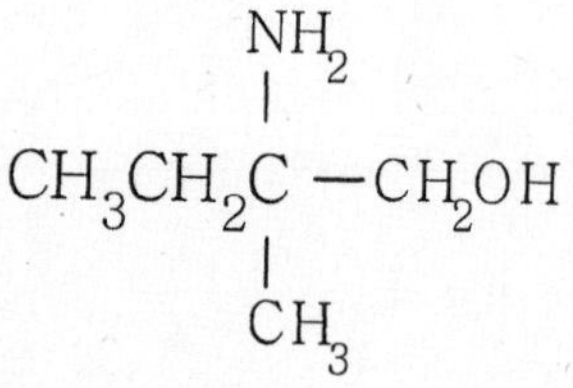
$$CH_3CH_2\underset{\underset{CH_3}{|}}{\overset{\overset{NH_2}{|}}{C}}-CH_2OH$$

e)   none of these

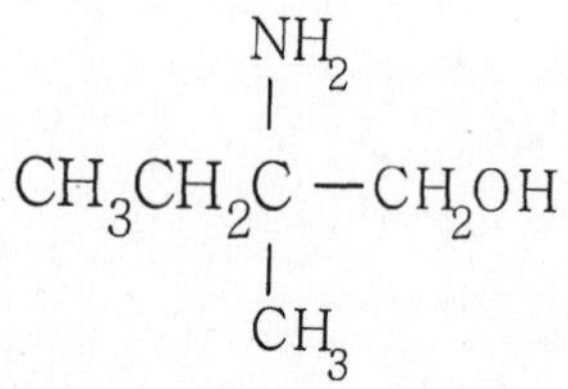

ANS: d)
$$CH_3CH_2\underset{\underset{CH_3}{|}}{\overset{\overset{NH_2}{|}}{C}}-CH_2OH$$

PAGE: 22.4

43. Identify all the functional groups present in the following organic compound. 1) ketone, 2) aldehyde, 3) acid, 4) alcohol, 5) ether, 6) ester, 7) amine

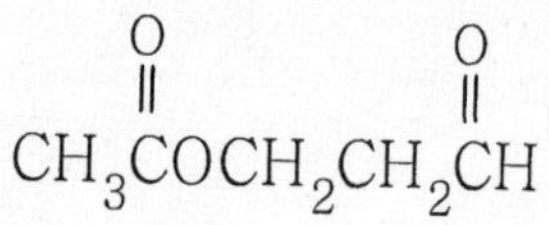

$$CH_3\overset{\overset{O}{\|}}{C}OCH_2CH_2\overset{\overset{O}{\|}}{C}H$$

a)   2,6
b)   2,5
c)   1,2
d)   1,2,5
e)   3,4

ANS: a) 2,6

PAGE: 22.4

534

44. Name the following:

H
|
H   O   H–C–H
| || |
H–C–C-O-C–H
| |
H   H–C–H
|
H

a) *n*-propyl acetate
b) isopropyl formate
c) isopropyl acetate
d) ethyl propanoate
e) none of these

ANS: c) isopropyl acetate

PAGE: 22.4

45. Name the following:

H H H
| | |
H–C—C-C—H
| | |
H OH H

a) methyl alcohol
b) ethyl alcohol
c) propyl alcohol
d) isopropyl alcohol
e) butanol

ANS: d) isopropyl alcohol

PAGE: 22.4

46. Name the following:

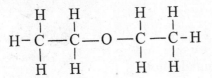

a) acetone
b) butyraldehyde
c) diethylketone
d) diethyl ether
e) none of these

ANS: d) diethyl ether

PAGE: 22.4

47. Name the following:

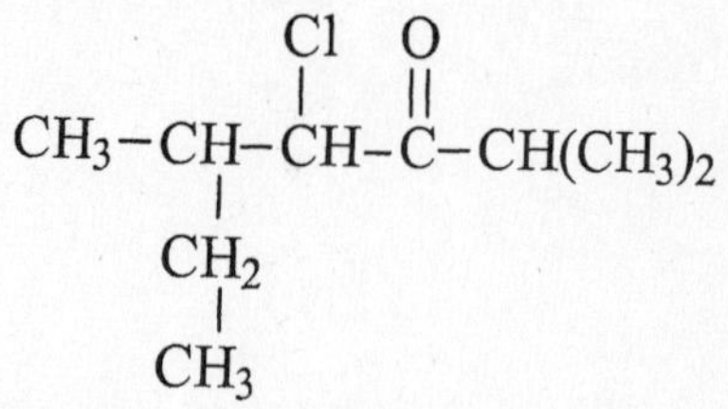

$$\underset{\underset{\underset{CH_3}{|}}{\underset{CH_2}{|}}{CH_3-CH-\overset{\overset{Cl}{|}}{CH}-\overset{\overset{O}{||}}{C}-CH(CH_3)_2}}$$

   a) 2-chloro-3-ethyl-1-isopropylbutanone
   b) isopropyl-chloro,methylbutyl ketone
   c) 2-butyl,chloro,isobutanoyl methane
   d) 4-chloro-2,5-dimethyl-3-heptanone
   e) 3-methyl-4-chloro-1-isopropylpentanone

   ANS: d) 4-chloro-2,5-dimethyl-3-heptanone

PAGE: 22.4

48. Oxidation of 2-methyl-*l*-butanol could yield

   a) 2-methyl-*l*-butanone
   b) 2-methyl-*l*-butanol
   c) 2-methylbutanoic acid
   d) both b and c
   e) both a and c

   ANS: d) both b and c

PAGE: 22.4

49. Which of the following is known as wood alcohol?

   a) methanol
   b) ethanol
   c) propanol
   d) isopropanol
   e) none of these

   ANS: a) methanol

PAGE: 22.4

50. Which of the following is known as rubbing alcohol?

   a) methanol
   b) ethanol
   c) propanol
   d) isopropanol
   e) none of these

   ANS: d) isopropanol

PAGE: 22.4

51. Which of the following is found in beverages such as wine?

   a) methanol
   b) ethanol
   c) propanol
   d) isopropanol
   e) none of these

   ANS: b) ethanol

   PAGE: 22.4

52. Oxidation of a primary alcohol results in a(n) _____ and oxidation of a secondary alcohol results in a(n) _____.

   a) carboxylic acid, amine
   b) aldehyde, ketone
   c) ester, ether
   d) ketone, aldehyde
   e) amine, carboxylic acid

   ANS: b) aldehyde, ketone

   PAGE: 22.4

53. Which of the following has a double C-O bond and a single C-O bond?

   a) ketone
   b) ester
   c) alcohol
   d) amine
   e) aldehyde

   ANS: b) ester

   PAGE: 22.4

54. Which of the following has only one single C-O bond?

   a) ketone
   b) alcohol
   c) ether
   d) ester
   e) aldehyde

   ANS: b) alcohol

   PAGE: 22.4

55. Teflon is an example of a

   a) copolymer
   b) homopolymer
   c) dimer
   d) two of these
   e) none of these

   ANS: b) homopolymer

   PAGE: 22.5

56. The boiling point of methanol is much higher than that of ethane. This is primarily due to

   a)   the difference in molar masses of methanol and ethane.
   b)   the hydrogen bonding in methanol.
   c)   the significant molecular size difference between methanol and ethane.
   d)   the carbon oxygen double bond in the methanol.
   e)   none of these.

   ANS: b)   the hydrogen bonding in methanol.   **PAGE:** 22.4

57. Aspirin is formed via a(n) _____ reaction.

   a)   combustion
   b)   hydrogenation
   c)   addition
   d)   condensation
   e)   substitution

   ANS: d)   condensation   **PAGE:** 22.4

58. Referring to the structures below, which statement is true?

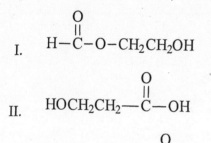

   a)   I and II have different molecular formulas.
   b)   I and III are structural isomers of each other.
   c)   II and III are stereoisomers of each other.
   d)   II and III are different conformations of the same compound.
   e)   I and III are the same compound.

   ANS: e)   I and III are the same compound.   **PAGE:** 22.4

538

59. Identify the functional group present in the following organic compound:

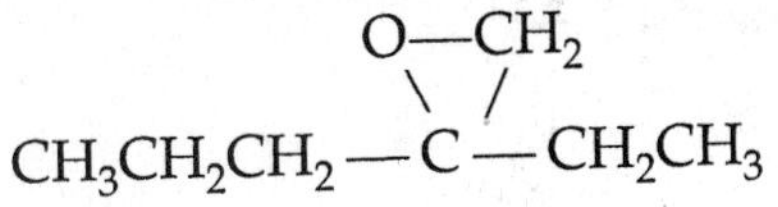

$$CH_3CH_2CH_2 - \underset{\underset{\displaystyle \overset{O-CH_2}{\diagdown \diagup}}{}}{C} - CH_2CH_3$$

a) ester
b) aldehyde
c) ether
d) ketone
e) none of these

ANS: c) ether

PAGE: 22.4

60. Identify the type of organic compound shown:

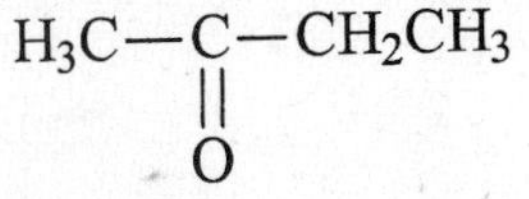

$$H_3C - \underset{\underset{\displaystyle O}{||}}{C} - CH_2CH_3$$

a) aldehyde
b) ester
c) amine
d) alcohol
e) none of these

ANS: e) none of these

PAGE: 22.4

61. Identify the type of organic compound shown:

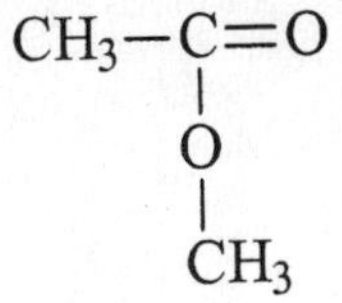

$$CH_3 - \underset{\underset{\displaystyle \underset{\displaystyle CH_3}{|}}{\overset{\displaystyle O}{|}}}{C} = O$$

a) aldehyde
b) ester
c) amine
d) ketone
e) none of these

ANS: b) ester

PAGE: 22.4

62. Identify the type of organic compound shown:

$$(CH_3)_3N$$

a) aldehyde
b) ester
c) amine
d) ketone
e) none of these

ANS: c) amine

PAGE: 22.4

63. Identify the type of organic compound shown:

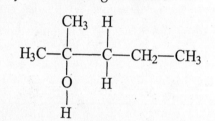

   a) aldehyde
   b) ester
   c) amine
   d) ketone
   e) none of these

   ANS: a) aldehyde

PAGE: 22.4

64. Classify the following molecule:

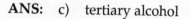

   a) primary alcohol
   b) secondary alcohol
   c) tertiary alcohol
   d) ether
   e) phenol

   ANS: c) tertiary alcohol

PAGE: 22.4

65. Which molecule is an amine?

   a) $CH_3CH_2\overset{\overset{\displaystyle O}{\|}}{C}OCH_3$

   b) $CH_3CH_2OCH_3$

   c) $CH_3CH_2\overset{\overset{\displaystyle O}{\|}}{C}CH_3$

   d) $CH_3CH_2NH_2$

   e) none of these

   ANS: d) 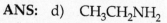

PAGE: 22.4

66. Which molecule is an ester?

    a) $CH_3CH_2\overset{\overset{\textstyle O}{\|}}{C}OCH_3$

    b) $CH_3CH_2OCH_3$

    c) $CH_3CH_2\overset{\overset{\textstyle O}{\|}}{C}CH_3$

    d) $CH_3CH_2NH_2$

    e)   none of these

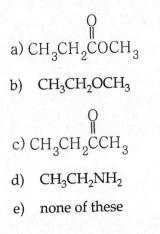

ANS: a)

PAGE: 22.4

67. Which molecule is a ketone?

    a) $CH_3CH_2\overset{\overset{\textstyle O}{\|}}{C}OCH_3$

    b) $CH_3CH_2OCH_3$

    c) $CH_3CH_2\overset{\overset{\textstyle O}{\|}}{C}CH_3$

    d) $CH_3CH_2NH_2$

    e)   none of these

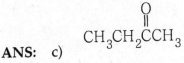

ANS: c)

PAGE: 22.4

68. Which molecule is an ether?

a) $CH_3CH_2\overset{\overset{\displaystyle O}{\|}}{C}OCH_3$

b) $CH_3CH_2OCH_3$

c) $CH_3CH_2\overset{\overset{\displaystyle O}{\|}}{C}CH_3$

d) $CH_3CH_2NH_2$

e) none of these

ANS: b) $CH_3CH_2OCH_3$

PAGE: 22.4

69. Classify the following molecule:

$$CH_3-\underset{\underset{\displaystyle NH_2}{|}}{C}H-CH_3$$

a) primary amine
b) secondary amine
c) tertiary amine
d) amino acid
e) peptide

ANS: a)   primary amine

PAGE: 22.4

70. Identify the secondary amine.

a) CH_3NH_2

b) $(CH_3)_2NH$

c) 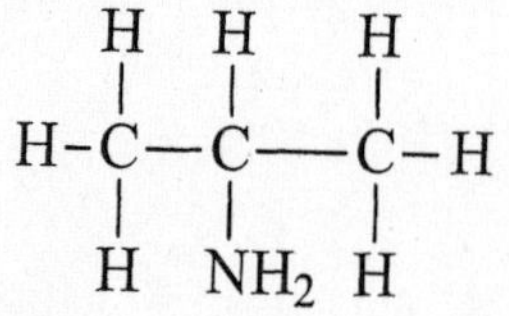
$$H-\underset{\underset{\displaystyle H}{|}}{\overset{\overset{\displaystyle H}{|}}{C}}-\underset{\underset{\displaystyle NH_2}{|}}{\overset{\overset{\displaystyle H}{|}}{C}}-\underset{\underset{\displaystyle H}{|}}{\overset{\overset{\displaystyle H}{|}}{C}}-H$$

d) NH_3

e) $(CH_3)_3N$

ANS: b) $(CH_3)_2NH$

PAGE: 22.4

71.   Classify the following molecule:

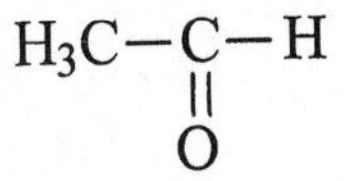

$$H_3C-C-H$$
with a double bond to O below the C

a)   acid
b)   aldehyde
c)   amine
d)   ketone
e)   carbonyl

ANS: b)   aldehyde

PAGE: 22.4

72.   Classify the following molecule:

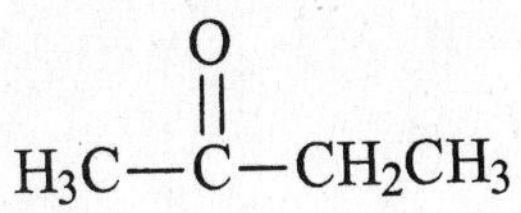

$$H_3C-C-CH_2CH_3$$
with a double bond to O above the C

a)   acid
b)   aldehyde
c)   amine
d)   ketone
e)   carbonyl

ANS: d)   ketone

PAGE: 22.4

73.   Which of the following functional groups does not contain a doubly bonded oxygen?

a)   aldehyde
b)   carboxyl
c)   ketone
d)   carboxylic acid
e)   all contain a double bond

ANS: e)   all contain a double bond

PAGE: 22.4

74. Which structure represents an optically active aldehyde?

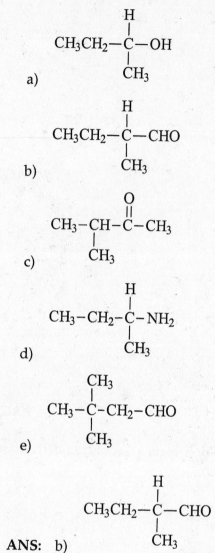

a)

b)

c)

d)

e)

ANS: b)

PAGE: 22.4

75. Pick the optically active molecule among the following:

a)
```
    H   H
    |   |
H−C−C−H
    |   |
    H   H
```

b)
```
    H
    |
H−C−O−H
    |
    H
```

c)
```
   HO   H
    |   |
H−C−C−H
    |   |
   Cl   H
```

d)
```
   HO   H
    |   |
H−C−C−H
    |   |
   HO   H
```

e)   none of these

ANS: c)

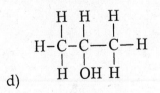

PAGE: 22.4

76. Which of the following molecules exhibits chirality?

a) CH_4

b) CH_3OH

c) CH_3CH_2OH

d)
```
    H   H   H
    |   |   |
H−C−C−C−H
    |   |   |
    H   OH  H
```

e)   none of these

ANS: e)   none of these

PAGE: 22.4

77. Which of the following is optically active (i.e., chiral)?

    a) $HN(CH_3)_2$
    b) CH_2Cl_2
    c) 2-chloropropane
    d) 2-chlorobutane
    e) 3-chloropentane

    ANS: d)   2-chlorobutane

    PAGE: 22.4

78. Which of the following becomes more soluble in water upon addition of NaOH?

    a) an amine
    b) a carboxylic acid
    c) an amine
    d) an aromatic hydrocarbon
    e) an alkane

    ANS: b)   a carboxylic acid

    PAGE: 22.4

79. Which of the following yields a primary alcohol upon reduction?

    a) a ketone
    b) an alkene
    c) an amine
    d) an aldehyde
    e) an ether

    ANS: d)   an aldehyde

    PAGE: 22.4

80. When C_4H_8 is treated with water and H_2SO_4 a tertiary alcohol is produced. Which of the following structures could represent C_4H_8 in this reaction?

    a) $CH_3CH = CHCH_3$

    b) $CH_3CH_2CH = CH_2$

    c) 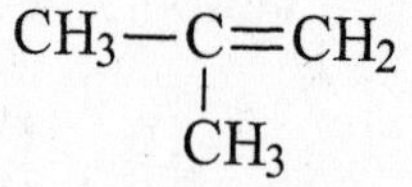 $$CH_3-\underset{\underset{\displaystyle CH_3}{|}}{C}=CH_2$$

    d) $CH_3CH_2CH_2CH_3$

    e) none of these

    ANS: c) 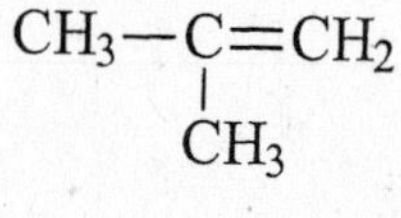 $$CH_3-\underset{\underset{\displaystyle CH_3}{|}}{C}=CH_2$$

    PAGE: 22.4

81. When the following organic compound is oxidized, what is the major organic product?

$$CH_2CH_3$$
$$|$$
$$CH_3CH_2CHOH \ + \ KMnO_4$$

   a) 3-pentanoic acid
   b) 3-pentanol
   c) 3-pentanone
   d) 3-pentanol
   e) no reaction takes place

   ANS: c)   3-pentanone

PAGE: 22.4

82. Which of the following will yield a carboxylic acid upon oxidation?

   a) a secondary alcohol
   b) an aldehyde
   c) a cycloalkane
   d) a ketone
   e) tertiary alcohol

   ANS: b)   an aldehyde

PAGE: 22.4

83. If you were to heat pentanoic acid and 2-butanol with a strong acid, you would most likely discover in your flask:

   a) a ketone
   b) an ester
   c) an amine
   d) an alkane
   e) an aldehyde

   ANS: b)   an ester

PAGE: 22.4

84. No atoms are lost from starting material in making which kind of polymer?

   a) condensation polymer
   b) polyester polymer
   c) addition polymer
   d) vulcanized polymer
   e) branched polymer

   ANS: c)   addition polymer

PAGE: 22.5

85. Which of the following pairs of substances could form a polyester?

   a) $H_2C=CHCH_3 + HOCH_2CH_2COOH$

   b) $HO(CH_2)_4COOH + HOCH_2CH=CHCH_3$

   c) $H_2C=CHCN + H_2C=CHCH_3$

   d) $HOCH_2CH_2OH + HOOCCOOH$

   e) $H_2NCH_2COOH + H_2NCH_2CH_2COOH$

   ANS: d) $HOCH_2CH_2OH + HOOCCOOH$ **PAGE:** 22.5

86. Consider the polymer drawn below:

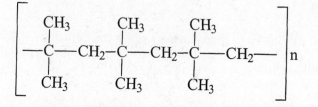

   What monomer(s) is (are) needed to produce the above polymer?

   a) $CH_2 = CH_2$ and $CH_3CH = CH_2$

   b) $CH_2 = C(CH_3)_2$

   c) $CH_3CH = CHCH_3$

   d) CO and $CH_2 = CH_2$

   e) none of the above

   ANS: b) $CH_2 = C(CH_3)_2$ **PAGE:** 22.5

87. The polymer $(-CH-CH-CH-CH-)_n$
    with CH_3, CH_3, CH_3, CH_3 substituents

    is formed by addition of

    a) $CH_2 = CH - CH_3$

    b) $CH_3CH_2CH_3$

    c) $CH_3 - CH = CH - CH_3$

    d) $H_2C = CH - CH - CH_2$

    e) $CH_3CH = C(CH_3)_2$

    ANS: c) $CH_3 - CH = CH - CH_3$ **PAGE: 22.5**

88. Which of the following pairs of substances could form an addition copolymer?

    a) $H_2C = CHCH_3 + HOCH_2CH_2COOH$

    b) $HO(CH_2)_4COOH + HOCH_2CH = CHCH_3$

    c) $H_2C = CHCH + H_2C = CHCH_3$

    d) $HOCH_2CH_2OH + HOOCCOOH$

    e) $H_2NCH_2COOH + H_2NCH_2CH_2COOH$

    ANS: c) $H_2C = CHCH + H_2C = CHCH_3$ **PAGE: 22.5**

89. What organic compounds typically have strong odors?

    a) aldehydes
    b) alkynes
    c) carboxylic acids
    d) amines
    e) two of these

    ANS: e)   two of these **PAGE: 22.4**

90. What is the common name for acetylsalicylic acid?

    a) orange juice
    b) aspirin
    c) acetone
    d) bananas
    e) vinegar

    ANS: b)   aspirin **PAGE: 22.4**

91. What organic molecules have the general formula RCOOH?

    a) esters
    b) alcohols
    c) carboxylic acids
    d) ketones
    e) aldehydes

    ANS: c)   carboxylic acids

    PAGE: 22.4

92. A carboxylic acid will react with an alcohol to form a(n) _____ and a water molecule.

    a) ester
    b) amine
    c) polymer
    d) ketone
    e) aldehyde

    ANS: a)   ester

    PAGE: 22.4

93. When sulfur is added to rubber and the mixture is heated, the resulting rubber is still elastic but much stronger. This process is called

    a) addition polymerization.
    b) isomerization.
    c) oligomerization.
    d) vulcanization.
    e) halogenation.

    ANS: d)   vulcanization.

    PAGE: 22.5

94. The structure of the polymer used in a freezer wrap can mainly be described as follows:

    $$[CCl_2 - CH_2 - CCl_2 - CH_2 - CCl_2 - CH_2 - CCl_2 - CH_2]_n$$

    The chief monomer of this wrap would have which structure?

    a) $CCl_2 = CH_2$
    b) $Cl_2C - CH_2$
    c) $Cl_2C = CH_2 = CCl_2$
    d) CCl_2
    e) none of these

    ANS: a) $CCl_2 = CH_2$

    PAGE: 22.5

550

95. Which of the following monomers are used to produce the polymer:

$$\left[-O-\underset{\underset{CH_3}{|}}{CH}-\underset{\overset{\parallel}{O}}{C}-O-\underset{\underset{CH_3}{|}}{CH}-\underset{\overset{\parallel}{O}}{C}-O-\underset{\underset{CH_3}{|}}{CH}-\underset{\overset{\parallel}{O}}{C}- \right]_n$$

I. $HOOC-\underset{\underset{CH_3}{|}}{CH}-COOH$

II. $HO-\underset{\underset{CH_3}{|}}{CH}-COOH$

III. $HO-\underset{\underset{CH_3}{|}}{CH}-\underset{\overset{\overset{H}{|}}{\underset{H}{|}}}{C}-OH$

a)   I
b)   II
c)   III
d)   I and III
e)   II and III

ANS: b)   II

PAGE: 22.5

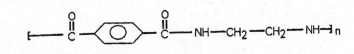

96. The formula above is the repeating unit of a

a)   homopolymer formed by an addition reaction.
b)   homopolymer formed by a condensation reaction.
c)   copolymer formed by an addition reaction.
d)   copolymer formed by a condensation reaction.
e)   polyester formed by an addition reaction.

ANS: d)   copolymer formed by a condensation reaction.

PAGE: 22.5

97.

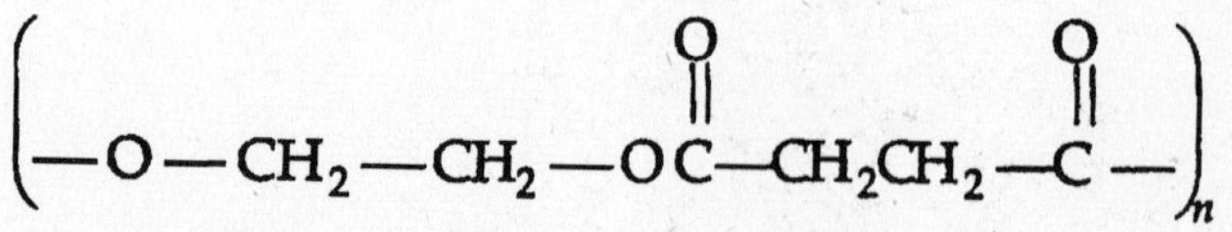

$$\left(-O-CH_2-CH_2-O\overset{\overset{\displaystyle O}{\|}}{C}-CH_2CH_2-\overset{\overset{\displaystyle O}{\|}}{C}-\right)_n$$

What monomer(s) is (are) needed to make the polymer shown above?

I. $HOCH_2CH_2OH$
II. $HOOCCH_2CH_2COOH$
III. $HOCH_2CH_2COOH$
IV. $HOCH = CHOH$
V. $HOOCCH = CHCOOH$

a) II
b) III
c) I and II
d) IV and V
e) II and III

ANS: c)   I and II

PAGE: 22.5

98. In condensation polymerization, a common by-product is:

a) ethylene
b) alcohol
c) aldehyde
d) water

ANS: d)   water

PAGE: 22.5

99. Nylon is an example of a

a) copolymer.
b) homopolymer.
c) dimer.
d) two of these
e) none of these.

ANS: a)   copolymer.

PAGE: 22.5

100. Which of the following polymers is not based on a substituted ethylene monomer?

a) nylon
b) polyvinylchloride
c) Teflon
d) polystyrene
e) polypropylene

ANS: a)   nylon

PAGE: 22.5

101. The greatest single use for PVC is

    a)   credit cards.

    b)   table cloths and mats.

    c)   pipe and pipe fittings.

    d)   garden hose.

    e)   toys.

    ANS: c)   pipe and pipe fittings.   **PAGE:** 22.5

102. In each pair below the relative strength of the polymer types is indicated with the stronger polymer on the right. Which comparison is wrong?

    a)   low molecular weight < high molecular weight

    b)   polyamide (e.g., nylon) < polyhydrocarbon (e.g., polyethylene)

    c)   branched < linear

    d)   low density < high density

    e)   atactic < isotactic

    ANS: b)   polyamide (e.g., nylon) < polyhydrocarbon (e.g., polyethylene)   **PAGE:** 22.5

103. Which factor is not characteristic of a strong polymer?

    a)   high crystallinity

    b)   branching

    c)   strong intermolecular forces

    d)   high molecular weight

    e)   isotactic

    ANS: c)   branching   **PAGE:** 22.5

104. Plasticizers are added to polymers to

    a)   increase crystallinity.

    b)   increase fire retardance.

    c)   increase cross-linking.

    d)   increase flexibility.

    e)   none of the above

    ANS: d)   increase flexibility.   **PAGE:** 22.5

105. The major use for linear low-density polyethylene (LDPE) is in the manufacturing of

    a)   pipes.

    b)   film for packaging.

    c)   Teflon.

    d)   rubber

    e)   carpets

    ANS: b)   film for packaging.   **PAGE:** 22.5

106.   HDPE, or high-density polyethylene, is a highly recyclable material because

    a)   it has a high molecular weight (molar mass).

    b)   it is both strong and tough.

    c)   it is a thermoplastic polymer.

    d)   it is a thermoset polymer.

    e)   none of these

    ANS: c)   it is a thermoplastic polymer.

                                                                           PAGE: 22.5

107.   _____ are materials that recover their shape after a deforming force.

    a)   Elastomers

    b)   Plasticizers

    c)   Thermoplastic polymers

    d)   Thermoset polymers

    e)   Inhibitors

    ANS: a)   Elastomers

                                                                           PAGE: 22.5

108.   What substances are most often used to decrease the flammability of a polymer itself?

    a)   plasticizers

    b)   inhibitors

    c)   sulfur

    d)   halogens

    e)   ethylene

    ANS: d)   halogens

                                                                           PAGE: 22.5

109.   Which of the following will increase the rigidity of a polymer?

    a)   shorter polymer chains

    b)   make chains more branched

    c)   decrease cross-linking

    d)   introduce the possibility of hydrogen bonding between chains

    e)   use atactic instead of isotactic chains

    ANS: d)   introduce the possibility of hydrogen bonding between chains

                                                                           PAGE: 22.5

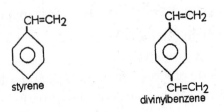

styrene

divinylbenzene

110. Polystyrene is an addition polymer of styrene. What would be the effect if some divinylbenzene was added to styrene and then polymerized?

   a) The second polymer would be made less flammable than pure polystyrene.
   b) The polymer would be more flexible. Divinylbenzene acts as a plasticizer.
   c) Divinylbenzene would act as a cross-linking agent, making the polymer stronger.
   d) There would be no effect on the properties of the polymer.
   e) There would be an effect, but it cannot be predicted.

   ANS: c) Divinylbenzene would act as a cross-linking agent, making the polymer stronger.   **PAGE:** 22.5

111. Teflon is a type of

   a) nylon.
   b) PVC.
   c) elastomer.
   d) polymer.

   ANS: d) polymer.   **PAGE:** 22.5

112. Draw the isomers for C_4H_{10}.

   ANS: See Sec. 22.1 of Zumdahl, *Chemistry*.   **PAGE:** 22.1

113–116. Write molecular equations for the following reactions:

113. halogenation of ethane

   ANS: $C_2H_6 + HCl \rightarrow C_2H_5Cl + H_2$ **PAGE:** 22.1

114. formation of dipropyl ester

   ANS: $C_3H_6OH + C_2H_5COOH \rightarrow CH_3CH_2COOCH_2CH_2CH_3 + H_2O$ **PAGE:** 22.4

115. hydration of pentane

   ANS: $C_5H_{12} + H_2O \rightarrow C_5H_{11}OH + H_2$ **PAGE:** 22.4

116. methyl substitution of benzene

   ANS: $C_6H_6 + CH_4 \rightarrow C_6H_5CH_3 + H_2$ **PAGE:** 22.3

117.   Which one of the following statements about the structure of proteins is incorrect?

   a)   Disulfide bonds provide strong intrachain interactions.
   b)   Hydrogen bonding stabilizes the α-helix proteins.
   c)   Nonpolar groups tend to face the outside of a protein in an aqueous solution.
   d)   Ionized amino acid side chains can form salt bridges within a protein.
   e)   Heat can disrupt tertiary structure.

   ANS: c)   Nonpolar groups tend to face the outside of a protein in an aqueous solution.

PAGE: 22.5

118.   The structures of proteins are partially determined by the order of various amino acids in the macromolecule. This level of structural determination is known as

   a)   primary structure.
   b)   secondary structure.
   c)   tertiary structure.
   d)   quaternary structure.
   e)   order of bases.

   ANS: a)   primary structure.

PAGE: 22.6

119.   A polypeptide is

   a)   an addition polymer of amino acids.
   b)   a condensation polymer of amino acids.
   c)   a polymer of sugar molecules.
   d)   a part of nucleic acids.
   e)   none of these

   ANS: b)   a condensation polymer of amino acids.

PAGE: 22.6

120.   Which of the following is the best description of a protein?

   a)   an alternating chain of amino acids and nucleic acids
   b)   a chain of amino acids connected by ester bonds
   c)   two antiparallel chains of nucleic acids connected by hydrogen bonding
   d)   a chain of amino acids formed by condensation polymerization
   e)   a chain of nucleotides connected by phosphodiester bonds

   ANS: d)   a chain of amino acids formed by condensation polymerization

PAGE: 22.6

121. The building blocks of all proteins are
     a)   pleated sheets.
     b)   alpha amino acids.
     c)   alpha helices.
     d)   tertiary structures.
     e)   none of these (a-d)
     ANS: b)   alpha amino acids

PAGE: 22.6

122. In order to give someone a "permanent" (permanent waving of hair), these must be broken and reformed.
     a)   disulfide linkages
     b)   pleated sheets
     c)   alpha helices
     d)   alpha amino acids
     e)   globular proteins
     ANS: a)   disulfide lnkages

PAGE: 22.6

123. How many of the following apply to globular proteins?
     I.   Provide structural integrity and strength for many types of tissues.
     II. Transport and store oxygen and nutrients,
     III. Act as catalysts.
     IV. Are the main components of muscle, hair, and cartilage.
     V.   Fight invasion of the body by foreign objects.
     a)   1
     b)   2
     c)   3
     d)   4
     e)   5
     ANS: c)   3

PAGE: 22.6

124. How many of the following apply to fibrous proteins?
     I.   Provide structural integrity and strength for many types of tissues.
     II. Transport and store oxygen and nutrients,
     III. Act as catalysts.
     IV. Are the main components of muscle, hair, and cartilage.
     V.   Fight invasion of the body by foreign objects.
     a)   1
     b)   2
     c)   3
     d)   4
     e)   5
     ANS: b)   2

PAGE: 22.6

125. Nonpolar amino acid side chains contain mostly what atoms?

a)   carbon and hydrogen
b)   nitrogen and oxygen
c)   carbon and nitrogen
d)   carbon and oxygen
e)   nitrogen and hydrogen

ANS: a)   carbon and hydrogen

PAGE: 22.6

126. Polar amino acid side chains contain mostly what atoms?

a)   carbon and hydrogen
b)   nitrogen and oxygen
c)   carbon and nitrogen
d)   carbon and oxygen
e)   nitrogen and hydrogen

ANS: b)   nitrogen and oxygen

PAGE: 22.6

127. Which of the following is *not* a function of proteins?

a)   structure
b)   catalysis
c)   oxygen transport
d)   energy transformation
e)   All of these are functions of proteins.

ANS: e)   All of these are functions of proteins.

PAGE: 22.6

128. The condensation product of two amino acids is a(n)

a)   peptide.
b)   ketone.
c)   ether.
d)   ester.
e)   alcohol.

ANS: a)   peptide.

PAGE: 22.6

129. Which of the following statements is correct?

a)   No one has ever made a polymer using amide bonds.
b)   Nucleic acids are made of nucleotides joined together with amide bonds.
c)   The primary structure of proteins is determined by 3'–5'.
d)   All of the above (a-c) statements are true.
e)   none of these

ANS: e)   none of these

PAGE: 22.6

130. Which statement (a–d) is false with respect to proteins?

a) Primary structure refers to the sequence of nucleotides.
b) Secondary structure includes α-helixes.
c) Tertiary structure includes disulfide bonds.
d) The overall shape of a protein is related to the tertiary structure.
e) All are false.

ANS: a)   Primary structure refers to the sequence of nucleotides.   PAGE: 22.6

131. Which statement is true?

a) Protein synthesis takes place in the cytoplasm of the cell.
b) Each gene in the DNA molecule codes for a specific protein.
c) Messenger RNA can be found in both the nucleus and the cytoplasm of each cell.
d) When a peptide bond is formed, H_2O is produced.
e) all of these

ANS: e)   all of these   PAGE: 22.6

132. Hydrogen bonding between —C=O groups and NH–groups in the backbone of a protein determines the

a) primary structure.
b) secondary structure.
c) tertiary structure.
d) quaternary structure.
e) all of these

ANS: b)   secondary structure   PAGE: 22.6

133. The secondary and tertiary structures of most biomolecules are determined by

a) hydrophobic bonding.
b) hydrogen bonding.
c) salt bridges.
d) disulfide bonds.
e) all of these

ANS: e)   all of these   PAGE: 22.6

134. When heat is added to proteins, the hydrogen bonding in the secondary structure breaks apart. What are the algebraic signs of ΔH and ΔS for the denaturation process?

   a)   Both ΔH and ΔS are positive.
   b)   Both ΔH and ΔS are negative.
   c) ΔH is positive and ΔS is negative.
   d) ΔH is negative and ΔS is positive.
   e) ΔH is positive and ΔS is 0.

   ANS: a)   Both ΔH and ΔS are positive.

   PAGE: 22.6

135. The process of breaking down the three-dimensional structure of a protein is called

   a)   degradation.
   b)   denaturation.
   c)   decomposition.
   d)   fission.
   e)   none of these.

   ANS: b)   denaturation.

   PAGE: 22.6

136. The overall shape of a protein is maintained by

   a)   hydrogen bonding.
   b)   ionic bonds.
   c)   dipole-dipole bonding.
   d)   covalent bonds.
   e)   all of these

   ANS: e)   all of these

   PAGE: 22.6

137. The analysis of a protein for its amino acid content is valuable in determining the protein's

   a)   tertiary structure.
   b)   secondary structure.
   c)   quaternary structure.
   d)   primary structure.
   e)   main structure.

   ANS: d)   primary structure.

   PAGE: 22.6

138.   The alpha helix of a protein is held in a coiled conformation partly because of

    a)   hydrogen bonding.
    b)   optical activity.
    c)   active sites.
    d)   double bonding.
    e)   ionization energies.

    ANS: a)   hydrogen bonding.   **PAGE:** 22.6

139.   What are the building blocks of proteins?

    a)   nucleotides
    b)   glucose and sucrose
    c)   lipids
    d)   amino acids
    e)   esters

    ANS: d)   amino acids   **PAGE:** 22.6

140.   The monomers that make up a starch molecule are:

    I.   optically active
    II.   not optically active
    III.   aldehydes
    IV.   ketones

and the polymer itself is formed primarily by

    V.   addition.
    VI.   condensation
    a)   I, III, V
    b)   II, IV, VI
    c)   I, III, VI
    d)   II, IV, V
    e)   I, IV, VI

    ANS: c)   I, III, VI   **PAGE:** 22.6

141.   Which of the following is incorrect?

    a)   Nonpolar amino acid side chains are hydrophobic.
    b)   Polar amino acid side chains are hydrophilic.
    c)   Nonpolar amino acid side chains contain hydrogen.
    d)   Polar amino acid side chains contain nitrogen.
    e)   Both polar and nonpolar amino acid side chains contain oxygen atoms.

    ANS: e)   Both polar and nonpolar amino acid side chains contain
            oxygen atoms.   **PAGE:** 22.6

142. How many possible sequences can be made for a polypeptide with six different amino acids?

    a) 6

    b) 36

    c) 64

    d) 720

    e) none of these (a-d)

    ANS: d)   720

PAGE: 22.6

143. The primary structure of a protein chain is

    a) the order of amino acids.

    b) the arrangement of the chain in the long molecule.

    c) the overall shape of the protein.

    d) determined by the types of bonds it contains.

    e) determined by the side chains.

    ANS: a)   the order of amino acids.

PAGE: 22.6

144. A pleated sheet arrangement of proteins

    a) is found in muscle fibers.

    b) contains interchain hydrogen bonds.

    c) is found in silk fibers.

    d) results when hydrogen bonds occur between protein chains.

    e) all of these

    ANS: e)   all of these

PAGE: 22.6

145. Which of the following statements about enzymes is incorrect?

    a) They are proteins that catalyze specific biologic reactions.

    b) Several hundred are now known.

    c) The molecules they react with are called substrates.

    d) They are equal to inorganic catalysts in efficiency.

    e) All of these are correct.

    ANS: d)   They are equal to inorganic catalysts in efficiency.

PAGE: 22.6

146. An example of a secondary structure of a protein is

    a) an alpha amino acid.

    b) a peptide linkage.

    c) a pleated sheet.

    d) serine.

    e) none of these

    ANS: c)   a pleated sheet.

PAGE: 22.6

147. Which of the following is not a monosaccharide?

    a) sucrose
    b) glucose
    c) fructose
    d) galactose
    e) All of the above (a-d) are monosaccharides.

    ANS: a) sucrose

PAGE: 22.6

148. Which of the following is a carbohydrate reservoir for animals?

    a) starch
    b) cellulose
    c) glycogen
    d) two of these
    e) none of these

    ANS: c) glycogen

PAGE: 22.6

149. Table sugar is a disaccharide formed from

    a) alpha-D-glucose and fructose
    b) beta-D-glucose and fructose
    c) D-galactose and D-ribose
    d) D-galactose and fructose
    e) none of these

    ANS: a) alpha-D-glucose and fructose

PAGE: 22.6

150. What type of bonding occurs between two consecutive nucleotides in RNA?

    a) ester
    b) amide
    c) hydrogen
    d) ionic
    e) hydrophobic

    ANS: a) ester

PAGE: 22.6

151. Protein synthesis in a human occurs

    a) in the nucleus.
    b) on the ribosomes in the cytoplasm.
    c) on the cell membranes.
    d) by reading pairs of tRNA nucleotides called codons.
    e) none of these

    ANS: b) on the ribosomes in the cytoplasm.

PAGE: 22.6

152. Which of the following has the smallest molar mass?

    a) mRNA
    b) dRNA
    c) rRNA
    d) sRNA
    e) tRNA

    ANS: e) tRNA

PAGE: 22.6

153. Which of the following is (are) not necessary for protein synthesis at the time and place where synthesis occurs?

    a) amino acids
    b) mRNA
    c) DNA
    d) tRNA
    e) ribosomes

    ANS: c) DNA

PAGE: 22.6

154. All of the following statements about carbohydrates are true except which one?

    a) They serve as a food structure for most organisms.
    b) They are used as a structural material for plants.
    c) Many have the empirical formula CH_2O.
    d) Starch and cellulose are two important carbohydrates made of monosaccharides.
    e) Fructose, a sugar found in fruit, has five carbon atoms.

    ANS: e)   Fructose, a sugar found in fruit, has five carbon atoms.

PAGE: 22.6

155. Which of the following pairs is incorrect?

    a) sucrose – disaccharide
    b) starch – polysaccharide
    c) glycogen – disaccharide
    d) cellulose – polysaccharide
    e) fructose – monosaccharide

    ANS: c)   glycogen – disaccharide

PAGE: 22.6

156. What carbohydrate is the form in which plants store glucose for future use as cellular fuel?

    a) starch
    b) cellulose
    c) glycogen
    d) sucrose
    e) fructose

    ANS: a) starch

    PAGE: 22.6

157. What carbohydrate breaks down rapidly when energy is needed?

    a) starch
    b) cellulose
    c) glycogen
    d) sucrose
    e) fructose

    ANS: c) glycogen

    PAGE: 22.6

158. The complimentary nucleic acid sequence for the following DNA sequence—GAC TAC GTT AGC—is

    a) GAC TAC GTT AGC
    b) TCA GCA TGG CTA
    c) CGA TTG CAT CAG
    d) CTG ATG CAA TCG
    e) none of these

    ANS: d) CTG ATG CAA TCG

    PAGE: 22.6

159. The complimentary nucleic acid sequence for the following DNA sequence—ATG GAC GTA TTC—is

    a) ATG GAC GTA TTC
    b) TAC CTG CAT AAG
    c) CGT TCA TGC GGA
    d) CTT ATG CAG GTA
    e) none of these

    ANS: b) TAC CTG CAT AAG

    PAGE: 22.6

160. The complimentary nucleic acid sequence for the following DNA sequence—CTG ACT TAC GCT—is

    a) AGT CAG GCA TAG
    b) CTG ACT TAC GCT
    c) GAC TGA ATG CGA
    d) TCG CAT TCA GTC
    e) none of these

    ANS: c) GAC TGA ATG CGA

    PAGE: 22.6